GROWING OLD
IN AMERICA

ISSN 1538-6686

GROWING OLD IN AMERICA

Barbara Wexler

INFORMATION PLUS® REFERENCE SERIES
Formerly Published by Information Plus, Wylie, Texas

Detroit • New York • San Francisco • San Diego • New Haven, Conn. • Waterville, Maine • London • Munich

Growing Old in America
Barbara Wexler
Paula Kepos, Series Editor

Project Editor
John McCoy

Permissions
Margaret Abendroth, Edna Hedblad, Emma Hull

Composition and Electronic Prepress
Evi Seoud

Manufacturing
Drew Kalasky

ISBN 0-7876-5103-6 (set)
ISBN 1-4144-0416-6
ISSN 1538-6686

This title is also available as an e-book.
ISBN 1-4144-1043-3 (set)
Contact your Thomson Gale sales representative for ordering information.

Printed in the United States of America
10 9 8 7 6 5 4 3 2 1

TABLE OF CONTENTS

in the fabric of American society. It also includes descriptions of programs aimed at supporting caregivers.

CHAPTER 10
Health-Care Use, Expenditures, and Financing 151

Older adults account for about 12% of the U.S. population, but they are responsible for disproportionate health-care expenditures. This chapter describes trends in health-care use, expenditures, and financing, and it provides in-depth coverage of government entitlement programs—Medicare and Medicaid. The challenges of long-term care are discussed along with in-home services that enable older adults to remain in the community—"aging in place."

CHAPTER 11
Crime and Abuse of Older Adults. 171

Chapter 11 enumerates the rates and types of crime against older Americans, including characteristics of older crime victims. It also describes domestic abuse, mistreatment, institutional abuse, and frauds perpetrated against the older population.

PREFACE

Growing Old in America is part of the *Information Plus Reference Series*. The purpose of each volume of the series is to present the latest facts on a topic of pressing concern in modern American life. These topics include today's most controversial and most studied social issues: abortion, capital punishment, care for the elderly, crime, the environment, health care, immigration, minorities, national security, social welfare, women, youth, and many more. Although written especially for the high school and undergraduate student, this series is an excellent resource for anyone in need of factual information on current affairs.

By presenting the facts, it is Thomson Gale's intention to provide its readers with everything they need to reach an informed opinion on current issues. To that end, there is a particular emphasis in this series on the presentation of scientific studies, surveys, and statistics. These data are generally presented in the form of tables, charts, and other graphics placed within the text of each book. Every graphic is directly referred to and carefully explained in the text. The source of each graphic is presented within the graphic itself. The data used in these graphics are drawn from the most reputable and reliable sources, in particular from the various branches of the U.S. government and from major independent polling organizations. Every effort has been made to secure the most recent information available. The reader should bear in mind that many major studies take years to conduct, and that additional years often pass before the data from these studies are made available to the public. Therefore, in many cases the most recent information available in 2006 dated from 2003 or 2004. Older statistics are sometimes presented as well if they are of particular interest and no more recent information exists.

Although statistics are a major focus of the *Information Plus Reference Series*, they are by no means its only content. Each book also presents the widely held positions and important ideas that shape how the book's subject is discussed in the United States. These positions are explained in detail and, where possible, in the words of their proponents. Some of the other material to be found in these books includes: historical background; descriptions of major events related to the subject; relevant laws and court cases; and examples of how these issues play out in American life. Some books also feature primary documents or have pro and con debate sections giving the words and opinions of prominent Americans on both sides of a controversial topic. All material is presented in an even-handed and unbiased manner; the reader will never be encouraged to accept one view of an issue over another.

HOW TO USE THIS BOOK

The percentage of Americans over the age of sixty-five has increased over the past century and will continue to increase as the children born during the mid–twentieth century baby boom age. This book explores the current condition of growing old in the United States. Included is a general overview on growing old in America; the economic status of older people; the Social Security program; Medicare and Medicaid; the living arrangements of the elderly; working and retirement; and the education levels, voting trends, and political behavior of the elderly. Physical and mental health and health problems; drug and alcohol abuse; care for the elderly; and crime are also covered.

Growing Old in America consists of eleven chapters and three appendices. Each of the chapters is devoted to a particular aspect of growing old. For a summary of the information covered in each chapter, please see the synopses provided in the Table of Contents at the front of the book. Chapters generally begin with an overview of the basic facts and background information on the chapter's topic, then proceed to examine subtopics of particular interest. For example, Chapter 7: The Health and Medical Problems of Older Adults begins with a discussion of the general health of older Americans. It then goes on to detail the chronic physical problems of the elderly, among them arthritis, diabetes, malnutrition, and hearing and vision loss. This is followed by discussion of the threat that influenza and pneumonia pose to the elderly. Many older Americans are disabled by these and other conditions; the meaning of "disabled," its prevalence, and its impact are examined. Drug use among the elderly, health maintenance, sexuality in aging, causes of death among the elderly, and the state of geriatric medicine are also included. Readers can find their way through a chapter by looking for the section and subsection headings, which are clearly set off from the text. They can also refer to the book's extensive Index if they already know what they are looking for.

Statistical Information

The tables and figures featured throughout *Growing Old in America* will be of particular use to the reader in learning about this issue. These tables and figures represent an extensive collection of the most recent and important statistics on growing old and related issues—for example, graphics in the book cover voting rates, the cost of housing, the marital status of older Americans, alcohol-related chronic health conditions, crimes against the elderly, actions taken by senior citizens to plan for their own long-term needs, and the percentage of older Americans participating in any type of learning activity. Thomson Gale believes that making this information available to the reader is the most important way in which we fulfill the goal of this book: to help readers understand the issues and controversies surrounding growing old in the United States and to reach their own conclusions.

Each table or figure has a unique identifier appearing above it for ease of identification and reference. Titles for the tables and figures explain their purpose. At the end of each table or figure, the original source of the data is provided.

In order to help readers understand these often complicated statistics, all tables and figures are explained in the text. References in the text direct the reader to the relevant statistics. Furthermore, the contents of all tables and figures are fully indexed. Please see the opening section of the Index at the back of this volume for a description of how to find tables and figures within it.

Appendices

In addition to the main body text and images, *Growing Old in America* has three appendices. The first is the Important Names and Addresses directory. Here the reader will find contact information for a number of government and private organizations that can provide further information on growing old. The second appendix is the Resources section, which can also assist the reader in conducting his or her own research. In this section the author and editors of *Growing Old in America* describe some of the sources that were most useful during the compilation of this book. The final appendix is the detailed Index, which facilitates reader access to specific topics in this book.

ADVISORY BOARD CONTRIBUTIONS

The staff of Information Plus would like to extend its heartfelt appreciation to the Information Plus Advisory Board. This dedicated group of media professionals provides feedback on the series on an ongoing basis. Their comments allow the editorial staff who work on the project to make the series better and more user-friendly. Our top priority is to produce the highest-quality and most useful books possible, and the Advisory Board's contributions to this process are invaluable.

The members of the Information Plus Advisory Board are:

- Kathleen R. Bonn, Librarian, Newbury Park High School, Newbury Park, California

- Madelyn Garner, Librarian, San Jacinto College—North Campus, Houston, Texas

- Anne Oxenrider, Media Specialist, Dundee High School, Dundee, Michigan

- Charles R. Rodgers, Director of Libraries, Pasco–Hernando Community College, Dade City, Florida

- James N. Zitzelsberger, Library Media Department Chairman, Oshkosh West High School, Oshkosh, Wisconsin

COMMENTS AND SUGGESTIONS

The editors of the *Information Plus Reference Series* welcome your feedback on *Growing Old in America*. Please direct all correspondence to:

Editors
Information Plus Reference Series
27500 Drake Rd.
Farmington Hills, MI 48331-3535

CHAPTER 1

OLDER AMERICANS—A DIVERSE AND GROWING POPULATION

Old age is the most unexpected of all the things that happen to a man.

—Leon Trotsky, Russian Communist revolutionary and Soviet politician (1879–1940)

THE UNITED STATES GROWS OLDER

The United States is aging. During the twentieth century the country's older population—adults age sixty-five and over—increased significantly. According to the U.S. Census Bureau, the number of older adults grew from 3.1 million in 1900 to 35.9 million in 2003 (the most recent year for which data, as opposed to estimates or projections, are available). Of an estimated U.S. population of 296.2 million people in 2005, about 12%, or slightly more than thirty-six million, were over the age of sixty-five. Between 2000 and 2050 the percentage increase of adults age sixty-five and over is projected to be 147%, compared to just a 49% increase in the population as a whole.

By 2030 there will be about 71.5 million people age sixty-five and older, more than twice the number in 2000, and by 2050 the ranks of older adults will increase to nearly eighty-seven million. (See Figure 1.1.) In 2050, 21%—one in five Americans—will be age sixty-five and over. Even as the percentage of older adults approaches 13%, however, the United States is relatively young among developed countries. In 2003 older adults comprised at least 15% of the population of almost twenty such countries, including nearly 19% in both Italy and Japan. (See Table 1.1.)

Fewer children per family and longer life spans have shifted the proportion of older adults in the population. The growth in the population segment of older adults in the United States, often termed "the graying of America," is considered one of the most significant issues facing the country in the twenty-first century. The swelling population of persons age sixty-five and over has an impact on every aspect of society—challenging policymakers, health-care providers, employers, families, and others to meet the needs of older Americans.

Many of the findings and statistics cited in this chapter, as well as a number of the tables and charts presented, were drawn from *Older Americans 2004: Key Indicators of Well-Being* (http://www.agingstats.gov/chartbook2004/default.htm), a report prepared in 2004 by the Federal Interagency Forum on Aging-Related Statistics. The group is a consortium of thirteen federal entities—Administration on Aging; Agency for Healthcare Research and Quality; Bureau of Labor Statistics; Census Bureau; Centers for Medicare & Medicaid Services; Department of Veterans Affairs; Environmental Protection Agency; National Center for Health Statistics; National Institute on Aging; Office of the Assistant Secretary for Planning and Evaluation, U.S. Department of Health and Human Services; Office of Management and Budget; Social Security Administration; and Substance Abuse and Mental Health Services Administration—dedicated to encouraging cooperation and collaboration among federal agencies to improve the quality and utility of data on the aging population.

To understand the aging of America it is not only important to consider the current population of older adults but also to look at how the older population will fare over time. In order to anticipate the needs of this growing segment of society, policymakers, planners, and researchers rely on projections and population estimates. Population estimates and projections are made at different times and based on different assumptions. As a result it is not surprising to find considerable variation in the statistics cited by different agencies and investigators. This chapter contains estimates and projections of demographic changes from several different sources, and as such there is some variability in the data presented.

FIGURE 1.1

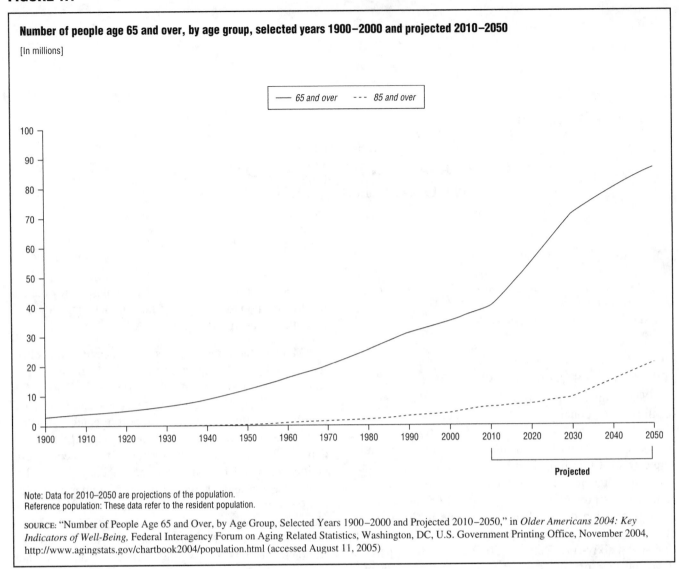

Number of people age 65 and over, by age group, selected years 1900–2000 and projected 2010–2050

[In millions]

Note: Data for 2010–2050 are projections of the population.
Reference population: These data refer to the resident population.

SOURCE: "Number of People Age 65 and Over, by Age Group, Selected Years 1900–2000 and Projected 2010–2050," in *Older Americans 2004: Key Indicators of Well-Being,* Federal Interagency Forum on Aging Related Statistics, Washington, DC, U.S. Government Printing Office, November 2004, http://www.agingstats.gov/chartbook2004/population.html (accessed August 11, 2005)

HOW DO POPULATIONS AGE?

Unlike people, populations can not only age but become younger. There are key indicators of the age structure of a given population. Populations age or grow younger because of changes in fertility (birth rates expressed as the number of births per one thousand population per year) and/or mortality (death rates expressed as the number of deaths per one thousand population per year) or in response to migration—people entering or leaving the population.

The aging of the United States resulted from changes in fertility and mortality that occurred over the past century. Such shifts in birth and death rates are termed "demographic transition." Generally, population aging is primarily a response to long-term declines in fertility, and declining fertility is the basic cause of the aging of the U.S. population. Reduced infant and child mortality, chiefly as a result of public health measures, fueled the decline in the fertility rate—the increased survival of

children prompted families to have fewer offspring. The birth of fewer babies resulted in fewer young people.

According to estimates presented in *The World Factbook* (Washington, DC: Central Intelligence Agency, 2005, http://www.cia.gov/cia/publications/factbook/index.html), the U.S. total fertility rate in 2005 was 2.08 children born per woman. This rate, which has not changed significantly since the mid-1980s, is sharply lower than the fertility rates during the nearly two decades following the end of World War II (1946–64). Victorious American soldiers returning home after the war were eager to start families, and this was facilitated by the relatively prosperous post–war economy.

During this period following the war, which came to be known as the "baby boom," U.S. fertility rates exploded, at one point approaching four children born per woman, according to Census Bureau statistics. Children born during the 1946–64 baby boom became known as "baby boomers," and it is this huge cohort (a group of

TABLE 1.1

Population of countries with at least 10 percent age 65 and over, 2003

Region or country	Total Number	65 and over Number	65 and over Percent
Italy	57,998,353	10,893,973	18.8
Japan	127,214,499	23,720,030	18.6
Greece	10,625,945	1,947,336	18.3
Germany	82,398,326	14,643,067	17.8
Spain	40,217,413	7,075,743	17.6
Sweden	8,970,306	1,545,515	17.2
Belgium	10,330,824	1,777,398	17.2
Bulgaria	7,588,399	1,293,949	17.1
Portugal	10,479,955	1,749,225	16.7
France	60,180,529	9,801,524	16.3
Croatia	4,497,779	723,788	16.1
Estonia	1,350,722	217,199	16.1
Austria	8,162,656	1,282,955	15.7
United Kingdom	60,094,648	9,429,087	15.7
Finland	5,204,405	805,215	15.5
Latvia	2,322,943	358,400	15.4
Switzerland	7,408,319	1,131,164	15.3
Ukraine	48,055,439	7,212,722	15
Georgia	4,710,921	706,380	15
Denmark	5,394,138	802,456	14.9
Norway	4,555,400	676,160	14.8
Hungary	10,057,745	1,492,216	14.8
Slovenia	2,011,604	298,344	14.8
Serbia and Montenegro	10,823,280	1,592,794	14.7
Lithuania	3,620,094	530,425	14.7
Luxembourg	456,764	65,985	14.4
Belarus	10,322,151	1,478,835	14.3
Romania	22,380,273	3,169,849	14.2
Czech Republic	10,251,087	1,432,188	14
Netherlands	16,223,248	2,241,317	13.8
Russia	144,457,596	19,203,848	13.3
Malta	395,178	51,969	13.2
Uruguay	3,381,606	442,733	13.1
Canada	32,207,113	4,167,291	12.9
Poland	38,622,660	4,924,081	12.7
Australia	19,731,984	2,502,665	12.7
United States	290,342,554	35,878,341	12.4
Hong Kong S.A.R	6,809,738	836,153	12.3
Puerto Rico	3,878,679	461,501	11.9
Iceland	291,064	34,055	11.7
Slovakia	5,416,406	630,190	11.6
New Zealand	3,951,307	457,805	11.6
Ireland	3,924,023	447,070	11.4
Cyprus	771,657	85,629	11.1
Macedonia	2,063,122	217,965	10.6
Argentina	38,740,807	4,042,311	10.4
Martinique	425,966	43,818	10.3
Armenia	3,001,712	306,182	10.2
Moldova	4,439,502	452,797	10.2
Bosnia and Herzegovina	3,989,018	401,929	10.1

SOURCE: "Population of Countries with at Least 10 Percent of Their Population Age 65 and Over, 2003," in *Older Americans 2004: Key Indicators of Well-Being*, Federal Interagency Forum on Aging Related Statistics, Washington, DC, U.S. Government Printing Office, November 2004, http://www.agingstats.gov/chartbook2004/tables-population.html #Indicator%202 (accessed August 11, 2005)

individuals that share a common characteristic such as birth years and is studied over time) that is responsible for the tremendous increase projected in the number of people age sixty-five and over, and especially age sixty-five to seventy-four, after 2010. The older adult segment of the population is expected to swell between 2010 and 2030 as the baby boom cohort completes its transition from "middle age" to "old age."

The decline in death rates, especially at the older ages, has also contributed to the increase in the number of older adults. Death rates of older adults began to plummet during the late 1960s and continued to decline through the early years of the twenty-first century. Advances in medical care have produced declining death rates for all three of the leading causes of death—heart disease, malignancies (cancer), and cerebrovascular diseases that cause strokes. (See Table 1.2.) According to the Centers for Disease Control and Prevention (CDC) National Center for Health Statistics, the age-adjusted death rate in the United States reached an all-time low in 2003 of 831.2 deaths per one hundred thousand population. Table 1.3 shows that the death rate declined between 2002 and 2003 among adults age sixty-five to seventy-four, from 2,315 to 2,254; among adults age seventy-five to eighty-four the death rate dropped from 5,557 to 5,460; and among the oldest old (eighty-five years and over) the death rate fell from 14,828 to 14,596.

Projections of an increasing proportion of older adults from 2010 to 2030 are based on three assumptions—historic low fertility and the prospect of continuing low fertility until 2030; aging of the baby boom cohort; and continued declines in mortality at older ages and low mortality until 2030. Demographers (those who study population statistics) anticipate that when the entire baby boom group has attained age sixty-five in 2030, the proportion of older people in the U.S. population will stabilize.

DEFINING OLD AGE

Forty is the old age of youth, fifty the youth of old age.

—Victor Hugo, French poet, dramatist, and novelist (1802–85)

When does old age begin? The challenge of defining old age is reflected in the terminology used to describe adults age fifty and older—for example, middle-aged, elder, elderly, older, aged, mature, or senior. AARP (formerly American Association of Retired Persons), the nonprofit, nonpartisan, national advocacy organization for older adults, invites members to join its ranks at age fifty. Many retailers offer "senior discounts" to persons beginning at age fifty or fifty-five, and federal entitlement programs such as Social Security and Medicare extend benefits to persons at age sixty-two, sixty-five, or sixty-seven. Despite the varying definitions of old age and the age at which one assumes "older adult status," in this text, unless otherwise specified, the term older adults is used to refer to persons age sixty-five and older.

Gerontology, the field of study that considers the social, psychological, and biological aspects of aging, distinguishes between three groups of older adults: the young-old are considered to be those persons age sixty-five to seventy-four, the middle-old includes those age seventy-five to eighty-four, and the oldest-old are persons

TABLE 1.2

Death rate statistics, 2002–03

[Data are based on a continuous file of records received from the states. Rates are per 100,000 population; age-adjusted rates per 100,000 U.S. standard population based on the year 2000 standard. Figures for 2003 are based on weighted data rounded to the nearest individual, so categories may not add to totals.]

Rank*	Cause of death	Number	Death rate	Age-adjusted death rate 2003	Age-adjusted death rate 2002	Percent change
...	All causes	2,443,930	840.4	831.2	845.3	−1.7
1	Diseases of heart	684,462	235.4	232.1	240.8	−3.6
2	Malignant neoplasms	554,643	190.7	189.3	193.5	−2.2
3	Cerebrovascular diseases	157,803	54.3	53.6	56.2	−4.6
4	Chronic lower respiratory diseases	126,128	43.4	43.2	43.5	−0.7
5	Accidents (unintentional injuries)	105,695	36.3	36.1	36.9	−2.2
6	Diabetes mellitus	73,965	25.4	25.2	25.4	−0.8
7	Influenza and pneumonia	64,847	22.3	21.9	22.6	−3.1
8	Alzheimer's disease	63,343	21.8	21.4	20.2	5.9
9	Nephritis, nephrotic syndrome and nephrosis	42,536	14.6	14.5	14.2	2.1
10	Septicemia	34,243	11.8	11.7	11.7	—
11	Intentional self-harm (suicide)	30,642	10.5	10.5	10.9	−3.7
12	Chronic liver disease and cirrhosis	27,201	9.4	9.2	9.4	−2.1
13	Essential (primary) hypertension and hypertensive renal disease	21,841	7.5	7.4	7.0	5.7
14	Parkinson's disease	17,898	6.2	6.1	5.9	3.4
15	Pneumonitis due to solids and liquids	17,457	6.0	5.9	6.1	−3.3
...	All other causes	421,226	144.8	...	...	...

— Quantity zero.
... Category not applicable.
*Rank based on number of deaths.

SOURCE: Donna L. Hoyert, Hsiang-Ching Kung, and Betty L. Smith, "Deaths and Death Rates for 2003 and Age-Adjusted Death Rates and Percent Changes in Age-Adjusted Death Rates from 2002 to 2003 for the 15 Leading Causes of Death in 2003: United States, Final 2002 and Preliminary 2003," in "Deaths: Preliminary Data for 2003," *National Vital Statistics Report*, vol. 53, no. 15, National Center for Health Statistics, Hyattsville, MD, February 28, 2005, http://www.cdc.gov/nchs/data/nvsr/nvsr53/nvsr53_15.pdf (accessed August 11, 2005)

age eighty-five and over. Figure 1.1 shows that the oldest segment of older adults, the oldest-old, grew from just over one hundred thousand in 1900 to 4.2 million in 2000 and is projected to steadily increase from 2010 to 2050.

LIFE EXPECTANCY

Life expectancy (the anticipated average length of life) has increased dramatically since 1900, when the average age of death for men and women combined was forty-seven. Most projections see life expectancy continuing to rise; according to the National Center for Health Statistics, the life expectancy of a baby born in the United States in 2005 was eighty years for females and 74.5 years for males.

Some researchers caution, however, that the historic trend of increasing longevity has ended, with life expectancy at birth beginning to decline by as much as five years as a direct result of the obesity epidemic in the United States. An analysis by S. Jay Olshansky, PhD, of the University of Illinois at Chicago; Leonard Hayflick, PhD, of the University of California, San Francisco; Robert N. Butler, MD, of the International Longevity Center in New York, and their colleagues suggests that the methods used to establish life expectancy projections, which have long been based on historic trends, need to be reassessed in view of increasing obesity-related mortality ("A Potential Decline in Life Expectancy in the United States in the 21st Century," *New England Journal of Medicine*, vol. 352, no. 11, March 17, 2005).

The investigators based their projections on an analysis of body mass index (BMI is a number that shows body weight adjusted for height) and other factors that could potentially affect the health and well-being of the current generation of children and young adults, and they determined that obesity currently reduces life expectancy by approximately four to nine months. The investigators assert that unless steps are taken to curb excessive weight gain, younger Americans will likely face a greater risk of mortality throughout life than previous generations.

Global Life Expectancy

The more developed regions of the world have lower death rates than the less developed regions and, as such, have higher life expectancies. The World Health Organization (WHO) observes that life expectancy at birth has increased globally from 46.5 years in the early to mid-1950s to 65.2 years in 2002. The exceptions to this trend are Africa and the former Soviet Union, both of which experienced declines in life expectancy of 2.9 years and one year respectively between 1990 and 2000.

Although the gap in life expectancy is expected to narrow during the first half of the twenty-first century, the developed world will still be far ahead. From 2045 to

TABLE 1.3

Deaths and age-adjusted death rates, by sex, final 2002 and preliminary 2003

[Data are based on a continuous file of records received from the states. Age-specific rates are per 100,000 population in specified group. Age-adjusted rates are per 100,000 U.S. standard population. Figures for 2003 are based on weighted data rounded to the nearest individual, so categories may not add to totals.]

Age, race, and sex	2003		2002	
	Number	Rate	Number	Rate
All ages, both sexes				
All ages	2,443,908	840.4	2,443,387	847.3
Under 1 year*	28,428	710.1	28,034	695.0
1–4 years	4,905	31.1	4,858	31.2
5–14 years	6,903	16.8	7,150	17.4
15–24 years	33,050	80.2	33,046	81.4
25–34 years	40,731	102.2	41,355	103.6
35–44 years	88,433	199.3	91,140	202.9
45–54 years	175,591	430.3	172,385	430.1
55–64 years	261,505	937.3	253,342	952.4
65–74 years	413,227	2,253.5	422,990	2,314.7
75–84 years	702,641	5,460.1	707,654	5,556.9
85 years and over	687,959	14,595.6	681,076	14,828.3
Not stated	533	...	357	...
Age-adjusted rate	...	831.2	...	845.3
All races, male				
All ages	1,198,454	837.9	1,199,264	846.6
Under 1 year*	16,131	788.6	15,717	761.5
1–4 years	2,807	34.8	2,806	35.2
5–14 years	4,116	19.6	4,198	20.0
15–24 years	24,232	114.4	24,416	117.3
25–34 years	28,216	139.5	28,736	142.2
35–44 years	55,839	252.3	57,593	257.5
45–54 years	109,830	548.0	107,722	547.5
55–64 years	155,748	1,160.2	151,363	1,184.0
65–74 years	231,375	2,771.2	237,021	2,855.3
75–84 years	341,875	6,632.9	343,504	6,760.5
85 years and over	227,932	15,774.7	225,906	16,254.5
Not stated	354	...	282	...
Age-adjusted rate	...	991.7	...	1,013.7
All races, female				
All ages	1,245,454	842.8	1,244,123	848.0
Under 1 year*	12,297	628.0	12,317	625.3
1–4 years	2,098	27.2	2,052	27.0
5–14 years	2,787	13.9	2,952	14.7
15–24 years	8,818	44.0	8,630	43.7
25–34 years	12,516	63.7	12,619	64.0
35–44 years	32,594	146.6	33,547	148.8
45–54 years	65,762	316.8	64,663	316.9
55–64 years	105,757	730.6	101,979	738.0
65–74 years	181,852	1,820.8	185,969	1,864.7
75–84 years	360,766	4,676.5	364,150	4,757.9
85 years and over	460,027	14,074.4	455,170	14,209.6
Not stated	179	...	75	...
Age-adjusted rate	...	705.4	...	715.2

... Category not applicable.
*Death rates for "Under 1 year" (based on population estimates) differ from infant mortality rates (based on live births).
Note: Data are subject to sampling or random variation.

SOURCE: Adapted from Donna L. Hoyert, Hsiang-Ching Kung, and Betty L. Smith, "Table 1. Deaths and Death Rates by Age, Sex, and Race and Hispanic Origin and Age-Adjusted Death Rates, by Sex and Race and Hispanic Origin: United States, Final 2002 and Preliminary 2003," in "Deaths: Preliminary Data for 2003," *National Vital Statistics Report*, vol. 53, no. 15, National Center for Health Statistics, Hyattsville, MD, February 28, 2005, http://www.cdc.gov/nchs/data/nvsr/nvsr53/nvsr53_15.pdf (accessed August 11, 2005)

2050 the more developed regions will have a life expectancy of 82.1 years, compared with seventy-five years for less developed regions and 69.7 for the least developed.

OLDER ADULTS IN THE UNITED STATES

According to U.S. Census Bureau statistics, more than half of the older population in 2000 was in the young-old bracket (age sixty-five to seventy-four). There

were 18.4 million people in this age group, comprising 53% of the sixty-five and over population. Thirty-five percent of the older adult population was in the middle-old bracket (age seventy-five to eighty-four). This group numbered 12.4 million. Twelve percent (4.2 million) were the oldest-old (age eighty-five and over).

By 2010 the number of young-old is projected to rise to more than twenty-one million, the middle-old will be

TABLE 1.4

Projections of the population, by age and sex, 1995–2050

[Numbers in thousands. Minus sign denotes a decrease.]

Age group and year	Both sexes			Sex		
	Number	Percent of all ages	Percent increase from 1995	Male	Female	Sex ratio*
All ages						
1995	262,820	x	x	128,311	134,509	95.4
2000	274,634	x	4.5	134,181	140,453	95.5
2010	297,716	x	13.3	145,584	152,132	95.7
2030	346,899	x	32	169,950	176,949	96
2050	393,931	x	49.9	193,234	200,696	96.3
55–64						
1995	21,138	8	x	10,045	11,093	90.6
2000	23,961	8.7	13.4	11,433	12,528	91.3
2010	35,283	11.9	66.9	16,921	18,362	92.2
2030	36,348	10.5	72	17,441	18,907	92.2
2050	42,368	10.8	100.4	20,403	21,965	92.9
65–74						
1995	18,758	7.1	x	8,337	10,421	80
2000	18,136	6.6	−3.3	8,180	9,956	82.2
2010	21,058	7.1	12.3	9,753	11,305	86.3
2030	37,407	10.8	99.4	17,878	19,529	91.5
2050	34,732	8.8	85.2	16,699	18,033	92.6
75–84						
1995	11,151	4.2	x	4,326	6,825	63.4
2000	12,316	4.5	10.4	4,938	7,378	66.9
2010	12,680	4.3	13.7	5,363	7,317	73.3
2030	23,517	6.8	110.9	10,818	12,699	85.2
2050	25,905	6.6	132.3	12,342	13,563	91
85+						
1995	3,634	1.4	x	1,015	2,619	38.8
2000	4,259	1.6	17.2	1,228	3,031	40.5
2010	5,670	1.9	56	1,771	3,899	45.4
2030	8,454	2.4	132.7	3,021	5,433	55.6
2050	18,224	4.6	401.5	7,036	11,188	62.9
65+						
1995	33,544	12.8	x	13,678	19,866	68.9
2000	34,710	12.6	3.5	14,346	20,364	70.4
2010	39,409	13.2	17.5	16,887	22,522	75
2030	69,379	20	106.8	31,718	37,661	84.2
2050	78,859	20	135.1	36,076	42,783	84.3

*Males per 100 females.
x=Not applicable

SOURCE: Jacob Siegel, "Projections of the Population, by Age and Sex: 1995 to 2050," in *Aging into the 21st Century*, Administration on Aging, Department of Health and Human Services, Washington, DC, May 31, 1996, http://www.aoa.gov/prof/Statistics/future_growth/aging21/table1.asp (accessed August 11, 2005)

nearing thirteen million, and the oldest-old will approach six million. (See Table 1.4.) Women are expected to outnumber men in all three age brackets. Table 1.2 shows how the projected distribution of older adults by gender— the number of males per one hundred females—declines in 2010 from 86.3 in the young-old bracket to 73.3 in the middle-old and 45.4 among the oldest-old. Longer female life expectancy, combined with the fact that men generally marry younger women, contributes to a higher proportion of older women living alone—widowed or unmarried.

The Oldest-Old

In the Census 2000 Brief *The 65 Years and Over Population: 2000* (Lisa Hetzel and Annetta Smith;

Washington, DC) released in October 2001, the U.S. Census Bureau reported that during the 1990s the oldest age group grew more rapidly than did the young-old and middle-old segments of the population. The eighty-five and older population grew from 3.1 million in 1990 to 4.2 million in 2000, an increase of 38%. In contrast, the middle-old increased by 23%, from 10.1 million in 1990 to 12.4 million in 2000, and the number of young-old rose less than 2%, from 18.1 million to 18.4 million.

According to Census Bureau estimates, as of July 1, 2004, there were 4.9 million people age eighty-five and older in the United States. By 2050 the eighty-five and over age group could number nearly twenty-one million—5% of the total U.S. population. The Federal Interagency Forum on Aging-Related Statistics report noted that some researchers believe that death rates at older ages will decline more rapidly than is reflected in U.S. Census Bureau projections, which would result in even faster growth of this population segment.

Among the oldest-old, women dramatically outnumber men—there are just forty-five men per one hundred women. Because it is anticipated that women will continue to live longer into the middle of the twenty-first century, they will comprise an even larger proportion of the older population and the overall U.S. population in the future.

THE WORLD'S EIGHTY-PLUS POPULATION. People age eighty and over make up the fastest-growing population segment in the world. As the U.S. Census Bureau reported in *Global Population Profile: 2002* (Washington, DC; March 2004), there were 77.1 million people in this age group in the world in 2002. By 2025 the eighty-plus population is expected to more than double to 164.4 million. Although this age group represented a very small portion of the world population (1%) in 2002, the proportion is expected to increase significantly by 2050.

Centenarians

During the first half of the twenty-first century, the United States will experience a "centenarian boom." The chances of living to age one hundred have increased by 40% since 1900. The centenarian population more than doubled during the 1980s, and as of August 1, 2004, the U.S. Census Bureau estimated that the country had 64,658 centenarians. According to the Census Bureau's middle-series projections, the United States will have 131,000 centenarians by 2010 and 834,000 by 2050, a phenomenal growth when compared with the four thousand centenarians living in the United States in 1960. (Figure 1.2 shows the projected population distribution in 2025; Figure 1.3 and Figure 1.4 contain comparable data for 2050 and 2100 respectively.) Not surprisingly, most centenarians do not live long after age one hundred; 90% do not reach 105 years of age.

Racial and Ethnic Diversity

The older population is becoming more ethnically and racially diverse, although at a slower pace than the overall population of the United States. As Figure 1.5 shows, in 2003 approximately 83% of the older population was comprised of non-Hispanic whites, African-Americans made up around 8%, Asians contributed about 3%, and Hispanics accounted for approximately 6% of older adults. By 2050 the composition of the older population is projected to be more racially and ethnically diverse, with 61% non-Hispanic white, 18% Hispanic, 12% African-American, and 8% Asian. Although the older population will increase among all racial and ethnic groups, the older Hispanic population will grow fastest, from slightly more than two million in 2003 to fifteen million in 2050. Similarly the older Asian population is expected to increase dramatically from nearly one million in 2003 to almost seven million in 2050.

Marital Status

As in previous years, in 2003 older men were much more likely than women to be married. More than three-quarters (78%) of men age sixty-four to seventy-five were married compared with 56% of women in the same age group. The proportion married decreases with advancing age. Thirty-six percent of women age seventy-five to eighty-four and 14% of women age eighty-five and over were married. Among men the proportion married decreases with advancing age but not as sharply. Even among the oldest-old the majority of men (59%) were married. (See Figure 1.6.)

As older women outnumber older men in all age groups, it is not surprising that there are more widows than widowers. In 2003 more than three times as many women as men age sixty-five to seventy-four were widowed—29% of women compared with 9% of men. Although the gap narrows in older age groups, there were still about twice as many women as men age eighty-five and over who were widowed—78% of women as opposed to 35% of men. A fairly small proportion of older adults were divorced, while an even smaller proportion had never married. (See Figure 1.6.)

Foreign-Born Older Adults

The nation's foreign-born population numbered 34.2 million in 2004, accounting for 12% of the total U.S. population according to U.S. Census Bureau survey data. The same survey identified 3.7 million older adult U.S. residents as foreign-born. Table 1.5 shows that the percentage of foreign-born older adults declines with age, from 3.5% in the sixty-five to sixty-nine age group to a scant 1.1% among older adults age eighty-five and over. Among the foreign-born older population, somewhat more than 1.9 million people, or 52%, entered the United States before 1970. Less than 135,000, or 3.6%, arrived in 2000 or later.

WHERE OLDER AMERICANS LIVE

From 2003 to 2004 the older adult population grew by 351,000 people, according to July 1, 2004, estimates by the U.S. Census Bureau. California was estimated to have the highest number of people sixty-five and older (3.8 million) in 2004, followed by Florida (2.9 million), New York (2.5 million), Texas (2.2 million), Pennsylvania (1.9 million), and Ohio and Illinois (1.5 million each). California's older population increased by fifty-seven thousand between 2003 and 2004, Texas added thirty-seven

FIGURE 1.2

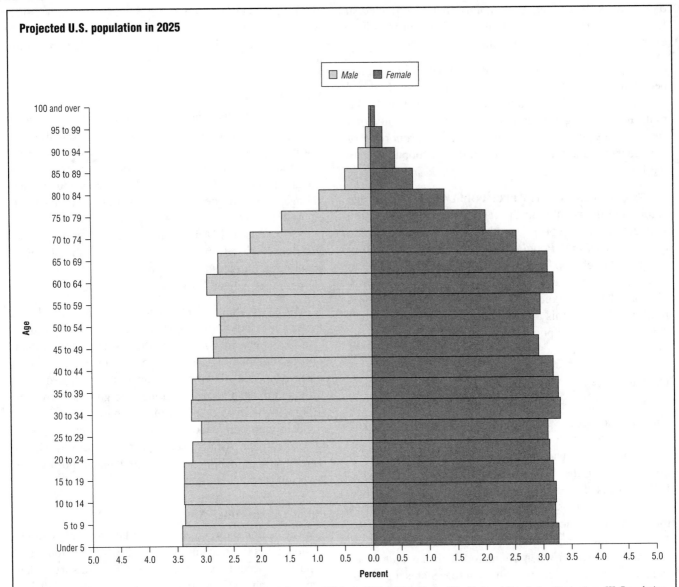

Projected U.S. population in 2025

SOURCE: "(NP-P3) Projected Resident Population of the United States as of July 1, 2025, Middle Series," in *National Population Projections III. Population Pyramids Total Resident Population of the United States by Sex, Middle Series*, U.S. Census Bureau, Population Division, Population Projections Branch, Washington, DC, http://www.census.gov/population/www/projections/np_p3.pdf (accessed August 11, 2005)

thousand older adults, and Florida's older population grew by thirty-two thousand.

The highest rates of increase in the sixty-five and older population between 2003 and 2004 occurred in Nevada and Alaska, with 4.2% and 3.8% respectively. The states with the highest proportions of their total population in the sixty-five and older age group were Florida with 16.8%, West Virginia and Pennsylvania with 15.3% each, and both North Dakota and Iowa with 14.7%.

The proportion of the population age sixty-five and over varies by state. By 2010 nearly 18% of Florida's population will be older adults, and by 2030 that percentage is projected to rise to more than 27%. Five other states in which the older population is predicted to exceed

25% by 2030 are Maine (26.5%), Wyoming (26.5%), New Mexico (26.4%), Montana (25.8%), and North Dakota (25.1%). In 2030 the states in which older adults will constitute the lowest percentage of the population are Utah (13.2%), Alaska (14.7%), Texas (15.6%), and Georgia (15.9%). (See Table 1.6.)

The proportion of the population age sixty-five and over also varies by county. According to the Federal Interagency Forum on Aging-Related Statistics, McIntosh County, North Dakota, had the highest proportion (35%) of older population in 2002, and several Florida counties exceeded 30%. By contrast, in Chattahoochee County, Georgia, just 2% of the population was age sixty-five and over.

FIGURE 1.3

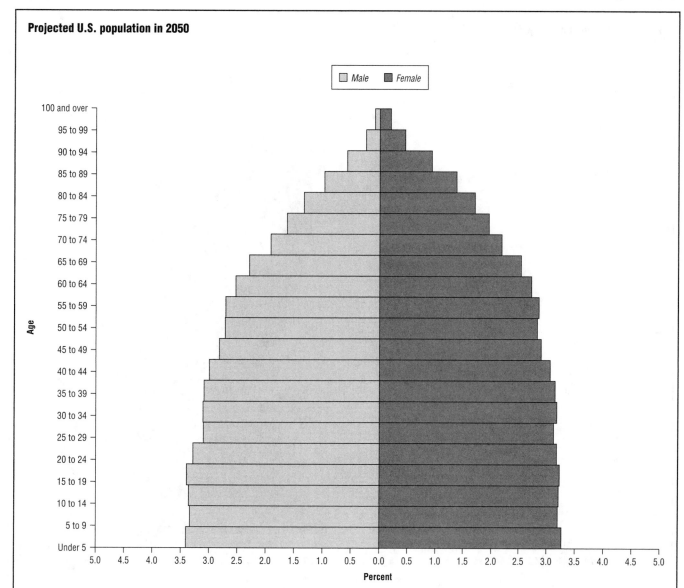

Projected U.S. population in 2050

SOURCE: "(NP-P4) Projected Resident Population of the United States as of July 1, 2050, Middle Series," in *National Population Projections III. Population Pyramids Total Resident Population of the United States by Sex, Middle Series*, U.S. Census Bureau, Population Division, Population Projections Branch, Washington, DC, http://www.census.gov/population/www/projections/np_p4.pdf (accessed August 11, 2005)

ENJOYMENT OF OLDER AGE

The average person can get younger in the sense that he or she can have even more years to live as time goes on.

—Warren Sanderson of State University of New York at Stony Brook in "Forty May Be the New 30 as Scientists Redefine Age" (Patricia Reaney, *Reuters Health*, June 8, 2005)

Highlights from the NCOA Study

According to a study conducted by the National Council on the Aging (NCOA) titled *Myths and Realities of Aging 2000*, almost half (44%) of respondents age sixty-five years and over said that their current years were the best years of their lives. The survey of more than three thousand adults found that the vast majority of

Americans of all ages (84%) said they would be happy to live to age ninety.

The number of older Americans who agreed with the statement "these are the best years of my life" rose dramatically since the NCOA first conducted this survey in 1974, when only 32% of older Americans concurred with this sentiment. The 2000 survey found that compared with older whites, much larger proportions of older African-Americans and Hispanics agreed with that statement. The NCOA researchers suggest that this may be because some ethnic groups are more likely than whites to have strong family and religious ties that provide a sense of connection and purpose, which are especially important in older years.

FIGURE 1.4

Projected U.S. population in 2100

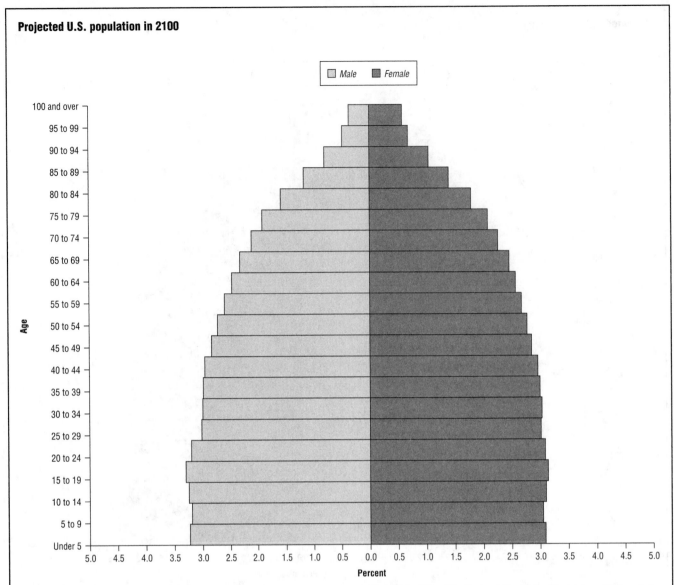

SOURCE: "(NP-P5) Projected Resident Population of the United States as of July 1, 2100, Middle Series," in *National Population Projections III. Population Pyramids Total Resident Population of the United States by Sex, Middle Series*, U.S. Census Bureau, Population Division, Population Projections Branch, Washington, DC, http://www.census.gov/population/www/projections/np_p5.pdf (accessed August 11, 2005)

Other important findings from the NCOA survey included the following:

- Most Americans favored spending more—not less—money on older people.

- Older people were less worried about their health, their finances, and the threat of crime than they were twenty-five years ago.

- For many respondents, "old age" begins with a decline in physical or mental ability, rather than with the arrival of a specific birthday.

- Younger people tended to overstate the social isolation and financial problems of older people.

- Sixty percent of respondents took responsibility for key financial decisions.

- Forty-four percent of married respondents had never discussed with their spouse when they would retire, 40% had never discussed where they would live when they retired, and 45% had never talked about how much money they would need.

A 2002 update of the NCOA survey examined Americans' perceptions of aging and found that almost half of people age sixty-five and older described themselves as middle-aged or young, and just 15% of those age seventy-five and over described themselves as "very old."

FIGURE 1.5

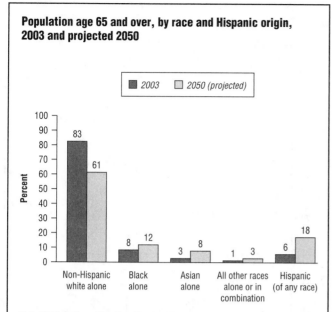

Population age 65 and over, by race and Hispanic origin, 2003 and projected 2050

Note: The term "non-Hispanic white alone" is used to refer to people who reported being white and no other race and who are not Hispanic. The term "black alone" is used to refer to people who reported being black or African American and no other race, and the term "Asian alone" is used to refer to people who reported only Asian as their race. The use of single-race populations in this report does not imply that this is the preferred method of presenting or analyzing data. The U.S. Census Bureau uses a variety of approaches. The race group "All other races alone or in combination" includes American Indian and Alaska Native, alone; Native Hawaiian and Other Pacific Islander, alone; and all people who reported two or more races. Reference population: These data refer to the resident population.

SOURCE: "Population Age 65 and Over, by Race and Hispanic Origin, 2003 and Projected 2050," in *Older Americans 2004: Key Indicators*, Federal Interagency Forum on Aging Related Statistics, Washington, DC, U.S. Government Printing Office, November 2004, http://www.agingstats.gov/chartbook2004/population.html#Indicator%202 (accessed August 11, 2005)

Positive Perceptions of Aging Influence Longevity

Research conducted at the Yale University Department of Epidemiology and Public Health found that older people with more positive self-perceptions of aging lived 7.5 years longer than those with less positive self-perceptions of aging even after taking into account other factors, including age, gender, socioeconomic status, loneliness, and overall health. Analyzing data from the 660 participants age fifty and older in the Ohio Longitudinal Study of Aging and Retirement (OLSAR), researchers compared mortality rates with responses made twenty-three years earlier by the participants (338 men and 322 women). The responses included agreeing or disagreeing with such statements as, "As you get older, you are less useful."

The investigators asserted that "the effect of more positive self-perceptions of aging on survival is greater than the physiological measures of low systolic blood pressure and cholesterol, each of which is associated with a longer lifespan of four years or less. . . . [It] is also greater than the independent contribution of lower body mass index, no history of smoking, and a tendency to

exercise; each of these factors has been found to contribute between one and three years of added life." They concluded that negative self-perceptions can diminish life expectancy, while positive self-perceptions can prolong it (Becca R. Levy, et al, "Longevity Increased by Positive Self-Perceptions of Aging," *Journal of Personality and Social Psychology*, vol. 83, no. 2, August 2002).

Happiness in the Face of Trauma

Detailed demographic data from the federal government outlined in the third edition of *Americans 55 & Older: A Changing Market* (Sharon Yntema, ed., American Generations Series, Ithaca, NY: New Strategist Publications, 2001) characterized older Americans as the happiest of any age group. In fact, the percentage of survey respondents that said they were "very happy" peaked in the sixty-five to seventy-four age group. Older Americans are also the most happily married. Seventy-two percent of couples age sixty-five to seventy-four said their marriage was "very happy," compared with 61% of all couples.

In contrast to the good news about marriage later in life, those age sixty-five to seventy-four suffered a high rate of traumatic events, including death, divorce, unemployment, hospitalization, and disability. Of persons age sixty-five to seventy-four, more than half (52%) had experienced at least one such traumatic event in the past five years, compared with 35% for all adults. Another 27% had experienced two or more such events, and 52% had experienced the death of one or more relatives in the past five years.

A 2003 NCOA survey examined the concerns of older Americans. The survey, part of an NCOA/MetLife Foundation initiative to increase civic involvement of older Americans, revealed that more than 40% of people over the age of sixty worry (very much or somewhat) about physically caring for themselves (44%) or losing their memory (42%). Older Americans also worry that their children, grandchildren, or youth in general will be exposed to drugs (63%) or face a lack of employment opportunities (54%).

The older Americans surveyed also said that "having something meaningful to do" (27%) or "having some good friends" (26%) were the activities that would have the most favorable impact on their future quality of life. When queried about the most important things to do within a year of retirement, the respondents' top choices included participating in a meaningful volunteer experience (27%) and visiting family and friends (22%). Very few selected "take it easy and relax most days." When asked about valued activities after five years of retirement, volunteering and visiting with family and friends were still the top choices.

FIGURE 1.6

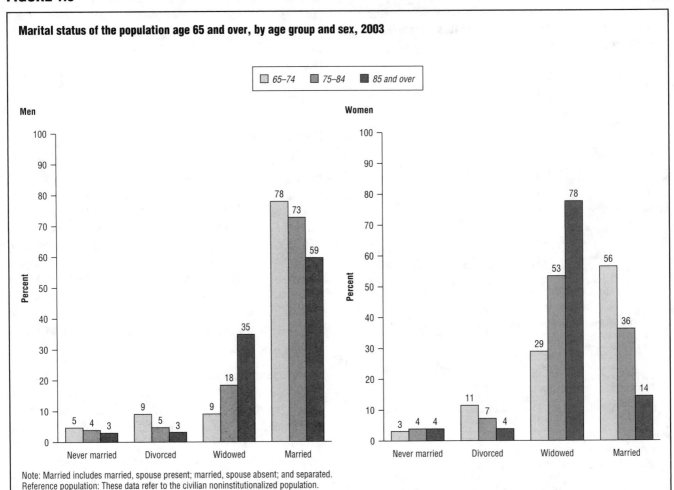

Marital status of the population age 65 and over, by age group and sex, 2003

Legend: 65–74, 75–84, 85 and over

Note: Married includes married, spouse present; married, spouse absent; and separated.
Reference population: These data refer to the civilian noninstitutionalized population.

SOURCE: "Marital Status of the Population Age 65 and Over, by Age Group and Sex, 2003," in *Older Americans 2004: Key Indicators*, Federal Interagency Forum on Aging Related Statistics, Washington, DC, U.S. Government Printing Office, November 2004, http://www.agingstats.gov/chartbook2004/population.html#Indicator%203 (accessed August 11, 2005).

ATTITUDES ABOUT AGING

People of all ages hold beliefs and attitudes about aging and older adults. Even very young children can distinguish age differences, and they display attitudes that appear to be characteristic of their generation. Because attitudes strongly influence behavior and because more Americans reach older ages than ever before, interaction with older persons and deeply held beliefs about growing old are likely influenced by cultural and societal attitudes about aging and older adults. The availability, accessibility, adequacy, and acceptability of health care and other services intended to meet the needs of older persons are similarly influenced by the attitudes of younger persons. The prevailing attitudes of opinion-leaders, decision makers, health and human services personnel, and taxpayers are particularly important in shaping policy, programs, services, and public sentiment.

In nonindustrialized countries, older people are often held in high esteem. Older adults are respected because they often have endured and persevered in harsh living conditions and because they have accumulated wisdom and knowledge that younger generations need in order to survive and carry on the traditions of their cultures. In many industrialized societies, including the United States, a person's worth may be measured in terms of income and the amount of wealth accumulated. When older adults retire from full-time employment, they may lose status because they are no longer working, earning money, or "contributing" to society. When an individual's sense of self-worth and identity is closely bound to employment or occupation, upon retirement from the workforce he or she may feel worthless.

Stereotypes Fuel Worries of Older Adults

While people of all ages worry about the future, for older adults, aging may signify a future threat to their health and well-being, diminished social status, a loss of power, and the possibility of loss of control over their lives. Researchers posit that social stereotypes, such as media portrayals of older adults as weak and helpless and

TABLE 1.5

Foreign-born population by sex, age, and year of entry, 2004

[Numbers in thousands]

	Foreign born		Year of entry 2000 or later*		1990–1999		1980–1989		1970–1979		Before 1970	
Sex and age	Number	Percent	Number	Percent	Number	Percent	Number	Percent	Number	Percent	Number	Percent
Total male and female	***34,244**	**100.0**	**6,052**	**100.0**	**11,968**	**100.0**	**7,865**	**100.0**	**4,499**	**100.0**	**3,861**	**100.0**
0 to 4 years	334	1.0	321	5.3	13	0.1	(X)	(X)	(X)	(X)	(X)	(X)
5 to 9 years	709	2.1	410	6.8	299	2.5	(X)	(X)	(X)	(X)	(X)	(X)
10 to 14 years	1,113	3.3	387	6.4	711	5.9	16	0.2	(X)	(X)	(X)	(X)
15 to 19 years	1,677	4.9	496	8.2	872	7.3	309	3.9	(X)	(X)	(X)	(X)
20 to 24 years	2,884	8.4	1,002	16.6	1,305	10.9	571	7.3	5	0.1	(X)	(X)
25 to 29 years	3,751	11.0	1,095	18.1	1,868	15.6	598	7.6	191	4.2	(X)	(X)
30 to 34 years	4,033	11.8	828	13.7	1,936	16.2	896	11.4	371	8.2	3	0.1
35 to 39 years	3,873	11.3	556	9.2	1,487	12.4	1,229	15.6	495	11.0	105	2.7
40 to 44 years	3,686	10.8	327	5.4	1,131	9.4	1,406	17.9	575	12.8	248	6.4
45 to 49 years	3,049	8.9	230	3.8	778	6.5	1,044	13.3	687	15.3	310	8.0
50 to 54 years	2,267	6.6	135	2.2	500	4.2	634	8.1	683	15.2	316	8.2
55 to 59 years	1,811	5.3	73	1.2	342	2.9	409	5.2	546	12.1	440	11.4
60 to 64 years	1,360	4.0	59	1.0	205	1.7	242	3.1	340	7.6	513	13.3
65 to 69 years	1,195	3.5	51	0.8	162	1.4	147	1.9	274	6.1	560	14.5
70 to 74 years	897	2.6	36	0.6	170	1.4	149	1.9	134	3.0	407	10.5
75 to 79 years	755	2.2	32	0.5	114	0.9	88	1.1	97	2.2	424	11.0
80 to 84 years	476	1.4	6	0.1	48	0.4	58	0.7	37	0.8	328	8.5
85 years and over	374	1.1	9	0.1	27	0.2	68	0.9	65	1.4	205	5.3
Under 15 years	2,156	6.3	1,118	18.5	1,023	8.5	16	0.2	(X)	(X)	(X)	(X)
15 years and over	32,088	93.7	4,934	81.5	10,945	91.5	7,849	99.8	4,499	100.0	3,861	100.0
Under 16 years	2,421	7.1	1,195	19.8	1,172	9.8	54	0.7	(X)	(X)	(X)	(X)
16 years and over	31,823	92.9	4,857	80.2	10,796	90.2	7,811	99.3	4,499	100.0	3,861	100.0
Under 18 years	3,098	9.0	1,381	22.8	1,531	12.8	185	2.4	(X)	(X)	(X)	(X)
18 years and over	31,146	91.0	4,671	77.2	10,437	87.2	7,680	97.6	4,499	100.0	3,861	100.0
Under 21 years	4,359	12.7	1,790	29.6	2,134	17.8	435	5.5	(X)	(X)	(X)	(X)
21 years and over	29,885	87.3	4,262	70.4	9,833	82.2	7,430	94.5	4,499	100.0	3,861	100.0
Under 55 years	27,376	79.9	5,786	95.6	10,900	91.1	6,702	85.2	3,006	66.8	982	25.4
55 years and over	6,868	20.1	266	4.4	1,068	8.9	1,162	14.8	1,493	33.2	2,878	74.6
Under 65 years	30,547	89.2	5,918	97.8	11,447	95.7	7,354	93.5	3,892	86.5	1,936	50.1
65 years and over	3,697	10.8	134	2.2	520	4.3	511	6.5	607	13.5	1,925	49.9
Median age (years)	38.4	(X)	26.9	(X)	32.4	(X)	41.1	(X)	49.5	(X)	64.9	(X)
Total male	**17,221**	**100.0**	**3,258**	**100.0**	**6,000**	**100.0**	**4,080**	**100.0**	**2,213**	**100.0**	**1,670**	**100.0**
0 to 4 years	173	1.0	164	5.0	9	0.1	(X)	(X)	(X)	(X)	(X)	(X)
5 to 9 years	376	2.2	233	7.2	142	2.4	(X)	(X)	(X)	(X)	(X)	(X)
10 to 14 years	537	3.1	175	5.4	353	5.9	9	0.2	(X)	(X)	(X)	(X)
15 to 19 years	870	5.0	268	8.2	436	7.3	166	4.1	(X)	(X)	(X)	(X)
20 to 24 years	1,589	9.2	589	18.1	680	11.3	317	7.8	3	0.2	(X)	(X)
25 to 29 years	2,024	11.8	583	17.9	1,014	16.9	325	8.0	101	4.6	(X)	(X)
30 to 34 years	2,121	12.3	470	14.4	978	16.3	500	12.3	170	7.7	2	0.1
35 to 39 years	1,965	11.4	286	8.8	725	12.1	676	16.6	231	10.4	46	2.8
40 to 44 years	1,916	11.1	180	5.5	555	9.2	738	18.1	335	15.1	108	6.5
45 to 49 years	1,524	8.9	125	3.8	365	6.1	502	12.3	384	17.4	148	8.9
50 to 54 years	1,112	6.5	71	2.2	247	4.1	300	7.4	329	14.9	164	9.8
55 to 59 years	846	4.9	34	1.1	160	2.7	220	5.4	249	11.3	182	10.9
60 to 64 years	638	3.7	29	0.9	101	1.7	109	2.7	164	7.4	236	14.1
65 to 69 years	490	2.8	24	0.7	67	1.1	66	1.6	122	5.5	211	12.6
70 to 74 years	386	2.2	12	0.4	76	1.3	70	1.7	58	2.6	169	10.1
75 to 79 years	305	1.8	11	0.3	61	1.0	23	0.6	32	1.4	179	10.7
80 to 84 years	214	1.2	2	0.1	13	0.2	30	0.7	15	0.7	154	9.2
85 years and over	136	0.8	—	0.0	16	0.3	29	0.7	19	0.9	72	4.3

of old age as a time of hardship, loss, and pain, have a powerful influence on attitudes and may be another source of worry for older adults. They contend that the image of a tragic old age has the potential to create worries about having a tragic old age. Worse still, the negative image of old age can become a self-fulfilling prophecy, thereby confirming negative stereotypes and promoting ageism (discrimination or unfair treatment based on age).

In view of the myriad difficulties and challenges facing older adults, including ill health, inadequate financial resources, and the loss of friends and loved ones, it seems natural to assume that advancing age would be associated with less overall happiness and more worry. Several studies, however, have refuted this premise. Researchers found less worry among older adults than anticipated, little decrease in life satisfaction across the life span, and a remarkable ability of older adults to adapt to their changing life conditions.

TABLE 1.5

Foreign-born population by sex, age, and year of entry, 2004 [CONTINUED]

[Numbers in thousands]

Sex and age	Foreign born Number	Percent	2000 or later* Number	Percent	1990–1999 Number	Percent	1980–1989 Number	Percent	1970–1979 Number	Percent	Before 1970 Number	Percent
Under 15 years	1,086	6.3	572	17.6	505	8.4	9	0.2	(X)	(X)	(X)	(X)
15 years and over	16,135	93.7	2,685	82.4	5,495	91.6	4,071	99.8	2,213	100.0	1,670	100.0
Under 16 years	1,210	7.0	605	18.6	570	9.5	35	0.9	(X)	(X)	(X)	(X)
16 years and over	16,011	93.0	2,652	81.4	5,431	90.5	4,045	99.1	2,213	100.0	1,670	100.0
Under 18 years	1,541	8.9	699	21.5	740	12.3	102	2.5	(X)	(X)	(X)	(X)
18 years and over	15,680	91.1	2,559	78.5	5,261	87.7	3,978	97.5	2,213	100.0	1,670	100.0
Under 21 years	2,265	13.2	945	29.0	1,071	17.8	249	6.1	(X)	(X)	(X)	(X)
21 years and over	14,957	86.8	2,313	71.0	4,930	82.2	3,831	93.9	2,213	100.0	1,670	100.0
Under 55 years	14,206	82.5	3,145	96.5	5,506	91.8	3,533	86.6	1,554	70.2	469	28.1
55 years and over	3,015	17.5	113	3.5	495	8.2	547	13.4	659	29.8	1,201	71.9
Under 65 years	15,690	91.1	3,208	98.5	5,766	96.1	3,862	94.7	1,968	88.9	886	53.1
65 years and over	1,531	8.9	50	1.5	234	3.9	218	5.3	246	11.1	784	46.9
Median age (years)	37.3	(X)	26.7	(X)	31.9	(X)	40.3	(X)	48.5	(X)	63.9	(X)
Total female	**17,023**	**100.0**	**2,794**	**100.0**	**5,968**	**100.0**	**3,785**	**100.0**	**2,286**	**100.0**	**2,191**	**100.0**
0 to 4 years	161	0.9	157	5.6	4	0.1	(X)	(X)	(X)	(X)	(X)	(X)
5 to 9 years	333	2.0	176	6.3	157	2.6	(X)	(X)	(X)	(X)	(X)	(X)
10 to 14 years	576	3.4	212	7.6	357	6.0	6	0.2	(X)	(X)	(X)	(X)
15 to 19 years	807	4.7	228	8.2	436	7.3	143	3.8	(X)	(X)	(X)	(X)
20 to 24 years	1,295	7.6	414	14.8	625	10.5	255	6.7	1	0.1	(X)	(X)
25 to 29 years	1,727	10.1	511	18.3	854	14.3	273	7.2	90	3.9	(X)	(X)
30 to 34 years	1,912	11.2	358	12.8	957	16.0	395	10.4	200	8.8	2	0.1
35 to 39 years	1,908	11.2	270	9.7	762	12.8	553	14.6	264	11.5	59	2.7
40 to 44 years	1,771	10.4	146	5.2	576	9.7	668	17.7	240	10.5	140	6.4
45 to 49 years	1,524	9.0	105	3.8	413	6.9	542	14.3	303	13.3	162	7.4
50 to 54 years	1,155	6.8	64	2.3	253	4.2	334	8.8	353	15.5	152	6.9
55 to 59 years	965	5.7	39	1.4	182	3.1	189	5.0	297	13.0	258	11.8
60 to 64 years	722	4.2	30	1.1	105	1.8	134	3.5	176	7.7	278	12.7
65 to 69 years	704	4.1	27	1.0	95	1.6	81	2.1	152	6.7	350	16.0
70 to 74 years	512	3.0	24	0.9	94	1.6	79	2.1	76	3.3	238	10.9
75 to 79 years	450	2.6	21	0.8	53	0.9	65	1.7	65	2.9	246	11.2
80 to 84 years	261	1.5	3	0.1	34	0.6	28	0.7	22	0.9	174	7.9
85 years and over	238	1.4	9	0.3	10	0.2	40	1.1	46	2.0	134	6.1
Under 15 years	1,070	6.3	546	19.5	518	8.7	6	0.2	(X)	(X)	(X)	(X)
15 years and over	15,952	93.7	2,248	80.5	5,450	91.3	3,778	99.8	2,286	100.0	2,191	100.0
Under 16 years	1,211	7.1	590	21.1	602	10.1	18	0.5	(X)	(X)	(X)	(X)
16 years and over	15,812	92.9	2,204	78.9	5,365	89.9	3,766	99.5	2,286	100.0	2,191	100.0
Under 18 years	1,557	9.1	683	24.4	791	13.3	83	2.2	(X)	(X)	(X)	(X)
18 years and over	15,466	90.9	2,112	75.6	5,176	86.7	3,702	97.8	2,286	100.0	2,191	100.0
Under 21 years	2,094	12.3	845	30.2	1,064	17.8	185	4.9	(X)	(X)	(X)	(X)
21 years and over	14,928	87.7	1,949	69.8	4,904	82.2	3,599	95.1	2,286	100.0	2,191	100.0
Under 55 years	13,170	77.4	2,642	94.5	5,394	90.4	3,169	83.7	1,451	63.5	514	23.4
55 years and over	3,853	22.6	152	5.5	573	9.6	616	16.3	834	36.5	1,677	76.6
Under 65 years	14,857	87.3	2,710	97.0	5,681	95.2	3,492	92.3	1,924	84.2	1,050	47.9
65 years and over	2,166	12.7	84	3.0	286	4.8	293	7.7	361	15.8	1,141	52.1
Median age (years)	39.5	(X)	27.0	(X)	32.9	(X)	42.0	(X)	50.6	(X)	65.7	(X)

(X)=Not applicable
— Represents zero or rounds to zero.
*The category '2000 or later' includes 2000–2004.

SOURCE: "Table 2.1. Foreign-Born Population by Sex, Age, and Year of Entry: 2004 (Numbers in Thousands)," *Foreign-Born Population of the United States Current Population Survey—March 2004 Detailed Tables (PPL-176)*, U.S. Census Bureau, Population Division, Immigration Statistics Staff, Washington, DC, May 25, 2005, http://www.census.gov/population/socdemo/foreign/ppl-176/tab02–1.pdf (accessed August 11, 2005)

Interestingly, one survey of 761 older adults found that more than half reported feeling that their lives were better now than when they were forty-five to forty-nine years-old (S. M. Neikrug, "Worrying about a Frightening Old Age," *Aging & Mental Health*, vol. 7, no. 5, September 2003). Nearly three-quarters of those age eighty and older felt their lives were the same or better than their lives twenty years prior. The survey found far more sources of pleasure for older adults than sources of worry and concern. Worries about becoming a burden to others and about declining health predominated, and few older adults expressed concern about their own mortality. Although worries did increase among the oldest-old, overall, older adults appear to be more resilient than previously believed, even in the face of illness and loss.

TABLE 1.6

Ranking of states by projected percent of population age 65 and over, 2000, 2010, and 2030

2000 state	2000 percent	2000 rank	2010 state	2010 percent	2010 rank	2030 state	2030 percent	2030 rank
United States	12.4	(x)	United States	13.0	(x)	United States	19.7	(x)
Florida	17.6	1	Florida	17.8	1	Florida	27.1	1
Pennsylvania	15.6	2	West Virginia	16.0	2	Maine	26.5	2
West Virginia	15.3	3	Maine	15.6	3	Wyoming	26.5	3
Iowa	14.9	4	Pennsylvania	15.5	4	New Mexico	26.4	4
North Dakota	14.7	5	North Dakota	15.3	5	Montana	25.8	5
Rhode Island	14.5	6	Montana	15.0	6	North Dakota	25.1	6
Maine	14.4	7	Iowa	14.9	7	West Virginia	24.8	7
South Dakota	14.3	8	South Dakota	14.6	8	Vermont	24.4	8
Arkansas	14.0	9	Connecticut	14.4	9	Delaware	23.5	9
Connecticut	13.8	10	Arkansas	14.3	10	South Dakota	23.1	10
Nebraska	13.6	11	Vermont	14.3	11	Pennsylvania	22.6	11
Massachusetts	13.5	12	Hawaii	14.3	12	Iowa	22.4	12
Missouri	13.5	13	Delaware	14.1	13	Hawaii	22.3	13
Montana	13.4	14	Alabama	14.1	14	Arizona	22.1	14
Ohio	13.3	15	Rhode Island	14.1	15	South Carolina	22.0	15
Hawaii	13.3	16	New Mexico	14.1	16	Connecticut	21.5	16
Kansas	13.3	17	Wyoming	14.0	17	New Hampshire	21.4	17
New Jersey	13.2	18	Arizona	13.9	18	Rhode Island	21.4	18
Oklahoma	13.2	19	Missouri	13.9	19	Wisconsin	21.3	19
Wisconsin	13.1	20	Oklahoma	13.8	20	Alabama	21.3	20
Alabama	13.0	21	Nebraska	13.8	21	Massachusetts	20.9	21
Arizona	13.0	22	Ohio	13.7	22	Nebraska	20.6	22
Delaware	13.0	23	Massachusetts	13.7	23	Mississippi	20.5	23
New York	12.9	24	New Jersey	13.7	24	Ohio	20.4	24
Oregon	12.8	25	New York	13.6	25	Arkansas	20.3	25
Vermont	12.7	26	South Carolina	13.6	26	Missouri	20.2	26
Kentucky	12.5	27	Wisconsin	13.5	27	Kansas	20.2	27
Indiana	12.4	28	Kansas	13.4	28	New York	20.1	28
Tennessee	12.4	29	Tennessee	13.3	29	New Jersey	20.0	29
Michigan	12.3	30	Kentucky	13.1	30	Kentucky	19.8	30
District of Columbia	12.2	31	Oregon	13.0	31	Louisiana	19.7	31
South Carolina	12.1	32	Michigan	12.8	32	Michigan	19.5	32
Minnesota	12.1	33	Mississippi	12.8	33	Oklahoma	19.4	33
Illinois	12.1	34	Indiana	12.7	34	Tennessee	19.2	34
Mississippi	12.1	35	Louisiana	12.6	35	Minnesota	18.9	35
North Carolina	12.0	36	New Hampshire	12.6	36	Virginia	18.8	36
New Hampshire	12.0	37	North Carolina	12.4	37	Nevada	18.6	37
Wyoming	11.7	38	Virginia	12.4	38	Idaho	18.3	38
New Mexico	11.7	39	Illinois	12.4	39	Oregon	18.2	39
Louisiana	11.6	40	Minnesota	12.4	40	Washington	18.1	40
Maryland	11.3	41	Nevada	12.3	41	Indiana	18.1	41
Idaho	11.3	42	Washington	12.2	42	Illinois	18.0	42
Washington	11.2	43	Maryland	12.2	43	California	17.8	43
Virginia	11.2	44	Idaho	12.0	44	North Carolina	17.8	44
Nevada	11.0	45	California	11.5	45	Maryland	17.6	45
California	10.6	46	District of Columbia	11.5	46	Colorado	16.5	46
Texas	9.9	47	Colorado	10.7	47	Georgia	15.9	47
Colorado	9.7	48	Texas	10.5	48	Texas	15.6	48
Georgia	9.6	49	Georgia	10.2	49	Alaska	14.7	49
Utah	8.5	50	Utah	9.0	50	District of Columbia	13.4	50
Alaska	5.7	51	Alaska	8.1	51	Utah	13.2	51

SOURCE: "Table 3. Ranking of States by Projected Percent of Population Age 65 and Older: 2000, 2010, and 2030," in *State Interim Population Projections by Age and Sex: 2004–2030*, U.S. Census Bureau, Population Division, Washington, DC, April 21, 2005, http://www.census.gov/population/www/projections/projectionsagesex.html (accessed August 11, 2005)

Baby Boomers Challenge Stereotypes

Since its inception the baby boom generation has left its mark on every American institution. As teenagers and young adults, they created and championed a unique blend of music, pop culture, and political activism. The generation has witnessed remarkable technological and medical advancements in their lifetime and has come to expect, and even loudly demand, solutions to health and social problems.

As the baby boom generation has begun to join the ranks of older Americans, it has fomented a cultural revolution. The almost eighty million boomers approaching age sixty-five are not content to be regarded as "old." Accustomed to freedom and independence, they want to be recognized and treated as individuals rather than stereotypes. The aging boomers are healthier, better educated, and wealthier than any other older adult cohort in history. They are redefining old age— reinventing retirement, continuing to pursue health, and challenging the public's perception of what it is to be old.

CHAPTER 2
THE ECONOMICS OF GROWING OLD IN AMERICA

Security was attained in the earlier days through the interdependence of members of families upon each other and of the families within a small community upon each other. The complexities of great communities and of organized industry make less real these simple means of security. Therefore, we are compelled to employ the active interest of the Nation as a whole through government in order to encourage a greater security for each individual who composes it. . . . This seeking for a greater measure of welfare and happiness does not indicate a change in values. It is rather a return to values lost in the course of our economic development and expansion.

—Franklin D. Roosevelt, *Message of the President to Congress,* June 8, 1934

The economic status of older Americans is more varied than that of any other age group. While many older adults have limited resources, others are well off. Nonetheless, as a whole in the United States, the older population has a lower economic status than the overall adult population. Upon retirement most rely in some part on Social Security—a federal government program that provides retirement income and health care for older adults—supplemented by pensions and assets. Some must depend on Supplemental Security Income (SSI), a benefit for low-income people provided by federal and state governments.

With fixed incomes and sharply limited potential to improve their incomes through employment, many older persons become vulnerable to such circumstances as the loss of a spouse, prolonged illness, or even economic variations like inflation that further compromise their financial well-being, sometimes plunging them into poverty. One common scenario is that of a couple that has planned well for retirement but then runs through all of their assets to pay the health-care costs of a long-term illness. When the ill partner dies, the surviving spouse is impoverished.

THE ECONOMIC WELL-BEING OF OLDER ADULTS

There are two important measures of an individual's or household's economic well-being. One is income—the flow of money earned through employment, interest on investments, and other sources. The other is asset accumulation or wealth—the economic resources (property or other material possessions) owned by an individual or household.

Income Distribution

According to the report *Older Americans 2004: Key Indicators of Well-Being* (http://www.agingstats.gov/chartbook2004/default.htm) by the Federal Interagency Forum on Aging-Related Statistics (the Forum), the trend in median (the middle value—half are higher and half are lower) household income of the older population has been positive, and fewer older adults are living in poverty. From 1974 to 2002 the proportion of older adults living in poverty declined. In 2002 just 10% of the older population lived below the poverty threshold, compared with about 14% in 1974. The proportion of the older population in the low-income bracket also fell, from approximately 35% in 1974 to 28% in 2002. (See Figure 2.1.)

In 1974 the median household income for older adults was $16,882 in terms of 2002 dollars. By 2002 this figure had risen to $23,152. The largest proportion (34%) of the older population was in the middle-income bracket. The proportion of high-income older adults increased from 18% in 1974 to 26% in 2002. (See Figure 2.1.)

According to the U.S. Department of Health and Human Services Administration on Aging (AoA) report *A Profile of Older Americans: 2004* (http://www.aoa.gov/prof/statistics/profile/2004/profiles2004.asp), the median income for older adults in 2003 was $20,363 for men and $11,845 for women. Households headed by persons age

FIGURE 2.1

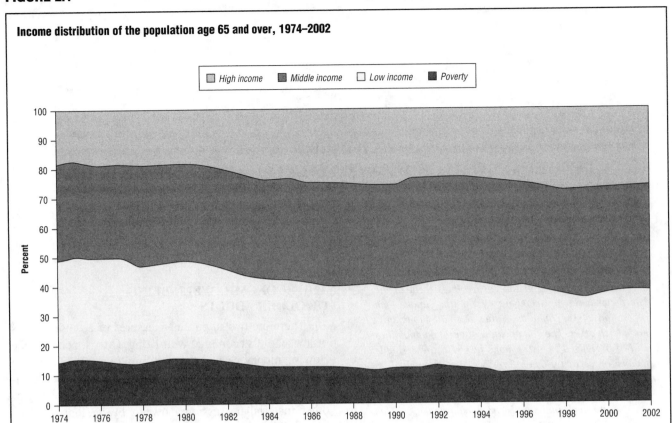

Income distribution of the population age 65 and over, 1974–2002

☐ High income ■ Middle income ☐ Low income ■ Poverty

Note: The income categories are derived from the ratio of the family's income (or an unrelated individual's income) to the corresponding poverty threshold. Being in poverty is measured as income less than 100 percent of the poverty threshold. Low income is between 100 percent and 199 percent of the poverty threshold. Middle income is between 200 percent and 399 percent of the poverty threshold. High income is 400 percent or more of the poverty threshold.
Reference population: These data refer to the civilian noninstitutionalized population.

SOURCE: "Income Distribution of the Population Age 65 and Over, 1974–2002," in *Older Americans 2004: Key Indicators*, Federal Interagency Forum on Aging Related Statistics, Washington, DC, U.S. Government Printing Office, November 2004, http://www.agingstats.gov/chartbook2004/economics .html#Indicator%208 (accessed August 11, 2005)

sixty-five and over had a median income of $35,310 in 2003, while individual median income for older adults that year was $14,664. (See Figure 2.2.) Median income was highest among non-Hispanic whites ($36,797), followed by Asians ($34,872), African-Americans ($28,407), and Hispanics ($25,355). Just over half of households headed by older adults (50.4%) had incomes in excess of $35,000, but nearly 10% had incomes of less than $15,000.

Sources of Income

Unlike younger adults, who derive most of their income from employment, older adults rely on a variety of sources of income to meet the expenses of daily living. Since the 1960s Social Security has provided the largest share of income for older Americans. In 2002 Social Security benefits were the major source of income— providing at least 50% of total income—for two-thirds (66%) of older adult beneficiaries. For more than one-third (34%) of Americans over age sixty-five in 2002, Social Security accounted for 90% of total income, and it

was the sole source of income for almost one-quarter (22%) of older adults. (See Figure 2.3.)

As reported in the Forum's *Older Americans 2004: Key Indicators of Well-Being*, the majority of older adults' income comes from four sources. In 2002, in addition to Social Security, which accounted for an average of 39%, earnings provided 25%, pensions contributed 19%, and asset income accounted for 14% of the older population's income. (See Figure 2.4.) The Forum report also stated that since the 1970s the percentage of older adults with pension coverage had remained relatively unchanged, and as of 2002 about half of all workers were covered by pension plans.

For older Americans in the lowest fifth of the income distribution, Social Security accounts for 83% of aggregate income (total income from all sources) and public assistance for another 9%. High-income older adults' aggregate income is about one-fifth each of pension, Social Security, and asset income, and nearly two-fifths are derived from income. (See Figure 2.5.) Among persons age eighty and

FIGURE 2.2

FIGURE 2.3

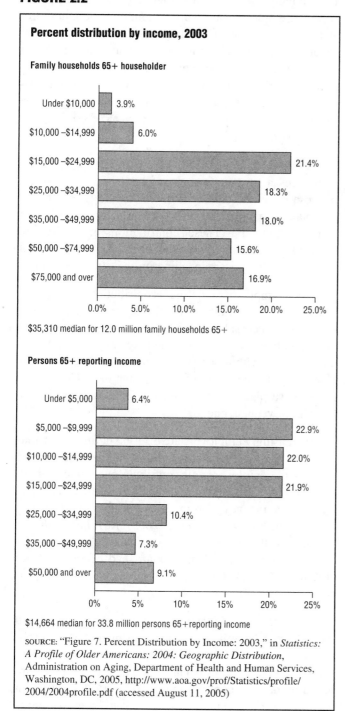

Percent distribution by income, 2003

Family households 65+ householder

$35,310 median for 12.0 million family households 65+

Persons 65+ reporting income

$14,664 median for 33.8 million persons 65+reporting income

SOURCE: "Figure 7. Percent Distribution by Income: 2003," in *Statistics: A Profile of Older Americans: 2004: Geographic Distribution*, Administration on Aging, Department of Health and Human Services, Washington, DC, 2005, http://www.aoa.gov/prof/Statistics/profile/2004/2004profile.pdf (accessed August 11, 2005).

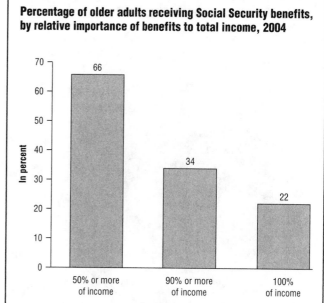

Percentage of older adults receiving Social Security benefits, by relative importance of benefits to total income, 2004

SOURCE: "Percentage of the Aged Receiving Social Security Benefits, by Relative Importance of Benefits to Total Income," in *Fast Facts & Figures About Social Security, 2004*, Social Security Administration, Office of Policy, Washington, DC, 2004, http://www.ssa.gov/policy/docs/chartbooks/fast_facts/2004/ff2004.html#agedpop (accessed August 11, 2005)

over, aggregate income is largely composed of Social Security and asset income, with earnings contributing a much smaller proportion compared with the youngest population of older adults, those age sixty-five to sixty-nine.

Expectations about Personal Finances Vary by Age

Every month Gallup Organization pollsters ask Americans to predict changes in their personal financial situation over the coming six months. They inquire about whether survey participants expect their income, savings, spending, and debt to increase, decrease, or remain the same in the next six months. Historically the Gallup data reveal that most Americans' finances remain pretty steady in the short term; there is practically no variation from month to month in Gallup's estimates of Americans' predictions for their short-term income, spending, savings, and debt. For example, the Gallup researchers usually find about the same proportion of Americans expecting their spending to increase or to decrease (25% for both) in the next six months and about 50% expecting it to stay the same.

The Gallup data shows that expectations of personal financial stability generally increase with age. Eighteen-to twenty-nine-year-olds expect the most change, thirty- to forty-nine-year-olds expect less change, and the majority of those age sixty-five and older expect all four aspects of personal financial stability—income, spending, savings, and debt—to remain unchanged. When older adults reach retirement age and rely on fixed incomes from Social Security benefits and work pensions, they anticipate little short-term change in their financial situation. In 2005 nearly three-quarters of older adults (70%) expected their income to remain the same in the next six months, while 61% also thought there would be no difference in their spending. (See Table 2.1.)

Pension (Retirement) Funds

Many large employers, along with most local and state governments and the federal government, offer pension plans for retirement. In the United States, American

FIGURE 2.4

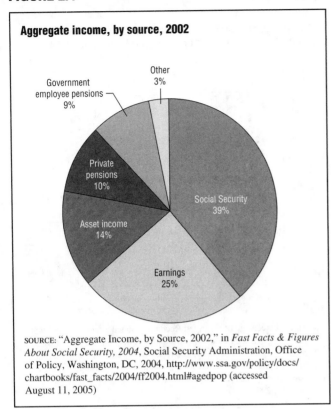

Aggregate income, by source, 2002

Other
3%

Government
employee pensions
9%

Private
pensions
10%

Asset income
14%

Social Security
39%

Earnings
25%

SOURCE: "Aggregate Income, by Source, 2002," in *Fast Facts & Figures About Social Security, 2004*, Social Security Administration, Office of Policy, Washington, DC, 2004, http://www.ssa.gov/policy/docs/chartbooks/fast_facts/2004/ff2004.html#agedpop (accessed August 11, 2005)

Express established the first private pension plan—an employer-run retirement program in 1875. General Motors Corp. provided the first modern plan in the 1940s.

Employers are not required to provide pensions, and pension plans do not have to include all workers; they may exclude certain jobs and/or individuals. Before 1976 pension plans could require an employee to work a lifetime for one company before becoming eligible for pension benefits. As required by the Employee Retirement Income Security Act of 1974 (ERISA; PL 93-406), starting in 1976 an employee became eligible after ten years of service. By the early 2000s most plans required five years of work before an employee became vested (eligible for benefits). In companies that offer pension plans, employees are eligible to begin receiving benefits when they retire or leave the company if they have worked for the requisite number of years and/or have reached the specified eligibility age.

The proportion of older adults' income from pensions grew rapidly during the 1960s and 1970s but leveled off from the 1980s to 2002. In contrast, the portion contributed by earned income declined until the mid-1980s and increased incrementally through 2002. The proportion of income from assets peaked in the mid-1980s and has declined since then. (See Figure 2.6.)

DEFINED BENEFIT PLANS AND DEFINED CONTRIBUTION PLANS. There are two principal types of pension plans—defined benefit plans and defined contribution plans.

Traditionally employers offered defined benefit plans that promised employees a specified monthly benefit at retirement. A defined benefit plan may stipulate the promised benefit as an exact dollar amount, such as $100 per month at retirement. More often, however, benefits are calculated using a plan formula that considers both salary and service—for example 1% of the average salary for the last five years of employment, for every year of service with the employer.

A defined contribution plan does not promise employees a specific amount of benefits at retirement. In these plans the employee and/or employer contribute to a plan account, sometimes at a set rate, such as 5% of earnings annually. These contributions generally are invested on the employee's behalf, and the amount of future benefits varies depending on investment earnings.

An example of a defined contribution plan is the 401(k) plan, which allows employees to defer receiving a portion of their salaries, which is instead contributed on their behalf to the plan. Income taxes are deferred until the money is withdrawn at retirement. In some instances employers match employee contributions. Created in 1978, these plans were named for section 401(k) of the Internal Revenue Code.

Increasingly employers are offering defined contribution plans, which stipulate how much the worker, and perhaps the employer, will contribute over time without specifying the exact amount of benefits at retirement. The Federal Interagency Forum on Aging-Related Statistics reported in *Older Americans 2004: Key Indicators of Well-Being* that between 1985 and 2003 the number of workers with defined benefit plans had decreased from 80% to 33%, while the proportion participating in defined contribution plans rose from 41% to 51%.

Since the mid-1990s many employers have converted their defined benefit plans to hybrid plans that incorporate elements of both defined benefit and defined contribution plans. Cash balance plans, for instance, are based on defined contributions of pay credits—based on an employee's compensation rate—and interest credits deposited annually by the employer into an account, the balance of which serves as the defined benefit. The profit or loss from the investment of the account is owned by the employer. Upon retirement the employee would have the right to an annuity (a series of regular payments) based on their account balance. For a balance of $100,000, such an annuity might be approximately $10,000 per year for life. In many cash balance plans, however, the worker could instead opt to receive a lump sum benefit equal to the entire account balance. Between 1997 and 2000 the popularity of cash balance plans skyrocketed from 6% of employers participating to 23%, according to the Forum report.

FIGURE 2.5

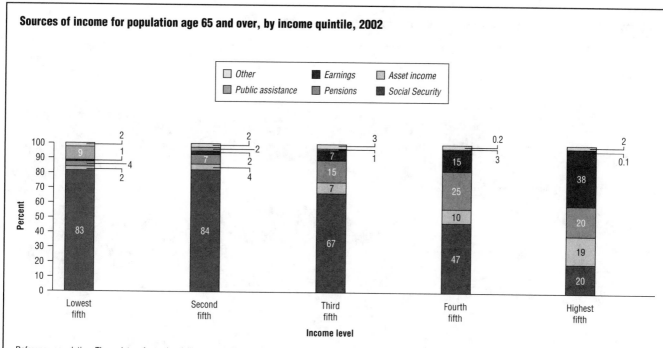

Sources of income for population age 65 and over, by income quintile, 2002

Reference population: These data refer to the civilian noninstitutionalized population.

SOURCE: "Sources of Income for the Population Age 65 and Over, by Income Quintile, 2002," in *Older Americans 2004: Key Indicators*, Federal Interagency Forum on Aging Related Statistics, Washington, DC, U.S. Government Printing Office, November 2004, http://www.agingstats.gov/chartbook2004/economics.html#Indicator%209 (accessed August 11, 2005)

PRIVATE PENSIONS AND PUBLIC PENSIONS. The Social Security Administration reported that in 1962 private pensions from employers accounted for just 3% of older adults' income. In 2002 private pensions supplied 10% of the income of older adults. Government employee public pensions contributed 9% of the total income of the older population. (See Figure 2.4.)

Because fewer employers are offering pension plans than in the past, the proportion of employees participating in these plans is decreasing. Testifying before the full House Committee on Ways and Means on May 19, 2005, Dallas L. Salisbury, president and chief executive officer of the nonpartisan Employee Benefit Research Institute (EBRI), asserted that just 13% of retirees receive annuity income from prior public-sector employment, while 20% receive such income from prior private-sector employment (http://waysandmeans.house.gov/hearings.asp?formmode=printfriendly&id=2665).

The EBRI reported that employees in larger firms are more likely to be covered by a pension plan than those in smaller firms. Highly paid employees and workers in industries covered by union contracts are most likely to have coverage. White-collar workers are somewhat more likely to receive pensions than blue-collar workers, and coverage is greater among whites than African-Americans or Hispanics and is strongly related to a worker's wage level. Employer pensions are more prevalent in goods-producing industries than in service industries.

TABLE 2.1

Public opinion on personal finance expectations, by age, 2005

	18–29 years %	30–49 years %	50–64 years %	65 years and older %
Income				
Increase	55	47	33	16
Stay the same	39	45	55	70
Decrease	6	7	11	11
Spending				
Increase	40	30	21	18
Stay the same	40	45	49	61
Decrease	20	24	29	20
Savings				
Increase	56	44	35	23
Stay the same	30	40	45	55
Decrease	13	14	17	15
Debt				
Increase	24	20	14	10
Stay the same	33	30	39	57
Decrease	42	49	45	25

SOURCE: Jeffrey M. Jones, "Personal Finance Expectations by Age, 2005," in *Young, Old Have Vastly Different Expectations for Short-Run Finances*, Poll Analyses, The Gallup Organization, Princeton, NJ, June 7, 2005, http://www.gallup.com/poll/content/?ci=16675 (accessed August 11, 2005). Copyright © 2005 by The Gallup Organization. Reproduced by permission of The Gallup Organization.

There are fewer government pension plans than private plans, but the average benefits of the public sector plans are substantially greater than those of private sector plans

FIGURE 2.6

Sources of income for the population age 65 and over, selected years 1962–2002

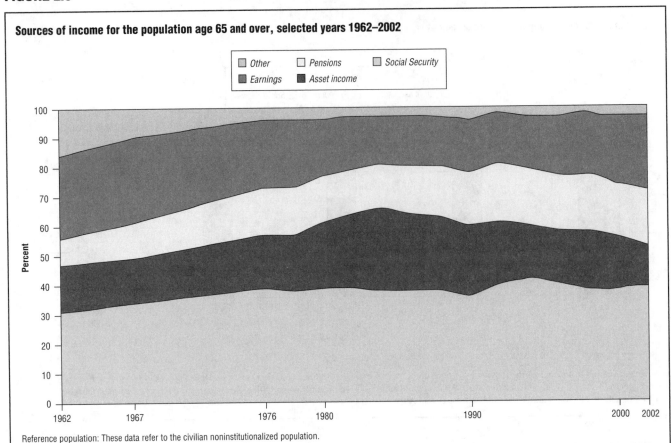

Reference population: These data refer to the civilian noninstitutionalized population.

SOURCE: "Distribution of Sources of Income for the Population Age 65 and Over, Selected Years 1962–2002," in *Older Americans 2004: Key Indicators*, Federal Interagency Forum on Aging Related Statistics, Washington, DC, U.S. Government Printing Office, November 2004, http://www.agingstats.gov/ chartbook2004/economics.html#Indicator%209 (accessed August 11, 2005)

(Ken McDonnell, "Retirement Annuity and Employment-Based Pension Income," *EBRI Notes*, vol. 26, no. 2, February 2005).

EBRI research confirmed that women do not fare as well as men in the pension system, primarily because women spend less time in the workforce and tend to hold lower-paying jobs than do men. In 2003 women age sixty-five or older were less than two-thirds as likely to receive pension payments or annuities as were older men. Furthermore, among women receiving benefits, the mean payment was roughly one-half that of payments received by older men. Widows fared least well, receiving the lowest mean retirement annuity or pension income; in 2003 the mean annuity or pension for widows was $9,215 per year, compared with $13,703 for women who had never married.

The research also found that educational attainment strongly influenced receipt and amount of benefits. Almost 30% of men over age fifty with graduate (post–college) education received an annuity or pension income in 2003. The median dollar amount of payments to men with graduate degrees was three-and-a-half times that for men without high school diplomas.

Unlike Social Security and many public plans, most private pension plans do not provide automatic cost-of-living adjustments. Without these adjustments many retirees' incomes and purchasing power erode. Military, government, and Railroad Retirement pensioners were more likely to receive cost-of-living increases than were pensioners in the private sector.

FEDERAL PENSION LAWS. Pension plan funds are often invested in vehicles such as stocks and bonds, much as banks invest their depositors' money. When the investment choice is a good one, the company makes a profit on the money in the fund; bad investments result in losses. During the early 1970s several major plans were terminated before they accumulated sufficient assets to pay employees and their beneficiaries retirement benefits. These "asset poor" plans were unable to make good on their promises, leaving retirees without benefits despite their years of service.

In order to protect retirement plan participants and their beneficiaries from these catastrophic losses, the Employee Retirement Income Security Act (ERISA) of 1974 was passed. ERISA established a new set of rules for participation, added mandatory and quicker vesting schedules, fixed minimum funding standards, and set standards of conduct for administering plans and handling plan assets. ERISA also required disclosure of plan information, established a system for insuring the payment of pension benefits and created the Pension Benefit Guaranty Corporation (PBGC), a federal corporation, to provide uninterrupted benefit payments when pension plans are terminated.

Prior to 1983 some plans paid lower monthly benefits to women because statistically women lived longer than men and, on average, collected pension benefits for a longer time. However, in 1983 the U.S. Supreme Court, in *Arizona Governing Committee for Tax Deferred Annuity and Deferred Compensation Plans v. Nathalie Norris* (463 U.S. 1073), ruled that pension plans must make payments based on gender-neutral actuarial tables (statistical calculations used for insurance purposes).

The Retirement Equity Act of 1984 (PL 98-397) requires pension plans to pay a survivor's benefit to the spouse of a deceased vested plan participant. Prior to 1984 some spouses received no benefits unless the employee was near retirement age at the time of death. Under the 1984 law, pension vesting begins at age twenty-one, or after five years on the job, and employees who have a break in employment for reasons such as maternity leave do not lose any time already accumulated.

CONGRESS SEEKS TO OVERHAUL PENSION FUNDING RULES. Fears in the early 2000s about the ailing airline industry and other troubled companies prompted the White House and Congress to agitate for an overhaul of pension-funding rules to prevent a crisis comparable to the pension fund collapses of the 1970s and 1980s. To campaign for change, members of Congress invoked memories of the savings and loan (referred to as S&L) crisis in the 1980s that resulted in government takeover of the insolvent plans. They also recounted the cost of the debacle—a 1996 congressional study estimated the price tag for the savings and loan bailout at $480.9 billion.

In January 2005 the White House proposed an overhaul of regulations dating to the 1974 establishment of ERISA and the PBGC. The White House proposal called for an increase in the PBGC premiums paid by employers, in addition to rewriting rules that have allowed companies to use favorable stock trends and interest rates to conceal under-funded plans. As of June 2005, legislation in keeping with the White House proposal was being drafted in the House by Republican Representative John Boehner of Ohio, who serves as chairman of the House Committee on Education and the Workforce (Glen Johnson, "Overhaul of Pension-Funding Rules Sought," Associated Press, June 7, 2005).

Personal Savings

One of the most effective ways to prepare for retirement is to save for it. The 2005 Retirement Confidence Survey, conducted by the Employee Benefit Research Institute (EBRI), the American Savings Education Council (ASEC), and Matthew Greenwald & Associates Inc., found that while 62% of workers claim they are currently saving for retirement, the amounts they have saved are low. The survey found that more than half (52%) of workers reported having total savings and investments, excluding the value of their homes, of less than $25,000. Despite the fact that this level of savings will render them woefully unprepared for retirement, one-quarter of workers are "very confident" and an additional 40% are "somewhat confident" that they will have enough money in retirement. The researchers determined that workers would find themselves better prepared for retirement by curbing their spending habits and eliminating consumer debt.

One popular way to save for retirement is to contribute to individual retirement plans. Individuals fund these retirement plans themselves. The money that they contribute can be tax deductible, the plans' earnings are not taxed, and contributors determine how the money is invested. Since 1974 one of the major types of individual retirement plans has been the individual retirement account (IRA). IRAs fall into several different categories, but the two most common types are traditional IRAs (deductible and nondeductible) and Roth IRAs; a variety of factors determine which kind of IRA will best serve an individual's needs. The Economic Growth and Tax Relief Reconciliation Act of 2001 contained many provisions affecting IRAs. Profit-sharing plans for the self-employed (formerly called Keogh plans) are another type of individual retirement plan.

Family Support

Older adults also may rely on their families for financial support and other types of assistance, such as transportation, shopping, and housekeeping. It is difficult to quantify the scope and extent of this support, though many studies have documented the responsibilities adult children assume for their aging parents. According to survey results reported in 2004 by the National Alliance for Caregiving (NAC) and AARP in *Caregiving in the U.S.*, more than three-quarters of the estimated 44.4 million caregivers in the United States provide care for an older adult age fifty or over. Excluding those caring for a spouse, 54% of the survey respondents reported contributing financial support to their care recipient. Caregivers providing financial support to an older adult typically contributed an average of $197 per month.

NET WORTH

Because the economic well-being of households depends on both income and wealth, assessment of income alone is not the best measure of older adults' financial health. To draw a more complete economic profile of the older population, it is necessary to evaluate older households in terms of such measures of wealth as home equity,

FIGURE 2.7

FIGURE 2.8

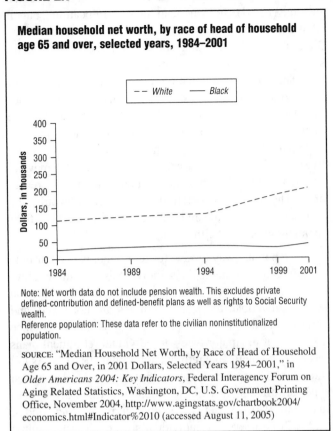

Median household net worth, by race of head of household age 65 and over, selected years, 1984–2001

Note: Net worth data do not include pension wealth. This excludes private defined-contribution and defined-benefit plans as well as rights to Social Security wealth.
Reference population: These data refer to the civilian noninstitutionalized population.

SOURCE: "Median Household Net Worth, by Race of Head of Household Age 65 and Over, in 2001 Dollars, Selected Years 1984–2001," in *Older Americans 2004: Key Indicators*, Federal Interagency Forum on Aging Related Statistics, Washington, DC, U.S. Government Printing Office, November 2004, http://www.agingstats.gov/chartbook2004/economics.html#Indicator%2010 (accessed August 11, 2005)

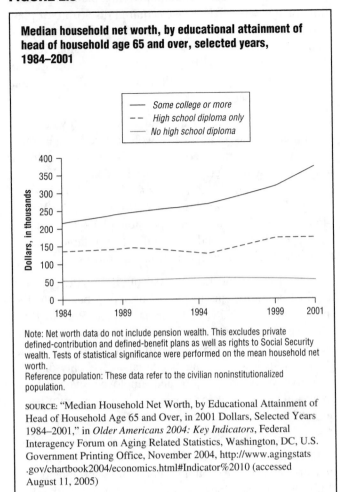

Median household net worth, by educational attainment of head of household age 65 and over, selected years, 1984–2001

Note: Net worth data do not include pension wealth. This excludes private defined-contribution and defined-benefit plans as well as rights to Social Security wealth. Tests of statistical significance were performed on the mean household net worth.
Reference population: These data refer to the civilian noninstitutionalized population.

SOURCE: "Median Household Net Worth, by Educational Attainment of Head of Household Age 65 and Over, in 2001 Dollars, Selected Years 1984–2001," in *Older Americans 2004: Key Indicators*, Federal Interagency Forum on Aging Related Statistics, Washington, DC, U.S. Government Printing Office, November 2004, http://www.agingstats.gov/chartbook2004/economics.html#Indicator%2010 (accessed August 11, 2005)

savings, and other assets and liabilities. For example, a household may be in the top one-fifth of the income distribution but be saddled with a large amount of debt.

Net worth is a measure of economic valuation and an indicator of financial security that is obtained by subtracting total liabilities from total assets. Greater net worth enables individuals and households to weather financial challenges such as illness, disability, job loss, divorce, widowhood, or general economic downturns.

According to *Older Americans 2004: Key Indicators of Well-Being*, median net worth grew from $98,000 to $179,800 (82%) between 1984 and 2001 among heads of household age sixty-five and over. As Figure 2.7 shows, however, the increase has been substantially greater for older white adults than for older African-American adults. During this period the median net worth of households headed by older white adults increased by more than 81%, from $113,400 to $205,000. While the median net worth of households headed by older African-American adults also grew—by 60%, from $25,000 to $41,000—the median net worth of white households was still five times greater than that of African-American households.

Households headed by older adults with some college or more were found to have a median net worth of $360,500 in 2001, which was more than six times greater than those headed by older adults without high school diplomas

($57,300). In addition the median net worth of households headed by college-educated older adults rose by 67% between 1984 and 2001, compared with a 4% increase in net worth among households headed by an older adult without a high school diploma. (See Figure 2.8.)

POVERTY

Poverty rates are measures of the economic viability of populations. Poverty standards were originally based on the "economy food plan," developed by the U.S. Department of Agriculture (USDA) in the 1960s. The plan calculated the cost of a minimally adequate household food budget for different types of households by age of householder. Since USDA surveys showed that the average family spent one-third of its income on food, it was decided that a household with an income three times the amount needed for food was living fairly comfortably. In 1963 the poverty level was calculated by simply multiplying the cost of a minimally adequate food budget by three. Later the U.S. Census Bureau began comparing family income before taxes with a set of poverty thresholds that vary based on family size and composition and are adjusted annually for inflation using the Consumer Price Index (CPI is a measure of the

TABLE 2.2

People in poverty, by selected characteristics, 2002–03

[Numbers in thousands. People as of March of the following year.]

Characteristic	2002 below poverty		2003 below poverty		Change in poverty (2003 less 2002)[a]	
	Number	Percentage	Number	Percentage	Number	Percentage
People						
Total	34,570	12.1	35,861	12.5	1,291	0.3
Family status						
In families	24,534	10.4	25,684	10.8	1,150	0.4
Householder	7,229	9.6	7,607	10.0	378	0.4
Related children under 18	11,646	16.3	12,340	17.2	694	0.9
Related children under 6	4,296	18.5	4,654	19.8	358	1.4
In unrelated subfamilies	417	33.7	464	38.6	46	4.9
Reference person	167	31.7	191	37.6	25	5.8
Children under 18	241	35.4	271	41.7	31	6.3
Unrelated individual	9,618	20.4	9,713	20.4	95	—
Male	4,023	17.7	4,154	18.0	131	0.3
Female	5,595	22.9	5,559	22.6	−36	−0.2
Race[b] and Hispanic origin						
White alone or in combination	24,074	10.3	24,950	10.6	876	0.3
White alone[c]	23,466	10.2	24,272	10.5	806	0.3
White alone, not Hispanic	15,567	8.0	15,902	8.2	335	0.2
Black alone or in combination	8,884	23.9	9,108	24.3	224	0.4
Black alone[d]	8,602	24.1	8,781	24.4	180	0.3
Asian alone or in combination	1,243	10.0	1,527	11.8	284	1.9
Asian alone[e]	1,161	10.1	1,401	11.8	240	1.8
Hispanic origin (of any race)	8,555	21.8	9,051	22.5	497	0.6
Age						
Under 18 years	12,133	16.7	12,866	17.6	733	0.9
18 to 64 years	18,861	10.6	19,443	10.8	582	0.2
65 years and older	3,576	10.4	3,552	10.2	−24	−0.2
Nativity						
Native	29,012	11.5	29,965	11.8	952	0.3
Foreign born	5,558	16.6	5,897	17.2	339	0.6
Naturalized citizen	1,285	10.0	1,309	10.0	24	—
Not a citizen	4,273	20.7	4,588	21.7	315	1.0
Region						
Northeast	5,871	10.9	6,052	11.3	182	0.4
Midwest	6,616	10.3	6,932	10.7	316	0.5
South	14,019	13.8	14,548	14.1	529	0.3
West	8,064	12.4	8,329	12.6	265	0.2
Residence						
Inside metropolitan areas	27,096	11.6	28,367	12.1	1,271	0.4
Inside central cities	13,784	16.7	14,551	17.5	767	0.8
Outside central cities	13,311	8.9	13,816	9.1	504	0.2
Outside metropolitan areas	7,474	14.2	7,495	14.2	20	—
Work experience						
All workers (16 years and older)	8,954	5.9	8,820	5.8	−134	−0.1
Worked full-time year-round	2,635	2.6	2,636	2.6	1	—
Not full-time year-round	6,318	12.4	6,183	12.2	−135	−0.3
Did not work at least one week	14,647	21.0	15,446	21.5	799	0.4

average change in consumer prices over time in a fixed market basket of goods and services).

According to the Census Bureau, the overall U.S. poverty rate in 2003 was 12.5%, up from 12.1% in 2002. This increase represents an additional 1.3 million Americans living in poverty in 2003. The poverty rate of adults age sixty-five and over in 2003 (10.2%) was essentially unchanged from the previous year and represented 3.6 million older adults living in poverty. The rates recorded for eighteen- to sixty-four-year-olds (10.8%) and children

under age eighteen (17.6%) both exceeded that of older adults. (See Table 2.2.) Census Bureau data reveal that in 1959 the poverty rate for people age sixty-five and over was 35%, well above the rates for the other age groups. The lowest level of poverty in the older population occurred in 1999, when the rate fell to 9.7%. (See Figure 2.9.)

As reported by the AoA in *A Profile of Older Americans: 2004* (http://www.aoa.gov/prof/Statistics/profile/2004/2004profile.doc), less than 9% of older whites lived in poverty in 2003, compared with 23.7% of older African-Americans,

TABLE 2.2

People in poverty, by selected characteristics, 2002–03 [CONTINUED]

[Numbers in thousands. People as of March of the following year.]

Characteristic	2002 below poverty		2003 below poverty		Change in poverty (2003 less 2002)[a]	
	Number	Percentage	Number	Percentage	Number	Percentage
Families						
Total	7,229	9.6	7,607	10.0	378	0.4
Type of family						
Married-couple	3,052	5.3	3,115	5.4	63	0.1
Female householder, no husband present	3,613	26.5	3,856	28.0	243	1.4
Male householder, no wife present	564	12.1	636	13.5	73	1.4

— Represents zero or round to zero.
[a]Details may not sum to total because of rounding.
[b]Data for American Indians and Alaska Natives, and Asian, Native Hawaiian and Other Pacific Islanders are not shown separately.
[c]The 2003 and 2004 CPS (Current Population Survey) asked respondents to choose one or more races. White alone refers to people who reported white and did not report any other race category. The use of this single-race population does not imply that it is the preferred method of presenting or analyzing data. The Census Bureau uses a variety of approaches. About 2.6 percent of people reported more than one race in Census 2000.
[d]Black alone refers to people who reported black and did not report any other race category.
[e]Asian alone refers to people who reported Asian and did not report any other race category.

SOURCE: Carmen DeNavas-Walt, Bernadette D. Proctor, and Robert J. Mills, "Table 3. People and Families in Poverty by Selected Characteristics: 2002 and 2003," in *Income, Poverty, and Health Insurance Coverage in the United States: 2003*, Current Population Reports Consumer Income, U.S. Census Bureau, Washington, DC, August 2004, http://www.census.gov/prod/2004pubs/p60-226.pdf (accessed August 11, 2005)

FIGURE 2.9

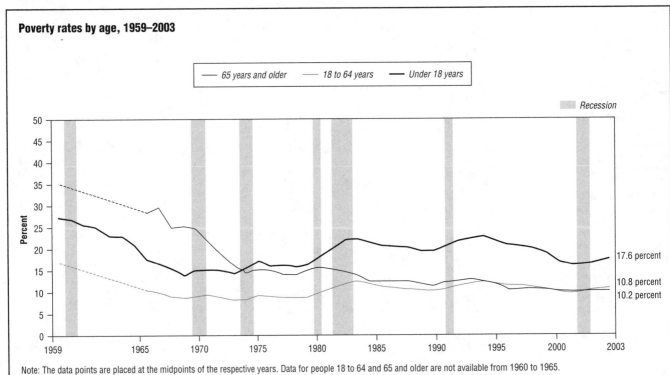

Poverty rates by age, 1959–2003

Note: The data points are placed at the midpoints of the respective years. Data for people 18 to 64 and 65 and older are not available from 1960 to 1965.

SOURCE: Carmen DeNavas-Walt, Bernadette D. Proctor, and Robert J. Mills, "Figure 4. Poverty Rates by Age: 1959 to 2003," in *Income, Poverty, and Health Insurance Coverage in the United States: 2003*, Current Population Reports Consumer Income, U.S. Census Bureau, Washington, DC, August 2004, http://www.census.gov/prod/2004pubs/p60-226.pdf (accessed August 11, 2005)

14.3% of older Asians, and 19.5% of older Hispanics. Poverty rates were higher than average for older residents of central cities (13.1%), rural areas (11.0%), and the South (11.9%). Older women were more likely to be poor (12.5%) than older men (7.3%) in 2003, and older adults living alone had a much higher poverty rate (18.6%) than those living with families (5.8%). Older Hispanic women who lived alone had a very high poverty rate in 2003—40.8%.

Poverty Thresholds Are Lower for Older Adults

The U.S. Census Bureau measures need for assistance using poverty thresholds—specific dollar amounts that determine poverty status. Each individual or family is assigned one out of forty-eight possible poverty thresholds. Thresholds vary according to family size and the ages of the members. The thresholds do not vary geographically, and they are updated annually for inflation using the Consumer Price Index.

One assumption used to determine poverty thresholds is that healthy older adults have lower nutritional requirements compared to younger persons and therefore require less money for food. This assumption has resulted in different poverty thresholds for the old and for the young. For example, in 2004 the poverty threshold for a single person under age sixty-five was $9,827, as opposed to $9,060 for a person age sixty-five or older. The 2004 poverty threshold for two persons including a householder under age sixty-five was $12,649, compared with $11,418 for two persons including a householder age sixty-five years or older.

This method of defining poverty fails to take into account the special financial problems older adults may face. For example, no household costs other than food are counted, even though older adults spend a much greater percentage of their income on health care than younger people do. Also the dollars allocated for food only consider the nutritional needs of healthy older adults; many are in poor health and may require more costly special diets or nutritional supplements.

WELL-OFF OLDER ADULTS

More older Americans live comfortably today than at any other time in history. Those in their seventies and eighties were children of the Great Depression, which began in 1929 and continued through the 1930s. The enforced Depression-era frugality taught them to economize and save. This generation returned from World War II to inexpensive housing and GI bills (legislation that made available for veterans low-interest loans for homes or small businesses and free or inexpensive college educations). During the 1940s and 1950s, their peak earning years, they enjoyed a period of unprecedented economic expansion. Since then many have raised their children, paid off their home mortgages, invested wisely, and become eligible to receive Social Security payments that are larger than ever.

While these factors have contributed to a more favorable economic status for this cohort of older adults than they would have otherwise enjoyed, the majority of older people are not wealthy. Figure 2.2 shows that in 2003 less than one-fifth (16.9%) of households headed by older adults had total incomes of $75,000 or more, and just

slightly more than 9% of individuals age sixty-five and over reported income in excess of $50,000.

CONSUMER EXPENSES

On average, older households spend less than younger households, because they generally have less money to spend, fewer dependents to support, and different needs and values. According to the 2003 Consumer Expenditure Survey conducted by the Bureau of Labor Statistics, the annual per capita expenditure for people age sixty-five to seventy-four was $33,629, while those who were age seventy-five or older spent just $25,016. Those under the age of twenty-five were the only group with a smaller expenditure, spending $22,396 per capita annually. (See Table 2.3.) The greatest amounts were spent on housing (including utilities), food, transportation, and health care. Not surprisingly, older adults spent more on health care than any other age group, both in actual dollars and as a percentage of expenditures. Older adults spent less on tobacco and smoking products, alcoholic beverages, apparel, and food away from home than other age groups.

Smaller Households Are More Expensive to Run

The majority of older adult households contain fewer persons than younger households. While larger households, in general, cost more to feed, operate, and maintain, they are less expensive on a per capita basis. According to the Census Bureau, the basic cost of living for two people was less than twice as much as the cost for one person living alone; the living cost of four people was significantly less than four times that of someone living alone.

Home maintenance, such as replacing a roof or major appliance, costs the same for any household, but in larger households the per capita cost is lower. Purchasing small quantities of food for one or two persons may be almost as costly as buying in bulk for a larger household. Because older adults often have limited transportation and mobility, they may be forced to buy food and other necessities at small neighborhood stores that generally charge more than supermarkets and warehouse stores. Larger households also may benefit from multiple incomes.

AGING CONSUMERS—A GROWING MARKET

Older adults have proven to be a lucrative market for many products. The January 2005 report *The U.S. Market for 55+ Consumers: Attitudes and Lifestyles in the New Retirement Paradigm* (Robert Brown and Ruth Washton, New York: Packaged Facts) concluded that the sixty-four million consumers age fifty-five and over wielded an estimated $2.4 trillion in purchasing power. Older adults are redefining aging—only a minority of Americans expects to retire as their parents did. Older adults are

TABLE 2.3

Average annual expenditures and characteristics, by age, 2003

Item	All consumer units	Under 25	25–34	35–44	45–54	55–64	65 and over	65–74	75 and over
Number of consumer units (in thousands)	115,356	8,584	19,737	24,413	23,131	16,580	22,912	11,495	11,417
Consumer unit characteristics									
Income before taxes[a]	$51,128	$20,680	$50,389	$61,091	$68,028	$58,672	$30,437	$35,314	$25,492
Income after taxes[a]	48,596	20,259	48,410	58,275	64,080	55,844	28,559	33,859	23,185
Age of reference person	48.4	21.3	29.7	39.7	49.4	59.0	75.1	69.2	81.1
Average number in consumer unit									
Persons	2.5	1.8	2.9	3.2	2.6	2.1	1.7	1.9	1.5
Children under 18	.6	.4	1.1	1.3	.6	.2	.1	.1	[b]
Persons 65 and over	.3	[b]	[b]	[b]	[b]	.1	1.4	1.4	1.3
Earners	1.3	1.2	1.5	1.6	1.8	1.4	.4	.6	.2
Vehicles	1.9	1.1	1.8	2.1	2.4	2.3	1.5	1.8	1.2
Percent distribution									
Sex of reference person									
Male	50	49	51	52	51	53	45	50	41
Female	50	51	49	48	49	47	55	50	59
Housing tenure									
Homeowner	67	15	48	69	76	82	80	83	78
With mortgage	41	9	42	57	56	44	17	27	8
Without mortgage	26	7	7	12	20	38	63	56	70
Renter	33	85	52	31	24	18	20	17	22
Race of reference person									
Black or African American	12	10	13	14	12	10	10	11	8
White, Asian, and all other races	88	90	87	86	88	90	90	89	92
Education of reference person									
Elementary (1–8)	6	2	3	4	4	6	14	11	18
High school (9–12)	36	30	30	37	34	36	46	45	47
College	57	68	66	59	62	57	39	43	35
Never attended and other	[c]	[c]	[c]	[c]	[c]	[c]	1	1	1
At least one vehicle owned or leased	88	71	89	91	92	91	82	87	76
Average annual expenditures	$40,817	$22,396	$40,525	$47,175	$50,101	$44,191	$29,376	$33,629	$25,016
Food	5,340	3,401	5,318	6,272	6,381	5,530	3,896	4,544	3,208
Food at home	3,129	1,766	2,976	3,600	3,693	3,315	2,575	2,888	2,241
Cereals and bakery products	442	256	421	523	509	427	387	414	358
Cereals and cereal products	150	96	156	183	168	140	120	129	110
Bakery products	292	160	265	340	341	287	267	285	248
Meats, poultry, fish, and eggs	825	438	769	933	1,002	914	661	758	558
Beef	246	131	227	265	320	287	178	226	128
Pork	171	88	142	188	208	192	157	165	147
Other meats	102	53	90	123	123	108	83	92	74
Poultry	145	85	151	174	171	142	105	114	94
Fish and seafood	124	57	124	139	140	148	103	122	82
Eggs	37	23	35	44	40	36	36	39	32
Dairy products	328	193	317	388	378	326	277	308	243
Fresh milk and cream	127	76	127	157	138	118	108	118	97
Other dairy products	201	116	191	230	240	209	169	190	146
Fruits and vegetables	535	272	495	593	621	593	484	537	428
Fresh fruits	171	75	157	190	204	189	153	172	133
Fresh vegetables	172	87	157	187	199	192	160	182	136
Processed fruits	108	66	104	123	122	115	95	99	92
Processed vegetables	84	44	77	93	96	97	76	84	68
Other food at home	$999	$607	$974	$1,164	$1,184	$1,054	$767	$872	$654
Sugar and other sweets	119	61	102	147	141	125	100	111	89
Fats and oils	86	44	76	95	101	93	80	89	70
Miscellaneous foods	490	331	509	562	570	498	366	416	313
Nonalcoholic beverages	268	159	256	317	329	291	191	217	164
Food prepared by consumer unit on out-of-town trips	36	12	31	43	43	47	29	39	19
Food away from home	2,211	1,636	2,342	2,672	2,688	2,215	1,321	1,656	968

now more likely to continue working, and working out, rather than retiring to the shuffleboard court or rocking chair on the front porch. As a result, they are considered an important market for an expanding array of services in addition to those traditionally marketed to older adults—health and life insurance plans and burial plots.

TABLE 2.3

Item	All consumer units	Under 25	25–34	35–44	45–54	55–64	65 and over	65–74	75 and over
Alcoholic beverages	391	509	446	424	477	372	184	237	128
Housing	13,432	7,095	14,392	16,098	15,624	13,714	9,729	10,761	8,678
Shelter	7,887	4,574	8,915	9,678	9,237	7,571	5,201	5,764	4,635
Owned dwellings	5,263	765	4,837	6,940	6,893	5,769	3,515	4,300	2,725
Mortgage interest and charges	2,954	449	3,373	4,541	4,088	2,739	851	1,349	350
Property taxes	1,344	230	910	1,479	1,625	1,770	1,399	1,472	1,325
Maintenance, repairs, insurance, other expenses	965	87	554	921	1,180	1,260	1,266	1,480	1,050
Rented dwellings	2,179	3,593	3,835	2,315	1,656	1,179	1,331	1,045	1,619
Other lodging	445	216	243	423	688	623	355	419	291
Utilities, fuels, and public services	2,811	1,329	2,580	3,142	3,335	3,089	2,484	2,723	2,244
Natural gas	392	118	341	427	468	432	396	411	380
Electricity	1,028	470	915	1,145	1,199	1,153	946	1,046	845
Fuel oil and other fuels	110	23	62	109	129	146	138	140	135
Telephone services	956	616	1,001	1,097	1,156	981	673	773	572
Water and other public services	326	102	261	365	383	376	332	352	312
Household operations	707	230	872	949	633	604	635	504	768
Personal services	294	135	571	521	121	71	206	37	377
Other household expenses	414	95	301	428	512	533	429	467	391
Housekeeping supplies	529	225	455	597	618	618	485	590	373
Laundry and cleaning supplies	132	73	140	149	154	139	103	123	81
Other household products	263	101	204	311	312	308	247	313	176
Postage and stationery	133	51	111	137	151	171	136	154	116
Household furnishings and equipment	1,497	737	1,571	1,731	1,801	1,831	923	1,180	657
Household textiles	113	42	109	108	155	140	90	124	54
Furniture	401	203	499	518	450	447	184	225	142
Floor coverings	52	8	32	61	62	76	48	55	40
Major appliances	196	67	216	209	217	231	165	219	110
Small appliances, miscellaneous housewares	88	48	69	92	111	127	63	79	47
Miscellaneous household equipment	648	369	647	743	807	810	373	477	265
Apparel and services	1,640	1,117	1,849	2,091	1,953	1,562	908	1,190	611
Men and boys	372	259	391	530	467	314	170	216	122
Men, 16 and over	282	233	274	349	372	273	150	186	112
Boys, 2 to 15	89	27	117	181	95	41	20	31	10
Women and girls	634	352	625	764	809	654	419	552	277
Women, 16 and over	529	326	485	547	708	602	386	496	268
Girls, 2 to 15	106	25	140	217	101	52	33	55	9
Children under	281	115	175	95	52	60	17	20	15
Footwear	294	206	331	413	334	237	167	214	116
Other apparel products and services	258	184	327	289	291	297	135	188	81
Transportation	7,781	4,674	8,106	8,892	9,766	8,680	4,824	6,015	3,622
Vehicle purchases (net outlay)	3,732	2,241	3,932	4,255	4,632	4,289	2,247	2,770	1,721
Cars and trucks, new	2,052	991	1,757	2,221	2,569	2,624	1,591	1,900	1,280
Cars and trucks, used	1,611	1,231	2,080	1,937	1,951	1,645	637	832	441
Other vehicles	68	419	96	98	113	420	419	438	41
Gasoline and motor oil	1,333	947	1,388	1,582	1,644	1,411	792	1,019	563
Other vehicle expenses	$2,331	$1,299	$2,446	$2,643	$3,013	$2,484	$1,487	$1,857	$1,112
Vehicle finance charges	371	224	483	476	485	336	125	191	57
Maintenance and repairs	619	352	558	677	782	728	467	601	330
Vehicle insurance	905	504	910	997	1,197	932	640	724	555
Vehicle rental, leases, licenses, other charges	436	218	495	493	549	488	255	340	170
Public transportation	385	187	340	411	476	495	298	370	226

Today's healthier, more affluent, older population clamors for products that promote health and ease, including stylish and comfortable clothing, customized travel services such as adventure tourism, and opportunities for recreation. The corporate world is responding to the needs and preferences of older adults with marketing and products aimed at this demographic. Examples include Sony commercials featuring a gray-haired astronaut using a digital camcorder and a grandmother taking underwater pictures of sharks. Another example is the Microsoft launch of a line of software tools to accommodate older workers who may have wrist, vision, or hearing problems.

TABLE 2.3

Average annual expenditures and characteristics, by age, 2003 [CONTINUED]

Item	All consumer units	Under 25	25–34	35–44	45–54	55–64	65 and over	65–74	75 and over
Health care	2,416	546	1,468	2,105	2,479	3,059	3,741	3,626	3,856
Health insurance	1,252	281	810	1,109	1,166	1,572	2,002	1,974	2,031
Medical services	591	129	394	598	718	742	688	681	695
Drugs	467	100	202	301	459	627	905	838	971
Medical supplies	107	37	62	97	137	118	146	133	159
Entertainment	2,060	950	1,958	2,519	2,407	2,414	1,469	2,016	909
Fees and admissions	494	233	402	638	624	597	314	383	244
Television, radios, sound equipment	730	463	780	874	865	744	488	560	415
Pets, toys, and playground equipment	378	139	403	438	450	381	309	451	159
Other entertainment supplies, equipment, and services	457	115	373	569	468	692	358	621	90
Personal care products and services	527	326	498	602	616	549	440	491	387
Reading	127	53	99	114	150	168	141	149	134
Education	783	1,490	684	694	1,377	743	129	176	81
Tobacco products and smoking supplies	290	230	285	312	385	337	162	219	105
Miscellaneous	606	251	532	601	830	675	533	547	519
Cash contributions	1,370	371	754	1,256	1,651	1,568	1,969	1,811	2,127
Personal insurance and pensions	4,055	1,382	4,137	5,196	6,003	4,819	1,251	1,847	651
Life and other personal insurance	397	40	200	382	600	570	388	504	270
Pensions and Social Security	3,658	1,342	3,937	4,814	5,403	4,249	864	1,342	382
Sources of income and personal taxes[a]									
Money income before taxes	51,128	20,680	50,389	61,091	68,028	58,672	30,437	35,314	25,492
Wages and salaries	41,200	18,525	47,430	55,795	59,835	45,121	7,501	12,359	2,575
Self-employment income	2,138	346	1,211	2,420	3,423	2,728	1,616	1,996	1,231
Social Security, private and government retirement	5,601	174	292	839	2,418	7,802	18,881	18,851	18,911
Interest, dividends, rental income, other property income	1,097	83	278	618	1,279	1,922	1,930	1,547	2,317
Unemployment and workers' compensation, veterans' benefits	269	78	296	350	357	319	109	110	109
Public assistance, supplemental security income, food stamps	314	262	342	371	300	386	214	243	184
Regular contributions for support	343	738	372	507	301	273	87	99	76
Other income	165	474	168	191	116	122	99	109	90
Personal taxes	2,532	421	1,979	2,817	3,949	2,827	1,878	1,455	2,307
Federal income taxes	1,843	261	1,336	1,988	2,914	2,010	1,535	1,044	2,032
State and local income taxes	502	144	544	658	814	511	114	152	77
Other taxes	187	15	99	170	221	306	228	259	197
Income after taxes	48,596	20,259	48,410	58,275	64,080	55,844	28,559	33,859	23,185
Addenda									
Net change in total assets and liabilities	−$14,376	−$2,556	−$21,532	−$20,302	−$20,363	−$7,462	−$5,284	−$7,736	−$2,816
Net change in total assets	6,451	4,074	13,436	9,678	6,101	6,512	−1,804	−1,830	−1,777
Net change in total liabilities	20,827	6,630	34,968	29,981	26,464	13,974	3,480	5,905	1,039
Other money receipts	530	109	141	425	507	1,449	495	529	461
Other financial information									
Mortgage principal paid on owned property	−1,565	−157	−1,078	−2,070	−2,391	−2,103	−749	−1,172	−322
Estimated market value of owned home	122,059	15,446	81,518	131,093	145,754	164,464	132,695	147,037	118,255
Estimated monthly rental value of owned home	750	124	539	838	898	930	791	852	730

The *Wall Street Journal* reported that Ford Motor Company was planning to market the Ford Five Hundred—a sedan with a trunk that holds eight golf bags—to empty-nesters who felt that sport utility vehicles (SUVs) no longer met their needs (Kelly Greene, "Marketing Surprise: Older Consumers Buy Stuff, Too," April 6, 2004).

TABLE 2.3

Average annual expenditures and characteristics, by age, 2003 [CONTINUED]

Item	All consumer units	Under 25	25–34	35–44	45–54	55–64	65 and over	65–74	75 and over
Gifts of goods and services	1,007	321	639	741	1,588	1,572	873	952	788
Food	78	19	23	40	140	180	49	72	26
Alcoholic beverages	16	10	21	16	22	17	8	11	6
Housing	220	75	139	204	322	310	198	213	181
Housekeeping supplies	42	17	31	54	49	52	31	41	21
Household textiles	13	2	5	10	21	23	10	15	6
Appliances and miscellaneous housewares	25	9	14	25	31	36	24	29	18
Major appliances	7	1	3	9	8	7	9	8	9
Small appliances and miscellaneous housewares	18	8	11	17	23	29	15	21	9
Miscellaneous household equipment	57	19	40	41	81	91	53	63	42
Other housing	85	28	48	73	140	107	79	65	94
Apparel and services	225	116	220	220	250	314	188	265	108
Males, 2 and over	56	30	38	55	71	80	48	57	39
Females, 2 and over	80	19	68	78	83	122	85	130	38
Children under	239	28	51	45	41	52	14	18	11
Other apparel products and services	50	39	65	42	56	59	40	60	20
Jewelry and watches	26	27	49	14	24	27	19	28	9
All other apparel products and services	25	12	15	28	32	33	21	31	11
Transportation	60	7	77	23	106	72	47	43	52
Health care	48	3	8	23	49	48	125	44	206
Entertainment	69	39	60	61	81	111	54	67	41
Toys, games, hobbies, and tricycles	26	8	23	21	30	45	23	33	14
Other entertainment	43	31	37	40	51	66	31	34	27
Personal care products and services	16	7	12	16	23	19	13	14	12
Reading	1	c	1	c	1	3	3	3	2
Education	200	23	31	97	510	373	83	111	54
All other gifts	74	22	47	41	84	126	106	110	101

aComponents of income and taxes are derived from "complete income reporters" only.
bValue less than 0.05.
cValue less than 0.5.

SOURCE: "Table 3. Age of Reference Person: Average Annual Expenditures and Characteristics, Consumer Expenditure Survey, 2003," in *Consumer Expenditure Survey*, U.S. Department of Labor Bureau of Labor Statistics, Branch of Information and Analysis, Washington, DC, December 2004, http://www.bls.gov/cex/2003/Standard/age.pdf (accessed August 11, 2005)

Similarly, the Pillsbury advertising campaign "Cooking for Two" targets empty-nesters adjusting to shopping, organizing, and cooking meals for a smaller household. Along with the advertising campaign, Pillsbury launched a Web site, a monthly electronic newsletter, and a public relations program featuring baby boomer and former Olympic figure skating champion Peggy Fleming.

Baby Boomers—The Emerging "Silver" Market

The aging baby boomers have been dubbed "zoomers" to reflect the generation's active lifestyle. Market researchers believe that the sheer size of the boomer cohort and its history of self-indulgence coupled with considerable purchasing power ensure that this group will be the most voracious older consumers ever.

The information in this section was drawn from the Boomer Marketing Report, a quarterly survey of fourteen hundred consumers by The Boomer Project/Survey Sampling International that aims to determine how this generation thinks, feels, and responds to marketing and advertising messages, and also from *50 Things Every Marketer Needs to Know about Boomers over 50* (Matt Thornhill, Richmond, VA: The Boomer Project, 2005). Included among the many insights that The Boomer Project research revealed were the following:

- Boomers at age fifty perceive themselves as twelve years younger and they expect to live thirty-five more years. They consider themselves to be in early "middle age" and view seventy-two as the onset of old age. (See Figure 2.10.)

- Boomers reject any and all age-related labels to describe themselves. They do not want to be called "seniors," "aged," or even "boomers," and they do not want to be compared with their parents' generation or any previous cohort of older adults.

FIGURE 2.10

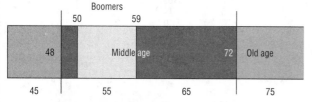

Older "baby boomers" see themselves as being in early middle age

QUESTIONS: WHAT AGE DOES "MIDDLE AGE" BEGIN?
WHAT AGE DOES "OLD AGE" BEGIN?

SOURCE: "Older Boomers See Themselves in Early 'Middle Age'," in *50 Things Every Marketer Needs to Know About Boomers Over 50*, The Boomer Project, Richmond, VA, 2005

- Boomers over age fifty do not want to reverse or stop the signs of aging, they simply want to postpone or slow the process. They are intent on seeking health rather than youth—feeling younger is as important as looking younger for boomers eager to age "on their own terms."

- Boomers want more time, which means that services that offer them free time to pursue work and leisure activities are likely to be in great demand. Examples of these include cleaning, home maintenance, and gardening services.

- Boomers are becoming less interested in material possessions and more interested in gaining a variety of experiences. Rather than embracing the premise that "he who has the most toys wins," boomers believe "he who chalks up the most experiences wins."

- Once dubbed the "me generation," boomers operate on the premise that they are entitled to special treatment, not because they have earned it by virtue of age, but simply because they deserve it. They want products and services that are relevant to them personally. They remain motivated to fulfill their own needs, whether these needs are for community, adventure, or a spiritual life.

- Boomers are life-long learners. Continuing education classes and opportunities to learn and enrich their lives through travel are important to this generation.

- Boomers are still interested in promoting social change. The generation known for protesting the Vietnam War and questioning authority and traditional American social mores continues to support global and local humanitarian and environmental action.

- Boomers do not want to relocate to traditional retirement enclaves and communities, preferring to "age in place" in their present homes or nearby. Having witnessed the institutionalization of their parents in nursing homes and other assisted living facilities, boomers are intent on remaining in their homes, and in the community, for as long as they can.

The Boomer Project predicts that adults over age fifty are poised to transform a variety of industries, including travel and tourism, health clubs, home improvement and maintenance services, apparel, personal care and beauty, financial services, education/learning, and family restaurants.

Pharmaceutical companies and health care providers will also rise to meet increasing demand from this generation. Boomers are more interested in health and in postponing aging than any generation before. They are purchasing a wide range of prescription and over-the-counter antiaging treatments, as well as vitamins, supplements, pharmaceutical products, and medical treatments to reduce the signs of aging and promote vitality.

THE U.S. SOCIAL SECURITY PROGRAM

We can never insure one hundred percent of the population against one hundred percent of the hazards and vicissitudes of life, but we have tried to frame a law which will give some measure of protection to the average citizen and to his family against the loss of a job and against poverty-ridden old age.

—President Franklin Roosevelt upon signing the Social Security Act

Social Security is a social insurance program funded through a dedicated payroll tax. It is also known as Old-Age, Survivors, and Disability Insurance (OASDI), which describes its three major classes of beneficiaries. In 2004 the program paid out nearly $500 billion in benefits.

During the Great Depression, poverty among the older population escalated. In 1934 more than half of older adults lacked sufficient income. Although thirty states had some form of old-age pension program, by 1935 these programs were unable to meet the growing need. Just 3% of the older population received benefits under these states' plans, and the average benefit amount was about sixty-five cents a day.

As advocated by President Franklin D. Roosevelt, social insurance would solve the problem of economic security for older adults by creating a work-related, contributory system in which workers would provide for their own future economic security through taxes paid while employed. By the time the Social Security Act was signed into law by President Roosevelt on August 14, 1935, thirty-four nations were already operating some form of social insurance program—government-sponsored efforts to provide for the economic well-being of a nation's citizens.

According to the U.S. Social Security Administration (SSA), as of June 2005 more than nine in ten persons age sixty-five or over received OASDI. Retired workers and their dependents accounted for more than two-thirds (69%) of total benefits paid, while survivors of deceased workers accounted for 14% of the total, and disabled workers and their dependents rounded out the total with 17% of benefits paid. An estimated 96% of the U.S. workforce was covered by Social Security.

Although Social Security was not initially intended as a full pension, 22% of older adults relied entirely on the program as of 2005. The SSA reported that the program enabled an estimated forty million Americans to live above the poverty level, making Social Security the country's most effective antipoverty program.

Benefits are funded through the Federal Insurance Contributions Act (FICA), which provided that a mandatory tax be withheld from workers' earnings and be matched by their employers. (Self-employed workers also pay FICA taxes.) When covered workers retire (or are disabled), they draw benefits based on the amount they contributed to the fund. The amount of the benefit is directly related to the duration of employment and earnings—persons who have worked longer and earned higher wages receive larger benefits.

Workers can retire as early as age sixty-two and receive reduced Social Security benefits, or they can wait until full retirement age and receive full benefits. Until 2003 the full retirement age was sixty-five, but beginning that year it began to increase gradually such that for persons born in 1960 or later, retirement age will be sixty-seven. A special credit is given to people who delay retirement beyond their full retirement age. This credit, which is a percentage added to the Social Security benefit, varies depending on the retiree's date of birth. Workers reaching full retirement age in 2008 or later can receive a credit of 8% per year.

Benefits and Beneficiaries

According to the *2005 Annual Report of the Board of Trustees of the Federal Old-Age and Survivors Insurance and Disability Insurance Trust Funds* issued by the SSA, at the close of 2004 nearly forty-eight million people were receiving benefits that totaled $493 billion for the year. The majority were older adults—thirty-three million retired workers and their dependents along with seven million survivors of deceased workers, and eight million disabled workers and their dependents. About 157 million people with earnings covered by Social Security during 2004 paid payroll taxes. Social Security income was $658 billion, while assets held in special issue U.S. Treasury securities reached $1.7 trillion. Table 2.4 shows the number of beneficiaries of all OASDI programs as well as the total and average monthly benefits paid for April 2004 through April 2005.

Social Security Amendments of 1977

Ever since 1940, the year that Americans began to receive Social Security checks, monthly retirement benefits have steadily increased, but during the 1970s they soared. Legislation enacted in 1973 provided for automatic cost-of-living adjustments (COLAs) that were intended to prevent inflation from eroding Social Security benefits. The average benefit was indexed to keep pace with inflation as reflected by the consumer price index. COLAs were nearly 10% in 1979 and peaked at 14.3% the following year. (See Table 2.5.) These increases threatened the continued financial viability of the entire system and prompted policymakers to reconsider the COLA formula.

Some legislators felt that indexing vastly overcompensated for inflation, causing relative benefit levels to rise higher than at any previous time in the history of the program. If the COLA formula had remained in effect, in many cases benefit levels for some future retirees would exceed their pre-retirement earnings. In an attempt to prevent future Social Security benefits from rising to what many considered excessive levels, Congress passed the Social Security Amendments of 1977 (PL 95-216) to restructure the benefit plan and design more realistic formulas for benefits. Along with redefining COLAs, the 1977 amendments raised the payroll tax slightly, increased the wage base, and reduced benefits slightly.

The Earnings Test

Legislation enacted on January 1, 2000, changed the way in which the amount that beneficiaries could earn while also receiving retirement or survivors' benefits was determined. The retirement earnings test applies only to people younger than normal retirement age, which ranges from age sixty-five to sixty-seven depending on year of birth. Social Security withholds benefits if annual retirement earnings exceed a certain level, called a retirement earnings test exempt amount, for persons who have not yet attained normal retirement age. These exempt amounts generally increase annually with increases in the national average wage index.

What the Public Knows about Social Security Eligibility

The results of the Employee Benefit Research Institute (EBRI) 2005 Retirement Confidence Survey show that workers' knowledge and understanding of Social Security retirement benefits is incomplete. The majority of workers either did not know or were incorrect in their belief about the age at which they would begin to receive full benefits. More than half (52%) believed they would be eligible for full retirement benefits earlier than the law permits, while 9% thought they would be ineligible until they were older than the law designates. One-fifth of workers surveyed did not know when they would become

TABLE 2.4

All OASDI (Old Age, Survivors, and Disability Insurance) benefits, by program and type of benefit, April 2004–April 2005

Month	Total, OASDI[a]	OASI			Subtotal, DI[c]
		Subtotal, OASI[b]	Retirement	Survivors	
			Number (thousands)		
2004					
April	47,301	39,531	32,736	6,795	7,770
May	47,378	39,571	32,767	6,803	7,807
June	47,369	39,558	32,792	6,766	7,810
July	47,330	39,542	32,823	6,720	7,788
August	47,379	39,559	32,842	6,717	7,821
September	47,468	39,618	32,893	6,724	7,850
October	47,533	39,648	32,919	6,729	7,885
November	47,618	39,697	32,960	6,737	7,921
December	47,688	39,738	33,005	6,734	7,949
2005					
January	47,821	39,843	33,140	6,703	7,979
February	47,916	39,903	33,199	6,704	8,013
March	47,999	39,946	33,234	6,713	8,052
April	48,087	39,988	33,268	6,720	8,099
			Total monthly benefits (millions of dollars)		
2004					
April	39,878	34,240	28,850	5,390	5,638
May	39,960	34,292	28,893	5,399	5,669
June	40,004	34,314	28,935	5,379	5,690
July	40,033	34,338	28,985	5,352	5,696
August	40,103	34,375	29,021	5,354	5,729
September	40,197	34,442	29,081	5,362	5,755
October	40,270	34,485	29,118	5,367	5,785
November	40,407	34,587	29,210	5,377	5,820
December	41,574	35,574	30,054	5,520	6,000
2005					
January	41,754	35,729	30,233	5,496	6,025
February	41,860	35,808	30,308	5,500	6,052
March	41,949	35,867	30,357	5,510	6,082
April	42,046	35,926	30,407	5,518	6,120
			Average monthly benefit (dollars)		
2004					
April	843.10	866.20	881.30	793.20	725.60
May	843.40	866.60	881.80	793.50	726.10
June	844.50	867.40	882.40	795.00	728.50
July	845.80	868.40	883.10	796.50	731.30
August	846.40	869.00	883.70	797.00	732.50
September	846.80	869.40	884.10	797.40	733.10
October	847.20	869.80	884.50	797.50	733.70
November	848.60	871.30	886.20	798.10	734.70
December	871.80	895.20	910.60	819.80	754.80
2005					
January	873.10	896.80	912.30	820.00	755.10
February	873.60	897.40	912.90	820.50	755.30
March	874.00	897.90	913.40	820.80	755.40
April	874.40	898.40	914.00	821.20	755.70

Notes: Data are for the end of the specified month.

Some Social Security beneficiaries are entitled to more than one type of benefit. In most cases, they are dually entitled to a worker benefit and a higher spouse or widow(er) benefit. If both benefits are financed from the same trust fund, the beneficiary is usually counted only once in the statistics, as a retired-worker or a disabled-worker beneficiary, and the benefit amount recorded is the larger amount associated with the auxiliary benefit. If the benefits are paid from different trust funds the beneficiary is counted twice, and the respective benefit amounts are recorded for each type of benefit.

OASDI is Old Age, Survivors, and Disability Insurance. OASI is Old Age Survivors Insurance. DI is Disability Insurance.

[a]Includes special age-72 beneficiaries.

Excludes a number of Railroad Retirement beneficiaries who would have been eligible for Social Security benefits had they applied. The reason they have not applied is that receipt of a Social Security benefit would reduce their Railroad Retirement benefit by a like amount. The number of Railroad Retirement beneficiaries who would be eligible for a Social Security benefit if they applied is not available, but is estimated to be less than 100,000.

[b]Benefits paid from the OASI trust fund to retired workers and their spouses and children and to all survivors.

[c]Benefits paid from the DI trust fund to disabled workers and their spouses and children.

SOURCE: "Table 1. All OASDI Benefits, by Program and Type of Benefit, April 2004–April 2005," in *OASDI Monthly Statistics, April 2005*, Office of Policy, Social Security Administration, Washington, DC, May 2005, http://www.ssa.gov/policy/docs/statcomps/oasdi_monthly/2005–04/table1.pdf (accessed August 11, 2005)

TABLE 2.5

Social Security cost-of-living adjustments, 1975–2004

Year	COLA	Year	COLA	Year	COLA
1975	8.00%	1985	3.10%	1995	2.60%
1976	6.40%	1986	1.30%	1996	2.90%
1977	5.90%	1987	4.20%	1997	2.10%
1978	6.50%	1988	4.00%	1998	1.30%
1979	9.90%	1989	4.70%	1999	2.50%
1980	14.30%	1990	5.40%	2000	3.50%
1981	11.20%	1991	3.70%	2001	2.60%
1982	7.40%	1992	3.00%	2002	1.40%
1983	3.50%	1993	2.60%	2003	2.10%
1984	3.50%	1994	2.80%	2004	2.70%

Note: The COLA for December 1999 was originally determined as 2.4 percent based on CPIs (Consumer Price Index) published by the Bureau of Labor Statistics. Pursuant to Public Law 106–554, however, this COLA is effectively now 2.5 percent.

SOURCE: "Social Security Cost-Of-Living Adjustments," in *Automatic Increases,* Actuarial Resources, History, Research & Data, Office of Policy, Social Security Administration, Washington, DC, October 19, 2004, http://www.ssa.gov/OACT/COLA/colaseries.html (accessed August 11, 2005)

eligible for retirement benefits. Just 19% of respondents were able to accurately describe age eligibility requirements for retirement benefits.

SUPPLEMENTAL SECURITY INCOME

Supplemental Security Income (SSI) is designed to provide monthly cash payments to those older, blind, and disabled persons who have low incomes. Although SSI is administered by the SSA, unlike Social Security benefits, SSI benefits are not based on prior work, and the funds come from general tax revenues rather than Social Security taxes.

In 1972 Congress passed the legislation establishing SSI in order to replace several state-administered programs and provide a uniform federal benefit based on uniform eligibility standards. While SSI is a federal program, some states provide a supplement to the federal benefit.

According to SSA data (http://www.ssa.gov/policy/docs/quickfacts/stat_snapshot/), of the 7.1 million people receiving SSI benefits in October 2005, nearly two million were sixty-five or older. While payments vary by age group, the average monthly benefit received by older adults was slightly more than $361.

Some researchers believe that the program could do more to help SSI beneficiaries, including older adults. Eileen P. Sweeney and Shawn Fremstad of the Center on Budget and Policy Priorities reported in *Supplemental Security Income: Supporting People with Disabilities and the Elderly Poor* (http://www.cbpp.org/7-19-05imm.htm) that SSI provided enough income in 2005 only to bring an individual to about 73% (and a couple to slightly more than 81%) of the poverty level. They suggest increasing benefits as well as easing stringent eligibility standards that require beneficiaries to have less than $2,000 in countable assets for individuals and less than $3,000 for couples. Such standards keep many older adults from obtaining benefits.

WHAT LIES AHEAD FOR SOCIAL SECURITY?

The Social Security program faces long-range financing challenges that, if left unresolved, threaten its solvency in the coming decades. Since the 1980s the program has been collecting more money than it has had to pay out and will continue to do so until 2017. The surplus is not, however, cash that is set aside. Rather it is loaned to the U.S. Treasury, which places it in the general revenue pool, and it is spent as the government sees fit.

In exchange for this infusion of cash, Social Security receives special Treasury bonds backed by the credit of the U.S. government. According to the SSA, these bonds were worth $1.7 trillion at the beginning of 2005 and paid $89 billion in interest in 2004.

According to the SSA in *The Future of Social Security* (http://www.ssa.gov/pubs/10055.html; March 2005), without changes to the system, the amount of benefits owed will exceed taxes collected by 2017, and Social Security will have to tap into trust funds to pay benefits. The SSA estimates that when the trust funds are depleted, which is projected to occur in 2041, Social Security will be able to pay only about 74% of benefits to older adult retirees and its other beneficiaries.

To a large extent, demographic changes precipitated this crisis. Social Security is a "pay-as-you-go" program, with the contributions of present workers paying the retirement benefits of those currently retired. The program is solvent at this time because the number of employees contributing funds to the system is sufficient. The earliest wave of baby boomers (persons born in the years 1946 through 1964) is still in the workforce and at its peak earning years. The large cohort of boomers is funding the smaller cohort of retirees born during the low birthrate cycle of the Great Depression during the 1930s. As a result there are still fewer retirees depleting funds than there are workers contributing.

In 2008 the seventy-eight million baby boomers will begin to retire, and in about twenty-five years there will be twice as many older Americans as there are in 2005. According to data in *The Future of Social Security*, as of 2005 there were 3.3 workers paying into Social Security per beneficiary, compared with 5.1 in 1960. The worker-to-beneficiary ratio dropped sharply until the mid-1970s, staying relatively level since that time. The SSA projects, however, that beginning in about 2010 the ratio of workers to beneficiaries will start to fall once again, and by 2031 there will be 2.1 workers contributing to the fund for each beneficiary.

Another factor that contributes to the projected shortfall is increased longevity. Along with the anticipated increase in the number of beneficiaries, those beneficiaries likely will live longer and collect more benefits than ever before. According to the SSA, when monthly Social Security benefits began in 1940, a person at age sixty-five could expect to live an average of about 13.7 additional years; by 2001 the typical sixty-five-year-old was likely to live on average another 17.6 years.

The *New York Times* reported that moves to reform the Social Security system are just beginning to come to grips with the issue of increased life expectancy (Robin Toner and David E. Rosenbaum, "In Overhaul of Social Security, Age Is the Elephant in the Room," June 12, 2005). The article observed that a simple way to offset the financial burden of greater longevity is to raise the retirement age, which now stands at sixty-five years and six months and which will gradually rise under current law to sixty-seven for people born in 1960 and later. This option, however, is fraught with peril for politicians, because it is not only unpopular—a 2005 *New York Times*/CBS News Poll found that eight out of ten respondents opposed raising the eligibility age for Social Security benefits—it also would be complicated to formulate an equitable solution that addressed the myriad demographic variables such as the fact that many low-income workers in physically taxing fields would be unable to work additional years. Another issue associated with increasing the retirement age is life expectancy; on average, women live longer than men, whites live longer than African-Americans, the rich live longer than the poor.

One approach to the problem is an automatic adjustment in the retirement age or the benefits received at each age to reflect increases in life expectancy, comparable to the automatic changes already made for average wage increases and price inflation. Using this approach, known as indexing for longevity, retirees' total lifetime benefits would remain more or less constant even as they lived longer. Indexing for longevity is not a short-term solution and is viewed as unlikely to reverse the Social Security solvency crisis in the immediate future, but it might prove helpful over seventy-five years or more.

Saving Social Security

According to predictions by the administration of President George W. Bush, by the year 2027 the government will have to come up with an extra $200 billion a year to maintain the viability of the Social Security system, and by 2033 the annual shortfall will be more than $300 billion a year (http://www.whitehouse.gov/infocus/social-security/). Without intervention to prevent its collapse, by 2041, when workers who are now in their mid-twenties begin to retire, the system will be bankrupt. Figure 2.11 graphically depicts the Bush administration's

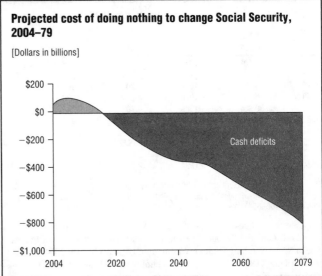

FIGURE 2.11

Projected cost of doing nothing to change Social Security, 2004–79

[Dollars in billions]

SOURCE: President George W. Bush, "Cost of Inaction," in *Strengthening Social Security for the 21st Century*, The White House, Washington, DC, February 2005, http://www.whitehouse.gov/infocus/social-security/200501/socialsecurity.pdf (accessed August 11, 2005)

analysis of the cost—increasing cash deficits—of failing to act to save Social Security.

There are three basic ways to resolve Social Security's financial problems—raise taxes, cut benefits, or make Social Security taxes earn more by investing the money. It is most likely that restoring Social Security's long-term financial balance will require a combination of increased revenues and reduced expenditures. Ways to reduce expenditures include:

- Reducing initial benefits to retirees

- Raising the retirement age (already slated to rise from sixty-five to sixty-seven by 2027)

- Lowering cost-of-living adjustments

- Limiting benefits based on beneficiaries' other income and assets

Ways to increase revenues include:

- Increasing Social Security payroll taxes

- Investing trust funds in securities with potentially higher yields than the government bonds in which they are currently invested

- Increasing income taxes on Social Security benefits

Personal Retirement Accounts

In the State of the Union Address given on February 2, 2005 (http://www.whitehouse.gov/news/releases/2005/02/20050202-11.html), President Bush asserted, "We must pass reforms that solve the financial problems of

Social Security once and for all." In his address the president called for an open, candid review of all available options to ensure the continued viability of Social Security and pledged to work with Congress to enact the most effective combination of measures to achieve this objective.

President Bush does not favor increasing payroll taxes, because he believes it would slow economic growth. Instead his administration favors partially "privatizing" Social Security by establishing voluntary personal retirement accounts for younger workers, which would give them the opportunity to establish "nest eggs" for retirement. Under his plan workers would be allowed to put as much as 4% of their wages, up to an annual capped amount, into private retirement accounts rather than into the Social Security trust funds. Guidelines and restrictions would help workers invest their money wisely and protect "near-retirees" from sudden shifts in market conditions. As workers approached retirement, investments would be shifted from high growth funds, which carry substantial downside risks, to secure bonds, which yield lower returns but carry less risk. In addition to receiving traditional Social Security benefits, the funds in the accounts would be paid out over time once retirement age was reached.

THE PROS AND CONS OF PERSONAL RETIREMENT ACCOUNTS. Advocates of personal retirement accounts contend that they can ensure the permanent solvency of Social Security, deliver demonstrably superior benefits to the vast majority of retirees, and allow for increased flexibility in the age of retirement. According to supporters of the plan, personal retirement accounts would offer younger workers a measure of ownership and control by providing them with options and allowing accounts to be passed on to others. They also believe that correcting Social Security's problems with the establishment of personal retirement accounts would cost far less than other plans. Citing analysis by the SSA, the Bush administration declared in the February 2005 pamphlet *Strengthening Social Security for the Twenty-First Century* (http://www.whitehouse.gov/infocus/social-security/200501/strengthening-socialsecurity.html) that permanently fixing the system could be achieved at a significant cost-savings by adopting reform measures incorporating personal retirement accounts.

Critics of personal retirement accounts—among them the AFL–CIO, a federation of labor organizations; and AARP, the national advocacy organization for older adults—feel that the accounts are excessively risky for workers, subjecting their retirement savings to a volatile stock market. The money in these personal retirement accounts would be invested in things like stocks and bonds that are not guaranteed to make money. It is even possible for them to decline in value if the stock market

suffers a downturn. Critics of President Bush's plan say it exposes retirees to too much risk and takes the "social" and the "security" out of Social Security. Another issue centers on the management fees and administrative costs associated with privately managed funds. Some detractors predict that the accounts would be so expensive to administer that any gains from investments would be offset by management fees.

While President Bush's critics do believe the long-term funding of Social Security needs to be addressed, some feel that the Bush administration has overstated the problem, making the situation appear more critical than it actually may be. In fact, according to Jessica Azulay's article in the *New Standard* ("New Social Security Figures Disprove Bush, Critics Say," http://newstandardnews.net/content/index.cfm/items/1580/, March 24, 2005), Jason Furman, a senior fellow with the Center on Budget and Policy Priorities, and Robert Greenstein, founder and executive director of the center, believe that private retirement accounts ultimately may increase the system's long-term shortfall. They contend that moving a portion of tax revenues into such accounts would divert funds necessary to pay the benefits of current recipients, possibly causing the deficit to occur sooner than anticipated. Most critics favor solutions aimed at increasing revenues.

Responding to concerns about exposing retirees to excessive risk, most Social Security reform proposals featuring personal retirement accounts would protect retirees with a guaranteed minimum benefit, and some proposals ensure that retirees would be no worse off than they would be under the present system. However, even some proponents of personal retirement accounts do not believe that they will completely resolve the Social Security crisis.

In the CNN/*Money* online article "What Privatization Alone Can't Do" (Jeanne Sahadi, http://money.cnn.com/2005/01/05/retirement/privatization_solvency/, February 4, 2005), University of Pennsylvania Wharton School professor Olivia Mitchell, who served on President Bush's Commission to Strengthen Social Security as well as the Congressional Budget Office's advisory board on Social Security, was quoted as stating, "Personal accounts are neither necessary nor sufficient." The article went on to cite a White House memo published in the *Wall Street Journal* in which Peter Wehner, deputy assistant to the president and director of strategic initiatives for the Bush administration, asserted, "We simply cannot solve the Social Security problem with Personal Retirement Accounts alone. If the goal is permanent solvency and sustainability . . . then Personal Retirement Accounts . . . are insufficient to the task."

Other Reform Proposals

There are other ideas about how to restore Social Security's economic prospects. According to the *New*

FIGURE 2.12

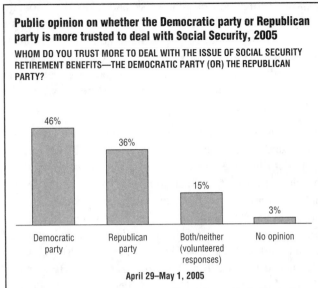

Public opinion on whether the Democratic party or Republican party is more trusted to deal with Social Security, 2005

WHOM DO YOU TRUST MORE TO DEAL WITH THE ISSUE OF SOCIAL SECURITY RETIREMENT BENEFITS—THE DEMOCRATIC PARTY (OR) THE REPUBLICAN PARTY?

April 29–May 1, 2005

SOURCE: Lydia Saad, "Whom Do You Trust More to Deal with the Issue of Social Security Retirement Benefits—the Democratic Party (or) the Republican Party?" in *Bush Fails to Ignite Public Support for Reform*, Poll Analyses, The Gallup Organization, Princeton, NJ, May 4, 2005, http://www.gallup.com/poll/content/?ci=16153&pg=1 (accessed August 11, 2005). Copyright © 2005 by The Gallup Organization. Reproduced by permission of The Gallup Organization.

Standard article, an increasingly popular solution would be to raise the cap on wages that can be taxed for Social Security. Under the present system the 6.2% Social Security tax is applied only to the first $90,000 of each person's income; progressive economists believe increasing that figure would have a significant positive impact on the system and help to ensure complete self-sufficiency.

In May 2005 Representative Robert Wexler, a Democrat from Florida, introduced a bill targeting the cap on wages. The Social Security Forever Act of 2005 would impose a 3% tax on all earnings in excess of $90,000. In a May 27, 2005, press release issued by Wexler's office ("Rep. Moran Becomes First Co-Sponsor of Wexler's Social Security Bill," http://www.wexler.house.gov/news.php?ID=9), Congressman Jim Moran, a Virginia Democrat who co-sponsored the bill, declared, "This bill meets the dual tests of simplicity and progressivity. It will keep Social Security solvent into perpetuity without burdening our children with increased national debt or deep benefit cuts." As of October 2005 the bill was being considered by the Ways and Means Committee and the Committee on Rules and the Budget.

Other approaches emphasize more tax-based savings incentives and programs that make it easier for workers and employers to set up retirement accounts. Among these are automatic enrollment in 401(k) plans, which has been demonstrated to increase participation; modified simple IRAs, which, unlike current IRAs, do not require employers to contribute matching funds; enhanced saver's credit

for low-income workers—either making the credit refundable or turning the credit into an IRA contribution; excluding some portion of annuity payments from income tax; and allowing taxpayers to split their tax refunds, depositing some portion into a checking account, another into savings, and the balance into an IRA.

Social Security Debate Continues

Despite a barnstorming tour of cities in May 2005 and a nationally televised, live address to garner public support, President Bush's Social Security reform plan remained stuck in Congress as of June of that year. A *New York Times* article (David E. Sanger, "Bush's Road Tour Rolls On in Push to Sell Social Security Changes," June 3, 2005) reported that the president vowed to tour the nation again to describe the benefits of using personal retirement accounts as part of a completely remodeled program of retirement benefits for younger workers.

The results of a CNN/*USA Today*/Gallup poll conducted in April 2005 and reported by Lydia Saad in a Gallup press release ("Bush Fails to Ignite Public Support for Reform," Gallup News Service, May 4, 2005) indicated that the president's plan to reform Social Security was declining in popularity. In fact, more Americans trusted Democrats (46%) rather than Republicans (36%) to deal with the issue of Social Security retirement benefits. (See Figure 2.12.) While the poll found that as many Americans (27%) would like to see a Democratic-sponsored Social Security plan pass in 2005 as they would a Republican-backed bill to pass, a full 46% feel it would be better if no plan passed at all. Furthermore only about one-third of Americans (35%) approved of the job President Bush was doing on Social Security and 58% disapproved. (See Figure 2.13.)

According to Gallup, the public reaction to the establishment of private retirement accounts was more negative than positive. More than half of Americans (52%) opposed allowing workers to invest part of their Social Security taxes in stocks or bonds, and 44% favored such private accounts. (See Figure 2.14.)

The survey respondents were even less enthusiastic about indexing Social Security benefits for future retirees so that benefits would be reduced using a sliding scale for middle- and upper-income Americans. The majority (54%) opposed the proposal, while somewhat more than one-third (38%) favored it. Americans oppose such means-testing so vigorously that, when offered a choice, more than half (53%) would rather endure higher taxes than have benefits cut (38%). Yet the majority of Americans (53%) believe that the president's proposed reforms will reduce their Social Security benefits.

While a large percentage of Americans feel that the Social Security system needs to be fixed (81%), the majority do not believe the need for action is that

FIGURE 2.13

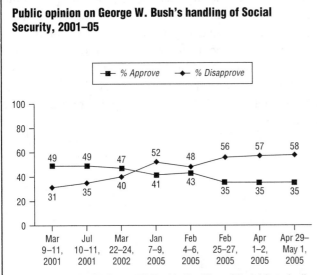

Public opinion on George W. Bush's handling of Social Security, 2001–05

SOURCE: Lydia Saad, "George W. Bush's Handling of Social Security," in *Bush Fails to Ignite Public Support for Reform*, Poll Analyses, The Gallup Organization, Princeton, NJ, May 4, 2005, http://www.gallup.com/poll/content/?ci=16153&pg=1 (accessed August 11, 2005). Copyright © 2005 by The Gallup Organization. Reproduced by permission of The Gallup Organization.

FIGURE 2.14

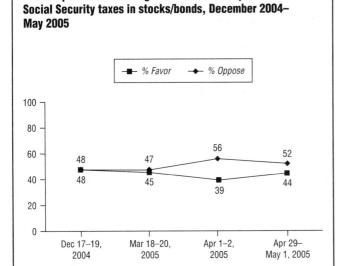

Public opinion on allowing workers to invest part of their Social Security taxes in stocks/bonds, December 2004–May 2005

SOURCE: Lydia Saad, "Allowing Workers to Invest Part of Their Social Security Taxes in Stocks/Bonds," in *Bush Fails to Ignite Public Support for Reform*, Poll Analyses, The Gallup Organization, Princeton, NJ, May 4, 2005, http://www.gallup.com/poll/content/?ci=16153&pg=1 (accessed August 11, 2005). Copyright © 2005 by The Gallup Organization. Reproduced by permission of The Gallup Organization.

FIGURE 2.15

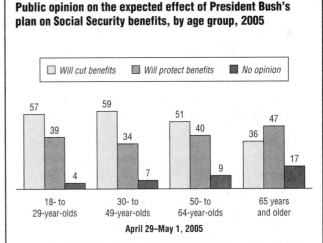

Public opinion on the expected effect of President Bush's plan on Social Security benefits, by age group, 2005

SOURCE: Lydia Saad, "Perceived Effect of Bush's Plan on Your Social Security Benefits," in *Bush Fails to Ignite Public Support for Reform*, Poll Analyses, The Gallup Organization, Princeton, NJ, May 4, 2005, http://www.gallup.com/poll/content/?ci=16153&pg=1 (accessed August 11, 2005). Copyright © 2005 by The Gallup Organization. Reproduced by permission of The Gallup Organization.

acknowledged that a painless solution to solving the Social Security crisis is impossible, but just over one-third (35%) felt the long-term future of Social Security could be secured without either raising their taxes or cutting their Social Security benefits.

America's older adults were the most critical of President Bush on the Social Security issue, and they were the least likely to support his various reform proposals. Only 29% of those age sixty-five and older, compared with 36% of those under age sixty-five, approved of how the president was handling Social Security. The percentage in favor of Bush's privatization plan dropped from 51% among those age eighteen to forty-nine, to 39% among those age fifty to sixty-four, and to 30% among those age sixty-five and older. Gallup analyst Lydia Saad observed that despite the extent of President Bush's efforts to convince older Americans that his plan would not reduce the benefits of those already receiving Social Security, 36% of people age sixty-five and over still believed their benefits will be cut, a number that could be seen as statistically significant. (See Figure 2.15.)

A June 2005 *New York Times*/CBS News poll found that a majority of Americans were worried about having enough money for retirement and pessimistic that Social Security will pay the benefits they expect when they retire (Robin Toner and Marjorie Connelly, "Poll Finds Broad Pessimism on Social Security Payments," June 19, 2005). Just over half (51%) of those surveyed did not think Social Security would have the money to pay the benefits they expect when they retire, and nearly three-quarters (70%) of respondents under age forty-five felt that way. More than three-quarters of the 1,111 survey

urgent—just 45% think such changes are needed in the next year or two. Thirty-six percent say changes should be made within the next ten years, and 16% believe changes are unnecessary. Most respondents (62%)

respondents, 781 of whom had not yet retired, said they felt it was the government's responsibility to provide a reasonable standard of living for older adults.

Most respondents supported raising the cap on income subject to the payroll tax and strongly opposed raising the age of eligibility for full benefits. A majority also opposed raising the tax rate for Social Security. The survey results imply that Americans may underestimate how important Social Security will be to their retirement.

Just one-fifth expected Social Security to be their main source of retirement income, while 29% said they would rely on an employer-sponsored pension plan as a primary source, and 45% felt they would depend on savings. If their predictions come to pass, the future retirees surveyed would be quite different from retirees in 2005—two-thirds rely on Social Security for the majority of their income, and for 20%, Social Security is their sole source of income.

CHAPTER 3
LIVING ARRANGEMENTS OF THE OLDER POPULATION

The vast majority of older Americans live independently in the community—they are not institutionalized in facilities such as nursing homes or retirement homes. According to data from the 2003 Current Population Survey (CPS) and the 2003 American Community Survey (ACS), the U.S. Census Bureau estimates that less than 5% of the population age sixty-five and over live in nursing homes. An additional 5% live in some type of senior housing, which frequently offers supportive services for residents. Although the overall numbers of older Americans living in nursing homes is small, the percentage of older adults in nursing homes increases dramatically with advancing age, from less than 1.5% of sixty-five- to seventy-four-year-olds to nearly 5% of persons age seventy-five to eighty-four, and more than 18% of those age eighty-five and older.

The living arrangements of older adults are important because they are closely associated with their health, well-being, and economic status. For example older adults who live alone are more likely to live in poverty than those who live with their spouse or other family members. Older adults living alone also may be socially isolated, and their health may suffer because there are no family members or others nearby to serve as caregivers.

LIVING WITH A SPOUSE OR OTHER RELATIVES

Table 3.1 shows that 22.7 million out of 111.3 million households—or one in five—were headed by a person age sixty-five or older in 2003. It also reveals that households headed by older adults were almost evenly divided between those composed of families (11.7 million) and nonfamily households (10.9 million).

According to data presented by the U.S. Department of Health and Human Services Administration on Aging (AoA) in *A Profile of Older Americans: 2004* (http://www.aoa.gov/prof/Statistics/profile/2004/profiles2004.asp), more than half (53.9%) of community-dwelling, civilian (noninstitutionalized) older adults lived with their spouse in 2003. Significantly more older men than women—10.3 million or 71.2% of older men compared with 8.1 million or 41.1% of older women—lived with their spouse. (See Table 3.2.) This disparity occurs because women live longer than men, are generally younger than the men they marry, and are far less likely to remarry after the death of a spouse, largely because there are relatively few available older men. In addition, the proportion of older adults living with their spouse decreased with age, and the gap between men and women widened. Among adults age seventy-five and older, slightly more than two-thirds (67.2%) of men and less than one-third (28.7%) of women were living with their spouse in 2003. (See Table 3.2.)

The AoA reported that in 2003, 30.8% of community-dwelling older adults (10.5 million) lived alone, including 7.8 million women and 2.7 million men. They represented 39.7% of older women and 18.8% of older men. Not surprisingly, the percentage of older adults who live alone rises with age. Nearly half of women age seventy-five and over (49.8%) and slightly less than one-quarter of men age seventy-five and over (22.9%) lived alone in 2003. (See Table 3.2.) The percentage of women age seventy-five and over living alone rose from 37% in 1970 to 54% in 1990 but decreased slightly by 2003, when the figure stood at just under 50%. During the same period the percentage of older men age seventy-five and over living alone remained relatively stable until 2000, when it increased somewhat from 21.4% to 22.9% in 2003. (See Figure 3.1.)

Race and ethnicity play a role in the living arrangements of older adults. Older non-Hispanic white and African-American women were twice as likely to live alone as older Asian and Hispanic women—about 40% each for non-Hispanic white and African-American women compared with about 20% for older Asian and

TABLE 3.1

Households by type and selected characteristics, 2003

[In thousands, except average size]

	All households	Family households				Nonfamily households		
					Other families			
				Married couple	Male house-holder	Female house-holder		Male house-holder	Female house-holder
Characteristic	Number	Total	Married couple	Male house-holder	Female house-holder	Total	Male house-holder	Female house-holder
All households	111,278	75,596	57,320	4,656	13,620	35,682	16,020	19,662
Age of householder								
15 to 24 years	6,611	3,551	1,379	789	1,383	3,060	1,507	1,552
25 to 34 years	19,056	13,438	9,536	1,011	2,892	5,617	3,343	2,274
35 to 44 years	24,069	18,741	14,001	1087	3,652	5,328	3,278	2,051
45 to 54 years	22,623	16,863	13,297	922	2,644	5,760	2,971	2,789
55 to 64 years	16,260	11,261	9,543	413	1,305	4,999	2,023	2,976
65 years and over	22,659	11,741	9,565	434	1,743	10,918	2,898	8,020
Race and ethnicity of householder								
White only	91,645	62,297	49,915	3,500	8,881	29,349	13,070	16,278
Non-Hispanic	81,166	53,845	44,101	2,674	7,070	27,321	11,968	15,353
Black only	13,465	8,928	4,165	762	4,000	4,538	2,043	2,495
Asian only	3,917	2,845	2,286	223	337	1,073	526	547
Hispanic (of any race)	11,339	9,090	6,189	872	2,029	2,249	1,228	1,021
Size of households								
1 person	29,431	(X)	(X)	(X)	(X)	29,431	12,511	16,919
2 people	37,078	32,047	24,310	1,992	5,745	5,031	2,660	2,371
3 people	17,889	17,076	11,526	1,403	4,147	813	556	257
4 people	15,967	15,672	12,754	733	2,185	295	212	83
5 people	7,029	6,969	5,719	296	955	60	42	17
6 people	2,521	2,489	2,004	142	344	31	19	12
7 or more people	1,364	1,343	1,007	90	246	22	19	2
Average size	2.57	3.19	3.22	3.11	3.12	1.24	1.32	1.17
Number of related children under 18								
No related children	72,367	36,685	30,261	2,240	4,183	35,682	16,020	19,662
With related children	38,911	38,911	27,059	2,416	9,437	(X)	(X)	(X)
1 child	16,511	16,511	10,378	1,429	4,704	(X)	(X)	(X)
2 children	14,333	14,333	10,800	683	2,850	(X)	(X)	(X)
3 children	5,771	5,771	4,235	220	1,317	(X)	(X)	(X)
4 or more children	2,296	2,296	1,646	84	566	(X)	(X)	(X)
Presence of own children under 18								
No own children	75,310	39,628	31,406	2,741	5,481	35,682	16,020	19,662
With own children	35,968	35,968	25,914	1,915	8,139	(X)	(X)	(X)
With own children under 12	26,251	26,251	19,168	1,295	5,788	(X)	(X)	(X)
With own children under 6	15,584	15,584	11,743	729	3,111	(X)	(X)	(X)
With own children under 3	9,081	9,081	7,014	451	1,615	(X)	(X)	(X)
With own children under 1	2,917	2,917	2,255	181	481	(X)	(X)	(X)
Tenure								
Owner	75,909	57,092	47,676	2,721	6,695	18,817	7,742	11,075
Renter	33,799	17,604	9,007	1,873	6,724	16,195	7,951	8,244
Occupies without payment	1,570	900	637	62	201	670	327	343

X Not applicable.
Note: Data are not shown separately for the other race groups because of the small sample sizes in the Current Population Survey in the 2003 Annual Social and Economic Supplement.

SOURCE: Jason Fields, "Table 1. Households by Type and Selected Characteristics: 2003," in *America's Families and Living Arrangements: 2003*, Current Population Reports P20-553, U.S. Department of Commerce, Economics and Statistics Administration, U.S. Census Bureau, Washington, DC, November 2004, http://www.census.gov/prod/2004pubs/p20-553.pdf (accessed August 11, 2005)

Hispanic women. Among the racial and ethnic groups, older Asian women were the most likely to live with relatives other than a spouse (36%). (See Figure 3.2.) The living arrangements of older men broke down somewhat differently along racial and ethnic lines than did those of older women. Older African-American men were more than three times as likely to live alone as older Asian men (30% versus 8%). Like older Asian women, however, older Asian men were the most likely

of any group of older men to live with relatives other than a spouse (31%). (See Figure 3.2.)

Multigenerational Households

The 2000 Census identified nearly four million multigenerational households (3.7% of all households), such as grandparents living with children and grandchildren in the United States. Many of these households include older relatives such as grandparents, great-grandparents,

TABLE 3.2

Living arrangements of younger and older adults, by age, 2003

[In thousands]

Characteristic	Number		Percent	
	Men	Women	Men	Women
Younger adults				
Total, 18 to 34 years				
Total	33,354	33,251	100.0	100.0
Living alone	2,934	2,411	8.8	7.3
Living with spouse	10,517	13,311	31.5	40.0
Child of the householder—not living with a spouse	10,200	7,590	30.6	22.8
Other living arrangement	9,703	9,939	29.1	29.9
18 to 24 years				
Total	13,811	13,592	100.0	100.0
Living alone	722	814	5.2	6.0
Living with spouse	1,211	2,191	8.8	16.1
Child of the householder—not living with a spouse	7,569	6,215	54.8	45.7
Other living arrangement	4,309	4,372	31.2	32.2
25 to 34 years				
Total	19,543	19,659	100.0	100.0
Living alone	2,212	1,597	11.3	8.1
Living with spouse	9,306	11,120	47.6	56.6
Child of the householder—not living with a spouse	2,631	1,375	13.5	7.0
Other living arrangement	5,394	5,567	27.6	28.3
Older adults				
Total, 65 years and over				
Total	14,521	19,695	100.0	100.0
Living alone	2,725	7,824	18.8	39.7
Living with spouse	10,341	8,086	71.2	41.1
Other living arrangement	1,455	3,785	10.0	19.2
65 to 74 years				
Total	8,268	9,831	100.0	100.0
Living alone	1,291	2,911	15.6	29.6
Living with spouse	6,141	5,257	74.3	53.5
Other living arrangement	836	1,663	10.1	16.9
75 years and over				
Total	6,253	9,864	100.0	100.0
Living alone	1,434	4,913	22.9	49.8
Living with spouse	4,200	2,829	67.2	28.7
Other living arrangement	619	2,122	9.9	21.5

SOURCE: Jason Fields, "Table 7. Living Arrangements of Younger and Older Adults by Age: 2003," in *America's Families and Living Arrangements: 2003*, Current Population Reports P20-553, U.S. Department of Commerce, Economics and Statistics Administration, U.S. Census Bureau, Washington, DC, November 2004, http://www.census.gov/prod/2004pubs/p20-553.pdf (accessed August 11, 2005)

and uncles and aunts. The Census Bureau analysis of multigenerational households found that such households are frequently located in areas where new immigrants live with relatives, where housing shortages or high costs force families to double up their living arrangements, or in areas with high rates of out-of-wedlock children where unwed mothers live with their parents and their children.

The concentration of mutigenerational families varies by geography, with the highest percentages in regions with significant Asian and Hispanic populations. For example Hawaii, with its large Asian population, had the highest proportion of multigenerational families (8.2%), followed by Puerto Rico with 7.4% and California with 5.6 %. In contrast, North Dakota had the smallest proportion—just 1.1%.

Almost two-thirds (65%, or 2.6 million households) of multigenerational households include the head of the household, a child or children, and a grandchild or grandchildren. The remaining third of multigenerational households (1.3 million households) consist primarily of a householder, the householder's parents or in-laws, and the householder's children. Four-generation households are rare, accounting for only 2% of multigenerational households.

An April 2004 CNN/*Money* online article asserted that while multigenerational households remain uncommon, they are growing in popularity in some parts of the United States, especially in areas with substantial immigrant populations and cities with higher than average costs of living (Sarah Max, "Living with the In-laws," http://money.cnn.com/2004/02/18/pf/yourhome/grannyflats/,

FIGURE 3.1

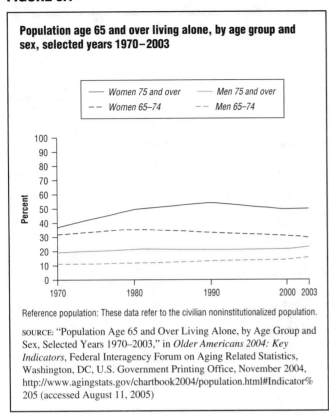

Population age 65 and over living alone, by age group and sex, selected years 1970–2003

Reference population: These data refer to the civilian noninstitutionalized population.

SOURCE: "Population Age 65 and Over Living Alone, by Age Group and Sex, Selected Years 1970–2003," in *Older Americans 2004: Key Indicators*, Federal Interagency Forum on Aging Related Statistics, Washington, DC, U.S. Government Printing Office, November 2004, http://www.agingstats.gov/chartbook2004/population.html#Indicator%205 (accessed August 11, 2005)

April 22, 2004). The article cited a poll conducted by homebuilder Del Webb in which 25% of baby boomers said they expected their children or grandchildren to live with them sometime during their retirement. Nicolas Retsinas, director of the Harvard University Joint Center for Housing Studies who was quoted in the article, believes that the multigenerational housing trend has been fueled by economics and has increased in recent years in response to increased housing prices.

Grandparents Raising Grandchildren

The 2000 Census found 5.6 million grandparents living with grandchildren under eighteen years of age. Forty-one percent of them (2.3 million, or 1.5 million grandmothers and more than 889,000 grandfathers) were responsible for their grandchildren—they had assumed the role of primary parents in their grandchildren's lives.

The AARP, a national advocacy organization for older adults, conducted a survey about grandparenting through its Grandparent Information Center and in conjunction with Roper ASW. According to data in *The Grandparent Study 2002 Report*, 6% of grandparents had grandchildren living with them, and parents were not present in more than 43% of these homes. Whether or not a parent lived in the home, these respondents were considered to be grandparents raising grandchildren (GRG). The survey estimated that 5% of white grandparents and 17% of African-American grandparents had grandchildren living in their home.

Nearly one-third (30%) of GRG households had annual incomes ranging from $20,000 to just under $40,000. Another third (33%) had annual incomes of $40,000 up to $60,000, while the rest had incomes of $60,000 or more. Nearly two-thirds (63%) of GRG respondents identified themselves as retired, but 13% of them still worked full- or part-time. About 30% of GRG respondents had not yet retired. Forty-five percent had a high school education or less, and the same percentage had attended college or earned a college degree. Grandparents with graduate degrees accounted for 9% of the total.

The majority (44%) of GRG grandparents were age sixty to sixty-nine, and 23% were between seventy and seventy-nine years-old. Almost one-third (28%) were age fifty to fifty-nine, and 3% each were age forty-five to forty-nine and age eighty or older. Almost three-quarters (70%) of the grandparents in GRG households were married.

In addition to the grandparents who live with and raise their grandchildren, about 15% of grandparents surveyed provided childcare for their grandchildren with working parents. Nearly 80% of these grandparents cared for one or two children, and 17% cared for as many as three or four grandchildren.

GRANDPARENTS' RIGHTS. The high rate of divorce in the United States has caused many grandparents to become separated from their grandchildren. As a result, some grandparents have sought visitation rights to their grandchildren. Since the 1980s a growing number of cases have been heard in the courts, prompting most states to enact legislation governing how and when grandparents may see their grandchildren. At issue is whether fit parents can be legally forced to allow grandparents to visit grandchildren. In most states grandparents must show that visitation is in the best interest of the child. In Georgia grandparents must show that the children would suffer harm if they were denied visits.

In the 2000 case *Troxel v. Granville* (530 U.S. 57) the U.S. Supreme Court heard arguments to decide whether nonparents, including grandparents, could legally sue for child visitation rights. Under a State of Washington statute that allows anyone to petition for the right to visit a child at any time, the Troxels petitioned for the right to visit their two granddaughters more often than the girls' mother desired. A Washington Superior Court, authorized under the statute to grant visitation rights when a child's best interest might be served, granted the Troxels additional visitation. Ms. Granville appealed the ruling, which was overturned based on the court's decision that nonparents could not sue under the statute. The Washington Supreme Court agreed with the ruling and declared the statute unconstitutional because it interfered with parents' right to rear

FIGURE 3.2

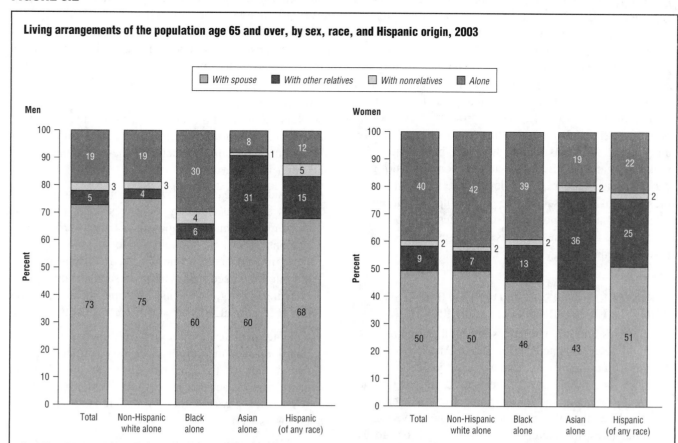

Living arrangements of the population age 65 and over, by sex, race, and Hispanic origin, 2003

Note: Living with other relatives indicates no spouse present. Living with nonrelatives indicates no spouse or other relatives present. The term "non-Hispanic white alone" is used to refer to people who reported being white and no other race and who are not Hispanic. The term "black alone" is used to refer to people who reported being black or African American and no other race, and the term "Asian alone" is used to refer to people who reported only Asian as their race. The use of single-race populations in this report does not imply that is the preferred method of presenting or analyzing data. The U.S. Census Bureau uses a variety of approaches.
Reference population: These data refer to the civilian noninstitutionalized population.

SOURCE: "Living Arrangements of the Population Age 65 and Over, by Sex and Race and Hispanic Origin, 2003," in *Older Americans 2004: Key Indicators*, Federal Interagency Forum on Aging Related Statistics, Washington, DC, U.S. Government Printing Office, November 2004, http://www.agingstats.gov/chartbook2004/population.html#Indicator%205 (accessed August 11, 2005)

their children. The question of the statute's constitutionality was brought before the U.S. Supreme Court, which concluded in a 6–3 decision that it violated the due process clause of the Fourteenth Amendment under which parents would have the right to make decisions about the care, custody, and control of their children. In her opinion, Justice Sandra Day O'Connor wrote that "[t]he liberty interest at issue in this case—the interest of parents in the care, custody, and control of their children—is perhaps the oldest of the fundamental liberty interests recognized by this Court" (FindLaw for Legal Professionals, http://caselaw.lp.findlaw.com/scripts/get-case.pl?court=us&vol=530&invol=57#section2). Essentially, the U.S. Supreme Court left grandparents with little or no recourse in trying to win visitation rights.

HOMELESSNESS

According to the U.S. Interagency Council on Homelessness, in 2003 the number of homeless adults age sixty-five and over was estimated to range from 10% to 15% of the total population of homeless Americans. In the early 2000s, as real estate values and rents have soared across the nation, some older adults have been forced to sleep in shelters and on the streets. Between 1999 and 2003 shelter use rose most rapidly among the age fifty-five and older population.

Among the concerns about homelessness are the inherent health-related issues. The relationship between homelessness, health, and illness is complex. Some health problems precede homelessness and contribute to it, while others are consequences of homelessness; in addition, homelessness often complicates access and adherence to treatment. For example mental illness or substance abuse (dependency on alcohol or drugs) may limit a person's ability to work, leading to poverty and homelessness. Without protection from the cold, rain, and snow, exposure to weather may result in illnesses such as bronchitis or pneumonia. Homelessness increases exposure to crime and violence, which could lead to trauma and injuries.

There are many reasons that homeless persons experience difficulties gaining access to health care services and receiving needed medical care. Lacking such essentials as transportation to medical facilities, money to pay for care, and knowledge about how to qualify for health insurance and where to obtain health care services makes seeking treatment complicated and frustrating. Psychological distress or mental illness may prevent homeless persons from attempting to obtain needed care, and finding food and shelter may take precedence over seeking treatment. Even when the homeless do gain access to medical care, following a treatment plan, filling prescriptions, and scheduling follow-up appointments often present insurmountable challenges to those who do not have telephone numbers, addresses, or safe places to store medications.

LONG-TERM CARE, SUPPORTIVE HOUSING, AND OTHER RESIDENTIAL ALTERNATIVES

Spouses and other relatives are still the major caretakers of older, dependent members of American society. However, the number of people age sixty-five and older living in long-term care facilities such as nursing homes is rising, because the older population is increasing rapidly. Even though many older adults now live longer, healthier lives, the increase in overall length of life has increased the need for long-term care facilities and supportive housing.

Growth of the home health care industry in the early 1990s only slightly slowed the increase in the numbers of Americans entering nursing homes. Supportive housing—assisted living, congregate housing, and continuing-care retirement communities—offer alternatives to nursing home care. The overarching goal of supportive housing is to enable older adults to receive needed assistance while retaining as much independence as possible.

There are three broad classes of supportive housing for older adults. The smallest, most affordable options usually house ten or fewer older adults and are often in homes in residential neighborhoods. Residents share bathrooms, bedrooms, and living areas. These largely unregulated facilities are alternately known as board and care facilities, domiciliary care, personal care homes, adult foster care, senior group homes, and sheltered housing.

Residential care facilities, assisted living residences, and adult congregate living facilities tend to be larger, more expensive, and offer more independence and privacy than board and care facilities. Most offer private rooms or apartments along with large common areas for activities and meals.

Continuing care retirement communities and life care communities are usually large complexes that offer a comprehensive range of services from independent living to skilled nursing home care. These facilities are specifically designed to provide nearly all needed care, except for hospital care, within one community. Facilities in this group tend to be the most costly.

Nursing Homes

Nursing homes fall into three broad categories: residential care facilities, intermediate care facilities, and skilled nursing facilities. Each provides a different range and intensity of services:

- A residential care facility (RCF) normally provides meals and housekeeping for its residents, plus some basic medical monitoring, such as administering medications. This type of home is for persons who are fairly independent and do not need constant medical attention but need help with tasks such as laundry and cleaning. Many RCFs also provide social activities and recreational programs for their residents.

- An intermediate care facility (ICF) offers room and board and nursing care as necessary for persons who can no longer live independently. As in the RCF, exercise and social programs are provided, and some ICFs offer physical therapy and rehabilitation programs as well.

- A skilled nursing facility (SNF) provides around-the-clock nursing care, plus on-call physician coverage. The SNF is for patients who need intensive nursing care, as well as such services as occupational therapy, physical therapy, respiratory therapy, and rehabilitation.

NURSING HOME RESIDENTS. The National Nursing Home Survey (NNHS) conducted by the National Center for Health Statistics is a continuing series of national sample surveys of nursing homes, their residents, and their staff. The surveys were conducted in 1973–74, 1977, 1985, 1995, 1997, and 1999. The latest survey was started in August 2004. While each survey has a different focus, all of them offer some basic data about nursing homes residents.

The nation's approximately eighteen thousand nursing homes had occupancy rates of almost 87% in 1999, and about 1.5 million adults age sixty-five and older were nursing home residents. Of those, the majority were white (87%) and female (74%). Most residents of nursing homes are the oldest-old; persons age eighty-five and older are the fastest-growing segment of the population, accounting for almost half (47%) of all nursing home residents. This compares with 35% in 1977 and 41% in 1985.

More than a quarter (27%) of the residents in nursing homes in 1999 had been there for three years or more, and another 30% had been in residence between one and three years. With the rise in age of those living in nursing homes, the level of such basic activities as eating, walking, dressing, and bathing that residents were able to perform themselves has declined. In 1999, 53% of residents were unable to eat without assistance compared with 67% in 1977 and 59% in 1985. While the number of residents able to bathe unassisted accounted for 13% in 1977 and 9% in 1985, only 6% were able to do so in 1999.

DIVERSIFICATION OF NURSING HOMES. To remain competitive with home health care and the increasing array of alternative living arrangements for older adults, many nursing homes have begun to offer alternative services and programs. New services include adult day care and visiting nurse services for persons who still live at home. Other programs include respite plans that allow caregivers who need to travel for business or vacation to leave an older relative in the nursing home temporarily.

INNOVATION IMPROVES QUALITY OF NURSING HOME CARE. Although industry observers and the media frequently decry the care provided in nursing homes, and the media publicize instances of elder abuse and other quality of care issues, several organizations have actively sought to develop models of health service delivery that improve the clinical care and quality of life for nursing home residents. In August 2002 the Commonwealth Fund, a New York City-based organization dedicated to improving health care services, published a report examining one such model in eastern Wisconsin. In *Evaluation of the Wellspring Model for Improving Nursing Home Quality*, researchers from the Institute for the Future of Aging Services and the American Association of Homes and Services for the Aging reported the findings of their evaluation of the Wellspring model of nursing home quality improvement.

Wellspring began in 1994 as an alliance of eleven not-for-profit nursing homes. The alliance, under the auspices of Wellspring Innovative Solutions Inc., aimed to simultaneously improve the clinical care delivered to its nursing home residents and the work environment for its employees. Education and collaboration are hallmarks of the Wellspring philosophy, and this program began by equipping nursing home personnel with the skills needed to perform their jobs and organizing employees in teams working toward shared goals. The Wellspring model of service delivery uses a multidisciplinary clinical team approach—including nurse practitioners, social services, food service personnel, nursing assistants, and facility and housekeeping personnel—to solve problems and develop approaches to better meet residents' needs. The teams represent an important innovation, because they allow health professionals and other workers to interact as peers and share resources, information, and decision-making in a cooperative, supportive environment.

Shared resources, training, ideas, and goals have had a powerful impact on care at the Wellspring facilities. The researchers observed more cooperation, responsibility, and accountability within the teams and the institutions than observed at other comparable facilities. In addition to finding a strong organizational culture committed to quality patient care, the researchers also documented measurable improvements in specific areas, including the following:

- Wellspring facilities had lower rates of staff turnover than comparable Wisconsin facilities during the same time period, probably because Wellspring workers felt valued by management and experienced greater job satisfaction than other nursing home personnel.

- No additional resources were required to institute the Wellspring model, and Wellspring facilities operated at lower costs than comparable facilities.

- Wellspring facilities' performance, as measured by a federal survey, improved.

- Generally, Wellspring personnel appeared more attentive to residents' needs and problems and sought to anticipate and promptly resolve any issues.

The researchers concluded that the organizational commitment to training and shared decision-making, along with improved quality of interactions and relationships among staff and between staff and residents, significantly contributed to enhanced quality of life for residents.

THE PIONEER NETWORK. In response to concerns about quality of life and quality of care issues in nursing homes, leaders in nursing home reform efforts from around the United States established the Pioneer Network in 2000 as a forum for the culture change movement. The culture change in this instance would be a focus on person-directed values that affirm and support each person's individuality and abilities and that apply to elders as well as those who work with them. Pioneers commit to the following values:

- Know each person.

- Each person can and does make a difference.

- Relationship is the fundamental building block of a transformed culture.

- Respond to spirit, as well as mind and body.

- Risk taking is a normal part of life.

- Put person before task.

- All elders are entitled to self-determination, wherever they live.

- Community is the antidote to institutionalization.

- Do unto others as you would have them do unto you.

- Promote the growth and development of all.

- Shape and use the potential of the environment in all its aspects: physical, organizational, and psycho-social/spiritual.

- Practice self-examination, searching for new creativity and opportunities for doing better.

- Recognize that culture change and transformation are not destinations but a journey, always a work in progress.

In August 2004 the Pioneer Network published *Getting Started: A Pioneering Approach to Culture Change in Long-Term Care Organizations*, a handbook designed to assist nursing home providers embarking on culture change journeys. The group also published *The Sanctity of Life and the Sacredness of Death: A Journey of Putting Pioneer Network Values into Practice* in 2004 and hosted its fifth national conference, "There's No Place Like Home," in Overland Park, Kansas, which was attended by 840 people from forty-four states.

THE EDEN ALTERNATIVE. Developed in 1991 by William Thomas, MD, the Eden Alternative is a movement that, like the Pioneer Network, seeks to transform nursing homes. The Eden Alternative strives to create nursing homes that are rich and vibrant human habitats where plants, children, and animals bring life-enriching energy to residents. The philosophy of the Eden Alternative is that providing a stimulant-rich environment will help to minimize the hopelessness often felt by nursing home residents. Nursing homes based on this model are being opened across the country.

By providing garden-like settings filled with plants and encouraging relationships with children and pets, the Eden Alternative hopes to improve the human spirit and dispel loneliness. The ten principles of an Eden Alternative nursing home are:

1. The three plagues of loneliness, helplessness, and boredom account for the bulk of suffering among our elders.

2. An elder-centered community commits to creating a Human Habitat where life revolves around close and continuing contact with plants, animals, and children. It is these relationships that provide the young and old alike with a pathway to a life worth living.

3. Loving companionship is the antidote to loneliness. Elders deserve easy access to human and animal companionship.

4. An elder-centered community creates opportunity to give as well as receive care. This is the antidote to helplessness.

5. An elder-centered community imbues daily life with variety and spontaneity by creating an environment in which unexpected and unpredictable interactions and happenings can take place. This is the antidote to boredom.

6. Meaningless activity corrodes the human spirit. The opportunity to do things that we find meaningful is essential to human health.

7. Medical treatment should be the servant of genuine human caring, never its master.

8. An elder-centered community honors its elders by deemphasizing top-down bureaucratic authority, seeking instead to place the maximum possible decision-making authority into the hands of the elders or into the hands of those closest to them.

9. Creating an elder-centered community is a never-ending process. Human growth must never be separated from human life.

10. Wise leadership is the lifeblood of any struggle against the three plagues. For it, there can be no substitute.

During 2004 the Eden Alternative trained 971 new Eden Associates, for a total of nearly ten thousand, and registered thirty-four new Eden homes, bringing the total registered homes to 277. The organization's second international conference was attended by seventy-five participants from outside the United States and another 275 professionals from thirty-eight states.

Thomas's initiatives also include the Green House Project. This effort comprises the design and construction of small group homes for older adults, built to a residential scale. Green Houses provide necessary clinical care within a social model in which primacy is given to the older adults' quality of life. The goal of the model is to provide frail older adults with an environment that promotes autonomy, dignity, privacy, and choice.

Green Houses are designed to feel more like homes than today's typical long-term care institutions and to blend easily into their community or surroundings. The first Green House in the nation opened in May 2003 in Tupelo, Mississippi, developed by United Methodist Senior Services of Mississippi. By mid-2005 fifteen additional Green House projects in thirteen states were in various stages of construction.

Assisted Living

Assisted living arose to bridge a gap in long-term care. It is intended to meet the needs of older adults who wish to live independently in the community but require some of the services—housekeeping, meals, transportation, and assistance with other activities of daily living—provided by a nursing home. (Activities of daily living are generally considered to include eating, bathing, dressing, getting to and using the bathroom, getting in or out of bed or a chair, and mobility.) Assisted living ideally offers a flexible array of services that enable older adults to maintain as much independence as they can, for as long as possible.

Since assisted living refers to a concept and philosophy as opposed to a regulated provider of health services such as a hospital or skilled nursing facility, there is no uniform description of the services an assisted living residence must offer, and as a result there is considerable variation among assisted living facilities. These residences are regulated on a state level, and each state has its own definition of what constitutes an assisted living facility as well as its own set of rules governing them. For the 2000 report *Understanding Medicaid Home and Community Services: A Primer* (Gary Smith et al., http://aspe.hhs.gov/daltcp/reports/primer.htm), the U.S. Department of Health and Human Services defined assisted living as "care that combines housing and supportive services in a homelike environment and seeks to promote maximal functioning and autonomy."

Members of the Assisted Living Federation of America (ALFA), the largest national association dedicated to operating assisted living communities for older adults, subscribe to a ten-point philosophy of care:

1. Offering cost-effective quality care that is personalized for individual needs

2. Fostering independence for each resident

3. Treating each resident with dignity and respect

4. Promoting the individuality of each resident

5. Allowing each resident choice of care and lifestyle

6. Protecting each resident's right to privacy

7. Nurturing the spirit of each resident

8. Involving family and friends, as appropriate, in care planning and implementation

9. Providing a safe, residential environment

10. Making the assisted living residence a valuable community asset

Assisted living residences may be located on the grounds of retirement communities or nursing homes, or they may be freestanding residential facilities. They vary in size and location as well as services. Some are high-rise apartment complexes, while others are converted private homes. Most facilities contain between twenty-five and 120 units, which vary in size from one room to a full apartment.

ALFA reports that in 2005 more than a million Americans lived in an estimated twenty thousand assisted living residences. ALFA characterizes the typical assisted living resident as a widowed or single woman in her eighties.

Assisted living licensing regulations vary from state to state. Most states require staff certification and training and all assisted living facilities must comply with local building codes and fire safety regulations.

COSTS OF ASSISTED LIVING. The cost of assisted living varies based on geography, unit size, and the services needed. According to ALFA, daily basic fees range from approximately $25 to $200 per day and may cover all services, or there may be additional charges for special services. Most assisted living facilities charge monthly rates and some require long-term lease arrangements.

Residents or their families generally pay for assisted living using their own financial resources. Some health insurance programs or long-term care insurance policies reimburse for specific health-related care provided by assisted living facilities, and some state and local governments offer subsidies for rent or services for low-income older adults. Others may provide subsidies in the form of an additional payment for those who receive Supplemental Security Income (SSI) or Medicaid.

Continuing Care Retirement Communities

Continuing care retirement communities (CCRCs), also known as life care communities, offer a continuum of care—independent living, assisted living, and nursing home care—in a single facility or on common grounds. The goal of CCRCs is to enable residents to "age in place." When residents become ill or disabled, for example, they do not have to relocate to a nursing home, because health care services are available on the CCRC campus.

Like assisted living facilities, CCRCs vary in location, design, and amenities. They range from urban high rises to semirural campuses and from one hundred residents to over a thousand. Most include common dining rooms, activity and exercise areas, indoor and outdoor recreation areas, and swimming pools.

Typically, residents enter into a contractual arrangement with the facility requiring that they pay an entrance fee and a fixed monthly fee in return for housing, meals, personal care, recreation, and nursing services. Many CCRCs offer other payment options, including both entrance fee and fee-for-service arrangements. In the past entrance fees were nonrefundable; however, by 2004 most newer CCRCs had instituted refundable or partially refundable entrance fees.

CCRCs may be operated by private, not-for-profit, and/or religious organizations. Entrance fees in these communities vary substantially, from $20,000 to $500,000, and monthly maintenance fees range from $600 to $2,000, depending on the size of the facility and the extent of services. With few exceptions, none of the costs of CCRCs are covered by government or private insurance.

Cohousing and Shared Housing

Older adults may share living quarters to reduce expenses, share household and home maintenance responsibilities, and gain companionship. Many choose to share the same homes in which they raised their families, because these houses are often large enough to accommodate more than one or two persons. Shared housing is often called "cohousing," but the phrases are not exactly the same. Cohousing usually refers to planned or intentional communities of private dwellings with shared common areas that include dining rooms, meeting rooms, recreation facilities, and lounges. Cohousing and shared housing are cost-effective alternatives for those who wish to remain in their own homes and for older adults who cannot afford private assisted living or continuing care retirement communities.

The cohousing concept originated in Denmark in the 1960s and spread to North America in the 1980s. According to the Cohousing Association of the United States, in 2005 there were more than one hundred cohousing communities in various stages of development in North America. Cohousing participants are involved in planning the community and maintaining it, and most cohousing groups make their decisions by consensus.

In contrast, most shared housing consists of a single homeowner taking a roommate to share living space and expenses. Shared housing can also include households with three or more roommates and family-like cooperatives in which large groups of people live together.

Intergenerational cohousing or shared housing also may meet the needs of younger as well as older people. Along with the benefits of cost-sharing and companionship, home sharers and cohousing residents may exchange services—for example, help with household maintenance in exchange for baby-sitting.

Matt Thornhill of The Boomer Project anticipates that aging baby boomers will embrace cohousing. The concept of a community with shared values, care, meals, transportation, and shared homes will likely appeal to many boomers, who enjoyed communes and group-living situations in the 1960s and 1970s. In an article for *The Boomer Project Newsletter* ("Cohabiting to Cohousing," June 2005), Thornhill predicted that cohousing communities will even be retrofitted from existing neighborhoods, enabling boomers to age in place.

ECHO Units or "Granny Flats"

Elder cottage housing opportunity (ECHO) units, or "granny flats," are small, freestanding, removable housing units that are located on the same lot as a single-family house. Another term used by local zoning authorities is "accessory apartments or units." Accessory apartments are self-contained second living units built into or attached to an existing single-family dwelling. They are private, generally smaller than the primary unit, and usually contain one or two bedrooms, a bathroom, sitting room, and kitchen.

Generally, families construct ECHO units and accessory apartments for parents or grandparents so that the older adults can be nearby while maintaining their independence. Existing zoning laws and concerns about property values and traffic patterns are obstacles to both cohousing and construction of ECHO units, but as these alternatives become more popular, local jurisdictions may be pressured to allow multifamily housing in neighborhoods that traditionally have had only single-family homes.

Retirement Communities

Developers such as industry leader Del Webb (a division of Pulte Homes) have created and constructed communities and even entire small "cities" exclusively for older adults. Examples include the Sun City communities in Florida, Arizona, and Texas. The Florida and Arizona locations opened in the 1960s and the Texas site in 1996.

In 2005 Del Webb boasted communities in nineteen states, which are home to more than two hundred thousand older adults. Homes in most of these properties are available only to those families in which at least one member is fifty-five or older, and no one under age nineteen is allowed to reside permanently. Sun City communities offer clubs, golf courses, social organizations, fitness clubs, organized travel, and recreational complexes. Medical facilities are located nearby.

The 2005 Del Webb Baby Boomer Survey (http://onlinepressroom.net/pulte/babyboomer/) conducted by Harris Interactive found that 59% of younger boomers (age forty-one to forty-nine) and half of older boomers (age fifty to fifty-nine) planned to buy a new home for their retirement. Among older boomers willing to relocate when they retire, 70% cited more affordable housing as their most important reason for moving, followed by more affordable location (67%). Two-thirds (66%) of older boomers said they would move for a better community lifestyle, and 54% would seek a warmer climate. Nearly half (47%) of all respondents (age forty-one to sixty-nine) who will move say staying within three hours of family is an important consideration when relocating. Among those willing to move to a different state, younger boomers preferred North Carolina while older boomers chose Florida.

While many older adults and baby boomers aspire to purchase new homes in active retirement communities or to relocate, it is likely that only those with considerable financial resources will be able to do so. Depending on location and size, in 2005 Del Webb home prices ranged from $123,990 in Sun City Texas to $573,900 in Sun City Lincoln Hills in northern California.

Board and Care Facilities

The U.S. Department of Health and Human Services defined board and care homes in the 1994 report *Licensed Board and Care Homes: Preliminary Findings from the 1991 National Health Provider Inventory* (Robert F. Clark, et al., http://aspe.hhs.gov/daltcp/reports/licbchom.htm) as "non-medical community-based facilities that provide protective oversight and/or personal care in addition to meals and lodging to one or more residents with functional or cognitive limitations." Typically, board and care residents have their own bedrooms and bathrooms or share them with one other person, while other living areas are shared.

Although many board and care homes offer residents safe, homelike environments and attentive caregivers, there have been many well-publicized instances of fraud and abuse. Entirely unregulated in many states, board and care facilities have frequently become dumping grounds for older adults.

In an attempt to stem abuses, the federal government passed the Keys Amendment in 1978. Under the terms of this legislation, residents living in board and care facilities that fail to provide adequate care are subject to reduced SSI payments. This move was intended to penalize substandard board and care operators, but advocates for older adults contend that it actually penalizes the SSI recipients and that it has not served to reduce reports of abuse. With the 1992 reauthorization of the Older Americans Act of 1965, Congress provided for long-term care ombudsman programs designed to help prevent the abuse, exploitation, and neglect of residents in long-term care facilities such as board and care residences and nursing homes. Paid and volunteer ombudsmen monitor facilities and act as advocates for the residents. In 2001 nearly 265,000 complaints were investigated.

OWNING AND RENTING A HOME

Data from the U.S. Census Bureau Housing Vacancies and Homeownership survey show the overall home ownership rate for 2003 was 68.3%, up from 67.9% in 2002. This is the highest rate since the U.S. Census Bureau began reporting these statistics in 1965. In the first quarter of 2005, 80.8% of adults age sixty-five and over owned their own homes. Homeownership peaked (83.3%) among adults age sixty-five to sixty-nine. (See Table 3.3.) These rates have risen steadily since the 1990s.

Older householders are less likely than those under age sixty-five to have mortgage indebtedness. According

TABLE 3.3

Homeownership rates, by age of householder, 2004 and 2005

Age of householder	First quarter 2004	First quarter 2005
United States	68.6	69.1
Under 25 years	23.6	25.2
25 to 29 years	40.0	41.5
30 to 34 years	56.4	57.2
35 to 39 years	66.0	67.4
40 to 44 years	71.3	72.5
45 to 49 years	76.2	75.3
50 to 54 years	77.8	77.8
55 to 59 years	81.2	81.1
60 to 64 years	82.4	82.6
65 to 69 years	82.5	83.3
70 to 74 years	82.3	83.0
75 years and over	78.9	78.5
Under 35 years	42.3	43.3
35 to 44 years	68.8	70.1
45 to 54 years	77.0	76.5
55 to 64 years	81.7	81.8
65 years and over	80.7	80.8

SOURCE: "Table 7. Homeownership Rates by Age of Householder: First Quarter: 2004 and 2005," in *Housing Vacancies and Homeownership (CPS/HVS)*, U.S. Census Bureau, Housing and Household Economic Statistics Division, Washington, DC, April 25, 2005, http://www.census.gov/hhes/www/housing/hvs/qtr105/q105tab7.html (accessed August 11, 2005)

to statistics presented by the Administration on Aging in *A Profile of Older Americans: 2004* (http://www.aoa.gov/prof/Statistics/profile/2004/profiles2004.asp), in 2003 approximately 72% of older homeowners owned their homes free and clear. However, even when there is no mortgage remaining on the home, homeowners must still pay property taxes, insurance premiums, and utility bills as well as the costs of home maintenance and repairs.

Renters generally pay a higher percentage of their income for housing than do homeowners. Unlike most homeowners who pay fixed monthly mortgage payments, renters often face annual rent increases. Many older adult renters living on fixed incomes are unprepared to pay these increases. Homeowners also benefit from their home equity and can borrow against it in times of financial need. In contrast, renters do not build equity and do not get a return on their investment. Also, while mortgage payments are tax deductible, rent payments are not.

Reverse Mortgages

To supplement their retirement incomes or pay for health care, many older Americans turn to "reverse" mortgages. Reverse mortgages allow older homeowners to convert some of their home equity into cash, making it possible for them to avoid selling their homes.

With a traditional mortgage homeowners make monthly payments to the lender. In a reverse mortgage the lender pays the homeowner in monthly installments and in most cases, no repayment is due until the homeowner dies, sells the house, or moves permanently. Reverse mortgages help homeowners who are house-rich—have considerable equity in their homes—but cash-poor stay in their homes and still meet their financial obligations.

Sale/Leaseback with Life Tenancy

Another option for older homeowners is a sale/lease-back in which the homeowner gives up ownership of a home and becomes a renter. The former homeowner frequently requests life tenancy—retaining the right to live in the house as a renter for the rest of his or her life. The buyer pays the former homeowner in monthly installments and also is responsible for property taxes, insurance, maintenance, and repairs.

Renting Is Often Unaffordable

The National Low-Income Housing Coalition (NLIHC) report *Out of Reach 2004* (Washington, DC; December 2004) documents income and rental housing cost data for the fifty states, the District of Columbia, and Puerto Rico. For each area, the coalition calculates the income needed to be able to afford the fair market rent (FMR) of the housing. The national median housing wage, based on each county's housing wage for a two-bedroom unit at the FMR, was $15.37 an hour in 2004. Housing wages ranged from a high of $29.60 in San Francisco, California, to $6.21 in Starr County, Texas, and $5.90 in parts of Puerto Rico.

The average monthly SSI payment, the federal income maintenance program that provides a base of support for about two million older adults, was just $353 for adults age sixty-five and over in December 2004. Older adults relying solely on SSI payments cannot afford rental housing anywhere in the United States. The NLIHC report described those people relying only on SSI as being "at the greatest disadvantage in today's housing markets." Even in West Virginia, the state with the smallest gap between fair market rents and rents afford-able to SSI recipients, affordable housing is well out of reach.

ADDITIONAL HOUSING CHALLENGES FOR OLDER ADULTS

Physical Hazards and Accommodations

Home characteristics considered desirable by younger householders may present challenges to older adults. For example, the staircase in a two-story house may become a formidable obstacle to an older adult suffering from arthritis, heart disease, or other disabling chronic conditions. Narrow halls and doorways cannot accommodate walkers and wheelchairs. High cabinets and shelves may be beyond the reach of an arthritis sufferer. While houses can be modified to meet the physical needs of older or disabled persons, some older houses cannot as easily be remodeled, and retrofitting them may be quite costly. Owners of condominiums in Florida, whose young-old residents once prized second- and third-floor units for their breezes and golf course views, are now considering installing elevators for residents in their eighties and nineties who find climbing stairs much more difficult.

Older adults, as well as advocates on their behalf, historically have expressed a strong preference for aging in place—remaining in their own homes rather than relocating to assisted living facilities or other supportive housing. The AARP reports that 85% of people over fifty-five want to remain in familiar surroundings rather than move to alternative housing. In order to live more comfortably, those older adults who have the means can redesign and reequip their homes to accommodate the physical changes associated with aging.

Simple adaptations include replacing doorknobs with levers that can be pushed downward with a fist or elbow, requiring no gripping or twisting; replacing light switches with flat "touch" switches; placing closet rods at adjustable heights; installing stoves with front- or side-mounted controls; and marking steps with bright colors. More complex renovations include replacing a bathroom with a wet room (a tiled space that is large enough to accommodate a wheelchair, and with a showerhead, waterproof chair, and sloping floor for a drain), placing electrical outlets higher than usual along walls, and widening passageways and doors for walkers, wheelchairs, or scooters.

Anticipating the increase in the older population in the coming years, some real estate developers are manufacturing houses designed to meet the needs of older adults and prolong their ability to live independently. These houses feature accommodations such as nonskid flooring, walls strong enough to support the mounting of grab bars, outlets at convenient heights, levers instead of knobs on doors and plumbing fixtures, and doors and hallways wide enough to allow wheelchair access.

PUBLIC HOUSING

Congress passed the United States Housing Act of 1937 (PL 75-412) to create low-income public housing, but according to the Housing Research Foundation (HRF) 2002 report *Public Housing for Seniors: Past, Present, and Future*, by 1952 only 6% of available housing was occupied by older adults. After 1956, when Congress authorized the development of dedicated public housing for the elderly and specifically made low-income older adults eligible for such housing, the situation began to improve. By 1999 about 20% of public housing was occupied by older adults, as reported in *A Quiet Crisis in America* prepared by the Commission on Affordable

Housing and Health Facility Needs for Seniors in the 21st Century (http://govinfo.library.unt.edu/seniorscommission/pages/final_report/index.html, 2002).

The HRF, a nonprofit institution dedicated to the study of public housing and its residents, estimated that approximately seven hundred thousand adults age sixty-two and older made their homes in public housing at the turn of the twenty-first century. The group's report described public housing's older residents as poorer and frailer than their age peers in the general population, disproportionately minority and female, and more likely to live alone. The residents who entered public housing as young-old have aged in place and are now the older-old and more in need of supportive and health services than they were two decades ago.

Given that public housing residents are more disadvantaged financially, in poorer health, and are more disabled than older adults in the general population, it is not surprising that about 20% require assistance with at least one activity of daily living, compared with just 12% of older adults in the general population. More than half of the older adults in public housing live below the poverty line.

Public housing itself has also aged—much of it is more than thirty years old. Many developments are badly run-down and in desperate need of renovation. Most are unequipped to offer the range of supportive services required by increasingly frail and dependent residents.

The HRF report concluded with the following recommendations for action that would enable public housing to better serve a growing number of older adults:

1. Immediately improving the current physical conditions of public housing

2. Securing the necessary funding to coordinate the delivery of social services to older adults wishing to age in place

3. Identifying various housing and assisted living models and associated amenities and the mechanisms for funding

4. Accurately projecting the number of older adults that will need assisted housing in the future

5. Collecting and analyzing information about public housing for older adults from various organizations and locations to create a comprehensive and cohesive picture of the status of public housing

6. Establishing a coalition composed of older public housing residents, housing interest groups, associations serving the older population, public entities, and other stakeholders to develop policy recommendations to address older residents' needs

CHAPTER 4

WORKING AND RETIREMENT: NEW OPTIONS
FOR OLDER ADULTS

Americans head off to their jobs each day as much for daily meaning as for daily bread.

—Studs Terkel in *Working*

Historically Americans age sixty-five and older have made substantial contributions to society. Examples of accomplished older adults include:

- Benjamin Franklin—writer, scientist, inventor, and statesman—helped draft the Declaration of Independence at age seventy.

- Thomas Alva Edison worked on inventions, including the light bulb, microphone, and the phonograph, until his death at the age of eighty-four.

- Rear Admiral Grace Hopper (Ret.), one of the early computer scientists and coauthor of the computer language COBOL, maintained an active speaking and consulting schedule until her death at age eighty-five.

- Margaret Mead, the noted anthropologist, returned to New Guinea when she was seventy-two and exhausted a much younger television film crew as they tried to keep up with her.

- Albert Einstein, who formulated the theory of relativity, was working on a unifying theory of the universe when he died at age seventy-six.

- Georgia O'Keeffe created masterful paintings when she was more than eighty years of age.

Older adults continue to play vital roles in industry, government, and the arts. Notable examples include:

- Former senator John Glenn, who piloted the first manned U.S. spacecraft to orbit Earth, returned to space at age seventy-seven as a payload specialist.

- Alan Greenspan, who turns eighty in 2006, was overseeing the U.S. economy in 2005 as the Federal Reserve chairman.

- U.S. Senator John McCain, a Republican from Arizona, will be seventy in 2006.

- James Watson, best known for his discovery of the structure of DNA, is chancellor of the Cold Spring Harbor Laboratory in New York and turned seventy-seven in 2005.

- Legendary actor and race car driver Paul Newman turned eighty in 2005 and is still working in the entertainment industry and driving fast cars.

DEFINING AND REDEFINING RETIREMENT

Retirement in the United States is usually defined by two actions—withdrawal from the paid labor force and receipt of income from pension plans, Social Security, or other retirement plans. There are, however, many people who may be viewed as "retired" even though they do not fulfill the criteria of the generally accepted definition of retirement. For example, workers who retire from military or other federal employment, which provide pension benefits after twenty years of service, may choose to continue to work and remain in the labor force for years, collecting both a salary and pension. Other workers retire from full-time employment but continue to work part-time to supplement their pension, Social Security, or retirement benefits. As a result, not all workers collecting pensions are retired, and some workers collecting salaries are retired.

In addition to expanding the definition of the term "retirement," an increasing number of older Americans are not subscribing to the traditional timing and lifestyle of retirement. Retirement is no longer an event, it is a process, and work and retirement are no longer mutually exclusive. While many older adults still choose to retire from full-time employment at age sixty-five, they remain active—exploring new careers, working part-time, volunteering, and engaging in a variety of leisure activities. An increasing proportion of older adults work well beyond age sixty-five, and some choose not to retire at all.

A 2000 survey conducted by Harris Interactive for the National Council on the Aging (NCOA), the results of which were published in *American Perceptions of Aging in the 21st Century* (Washington, DC; 2002), found that while 58% were "completely retired" (retired and not working), nearly one-quarter (23%) of persons age sixty-five and older described themselves as "both retired and working," and 19% were not retired at all. Respondents age seventy-five and over were more likely to describe themselves as completely retired than were those age sixty-five to seventy-four. The survey respondents named qualifying for Social Security benefits and accumulated savings as the most important factors in their decisions to retire.

RECASTING WORK AND RETIREMENT

Throughout much of human history, the average length of life was relatively short. In a world where most people did not expect to live beyond age fifty, it was essential that personal, educational, and professional milestones be attained by certain ages. Obtaining an education, job training, marriage, parenthood, and retirement not only were designated to particular periods of life but also were expected generally to occur only once in a lifetime.

This regimented pattern of life was maintained by tradition and, more recently, reinforced by laws and regulations. In the United States, government regulations and institutional rules prescribed the ages at which education began, work-life ended, and pension and Social Security benefits commenced. This timetable was based on the assumptions that these activities were to be performed "on time" and in sequence and that most growth and development occurred in the first half of life, while the second half was, in general, characterized by decline and disinvestment.

Social and demographic trends—including increased longevity and improved health—technological advances, and economic realities have transformed the size and composition of the labor force as well as the nature of family and work. Examples of these changes include:

• Marriage and childbearing often are postponed in favor of pursuing education and careers. Advances in reproductive technology have enabled women to delay having children by twenty years. The National Center for Health Statistics reported that the number of women age forty to forty-four giving birth more than doubled between 1981 and 2002, and increased by 5% from 2002 to 2003. The number of births to women over age forty exceeded one hundred thousand for the first time in 2003.

• Formal learning was once the exclusive province of the young; middle-aged and older adults, however, are increasingly returning to school. According to the National Center for Education Statistics, the number of students age thirty-five and over in degree-granting institutions more than doubled between 1970 and 2003. Distance learning programs and classes offered online have created additional opportunities for older adults who wish to continue their education.

• Career changes and retraining have become the norm rather than the exception. Americans once pursued a single career in their lifetimes; many workers now change jobs and even careers several times. The RAND Corporation, a California-based nonprofit research organization, predicts that by 2020 the average worker will retrain as many as thirteen times in his or her lifetime.

• Age-based mandatory retirement no longer exists in most private sector industries. Mandatory retirement ages historically were justified by the argument that some occupations were either too dangerous for older workers or required high levels of physical and mental acuity. Mandatory retirement is still compulsory for federal law enforcement, correctional officers, fire-fighters, air traffic controllers, and commercial airline pilots. Mandatory retirement ages have, however, been faulted because they are arbitrary and are not based on actual physical evaluations of individual workers. As a result, some detractors view the practice of age-based mandatory retirement as a form of age discrimination, or ageism.

While a conventional American life generally included education, work, and recreation/retirement, in that order, the current cohort of workers and retirees have the opportunity to blend, reorder, and repeat these activities as desired. Many gerontologists and other aging researchers posit that there is a "third age"—a stage of working life when older workers can actively renegotiate their relationships with the labor force. Their choices, depending on life circumstances, may include remaining in the workforce, retiring, or returning to work for periods of part-time, full-time, or part-season employment. Although not all workers and retirees will choose to stray from the conventional course, increasingly they have the option to do so.

A CHANGING ECONOMY AND CHANGING ROLES

From Agricultural . . .

When America's economy was predominantly agricultural, children were put to work as soon as they were able to contribute to the family upkeep. Similarly, workers who lived beyond age sixty-five did not retire; they worked as long as they were physically able. When older adults were no longer able to work, younger family members cared for them. Older people were valued and respected for their accumulated knowledge and experience and were integral members of the interconnected family and labor systems.

. . . to Industrial . . .

The Industrial Revolution shifted workers from the farm and into manufacturing jobs. The work was physically demanding, the hours long, and the tasks rigidly structured. Women labored in factories and at home caring for the family. Older people found themselves displaced—their skills and experience were not relevant to new technologies nor could they physically compete with the large number of young workers eager to exploit new economic opportunities.

As industrial workers matured, some were promoted to positions as supervisors and managers. For older workers who had been with the same company for many years, labor unions provided a measure of job security through the seniority system ("first hired, last fired"). In an increasingly youth-oriented society, however, older workers were often rejected in favor of younger laborers. Frequent reports of age discrimination prompted Congress to pass the Age Discrimination in Employment Act (ADEA; PL 90-202). Enacted in 1967 to protect workers age forty to sixty-five, the ADEA makes it illegal for employers or unions to discharge, refuse to hire, or otherwise discriminate on the basis of age. Victims are eligible for lost wages—the amount is doubled in the most blatant cases—and workers wrongfully terminated also may seek reinstatement. The Age Discrimination in Employment Act Amendments of 1978 (PL 95-256) made seventy the upper age limit and prohibited mandatory retirement for most workers in the private sector as well as many in government employment. In 1986 Congress again amended the act to eliminate the upper age limit.

. . . to Service and Information

The U.S. economy continued its dramatic shift away from smokestack industries such as mining and manufacturing to an economy in which service occupations and the production and dissemination of information predominate. As such, the demand for highly educated workers has grown, and demand has slackened for workers who perform physical labor. Many "information age" careers and service jobs such as those in the fields of health, law, information technology, and communications are ideally suited for older workers because they do not require physical labor, and employers benefit from the cumulative experience of older workers.

THE AGING LABOR FORCE

As the baby boom generation (persons born between 1946 and 1964) approaches retirement age, the proportion of the U.S. population age sixty-five and over will increase significantly between 2005 and 2035. The U.S. labor force, however, is already undergoing a shift toward a greater number of older workers and a relative scarcity of new entrants.

The U.S. Census Bureau estimates that there were 193 million Americans age twenty-five and over in 2005. By 2035 this number will increase by nearly one-third to 255 million. But the number of persons age twenty-five to fifty-four—the age range during which labor force participation rates are highest—will rise by just 11%. During the same period the number of persons age fifty-five to sixty-four is projected to increase by 30%, to nine million. So while the group of persons age twenty-five to sixty-four is anticipated to increase by 22.8 million between 2005 and 2035, as much as 40% of this increase is projected to occur among persons age fifty-five to sixty-four.

Older Adults in the Labor Force

The Bureau of Labor Statistics reported that in 2003 five million Americans age sixty-five and over (14.4% of older adults) were participating in the labor force—working or actively seeking work—while 3.6% of older adults were unemployed. The older adult labor force consisted of 3.3 million men (18.3% of employed men) and 2.1 million women (10.7% of employed women), and these older workers accounted for 3.4% of the entire U.S. labor force.

From 1963 to 2003 the labor force participation of men age fifty-five and over has generally declined. Among men age sixty-two to sixty-four, labor force participation decreased steadily from 76% to 50%, and among men age seventy and over, participation fell from 21% to 12%. (See Figure 4.1.) The observed decline in older adults' participation in the labor force during the 1970s and into the 1980s has been attributed to widespread mandatory retirement practices in many industries that forced workers to retire at age sixty-five. In addition, the eligibility age for Social Security benefits was reduced from sixty-five to sixty-two years of age in the 1960s, enabling workers to retire earlier. The relatively stable proportion of older workers in the labor force since that time is in part due to the relaxation and elimination of mandatory retirement and the liberalization of the Social Security earnings test—the earnings limits that prompt a reduction of Social Security benefits. Labor force participation of men age sixty-five to sixty-nine had dropped to about 24% in the mid-1980s; however, by 2003 it had risen to 33%. (See Figure 4.1.) This increase may reflect several factors, including economic necessity, the fact that older adults are seeking to remain vital and active into their seventies, a desire for the challenge and social interactions that work offers, or some combination of these.

FIGURE 4.1

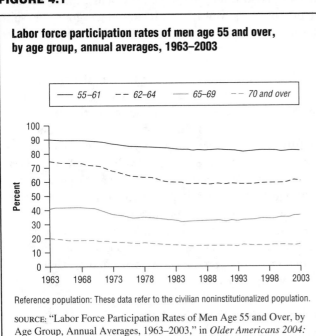

Labor force participation rates of men age 55 and over, by age group, annual averages, 1963–2003

Reference population: These data refer to the civilian noninstitutionalized population.

SOURCE: "Labor Force Participation Rates of Men Age 55 and Over, by Age Group, Annual Averages, 1963–2003," in *Older Americans 2004: Key Indicators*, Federal Interagency Forum on Aging Related Statistics, Washington, DC, U.S. Government Printing Office, November 2004, http://www.agingstats.gov/chartbook2004/economics.html#Indicator%2011 (accessed August 11, 2005)

FIGURE 4.2

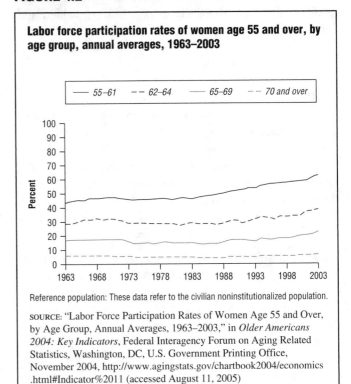

Labor force participation rates of women age 55 and over, by age group, annual averages, 1963–2003

Reference population: These data refer to the civilian noninstitutionalized population.

SOURCE: "Labor Force Participation Rates of Women Age 55 and Over, by Age Group, Annual Averages, 1963–2003," in *Older Americans 2004: Key Indicators*, Federal Interagency Forum on Aging Related Statistics, Washington, DC, U.S. Government Printing Office, November 2004, http://www.agingstats.gov/chartbook2004/economics.html#Indicator%2011 (accessed August 11, 2005)

Work Expectations after Age Sixty-Five

According to the 2005 Retirement Confidence Survey conducted by the Employee Benefit Research Institute (EBRI), the American Savings Education Council (ASEC), and Matthew Greenwald and Associates, Inc., more than half (56%) of workers expected to retire at age sixty-five or later, or never retire. In contrast to these expectations, however, most retirees (66%) reported actual retirement ages younger than sixty-five.

Retiring earlier than expected also had implications for workers' preparedness for retirement. The researchers found that putting off retirement and continuing paid employment even after retiring were two popular strategies cited by workers for making up shortfalls in retirement savings. These strategies may be unrealistic given that 40% of retirees cited retiring earlier than expected. Health issues (41%) and company changes such as closures and downsizing (34%) were among the negative reasons often reported for unexpected early retirement.

Older Women Opt to Work Rather Than Retire

Labor force participation rates generally rose among women age fifty-five and over from 1963 to 2003, with the largest increase among female workers age fifty-five to sixty-one—from 44% in 1963 to 63% in 2003. (See Figure 4.2.) These increases reflect an overall increase of women in the labor force with each successive generation. During the same period the participation rate for women age sixty-two to sixty-four rose from 29% to 39%, and among women age sixty-five to sixty-nine the rate increased from 17% to 23%. While the labor force participation of women age seventy and over has remained essentially stable, in recent years participation among women in the other age groups has increased at a faster rate. These increases also have served to narrow the gap in labor force participation rates between men and women.

Most of today's older women spent some time in the labor force when they were younger. The older the woman, however, the less likely she is to have ever worked outside the home. In the United States the group of women in their late fifties and early sixties that was the first to work outside the home in large numbers is approaching retirement. Women in this cohort who are single, widowed, or divorced often continue to work to support themselves because they do not have sufficient Social Security credits to retire.

Married older women increasingly are choosing to keep working after their husbands retire, breaking with the practice of joining their husbands in retirement. More often, in terms of retirement, older husbands and wives head in opposite directions. Among the reasons cited are:

- Older women have careers they find personally satisfying as well as financially rewarding.

- They need to secure their retirement to prevent the poverty that has historically afflicted widows.

- Their income helps to maintain the family standard of living and may be vital when their husbands have been pressured to retire by their employers or suffer failing health.

- They enjoy the social interactions at the workplace—women value relationships with coworkers more than do men, and as a result women often find retirement more isolating.

The Women's Bureau of the U.S. Department of Labor reported that women between the ages of fifty-five and sixty-four have steadily increased their labor force participation rates from 42% in 1985 to 56.6% in 2003. According to the National Economic Council Interagency Working Group on Social Security, the percentage of women receiving benefits based solely on their own earnings history is expected to rise from 40% in 2000 to 60% in 2060. In addition, 20% of these women will qualify for pensions higher than their husbands', up from less than 10% in 2003.

NONTRADITIONAL OCCUPATIONS FOR WOMEN. The U.S. Department of Labor's Bureau of Labor Statistics defines nontraditional occupations for women as those in which women comprise 25% or less of total employment. Nontraditional occupations span all major occupational groups and provide many employment options for women. Examples of nontraditional jobs for women include: architects, chefs, barbers, clergy, computer and office machine repairers, construction and building inspectors, railroad conductors, machinists, truck drivers, firefighters, aircraft pilots, construction occupations, and small engine mechanics.

Women continue to infiltrate nontraditional occupations. As more women enter industries and assume positions once dominated by men, many jobs that were considered nontraditional for women in the 1980s were no longer nontraditional by 2002. Examples of previously nontraditional occupations in which women accounted for more than 25% of total employment by 2002 are insurance sales, purchasing managers, photographers, physicians, chemists, postal service mail carriers, lawyers, and athletes.

Part-Time Work

In 2003 the AARP, a national, nonprofit advocacy organization for older adults, reported that seven out of ten workers age fifty-five and older continued to work full time, and those who worked part time did so by choice. In 2003 less than 3% of all nonagricultural older workers were employed part time because they could not find full-time work.

For employers, hiring part-time older workers is often an attractive alternative to hiring younger, full-time workers. Some employers value older workers' maturity,

dependability, and experience. Others hire older workers to reduce payroll expenses. This reduction is achieved when part-time workers are paid lower wages than full-time employees and are not provided benefits, such as health insurance, pensions, and profit sharing.

Job Tenure

Older people tend to be stable employees who stay in the same job longer than younger employees. Job tenure is measured as the median number of years workers have been with their current employer. According to the U.S. Bureau of Labor Statistics, workers age forty-five to fifty-four had double the median years of job tenure compared with those age twenty-five to thirty-four, and workers age fifty to sixty stay on the job an average of fifteen years. In January 2004 the median tenure of workers age fifty-five to sixty-four (9.6 years) was more than three times that of workers age twenty-five to thirty-four (2.9 years). (See Table 4.1.)

DISPELLING MYTHS AND STEREOTYPES ABOUT OLDER WORKERS

Older workers are often stereotyped by the mistaken belief that performance declines with age. Performance studies, however, reveal that older workers perform intellectually as well as or better than workers thirty years younger, maintaining their problem solving, communication, and creative skills. A survey of retail and industrial human resource managers found that workers age sixty and older performed as well or better than their younger counterparts. In fact, research confirms if any correlation exists between age and performance, it is that most performance improves with age (Juhani E. Ilmarinen, "Aging Workers," *Occupational Environmental Medicine*, vol. 58, no. 8, August 2001).

Myth: Older Workers Have Overly Increased Absenteeism

Since aging is associated with declining health, it is often mistakenly assumed that older workers have markedly higher rates of illnesses and absences from work. Somewhat surprisingly, the chronic health conditions older adults may suffer tend to be manageable and do not affect attendance records. In fact, absence rates for older full-time wage and salary workers differ only slightly from those of younger workers. According to the Bureau of Labor Statistics, in 2004 the absence rate for workers age fifty-five years and over was 3.5%, compared with 3.1% for those age twenty-five to fifty-four.

Myth: It Costs More to Hire Older Workers

One widely accepted myth is that hiring and training older workers is not a sound investment because they will not remain on the job very long. Yet according to the

TABLE 4.1

Median years of tenure with current employer for employed wage and salary workers, by age and sex, selected years, 1983–2004

Age and sex	Jan 1983	Jan 1987	Jan 1991	Feb 1996	Feb 1998	Feb 2000	Jan 2002	Jan 2004
Total								
16 years and over	3.5	3.4	3.6	3.8	3.6	3.5	3.7	4.0
16 to 17 years	.7	.6	.7	.7	.6	.6	.7	.7
18 to 19 years	.8	.7	.8	.7	.7	.7	.8	.8
20 to 24 years	1.5	1.3	1.3	1.2	1.1	1.1	1.2	1.3
25 years and over	5.0	5.0	4.8	5.0	4.7	4.7	4.7	4.9
25 to 34 years	3.0	2.9	2.9	2.8	2.7	2.6	2.7	2.9
35 to 44 years	5.2	5.5	5.4	5.3	5.0	4.8	4.6	4.9
45 to 54 years	9.5	8.8	8.9	8.3	8.1	8.2	7.6	7.7
55 to 64 years	12.2	11.6	11.1	10.2	10.1	10.0	9.9	9.6
65 years and over	9.6	9.5	8.1	8.4	7.8	9.4	8.6	9.0
Men								
16 years and over	4.1	4.0	4.1	4.0	3.8	3.8	3.9	4.1
16 to 17 years	.7	.6	.7	.6	.6	.6	.8	.7
18 to 19 years	.8	.7	.8	.7	.7	.7	.8	.8
20 to 24 years	1.5	1.3	1.4	1.2	1.2	1.2	1.4	1.3
25 years and over	5.9	5.7	5.4	5.3	4.9	4.9	4.9	5.1
25 to 34 years	3.2	3.1	3.1	3.0	2.8	2.7	2.8	3.0
35 to 44 years	7.3	7.0	6.5	6.1	5.5	5.3	5.0	5.2
45 to 54 years	12.8	11.8	11.2	10.1	9.4	9.5	9.1	9.6
55 to 64 years	15.3	14.5	13.4	10.5	11.2	10.2	10.2	9.8
65 years and over	8.3	8.3	7.0	8.3	7.1	9.0	8.1	8.2
Women								
16 years and over	3.1	3.0	3.2	3.5	3.4	3.3	3.4	3.8
16 to 17 years	.7	.6	.7	.7	.7	.6	.7	.6
18 to 19 years	.8	.7	.8	.7	.7	.7	.7	.8
20 to 24 years	1.5	1.3	1.3	1.2	1.1	1.0	1.1	1.3
25 years and over	4.2	4.3	4.3	4.7	4.4	4.4	4.4	4.7
25 to 34 years	2.8	2.6	2.7	2.7	2.5	2.5	2.5	2.8
35 to 44 years	4.1	4.4	4.5	4.8	4.5	4.3	4.2	4.5
45 to 54 years	6.3	6.8	6.7	7.0	7.2	7.3	6.5	6.4
55 to 64 years	9.8	9.7	9.9	10.0	9.6	9.9	9.6	9.2
65 years and over	10.1	9.9	9.5	8.4	8.7	9.7	9.5	9.6

Note: Data beginning 2000 reflect the introduction of Census 2000 population controls in January 2003 and are not strictly comparable with data for prior years. In addition, data for 2004 reflect the introduction of revised population controls in January 2003 and January 2004. Data for 1996 and 1998 are based on population controls from the 1990 census. Data for the period 1983–1991 are based on population controls from the 1980 census. Also, beginning in 1996, the figures incorporate the effects of the redesign of the Current Population Survey introduced in January 1994. Data exclude the incorporated and unincorporated self-employed.

SOURCE: "Table 1. Median Years of Tenure with Current Employer for Employed Wage and Salary Workers by Age and Sex, Selected Years, 1983–2004," in *Employee Tenure Summary*, U.S. Department of Labor Bureau of Labor Statistics, Washington, DC, September 21, 2004, http://www.bls.gov/news.release/tenure.t01.htm (accessed August 11, 2005)

Bureau of Labor Statistics, workers age forty-five to fifty-four had average job tenures twice as long as those of workers age twenty-five to thirty-four. AARP research has repeatedly demonstrated that workers between the ages of fifty and sixty work for an average of fifteen years. Furthermore, the Mature Workers Employment Alliance (MWEA), an organization dedicated to assisting older workers in transitioning to new positions, asserts that the future work life of employees over age fifty generally exceeds the life of the technology for which they are trained.

The AARP also observes that although older workers' health, disability, and life insurance costs are higher than those of younger workers, they are offset by lower costs due to fewer dependents. While older workers generally have earned more vacation time and have higher pension costs, they take fewer risks and as a result have lower accident rates. Workers over age fifty file fewer workers' compensation claims than younger workers—the largest number of claims are filed by workers between the ages of thirty and thirty-four. Fringe benefit costs for workers of all ages are about the same overall. Finally, retaining experienced older workers actually reduces employer costs associated with recruiting, hiring, and training new, younger workers.

Myth: Older Workers Are Technophobes

While older workers may require more time to learn new technologies, their improved attitudes, study habits, and diligence often help them to surpass younger workers in training courses. There is a pervasive myth that older adults are unable to learn or use new information technology. According to surveys conducted by Harris International, however, between 1999 and 2002 adults age fifty and over increased from one-fifth (20%) to more than one-quarter (26%) of Internet users.

Data from The Media Audit conducted by International Demographics Inc. showed that of the total Internet audience, adults age fifty-five to sixty-four increased from 9.5% to 11.3% between 2000 and 2003. The percentage of these older adults that access the Internet regularly rose from 45.8% in 2000 to 56.7% in 2003. During the same time period sixty-five- to seventy-four-year-olds increased as a percentage of the total Internet audience from 4.6% to 5.4%, and the percentage in that age group who access the Internet regularly increased from 26.2% to 35.9%. Adults age seventy-five and over have increased as a percentage of the Internet market from 1.3% to 1.6%, and the percentage of these older adults that is regularly accessing the Internet increased from 12.1% to 15.9%.

A study conducted by Dr. Tracey Rizzuto, an assistant professor of psychology at Louisiana State University, found that older workers were more willing to learn new technology than their younger coworkers. Dr. Rizzuto surveyed workers for the state of Pennsylvania after the state's computer system was upgraded; she discovered that not only did the older workers understand the benefits of the changes, they also were motivated to learn and implement the new system out of a sense of loyalty to their colleagues and obligation to their employer. "There is some research that shows older workers may not be as quick in learning new technology skills as younger people, but this study shows the commitment and willingness to learn is stronger among the older workers," Dr. Rizzuto was quoted as saying ("Study Shows Older Workers More Open to Change," Society for Industrial and Organizational Psychology, http://siop.org/media/news/olderworkers0305.htm, March 10, 2005). Older workers also were found to be more likely to support company initiatives and values, and as a result they tended to remain with their employer longer than did younger workers.

AGE DISCRIMINATION

But more and more, America will come to believe that there is no fixed age for retirement, that work is important to individuals and to organizations, and that age itself should not disqualify anyone from being hired nor discourage anyone from seeking work.

—William Novelli, AARP chief executive officer, "Seizing the Human Capital in Older Workers," speech, Wharton Impact Conference, The Wharton School, University of Pennsylvania, Philadelphia, PA, November 10, 2004

While the 1967 Age Discrimination in Employment Act (ADEA) and its amendments were enacted to ban discrimination against workers based on their age, the act also was intended to promote the employment of older workers based on their abilities. In addition to making it illegal for employers to discriminate based on age in hiring, discharging, and compensating employees, the act also prohibited companies from coercing older workers into accepting incentives to early retirement. In 1990 the ADEA was strengthened with the passing of the Older Workers Benefit Protection Act (PL 101-433). As well as prohibiting discrimination in employee benefits based on age, it provides that an employee's waiver of the right to sue for age discrimination, a clause sometimes included in severance packages, is invalid unless it is "voluntary and knowing."

Although age discrimination in the workplace is against the law, age bias and discrimination persists. More than fifteen thousand claims of age discrimination are filed with the Equal Employment Opportunity Commission (EEOC) each year. Although most cases involve older workers who believe they were terminated unfairly, a number of the cases involve workers who feel they have met age discrimination in hiring practices.

The number of claims received by the EEOC declined from the 1993 high of 19,809 to 14,141 in 1999, but the number has slowly resurged, climbing to 17,837 in 2004. The EEOC resolved 15,792 of these charges in 2004; however, agency data reveal that most claimants do not win. Of the claims that were resolved in 2004, the EEOC found "reasonable cause" that age discrimination may have occurred only 3.3% of the time and found "no reasonable cause" 60.6% of the time. The agency did garner $69 million in monetary benefits for charging parties and other aggrieved individuals (not including monetary benefits obtained through litigation). (See Table 4.2.)

Pressure to Retire

There are many forms of subtle discrimination against older workers as well as ways employers can directly or indirectly exert pressure on older employees to retire or resign. This form of discrimination is "under the radar" and in many instances violates the spirit, if not the letter, of the law of the ADEA.

From an employer's standpoint, age discrimination is simply the consequence of efforts to reduce payroll expenses. Employment decisions are not only based on how much an employee contributes to the company but also on the salary and benefits the company must provide the employee, relative to the cost of other employees. Since salary tends to increase with longevity on the job, older workers usually receive higher wages than younger ones. Thus if two employees are equally productive and the older one has a higher salary, a company has an economic incentive to lay off the older worker or strongly encourage early retirement.

Some policy makers assign a portion of the blame for employers' actions to the federal government, which by outlawing age discrimination has also inadvertently contributed to it. In a *New York Times* article ("The Adams

TABLE 4.2

Age Discrimination in Employment Act (ADEA) charges, FY 1992–FY 2004

	FY 1992	FY 1993	FY 1994	FY 1995	FY 1996	FY 1997	FY 1998	FY 1999	FY 2000	FY 2001	FY 2002	FY 2003	FY 2004
Receipts	19,573	19,809	19,618	17,416	15,719	15,785	15,191	14,141	16,008	17,405	19,921	19,124	17,837
Resolutions	19,975	19,761	13,942	17,033	17,699	18,279	15,995	15,448	14,672	15,155	18,673	17,352	15,792
Resolutions by type													
Settlements	963	774	585	571	452	642	755	816	1,156	1,006	1,222	1,285	1,377
	4.80%	3.90%	4.20%	3.40%	2.60%	3.50%	4.70%	5.30%	7.90%	6.60%	6.50%	7.40%	8.70%
Withdrawals with benefits	1,537	1,197	990	856	671	762	580	578	560	551	671	710	787
	7.70%	6.10%	7.10%	5.00%	3.80%	4.20%	3.60%	3.70%	3.80%	3.60%	3.60%	4.10%	5.00%
Administrative closures	4,957	5,556	5,021	6,571	5,028	4,986	4,175	3,601	3,232	3,963	6,254	2,824	3,550
	24.80%	28.10%	36.00%	38.60%	28.40%	27.30%	26.10%	23.30%	22.00%	26.10%	33.50%	16.30%	22.50%
No reasonable cause	12,075	11,481	6,872	8,309	11,081	11,163	9,863	9,172	8,517	8,388	9,725	11,976	9,563
	60.50%	58.10%	49.30%	48.80%	62.60%	61.10%	61.70%	59.40%	58.00%	55.30%	52.10%	69.00%	60.60%
Reasonable cause	443	753	474	726	467	726	622	1,281	1,207	1,247	801	557	515
	2.20%	3.80%	3.40%	4.30%	2.60%	4.00%	3.90%	8.30%	8.20%	8.20%	4.30%	3.20%	3.30%
Successful conciliations	121	147	97	52	96	74	119	184	241	409	208	166	139
	0.60%	0.70%	0.70%	0.30%	0.50%	0.40%	0.70%	1.20%	1.60%	2.70%	1.10%	1.00%	0.90%
Unsuccessful conciliations	322	606	377	674	371	652	503	1,097	966	838	593	391	376
	1.60%	3.10%	2.70%	4.00%	2.10%	3.60%	3.10%	7.10%	6.60%	5.50%	3.20%	2.30%	2.40%
Merit resolutions	2,943	2,724	2,049	2,153	1,590	2,130	1,957	2,675	2,923	2,804	2,694	2,552	2,679
	14.70%	13.80%	14.70%	12.60%	9.00%	11.70%	12.20%	17.30%	19.90%	18.50%	14.40%	14.70%	17.00%
Monetary benefits (millions)*	$57.30	$40.70	$42.30	$29.40	$31.50	$44.30	$34.70	$38.60	$45.20	$53.70	$55.70	$48.90	$69.00

*Does not include monetary benefits obtained through litigation.

Notes: The total of individual percentages may not always sum to 100% due to rounding.

Receipts include all charges filed under the ADEA as well as those filed concurrently under Title VII, ADA, and/or EPA. Therefore, the sum of receipts for all statutes will exceed total charges received.

Equal Employment Opportunity Commission (EEOC) total workload includes charges carried over from previous fiscal years, new charge receipts and charges transferred to EEOC from Fair Employment Practice Agencies (FEPAs). Resolution of charges each year may therefore exceed receipts for that year because workload being resolved is drawn from a combination of pending, new receipts and FEPA transfer charges rather than from new charges only.

SOURCE: "Age Discrimination in Employment Act (ADEA) Charges FY 1992–FY 2004," in Age Discrimination, The U.S. Equal Employment Opportunity Commission, Washington, DC, January 2005, http://www.eeoc.gov/stats/adea.html (accessed August 11, 2005)

Principle," June 21, 2005), John Tierney asserted that the ADEA was itself a reason not to hire an older worker. He asked, "Given a choice between two equally qualified candidates, whom would you hire, a thirty-five-year-old who could be quickly demoted or fired if he turns out to be incompetent, or a sixty-five-year-old who could sue you for age discrimination?" Tierney also observed that a sixty-five-year-old is more expensive than a younger worker to add to the company health plan and suggested that if federal policy was amended to permit older workers to rely primarily on Medicare rather than employer-sponsored health benefits, then more older adults would be hired and retained in the workforce.

For many workers, early retirement is untenable. Early retirement benefits are almost always less than regular retirement benefits and may be insufficient to allow a retiree to live comfortably without working. Finding a new job is more challenging for older workers, and they frequently are unemployed for longer periods than are younger job seekers. Workers who refuse to accept early retirement may find themselves without jobs at all, perhaps with no pension and no severance pay.

Some labor economists contend that early retirements, whether voluntary or coerced, deprive the nation of skilled workers needed for robust growth and deprive the government of the revenue that these workers would have contributed in income and payroll taxes.

Filing ADEA Claims—Suing the Company

If you're a 55-year-old male who's lost your $70,000 job, what do you do? The odds of finding any job, let alone a comparable job, are slim. So you fight.

—Howard Eglit, professor at Chicago-Kent College of Law and author of *Age Discrimination* in "Are You Ignoring Older Workers?" *HR Magazine* (Robert J. Grossman, vol. 48, no.8, August 2003)

The costs involved in filing an age discrimination suit are high. In addition to the financial outlay for legal representation, workers who sue their employers may be stigmatized and face further discrimination—future employers' reluctance to hire a worker who has filed a discrimination suit against a former employer. Workers caught in this scenario can suffer emotional and financial damage that may adversely affect them for the rest of their lives. Nonetheless, many workers do choose to sue their employers.

According to the Society for Human Resource Management, legal action based on allegations of age discrimination includes the following:

- Cases related to job loss
- Claims based on failure to hire
- Claims alleging harassment—antagonism or intimidation that creates a hostile work environment

The main classes of issues affecting older workers involve:

- The determination of whether being overqualified—having too much education or experience—may be grounds (or a pretext) for refusing to hire an older person
- Whether a senior worker's higher salary may be used as a basis for discharge
- Which preconditions employers can demand from older workers prior to hiring (for example, hiring an older worker with special exemptions from benefits)

Employment attorneys and industry observers conjecture that an aging population, coupled with low unemployment rates, strong demand for experienced workers, and managers who are themselves older, have already begun to deemphasize age as an issue in the marketplace.

A CHANGING FUTURE FOR OLDER WORKERS

Our nation has yet to rewrite the scripts around later life choice and chances in contemporary society.

—Phyllis Moen, McKnight Presidential Chair in Sociology at the University of Minnesota, in "Existing Scripts for Retirement Are Obsolete, but What's Next?" in *New Face of Work Survey* (San Francisco, CA: Civic Ventures, June 2005)

In *The 21st Century at Work: Forces Shaping the Future Workforce and Workplace in the United States* (Santa Monica, CA; 2004), a report prepared for the U.S. Department of Labor, RAND Corporation researchers Lynn A. Karoly and Constantijn W. A. Panis considered slower growth of the U.S. workforce, shifting workforce composition, and increased demand for highly skilled workers committed to lifelong learning as key forces shaping the future of the workplace in the United States. They observed that the aging U.S. population and rising proportion of working women has resulted in a workforce that is more balanced in terms of the distribution of workers by age, gender, race, and ethnicity, but the growth rate of the workforce is increasing at a considerably slower pace than it has in the past.

The researchers posit that one way to raise the rate of labor force growth is to motivate workers to retire later. Along with changes in incentives associated with pension plans and Social Security, the workplace itself has changed in ways that accommodate older workers. For example, technology has enabled many workers to enjoy nonstandard and increasingly flexible work locations and arrangements such as telecommuting, distance and online training, working from home, and part-time contractual employment.

Karoly and Panis also see indications that the participation of older workers will itself shape the face of the workforce and workplace. The need for these skilled workers may prompt employers to offer more flexibility in job responsibilities, number of hours worked, and rates of pay. Older workers also may precipitate changes in government policies that currently constrain employers' ability to adjust benefits for older workers in order to account for changes in preferences for compensation, health insurance, pension benefits, and other benefits as workers age.

AARP Project Aims to Help Older Adults Enter and Stay in the Workforce

In 2004 the AARP Foundation (the charitable organization affiliated with AARP) launched the Workforce Initiative in conjunction with the Home Depot to help Americans age fifty and over find jobs and stay in the workforce. The Workforce Initiative connects older workers with skills assessment tools, training resources, and job opportunities. It also helps match older workers seeking full- or part-time jobs or new careers with companies that will value their experience. In February 2005 the Workforce Initiative was expanded to include twelve additional major employers: Adecco, AlliedBarton Security Services, Borders Group Inc., Express Personnel Services, The Johns Hopkins Hospital and Health System, Kelly Services, Manpower Inc., MetLife Inc., Pitney Bowes, Principal Financial Group, Universal Health Services, and Walgreens.

Baby Boomers and Retirees Want to Do Good Work

People who were told from their birth about their own significance aren't ready to give it up just because they've hit a career ceiling called "retirement age."

—Rosabeth Moss Kanter, professor at Harvard Business School, in "Baby Boomers Still Want to Change the World," *New Face of Work Survey*

The results of a 2005 joint research project of Civic Ventures, a think tank dedicated to helping society realize the greatest return on people's life experience, and Princeton Survey Research Associates, which was funded by the MetLife Foundation, showed that Americans age fifty to seventy are not only intent on working and remaining active during the years traditionally spent in retirement but also want to perform work that benefits their communities. According to data in the *New Face of Work Survey*, the majority of Americans age fifty to seventy view retirement as a new chapter in their lives, and just 25% see it as "the end of their productive years."

The survey respondents had given considerable thought to their plans for retirement. Half reported that they had given it a great deal of thought, including what they would be doing and where they would live, and one-third said they had already explored the type of job they might pursue as a second career.

Americans planning to work in their retirement years want jobs that offer purpose and involvement with others

as well as income. Of the more than half of survey respondents who want to work in retirement, more than three-quarters are interested in "good work"—service careers in the helping professions—offering aid to the poor, disadvantaged youth, older adults, or others in need. The baby boomers (for survey purposes, respondents age fifty to fifty-nine) were the most emphatic about their intent to do good work—two-thirds said they would pursue careers in service. They are not, however, interested in traditional volunteer opportunities. Instead they want to lead efforts and wield as much influence as possible to create social change. Having challenged and changed many aspects of society in the past with the sheer force of their numbers and ambitions, baby boomers expect to generate a comparable impact on the issues they choose to tackle as older adults.

More than half of all respondents planning to work (56%) are interested in health issues and healthcare, and a similar proportion (55%) said they would like to teach or be involved in some aspect of education. While these older adults aspire to careers of service, they are not entirely confident that they will be able to obtain such positions. Nearly half feel that finding and obtaining "good work" could be either difficult (31%) or very difficult (17%).

Older adults' concerns about their inability to find meaningful work may be justified. In a commentary about the survey results, "Don't Fool Yourself: This Won't Be Easy for Employers," Peter Cappelli, the George W. Taylor Professor of Management and director of the Center for Human Resources at the Wharton School of Business of the University of Pennsylvania, cautions that there are still many prejudices against older workers. He also is uncertain that employers will adapt quickly enough to make use of the tremendous resource represented by retirement age boomers.

The majority (80%) of older Americans surveyed want to see the laws and policies that hinder work in retirement changed. Majorities of both Democrats and Republicans expressed support for measures to remove obstacles to employment. The responses of older adults to questions about some specific issues showed the following:

- Sixty percent favor tax credits for older Americans who work in schools or social service.

- Nearly half (48%) strongly support funding education and training to prepare older adults to work in schools or social service.

- Forty-six percent strongly support grants or tax credits for adults over fifty who spend a year training for, or working in, community service jobs.

In a commentary included in *New Face of Work Survey* ("Think Big: Make Aging Policy Equal to the

Aging Opportunity"), John S. Gomperts, chief executive officer of Experience Corps, a national service organization for older Americans, contends that to tap the human resource potential represented by the aging baby boomers federal policies must be revised to:

- Eliminate penalties for continuing to work or reentering the workforce

- Invest in education and training to help boomers help their communities

- Encourage experimentation with a wide range of opportunities to determine which are most effective in getting boomers into new jobs

- Provide incentives and recognition for good work in the second half of life

Gomperts also asserts that "just as investing in young people is critical to economic and social needs, investing now in capturing and channeling the energy and talent of older adults is in the greater national interest."

BABY BOOMERS WILL TRANSFORM RETIREMENT. In his introductory essay for *New Face of Work Survey* ("The Boomers, Good Work, and the Next Stage of Life"), Civic Ventures president Mark Freedman identified ten trends arising from analysis of the survey data:

1. The current cohort of older adults is more interested in gaining the *freedom to work* than *freedom from work*. The two-thirds of baby boomers intending to work in their retirement years are trailblazers, creating a new stage of life and a new stage of work.

2. Older adults want to do well by doing good—they will seek opportunities in social services, healthcare, and education that will enable them to generate income and improve the lives of others.

3. The timing of boomers' retirement and interest in service careers coincides with an urgent need for workers in the very sectors—health, education, and social services—they are interested in entering.

4. The coming generation of older adults may not pursue volunteer opportunities as vigorously as past generations. They are motivated to assume positions of leadership and equate paid work with being taken seriously.

5. Boomers heading into retirement may want flexible and part-time employment like opportunities currently available with retailers such as Wal-Mart and the Home Depot, but they are more interested in community service and social renewal than they are in entering the retail sector.

6. Boomers want second careers, not part-time jobs. While they may desire the flexibility of part-time employment, their commitment to meaningful work renders them willing to pursue education and training to prepare them for second careers that they anticipate lasting ten to twenty years. Also, while they may not have as many years to devote to second careers as they did to their first, they want to make comparable contributions.

7. Older adults are interested in achieving a satisfying work–life balance, but they have soundly rejected the notion that the years after age fifty represent a period of decline and disengagement.

8. The commitment to service of the current group of older adults is attributable not only to their idealism but also to the historic effort to find meaning and identity in work and the desire to work with others who share common goals.

9. Older adults are realistic about the fact that the opportunities they seek may not be readily available. While there is guidance to help workers plan their financial futures, there is no comparable "roadmap" to help them to navigate second careers. While older adults are lacking the preparation to obtain jobs in not-for-profit service organizations, this sector is similarly unprepared to accommodate the boomers poised to enter it.

10. Members of the baby boom generation are experienced at overcoming obstacles and breaking down barriers. Veterans of antiwar protests of the 1960s and the women's movement of the 1970s, boomers are used to speaking up and creating change. If the force of a social movement is required to create career opportunities for older adults, then these seasoned agitators may well be the ones to accomplish this objective.

Freedman concludes that fully realizing and benefiting from the experience, skill, and talent of older adults will be neither easy nor inevitable. However, he is confident that it will be worth the effort, asserting, "The payoff is nothing less than a society that makes sense, one that balances the joys and responsibility of engagement throughout the lifespan and across the generations. In other words, one that works better for everybody."

Volunteerism in Retirement

Millions of Americans who have years of productivity and service to offer are dormant. Retired teachers, craftsmen, tradesmen really don't want to go to the seashore to fade away. They want to help. So many of these people have come forward that I am convinced they can accomplish something unique in this country, something undone by all the federal, state, county and private agencies, something still to be done.

—Attorney General Robert Kennedy, in testimony in 1963 before a special congressional committee to determine the viability of establishing the National Service Corps

FIGURE 4.3

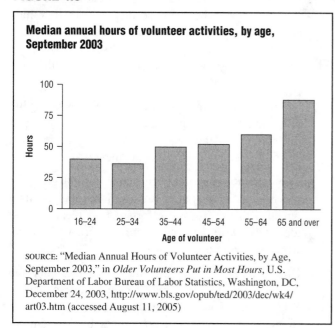

Median annual hours of volunteer activities, by age, September 2003

SOURCE: "Median Annual Hours of Volunteer Activities, by Age, September 2003," in *Older Volunteers Put in Most Hours*, U.S. Department of Labor Bureau of Labor Statistics, Washington, DC, December 24, 2003, http://www.bls.gov/opub/ted/2003/dec/wk4/art03.htm (accessed August 11, 2005)

Volunteerism among older adults is a relatively new phenomenon. Historically, older adults were seen as the segment of society most in need of care and support. As medical technology enables people to live longer, healthier lives, and as stereotypes about aging shatter, the older population is now recognized as a valuable resource for volunteer organizations.

Every day millions of older Americans perform volunteer work in their communities. Often having more free time as well as the wisdom and experience derived from years of living, they make ideal volunteers. Older adult volunteers increasingly are highly educated and skilled and can offer volunteer organizations many of the professional services they would otherwise have to purchase, such as legal, accounting, public relations, information systems support, and human resource management. Perhaps more importantly, they have empathy and compassion, having encountered many of the same problems faced by those they seek to help.

According to survey results reported in *America's Senior Volunteers* (Susan Saxon-Harrold, Michael McCormack, and Keith Hume; Washington, DC) published in June 2000 by Independent Sector, a national coalition of philanthropic organizations, about 48% of persons age fifty-five and over volunteered at least once a year. Older adults volunteered an average of 3.3 hours per week for service clubs, churches and synagogues, schools, and other groups and causes they support. The estimated five billion hours of time contributed by the twenty-eight million older volunteers translated into a value of $71.2 billion.

The survey found that older adult volunteers were motivated by the desire to help others less fortunate and the feeling that those who have more should help those with less. Giving back to society is the driving force for volunteerism among older adults. More than one-third of survey respondents said they volunteered because they wanted to give back to society some of the benefits they received individually.

In addition to coming from all age groups, volunteers come from all ethnic and racial groups as well. Growing numbers of African-American and Hispanic older adults are volunteering their time. According to the survey results, 47% of older African-Americans and 41% of older Hispanic adults did some type of volunteer work.

According to the U.S. Department of Labor's Bureau of Labor Statistics, volunteer rates in 2003 were lowest for people age sixty-five and over (23.7% of the population) and for those in their early twenties (19.7%). Among adults age sixty-five and over, volunteer rates decreased with increasing age. Volunteers age sixty-five and older did, however, devote the most time—a median of eighty-eight hours during the year—to volunteer activities. (See Figure 4.3.) Older volunteers were more likely to work for religious organizations than younger volunteers. Almost half (46.5%) of volunteers age sixty-five and older volunteered primarily for religious organizations, compared with 29.1% of volunteers age sixteen to twenty-four.

NATIONAL SERVICE ORGANIZATIONS. Efforts to establish a national senior service during the administration of President John F. Kennedy were described in *A History of National Service in America* (Peter Shapiro, ed., College Park, MD: Center for Political Leadership and Participation, 1994). In 1963 Kennedy proposed the National Service Corps (NSC) "to provide opportunities for service for those aged persons who can assume active roles in community volunteer efforts." When the NSC was proposed, a scant 11% of the older population was involved in any kind of volunteerism. The plan to engage older adults in full-time, intensive service, with a minimum one-year commitment, in order to combat urban and rural poverty was viewed as revolutionary. Although the NSC proposal was championed by the Kennedy administration and widely and enthusiastically supported in the public and private sectors, it was defeated in Congress, where reactionary lawmakers linked it to efforts aimed at promoting racial integration in the South.

Despite the defeat of the NSC, the idea of harnessing the volunteer power of older adults had caught on. The Economic Opportunity Act of 1964 gave rise to VISTA (Volunteers in Service to America) and eventually led to the launch of service programs involving low-income older adults—the Foster Grandparent, Senior Companion, and Senior Community Service Employment programs. The Foster Grandparent Program matched one thousand older adults age sixty and over with twenty-five hundred children living in orphanages and other institutions. The older adults would spend four hours a day, five days a week, feeding, cuddling, rocking, and exercising disabled children. In return they would receive stipends of $1.25 an hour.

The success of the Foster Grandparent Program exceeded all expectations. In 1971 the program was incorporated into the newly created ACTION agency, along with the Peace Corps, VISTA, the Service Corps of Retired Executives (SCORE), and the Active Corps of Executives (ACE). Foster Grandparents has since become part of Senior Corps, a network of programs that tap the experience, skills, and talents of older adults to meet community challenges. Through its three programs— Foster Grandparents, Senior Companions, and RSVP (Retired and Senior Volunteer Program)—more than half a million Americans age fifty-five and over assisted local nonprofits, public agencies, and faith-based organizations in 2001. The Corporation for National and Community Service administers Senior Corps as well as AmeriCorps and Learn and Serve America. By 2001 more than thirty thousand Foster Grandparents tended to the needs of 275,000 young children and teenagers. Participants in Foster Grandparents continue to serve twenty hours a week and now receive a stipend of $2.65 an hour (tax free), plus reimbursement for transportation, meals during service, annual physical examinations, and accident and liability insurance while on duty.

Another tremendously successful national volunteer program involving older adults is SCORE (Service Corps of Retired Executives), the first initiative to use retired business executives as counselors and consultants to small businesses. Established by the Small Business Administration (SBA) in 1964, the program works with recipients of SBA loans and other entrepreneurs, assisting them to draft business plans, evaluate profitability, and develop marketing and sales strategies. One objective of the program is to reduce default rates on these loans. SCORE mentors business owners and provides one-to-one counseling, consultation via e-mail, and training sessions conducted on topics ranging from pricing strategies to marketing. In fiscal year 2004 SCORE's 10,500 volunteers spent 1.42 million hours helping entrepreneurs.

CHAPTER 5
EDUCATION, POLITICAL BEHAVIOR, AND VOTING

EDUCATIONAL ATTAINMENT OF OLDER AMERICANS

Educational attainment influences employment and socioeconomic status, which in turn affect the quality of life of older adults. Higher levels of education are often associated with greater earning capacity, higher standards of living, and better overall health status.

As of 2003 more than 70% of the older population had earned high school diplomas, and 17% had obtained undergraduate college degrees. These figures are in contrast to those from 1950, when just 17% had earned high school diplomas and only 3% were college graduates. (See Figure 5.1.)

In 2003, the most recent year for which age, race, ethnicity, and gender-specific data were available from the U.S. Census Bureau, comparable percentages of older men and older women were high school graduates (72% and 71% respectively), however older men were more likely to have graduated from college (23% compared with 13%). This observed gender gap in educational attainment is likely to narrow in the future, because younger men and women are graduating from college at about the same rate.

Although educational attainment has increased among older adults, significant differences remain between racial and ethnic groups. Among adults age sixty-five and older in 2003, more than three quarters (76%) of non-Hispanic whites and 70% of Asians had graduated from high school, compared with 52% of African-Americans and 36% of Hispanics. (See Figure 5.2.) Older Asians were the most likely to have graduated from college (29%), followed by older non-Hispanic whites (19%); just 10% of African-Americans and 6% of Hispanics who were age sixty-five and older had earned bachelor's degrees.

Baby boomers—the people born between 1946 and 1964 who will comprise the next generation of older adults—have more education than any previous genera-

tion. Table 5.1 shows that in 2004 nearly 90% of adults age forty-five to fifty-nine (the range roughly corresponding to the baby boomer cohort) were high school graduates, while fewer than 80% of adults age sixty-five to seventy-four had graduated from high school. Approximately 30% of forty-five- to fifty-nine-year-olds held bachelor's degrees or higher; among adults age sixty-five to seventy-four this figure was about 20%.

Lifelong Learning

Live as if you were to die tomorrow. Learn as if you were to live forever.

—Mohandas Gandhi

Campuses are graying as a growing number of older people head back to school. Older adults, both working and retired, are major participants in programs once termed "adult education"—college courses that do not lead to a formal degree. Older adults also are increasingly attending two- and four-year colleges to pursue undergraduate and graduate degrees, as well as taking personal enrichment classes and courses that are sponsored by community senior centers and parks and recreation facilities.

In 2001 persons age fifty-five and older accounted for nearly 60% of overall participation in adult education programs. (See Table 5.2.) Older adults have the time and resources to seek learning for personal and social reasons. Some universities allow older people to audit courses (take classes without receiving credit toward a degree) for reduced or waived tuition and fees.

Older adults' motivations for returning to school have changed over time. While they once may have taken courses primarily for pleasure, today's older students are likely to return to school for work-related adult education. They are learning new skills, retraining for new careers, or enhancing their existing skills to remain competitive in their fields. Homemakers displaced by divorce

FIGURE 5.1

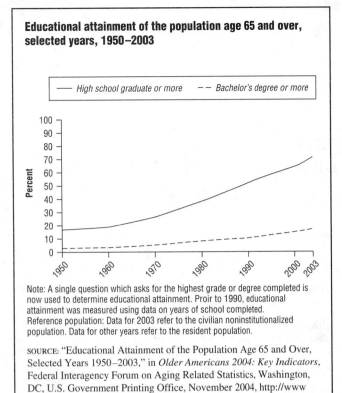

Educational attainment of the population age 65 and over, selected years, 1950–2003

Note: A single question which asks for the highest grade or degree completed is now used to determine educational attainment. Proir to 1990, educational attainment was measured using data on years of school completed.
Reference population: Data for 2003 refer to the civilian noninstitutionalized population. Data for other years refer to the resident population.

SOURCE: "Educational Attainment of the Population Age 65 and Over, Selected Years 1950–2003," in *Older Americans 2004: Key Indicators*, Federal Interagency Forum on Aging Related Statistics, Washington, DC, U.S. Government Printing Office, November 2004, http://www .agingstats.gov/chartbook2004/population.html#Indicator%204 (accessed August 11, 2005)

FIGURE 5.2

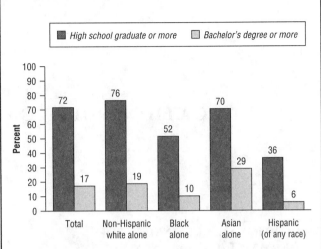

Educational attainment of the population age 65 and over, by race and Hispanic origin, 2003

Note: The term "non-Hispanic white alone" is used to refer to people who reported being white and no other race and who are not Hispanic. The term "black alone" is used to refer to people who reported being black or African American and no other race, and the term "Asian alone" is used to refer to people who reported only Asian as their race. The use of single-race populations in this report does not imply that this is the preferred method of presenting or analyzing data. The U.S. Census Bureau uses a varity of approaches.
Reference population: These data refer to the civilian noninstitutionalized population.

SOURCE: "Educational Attainment of the Population Age 65 and Over, by Race and Hispanic Origin, 2003," in *Older Americans 2004: Key Indicators*, Federal Interagency Forum on Aging Related Statistics, Washington, DC, U.S. Government Printing Office, November 2004, http://www.agingstats.gov/chartbook2004/population.html#Indicator%204 (accessed August 11, 2005)

or widowhood are often seeking education and training to enable them to reenter the workforce.

Forty percent of adults participated in some work-related adult education from 2002 to 2003. Among adults age forty-five to sixty-four, 39% took part in such education, while 7% of people age sixty-five and older did so. (See Table 5.3.) Adults age forty-five and older who participated in such education were much more likely to take work-related courses as opposed to getting a college degree, which was more likely among those age sixteen to forty-four.

The type of education older adults pursue varies with age. Students age fifty-five to sixty-four are nearly evenly divided between work-related coursework (23.1%) and personal interest courses (20.5%), while those age sixty-five and older are much more likely to be enrolled in personal interest courses (18.6%) than work-related courses (4.2%). (See Table 5.2.)

ELDERHOSTELS MEET OLDER ADULTS' NEEDS FOR EDUCATION AND ADVENTURE. Elderhostel is a not-for-profit organization that provides learning adventures for people fifty-five and older. Founded in 1975, it provides educational opportunities to nearly two hundred thousand older adults each year. More than ten thousand Elderhostel programs a year are conducted in ninety countries. The programs are diverse and range from three- to five-

day classes to field trips and cultural excursions. Traditional programs provide older adults with opportunities to study diverse cultures, explore ancient histories, study literature and art, and learn about modern peoples and issues. Some Elderhostel participants attend programs held on local college and university campuses, while others embark on more extensive programs that involve transcontinental travel.

Adventure programs feature outdoor sports such as walking, hiking, camping, kayaking, and biking. The programs combine adventure and learning. For example, a bicycle tour of the Netherlands also includes instruction about the country's history, art, and people. Shipboard programs explore history, art, ecology, and culture while aboard a floating classroom.

Service-learning programs involve both education and hands-on work to serve the needs of a community. Older adults conduct wildlife or marine research, tutor schoolchildren, and build affordable housing. The organization also offers a series of intergenerational programs in which older adults and their grandchildren explore subjects that appeal to both young and old, including dinosaurs, hot-air ballooning, and space travel.

TABLE 5.1

Percent of high school and college graduates, by selected characteristics, 2004

[Numbers in thousands. Civilian noninstitutionalized population.]

		High school graduate			Bachelor's degree		
		Total	Not high school graduate	High school graduate or higher	Total	Less than bachelor's degree	Bachelor's degree or higher
	Total	Percent	Percent	Percent	Percent	Percent	Percent
All races and both sexes							
15 years and over	227,529	100.0	20.4	79.6	100.0	76.2	23.8
15 to 17 years	12,829	100.0	98.3	1.7	100.0	100.0	0.0
18 to 19 years	7,485	100.0	43.9	56.1	100.0	100.0	0.0
20 to 24 years	20,339	100.0	14.1	85.9	100.0	88.5	11.5
25 to 29 years	19,008	100.0	13.4	86.6	100.0	71.3	28.7
30 to 34 years	20,193	100.0	12.5	87.5	100.0	68.4	31.6
35 to 39 years	20,791	100.0	11.9	88.1	100.0	69.4	30.6
40 to 44 years	22,782	100.0	12.1	87.9	100.0	71.4	28.6
45 to 49 years	21,823	100.0	10.6	89.4	100.0	70.3	29.7
50 to 54 years	19,246	100.0	10.1	89.9	100.0	68.5	31.5
55 to 59 years	16,158	100.0	12.1	87.9	100.0	69.8	30.2
60 to 64 years	12,217	100.0	15.6	84.4	100.0	74.4	25.6
65 to 69 years	9,818	100.0	21.8	78.2	100.0	79.1	20.9
70 to 74 years	8,420	100.0	25.8	74.2	100.0	80.1	19.9
75 years and over	16,421	100.0	30.6	69.4	100.0	83.3	16.7
15 to 17 years	12,829	100.0	98.3	1.7	100.0	100.0	0.0
18 years and over	214,700	100.0	15.8	84.2	100.0	74.8	25.2
15 to 24 years	40,652	100.0	46.2	53.8	100.0	94.2	5.8
25 years and over	186,877	100.0	14.8	85.2	100.0	72.3	27.7
15 to 64 years	192,870	100.0	19.3	80.7	100.0	75.3	24.7
65 years and over	34,659	100.0	26.9	73.1	100.0	81.3	18.7
All races and male							
15 years and over	110,158	100.0	21.3	78.7	100.0	75.3	24.7
15 to 17 years	6,411	100.0	98.4	1.6	100.0	99.9	0.1
18 to 19 years	3,928	100.0	48.6	51.4	100.0	100.0	0.0
20 to 24 years	10,262	100.0	16.0	84.0	100.0	91.1	8.9
25 to 29 years	9,543	100.0	14.8	85.2	100.0	73.9	26.1
30 to 34 years	10,056	100.0	13.8	86.2	100.0	70.1	29.9
35 to 39 years	10,309	100.0	12.9	87.1	100.0	70.1	29.9
40 to 44 years	11,222	100.0	13.7	86.3	100.0	71.2	28.8
45 to 49 years	10,693	100.0	11.3	88.7	100.0	69.4	30.6
50 to 54 years	9,389	100.0	10.4	89.6	100.0	67.0	33.0
55 to 59 years	7,852	100.0	12.0	88.0	100.0	65.7	34.3
60 to 64 years	5,699	100.0	16.4	83.6	100.0	70.0	30.0
65 to 69 years	4,566	100.0	21.3	78.7	100.0	72.9	27.1
70 to 74 years	3,789	100.0	24.2	75.8	100.0	73.3	26.7
75 years and over	6,441	100.0	30.2	69.8	100.0	76.6	23.4
15 to 17 years	6,411	100.0	98.4	1.6	100.0	99.9	0.1
18 years and over	103,747	100.0	16.5	83.5	100.0	73.7	26.3
15 to 24 years	20,600	100.0	47.8	52.2	100.0	95.5	4.5
25 years and over	89,558	100.0	15.2	84.8	100.0	70.6	29.4
15 to 64 years	95,361	100.0	20.5	79.5	100.0	75.4	24.6
65 years and over	14,797	100.0	25.9	74.1	100.0	74.6	25.4

OLDER ADULTS ARE ONLINE. Rapid technological change has intensified the need for computer and information management skills and ongoing training of the workforce. The growing importance of knowledge- and information-based jobs has created a workforce that is rapidly becoming accustomed to continuous education, training, and retraining throughout work-life.

Computer technology, especially use of the Internet, also has gained importance in Americans' lives outside of work, facilitating communication via email and enabling interactions and transactions that once required travel now to occur in their homes. Examples include online banking and shopping, email communication with physi-cians and other healthcare providers, and participation in online support groups.

The Pew Internet & American Life Project is an initiative of the nonprofit, nonpartisan think tank Pew Research Center. The project is designed to study the effect of the Internet on all aspects of life. According to project findings, the percentage of older adults that goes online rose by 47% between 2000 and 2004. In February 2004, 22% of adults age sixty-five and older—eight million Americans—said they had Internet access, up from 15% in 2000.

Nearly two-thirds (62%) of Americans age fifty to fifty-eight—older baby boomers—and 46% of adults age

TABLE 5.1

Percent of high school and college graduates, by selected characteristics, 2004 [CONTINUED]

[Numbers in thousands. Civilian noninstitutionalized population.]

		High school graduate			Bachelor's degree		
	Total	Total	Not high school graduate	High school graduate or higher	Total	Less than bachelor's degree	Bachelor's degree or higher
	Total	Percent	Percent	Percent	Percent	Percent	Percent
All races and female							
15 years and over	117,371	100.0	19.7	80.3	100.0	77.1	22.9
15 to 17 years	6,418	100.0	98.3	1.7	100.0	100.0	0.0
18 to 19 years	3,557	100.0	38.9	61.1	100.0	99.9	0.1
20 to 24 years	10,077	100.0	12.2	87.8	100.0	85.9	14.1
25 to 29 years	9,465	100.0	12.0	88.0	100.0	68.6	31.4
30 to 34 years	10,138	100.0	11.2	88.8	100.0	66.7	33.3
35 to 39 years	10,483	100.0	10.9	89.1	100.0	68.8	31.2
40 to 44 years	11,560	100.0	10.5	89.5	100.0	71.6	28.4
45 to 49 years	11,130	100.0	9.9	90.1	100.0	71.2	28.8
50 to 54 years	9,856	100.0	9.8	90.2	100.0	69.9	30.1
55 to 59 years	8,307	100.0	12.2	87.8	100.0	73.6	26.4
60 to 64 years	6,517	100.0	14.8	85.2	100.0	78.1	21.9
65 to 69 years	5,252	100.0	22.3	77.7	100.0	84.4	15.6
70 to 74 years	4,631	100.0	27.1	72.9	100.0	85.7	14.3
75 years and over	9,980	100.0	30.8	69.2	100.0	87.7	12.3
15 to 17 years	6,418	100.0	98.3	1.7	100.0	100.0	0.0
18 years and over	110,953	100.0	15.1	84.9	100.0	75.8	24.2
15 to 24 years	20,052	100.0	44.5	55.5	100.0	92.9	7.1
25 years and over	97,319	100.0	14.6	85.4	100.0	73.9	26.1
15 to 64 years	97,508	100.0	18.0	82.0	100.0	75.3	24.7
65 years and over	19,862	100.0	27.7	72.3	100.0	86.3	13.7

SOURCE: "Table 1a. Percent of High School and College Graduates of the Population 15 Years and Over, by Age, Sex, Race, and Hispanic Origin: 2004," in *Educational Attainment in the United States: 2004*, U.S. Census Bureau, Current Population Survey, Population Division, Education and Social Stratification Branch, Washington, DC, March 27, 2005, http://www.census.gov/population/www/socdemo/education/cps2004.html (accessed August 11, 2005)

fifty-nine to sixty-eight were online. As these proficient users reach retirement age, they will very likely continue their avid Internet use and will completely dispel the myth that older adults are technophobes unable to navigate the World Wide Web. This cohort of older adults also will be well prepared to avail themselves of technology-mediated learning—distance and online coursework—to support lifelong learning in order to enhance their personal lives and enable them to stay current in terms of job skills.

Although older Internet users are largely still highly educated, white, and living in households with above average incomes, the number of older adult users in households with moderate incomes rose dramatically since 2000, as did the number of older Internet users with just a high school education. In 2000 three-quarters of older adult Internet users had attended college, compared with slightly more than one-third of all older adults, and just one-quarter of older adult users had a high school education or less. In 2004 nearly two-thirds of older adult users had attended college, compared with 35% of all Americans age sixty-five and older, and 30% of older adult users had a high school education or less, compared with 58% of all older Americans. By 2004 the gender gap also closed, with as many older women (50%) going online as older men (50%).

Older adults are not only going online in record numbers, they also log on as frequently as younger users. Older users are as likely as younger ones to go online daily and to use email. Almost all older users (94%) have sent or received email, compared with 91% of all Internet users. Older adults have also learned to use search engines to perform research online. More than three-quarters (76%) reported using a search engine to find information, compared with 80% of all Internet users.

The research shows that along with email, instant messaging, and using search engines to seek information, older Internet users go online to read news, especially political news, and to look for religious or spiritual material. Because older users were more likely to describe their health as "fair" or "poor" than other users, it is not surprising that they also seek health and medical information online. In 2004 more than half (53%) of older users said they had visited Web sites that provided information or support for a specific medical condition. More than one-third of older users (36%) have researched their family's history or genealogy online, compared with about one-quarter of all Internet users.

Older Internet users were less likely to perform transactions online—just 20% had done banking on the Internet and less than half (47%) had made a purchase online. Older adults may be unwilling to conduct transactions

TABLE 5.2

Percentage of population participating in adult education activities, by type of activity and personal characteristics, 2001

Characteristic	Overall participation[a]	College or university credential programs[a]	Work-related courses	Personal interest courses	Other activities[b]
		Type of adult education activity			
Total	**47.4**	**7.3**	**29.7**	**21.3**	**3.8**
Sex					
Male	44.0	7.0	29.0	16.3	4.5
Female	50.5	7.5	30.4	25.9	3.3
Race/ethnicity[c]					
Asian/Pacific Islander	52.3	*	34.3	18.2	
Black	43.9	7.5	23.4	25.7	4.5
White	48.3	7.0	31.7	21.6	2.4
Hispanic	42.9	7.1	21.6	16.3	12.2
Education					
Less than high school	22.2	0.6	5.7	10.7	10.4
High school diploma or equivalent	34.2	4.0	19.6	15.4	2.7
Some college, including vocational/technical	58.8	11.7	36.5	26.2	3.8
Bachelor's degree or higher	68.1	10.9	50.6	30.4	1.4
Age					
16–24	53.2	12.7	22.3	27.6	13.0
25–34	56.4	15.5	35.1	20.7	6.0
35–44	54.6	7.1	40.9	19.8	3.2
45–54	54.0	4.8	41.4	22.5	1.8
55–64	37.9	*	23.1	20.5	*
65 and above	21.4	*	4.2	18.6	*
Household income					
$15,000 or less	28.4	4.5	10.7	15.5	6.4
$15,001–30,000	35.8	6.6	16.7	16.5	5.8
$30,001–50,000	48.0	8.3	29.0	21.4	3.9
$50,001–75,000	56.3	8.0	39.2	24.3	2.3
More than $75,000	60.3	7.9	44.6	26.2	1.9
Employment/occupation					
Employed in past 12 months	55.3	8.9	39.0	22.0	4.2
Professional or managerial	73.0	13.1	59.4	29.2	*
Services, sales, or support	55.9	9.2	36.0	23.3	4.7
Trades	34.6	3.9	21.3	11.9	7.1
Not employed in past 12 months	25.8	2.7	4.5	19.4	2.8

*Reporting standards not met (too few cases).

[a]Among those ages 16–24, full-time participation for all or part of the year in a college or university credential program or a vocational or technical diploma program was not counted as an adult education activity.

[b]Includes basic skills training, apprenticeships, and English as a Second Language (ESL) courses.

[c]Black includes African American, Pacific Islander includes Native Hawaiian, and Hispanic includes Latino. Race categories exclude Hispanic origin unless specified.

Note: The survey population includes civilian, noninstitutionalized individuals age 16 and above who are not enrolled in elementary or secondary school. The sample includes individuals who do not speak English, and this is likely to affect the participation rates for Hispanics. Percentages for individual activities do not sum to the overall participation because individuals may participate in multiple activities.

SOURCE: "Table 8–2. Percentage of Population Age 16 and Above Participating in Adult Education Activities, by Type of Activity and Personal Characteristics, 2001," in "Participation in Adult Education," *The Condition of Education 2003*, U.S. Department of Education, National Center for Education Statistics, U.S. Government Printing Office, Washington, DC, 2003, http://nces.ed.gov/programs/coe/2003/section1/tables/t08_2.asp (accessed August 11, 2005)

online because they have heard media reports and warnings about instances of credit card theft and identity fraud. Older Internet users are also the least likely to download music, video, or game files, but they are among the most likely to play games online.

THE POLITICS OF OLDER ADULTS

Older adults are vitally interested in politics and government, and they are especially interested in the issues that directly influence their lives, including Social Security eligibility and reform as well as Medicare ben-

efits and coverage. The AARP, a national, nonprofit advocacy organization for older adults, characterizes the twenty-six million Americans age seventy and older as generally conservative on economic and social issues. As reported in *Political Behavior and Values across the Generations: A Summary of Selected Findings* (Jeffrey Love, Washington, DC: AARP Knowledge Management, July 2004), about one-third of Americans age seventy and older say they have become more conservative on economic, social, foreign policy, moral, and legal issues as they have aged. Large majorities of these older Americans support prayer in school, the death penalty,

TABLE 5.3

Percentage of persons taking work-related adult education courses or activities in the past 12 months, by type of activity and selected characteristics, 2002–03

Characteristic	Number of adults (thousands)	Total	College or university degree/certificate program	Vocational or technical diploma program	Apprenticeship program	Work-related courses[a]
Characteristic						
Total	206,533	40	9	2	1	33
Sex						
Male	98,793	40	8	2	1	33
Female	107,740	40	10	2	*	33
Race/ethnicity[b]						
Asian/Pacific Islander	6,330	49	16	1	*	38
Black	23,145	39	10	3	1	31
White	149,135	41	9	2	1	35
Hispanic	24,248	31	6	2	1	25
Other	3,675	43	15	3	2	31
Education						
Less than high school	32,357	10	*	*	1	9
High school diploma or equivalent	61,194	28	5	2	1	23
Some college, including vocational/technical	58,055	49	16	3	1	36
Bachelor's degree	32,122	58	10	2	*	52
Graduate or professional degree	22,804	62	13	1	*	58
Age						
16–24	24,053	59	37	3	2	31
25–44	82,223	48	10	3	1	41
45–64	66,447	39	2	1	*	37
65 and above	33,810	7	*	*	*	7
Household income						
$25,000 or less	53,796	21	8	1	1	14
$25,001–50,000	55,435	38	9	3	1	31
$50,001–75,000	43,189	48	10	2	1	40
$75,001–100,000	24,286	54	9	2	*	49
$100,001 or more	29,826	54	9	1	1	49
Occupation[c]						
Professional or managerial	45,292	70	13	1	1	64
Service, sales, or support	65,769	49	12	3	1	40
Trades	34,969	32	5	2	3	26

*Rounds to zero.
[a]Formal work-related courses include trainings, workshops, seminars, courses, or classes taken for work-related reasons.
[b]Black includes African American, Pacific Islander includes Native Hawaiian, and Hispanic includes Latino. Racial categories exclude Hispanic origin.
[c]Includes only those who reported working in the previous 12 months.
Note: Detail may not sum to totals because of rounding. Participation in any adult education for work-related reasons includes apprenticeships, formal work-related courses, college or university degree or certificate programs for work-related reasons, and vocational/technical diploma programs for work-related reasons. Excludes informal learning (e.g., brown bag demonstrations, conferences, or self-paced study). Percentages of individual activities do not sum to the overall participation rate because individuals may have participated in multiple activities.

SOURCE: "Table 7-1. Percentage of Persons Ages 16 and Above Taking Work-Related Adult Education Courses or Activities in the Past 12 Months, by Type of Activity and Selected Characteristics: 2002–03," in "Adult Participation in Work-Related Learning," *The Condition of Education 2004*, U.S. Department of Education, National Center for Education Statistics, U.S. Government Printing Office, Washington, DC, 2004, http://nces.ed.gov/programs/coe/2004/section1/table.asp?tableID=40 (accessed August 11, 2005)

stricter prison sentences, and restricting civil liberties to deter terrorism. Although they support environmental regulation and welfare programs for low-income populations, they oppose legal abortions and gay marriage. Unlike some of the conservative policymakers they support, the majority of adults age seventy and older oppose proposals to privatize Social Security and Medicare.

The thirty million older adults age fifty-eight to sixty-nine share the conservative sentiments of adults age seventy and older, especially regarding such issues

as school prayer, stricter prison sentences, and curbing civil liberties to deter terrorist threats. The AARP findings, however, showed that the younger old were more likely to support legalized abortion, stem cell research, and gay marriage than the population age seventy and older. They describe themselves as more politically active than the older cohort, and one-quarter said they would like to become more politically active.

The seventy-eight million baby boomers (age forty-one to sixty) poised to begin entering the ranks of older

TABLE 5.4

Reported voting and registration of the voting-age population, by age, November 2004

[In thousands]

State and age	Population 18 and over	Total citizen		Total registered		Total voted	
		Total	Percent citizen (18+)	Total	Percent registered (18+)	Total	Percent voted (18+)
United States							
Total	215,694	197,005	91.3	142,070	65.9	125,736	58.3
18 to 24	27,808	24,899	89.5	14,334	51.5	11,639	41.9
25 to 44	82,133	71,231	86.7	49,371	60.1	42,845	52.2
45 to 64	71,014	67,184	94.6	51,659	72.7	47,327	66.6
65 to 74	18,363	17,759	96.7	14,125	76.9	13,010	70.8
75+	16,375	15,933	97.3	12,581	76.8	10,915	66.7

SOURCE: Adapted from "Table 4b. Reported Voting and Registration of the Total Voting-Age Population, by Age, for States: November 2004," in *Voting and Registration in the Election of November 2004*, U.S. Census Bureau, Current Population Survey, Population Division, Washington, DC, May 25, 2005, http://www.census.gov/population/www/socdemo/voting/cps2004.html (accessed August 11, 2005)

adults in 2011 are slightly less conservative than adults age seventy and older, but about 40% claim to have become more conservative on a variety of issues as they have aged. When the youngest boomers reach age sixty-five, they will comprise 25% of the electorate. Although they share many of the same political beliefs and values held by older adults, they diverge on key social issues. AARP research found that more boomers support legal abortion and stem cell research, and they are twice as likely as adults age seventy and older to support gay marriage. Some of the most striking differences include the following:

- Fifty-seven percent of boomers support abortion rights, compared with 43% of adults age seventy and older.

- Twenty-six percent of boomers support gay marriage, compared with only 11% of adults age seventy and older.

- Fifty-six percent of boomers, compared with 37% of adults age seventy and older, feel the United States needs a strong third political party.

- Boomers are almost evenly split on whether a candidate's personal qualities are more important than his or her positions on key issues, while adults age seventy and older said that personal qualities mattered most (by a margin of 62% to 25%).

- Twenty percent of boomers describe themselves as "very" or "moderately" liberal, compared with 15% of adults age seventy and older.

Another difference between the two cohorts is the way in which they view entitlements and obligations. The AARP survey found that boomers were more likely to count additional issues, such as provision of health care and social programs, among the "definite responsibilities" of government, but boomers do not want to be taxed for these entitlements. Boomers also are less likely to feel that they owe their country anything, such as military service or taxes, in return for government programs and protection.

Boomers are more inclined to view political participation as a means to achieving personal ends, and less for larger goals. Such self-interest is evident in this generation's feelings about entitlements; while they are more liberal on selected social issues than the current group of older adults, this does not necessarily translate into support for social welfare programs or traditional entitlements such as Social Security and Medicare. Boomers are less likely than adults age seventy and older to support welfare programs for lower income people and far more likely to favor privatizing Social Security and Medicare.

In the AARP report, Jeffrey Love, PhD, predicts that when boomers become older adults they will continue to behave much as they have throughout their lives. The director of strategic issues research at AARP contends that they will be "socially active but skeptical about politics; concerned with their communities or other things that directly affect them; results oriented with more regard for producing benefits than for achieving higher goals or fulfilling moral imperatives."

Voting Behavior

Americans are more likely to vote as they get older. U.S. Census Bureau data reveal that in 2004 nearly 77% of adults age sixty-five and older were registered to vote, compared with 51.5% of eighteen- to twenty-four-year-olds and 60.1% of twenty-five- to forty-four-year-olds. (See Table 5.4.) In the November 2004 elections the youngest group also had the lowest voting rate (41.9%), while the highest rate (70.8%) was among sixty-five- to seventy-four-year-olds. The voting rates of those age forty-five to sixty-four and age seventy-five and older were roughly the same at nearly 67%.

The November 2004 presidential election provided ample evidence that older adults can be swing voters. According to CBS exit polls, George Bush received support across the country from 53% of voters age sixty and older, compared with 46% of those voters for John Kerry. In swing states such as Florida, Ohio, and Colorado, Bush received support from a majority of older adults and won these states. However, in the battleground states of Pennsylvania, Michigan, and Minnesota, where Bush failed to secure a majority of older voters, he did not prevail (Alan Johnson, "The Gray Vote," *Global Report on Aging*, Spring 2005).

Party Affiliation

The 2003 Pew Research Center report *Evenly Divided and Increasingly Polarized: The 2004 Political Landscape* (The Pew Research Center for the People and the Press, http://people-press.org/reports/display.php3?Report ID=196) characterizes older Americans as more Democratic than Republican in terms of their political party affiliations. Along with a firm hold on adults age sixty-five and older, the Democratic party is favored among baby boomers in their mid-forties to late fifties. Younger boomers and adults in their thirties are somewhat more Republican, while adults under thirty are nearly evenly divided between Democrats and Republicans.

The survey results in AARP's *Political Behavior and Values across the Generations: A Summary of Selected Findings* showed that party affiliation and voting along party lines was strongest among adults age seventy and older. When asked, "Do you always vote for candidates from the same political party, nearly always vote for candidates from the same party, or do you switch parties?" more than half of adults age seventy and older said they always or nearly always vote for candidates from the same party. In contrast, 47% of voters age forty to fifty-seven and 43% of those age fifty-eight to sixty-nine said they always or nearly always vote for candidates from the same party.

The survey also found the fewest independents among persons age seventy and older. Just 8% of this age group labeled themselves "independents," compared with 11% of adults age forty to fifty-seven; an additional 7% said they were not members of any particular party.

"GRAY POWER"—A POLITICAL BLOC

> *AARP is dedicated to enhancing quality of life for all as we age. We lead positive social change and deliver value to members through information, advocacy and service.*
>
> —AARP mission statement

Adults age fifty-five to seventy-four vote more than any other age group, and it is inevitable that the increasing number of Americans in this cohort will wield an enormous political impact. AARP already exercises considerable influence in lobbying and in educating political leaders about the issues that concern older Americans.

With more than thirty-five million members (nearly half of all Americans over the age of fifty) and an annual budget in excess of $800 million, AARP is the world's second-largest nonprofit organization after the Catholic Church. The group's slogan, "The power to make it better," only hints at AARP's effectiveness at promoting its agenda for social and legislative change.

As part of its purpose, AARP advocates on behalf of older adults. To this end the organization monitors issues pertinent to the lives of older Americans, assesses public opinion on such issues, and keeps policymakers apprised of those opinions. Advocacy efforts also include becoming involved in litigation when the decision could have a significant effect on the lives of older Americans. In cases regarding age discrimination, pensions, health care, economic security, and consumer issues, AARP lawyers will file amicus briefs (legal documents filed by individuals or groups that are not actual parties to a lawsuit but that are interested in influencing the outcome of the lawsuit) and support third party lawsuits in order to promote the interests of older persons.

AARP is known as a powerful advocate on a range of legislative, consumer, and legal issues. In 2005 the association's advocacy work focused on two key issues:

- Ensuring the continued financial viability of Social Security—AARP opposed Social Security reform proposals that centered on privatization and the assumption that gains from individual investment accounts would guarantee benefits for future generations. AARP deemed dependence on private accounts too risky and described it as a strategy that would drain money out of Social Security, reduce benefits, and pass the bill to future generations.

- Opposing efforts to contain Medicaid costs by capping or cutting off federal spending for Medicaid— Medicaid is the federal–state safety net program that provides health services to one in six Americans, including older people needing long-term care (it covers about two-thirds of nursing home residents) as well as persons with disabilities. AARP contends that caps on spending simply serve to shift the cost burden to the states and health-care providers (hospitals and physicians forced to provide more uncompensated care), which in turn shifts costs to employers and employees in the form of higher health insurance premiums. AARP also opined that funding cuts might lead to unduly stringent eligibility requirements for Medicaid recipients, leaving many people in need without any health care coverage.

AARP has historically issued policy statements about topics such as age discrimination, quality of care in nursing facilities, Medicare and other health coverage, paying for prescription drugs and long-term care, nontraditional living arrangements, and pension plan reforms. It also offers pertinent information for older adults on such topics as health, travel, employment, technology, and volunteer and learning opportunities, as well as member discounts and benefits.

The political clout of AARP should not be underestimated. Over the course of two weeks in March 2005, AARP spent more than $5 million on advertising opposing President Bush's Social Security reform plan—close to three times as much money as supporters of the plan spent. AARP held forums in every state with a swing-vote senator—one who is publicly undecided—drawing an average of three hundred concerned citizens. AARP volunteers attended town meetings to protest the plan to institute individual accounts.

Silver-Haired Legislatures

As of 2005 twenty-nine states had "silver-haired legislatures"—activists age sixty and older who propose and track legislation affecting older adults. The legislature members are elected by their peers and endeavor to influence bills pertaining to medical care, pension plan reform, consumer protection, and age discrimination, often by educating the real legislators and policymakers about the issues. Their ranks include former teachers, judges, doctors, business owners, and even retired legislators.

CHAPTER 6
ON THE ROAD—OLDER ADULT DRIVERS

The number of older Americans is expected to double over the next 25 years. All but the most fortunate seniors will confront an array of medical and other constraints on their mobility even as they continue to seek an active community life.

—Sandra Rosenbloom in *The Mobility Needs of Older Americans: Implications for Transportation Reauthorization* (The Brookings Institution Series on Transportation Reform, Washington, DC: Center on Urban and Metropolitan Policy, The Brookings Institution, July 2003)

Readily available transportation is a vital factor in the quality of life of older adults. Transportation is essential for accessing health care, establishing and maintaining social and family relationships, obtaining food and other necessities, and preserving independence and self-esteem.

The ability to drive often determines whether an older adult is able to live independently. Driving is the primary mode of transportation in the United States, and personal vehicles remain the transportation mode of choice for almost all Americans, including older people. AARP surveys repeatedly confirm that persons over the age of sixty-five make nearly all of their trips in private vehicles, either as drivers or passengers. Even in urban areas where public transit is readily available, private vehicles are still used by most older people, with non-drivers relying heavily on family members or friends for transport. Figure 6.1 shows that two-thirds of adult non-drivers age seventy-five and older rely on rides from family or friends, and the other one-third use public transportation, walk, or ride in senior vans or taxicabs.

According to the Federal Highway Administration, the number of older drivers increased steadily from 1991 to 2001. (See Figure 6.2.) By 2003 the 28.6 million drivers age sixty-five and older accounted for almost 15% of all drivers. The percentage of older drivers is comparable for men and women age sixty-five to seventy-four, but from age seventy-five to eighty-four somewhat more women than men are licensed drivers,

then the figures are roughly equal again for drivers age eighty-five and older. (See Table 6.1.) As the huge cohort of baby boomers joins the ranks of older adults, the number of drivers age sixty-five and older will continue to grow, exceeding forty million by 2020.

Although many older adults drive and many more are expected to in the future, driving is not a viable alternative for a significant number of older persons. In 2004 an estimated seven million persons age sixty-five and older did not drive. Many older adults choose to stop or limit their driving for health or safety reasons.

Limited income also restricts many older adults' use of automobiles. According to the Bureau of Labor Statistics, car ownership costs are the second-largest household expense in the United States, and the average household spends nearly as much to own and operate a car as it does on food and health care combined. Table 6.2 shows that in 2003 the average costs associated with car ownership totaled $7,396 per year, while the average expenditures for food and health care were comparable, totaling $7,756. The cost of owning and operating an automobile, especially during periods of rising fuel prices, may be prohibitive for older adults living on fixed incomes. As a result, an ever-increasing proportion of the older population depend on alternative forms of transport in those areas where such transport is available, while some older adults remain isolated and immobilized by the absence of accessible, affordable transportation in their communities. According to the results of a survey conducted by AARP and reported by the U.S. Government Accountability Office (GAO) in *Transportation-Disadvantaged Seniors: Efforts to Enhance Senior Mobility Could Benefit from Additional Guidance and Information* (GAO-04-971; Washington, DC; August 2004), adults age seventy-five and older who live in small towns and rural areas are much less likely than residents of cities and suburbs to have access to public transportation. (See Figure 6.3.)

FIGURE 6.1

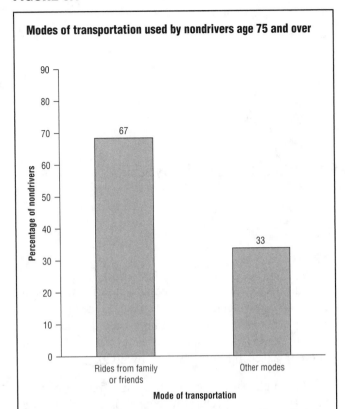

Modes of transportation used by nondrivers age 75 and over

Note: Other modes include public transportation, senior vans, walking, and taxicabs.

SOURCE: "Figure 3. Modes of Transportation Used by Nondrivers Aged 75 and Older," in *Transportation-Disadvantaged Seniors: Efforts to Enhance Senior Mobility Could Benefit from Additional Guidance and Information*, U.S. Government Accountability Office, Washington, DC, August 2004, http://www.gao.gov/new.items/d04971.pdf (accessed August 11, 2005)

FIGURE 6.2

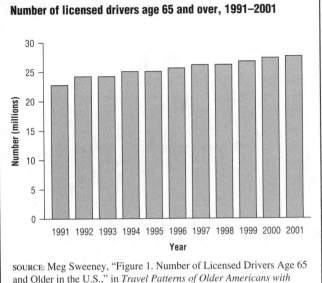

Number of licensed drivers age 65 and over, 1991–2001

SOURCE: Meg Sweeney, "Figure 1. Number of Licensed Drivers Age 65 and Older in the U.S.," in *Travel Patterns of Older Americans with Disabilities*, Bureau of Transportation Statistics, U.S. Department of Transportation, Washington, DC, 2003, http://www.bts.gov/programs/bts_working_papers/2004/paper_01/html/figure_01.html (accessed August 11, 2005)

THE NATIONAL HOUSEHOLD TRAVEL SURVEY

The 2001 National Household Travel Survey (NHTS) conducted by the U.S. Department of Transportation's Bureau of Transportation Statistics is the nation's inventory of daily and long-distance travel. The survey includes demographic characteristics of households, people, and vehicles, as well as detailed information on daily and longer-distance travel. The most recent NHTS data available confirm that the number of miles driven per licensed driver continues to increase. Among adults age sixty-five and older, the average number of miles driven annually increased by 48.6% from 1969 to 2001. While the average annual mileage of older men increased by 71.7% during that time period, older women's mileage increased by 31.1%. (See Table 6.3.)

Although adults age sixty-five and older make the fewest daily trips of all drivers, their average number of trips per person nearly doubled—from 1.8 in 1983 to 3.4 in 2001. Women age sixty-five and older took about 20% fewer trips than did older men. (See Table 6.4.) Although older adults traveled the fewest miles per day of any driving age group, their average daily miles traveled

more than doubled between 1983 and 2001, from 12 to 27.5 miles. (See Table 6.5.) Trips taken by women of all ages were considerably shorter than men's; in 2001 women age sixty-five and older logged an average of 23.5 miles per day, compared with older men's 32.9 miles. Older adults spent just under an hour a day in a vehicle in 2001, less than other adult age groups but more than children under age eighteen. (See Figure 6.4.)

MOTOR VEHICLE ACCIDENTS

The Insurance Institute for Highway Safety (IIHS) reports that, apart from the youngest drivers, older drivers have the highest rates of fatal crashes per mile driven. (The IIHS is a nonprofit, scientific, and educational organization supported by auto insurers that is dedicated to reducing the losses from motor vehicle accidents.) Although older drivers tend to limit their number of miles driven as they age and even though they drive at the safest times—in daylight and avoiding rush-hour traffic—their rate of accidents per mile is extremely high. From April 2001 through March 2002 drivers age eighty-five and older were involved in nearly nine times the number of fatal crashes as drivers age twenty-five to sixty-nine. The oldest and youngest drivers have the highest fatality rates on a per-mile-driven basis, but a key difference between the two age groups is that older drivers involved in crashes are less likely than younger drivers to hurt others—older drivers pose more of a danger to themselves. Drivers under the age of thirty are responsible for far more of the injuries and deaths of others than are older adult drivers.

TABLE 6.1

Licensed drivers, by sex and percentage in each age group and relation to population, 2003

Age	Male drivers			Female drivers			Total drivers		
	Number	Percent of total drivers	Drivers as percent of age group*	Number	Percent of total drivers	Drivers as percent of age group*	Number	Percent of total drivers	Drivers as percent of age group*
Under 16	19,027	0	0.9	18,382	0	0.9	37,409	0	0.9
16	642,541	0.7	30.6	620,358	0.6	31.1	1,262,899	0.6	30.8
17	1,112,082	1.1	52.9	1,066,350	1.1	53.5	2,178,432	1.1	53.2
18	1,423,653	1.4	67.6	1,342,145	1.4	67.5	2,765,798	1.4	67.5
19	1,549,037	1.6	73.6	1,469,642	1.5	74.5	3,018,679	1.5	74
(19 and under)	4,746,340	4.8	45.1	4,516,877	4.6	45.4	9,263,217	4.7	45.2
20	1,625,472	1.7	76.2	1,552,950	1.6	78.2	3,178,422	1.6	77.1
21	1,679,332	1.7	78.3	1,626,570	1.7	80.6	3,305,902	1.7	79.4
22	1,705,850	1.7	78.9	1,664,026	1.7	81.1	3,369,876	1.7	79.9
23	1,740,745	1.8	80.8	1,699,786	1.7	83.1	3,440,531	1.8	81.9
24	1,742,438	1.8	84.3	1,699,662	1.7	86.7	3,442,100	1.8	85.5
(20–24)	8,493,837	8.6	79.7	8,242,994	8.4	81.9	16,736,831	8.5	80.7
25–29	8,669,799	8.8	88.7	8,394,229	8.6	89.3	17,064,028	8.7	89
30–34	9,622,899	9.8	92.1	9,302,556	9.5	90.7	18,925,455	9.6	91.4
35–39	9,960,238	10.1	92.9	9,724,146	9.9	91	19,684,384	10	91.9
40–44	10,653,505	10.8	93.4	10,606,207	10.8	91.8	21,259,712	10.8	92.6
45–49	10,135,650	10.3	94.5	10,206,178	10.4	92.5	20,341,828	10.4	93.5
50–54	8,916,619	9.1	95.7	9,001,861	9.2	92.5	17,918,480	9.1	94.1
55–59	7,482,632	7.6	97.7	7,502,345	7.7	92.2	14,984,977	7.6	94.9
60–64	5,680,012	5.8	98.5	5,702,436	5.8	89.9	11,382,448	5.8	94
65–69	4,370,011	4.4	96.6	4,407,404	4.5	84.4	8,777,415	4.5	90.1
70–74	3,613,116	3.7	94.5	3,749,487	3.8	78.7	7,362,603	3.8	85.7
75–79	2,894,252	2.9	93.4	3,173,326	3.2	72.9	6,067,578	3.1	81.4
80–84	1,856,730	1.9	90.3	2,103,187	2.1	62.6	3,959,917	2	73.1
85 and over	1,132,725	1.2	81.5	1,304,069	1.3	39.9	2,436,794	1.2	51.7
Total	**98,228,365**	**100**	**89.5**	**97,937,302**	**100**	**82.9**	**196,165,667**	**100**	**85.3**

*These percentages are computed using population estimates of the Bureau of the Census. Under-16 age group is compared to 14 and 15-year old population estimates; the other age brackets coincide with those from the Bureau of the Census.

SOURCE: "Distribution of Licensed Drivers—2003 By Sex and Percentage In Each Age Group and Relation to Population," in *Highway Statistics 2003*, U.S. Department of Transportation Federal Highway Administration, Washington, DC, November 17, 2004, http://www.fhwa.dot.gov/policy/ohim/hs03/htm/dl20 .htm (accessed August 11, 2005)

Table 6.6 shows that in 2002 the death rate (the number of deaths per one hundred thousand people) for motor vehicle-related injuries for adults age sixty-five and older was 21.5%, compared with 14.5% for adults age forty-five to sixty-four. The higher fatality rates of adults age seventy-five to eighty-four and eighty-five and older who are involved in crashes—25.7% and 28% respectively—are attributable to older adults' fragility as opposed to the likelihood of being involved in an accident. Older people are more susceptible to injury, especially chest injuries, and are more likely to die as a result of those injuries. However, relatively few deaths—less than 1%—of adults age seventy and older are attributable to motor vehicle accidents.

The IIHS reports that in 2004, 81% of motor vehicle crash fatalities among people seventy and older involved occupants in passenger vehicles, and 15% were pedestrians. The death rate per one hundred thousand people for pedestrians age seventy and older in 2004 was higher than for pedestrians in all younger age groups. While older pedestrian deaths have declined by 44% since 1975, deaths of older passenger vehicle occupants increased by 77%. However, as the population of adults age seventy and older has increased, the death rate, which was twenty-six per one hundred thousand in 1975, generally has been declining, reaching a low of nineteen in 2004.

According to the IIHS, in 2004 about 78% of fatal crashes involving drivers eighty-five and older were multiple-vehicle accidents. Of those, two-thirds occurred at intersections. That year 37% of pedestrians age seventy and older were killed at intersections, compared with 21% of younger pedestrians. Drivers over the age of sixty-five are more likely than younger drivers to have accidents when making left turns. The IIHS attributes this to the fact that older drivers take longer to make turns, increasing the risk of a crash.

Older adults also suffer nonfatal injuries as drivers or passengers in motor vehicle crashes. In 2003 the National Center for Injury Prevention and Control recorded nearly 235,000 such nonfatal injuries in adults age sixty-five and older. (Table 6.7 shows the 188,278 injuries to occupants of vehicles and 46,507 injuries attributable to other transport.) Motor vehicle accidents (termed "unintentional MV-Occupant") were the third-leading cause of nonfatal injuries among adults age sixty-five and older in the United States in 2003.

TABLE 6.2

Average annual expenditures of all consumer units and percent changes, 2001–03

Item	2001	2002	2003	Percent change 2001–2002	Percent change 2002–2003
Number of consumer units (in thousands)	110,339	112,108	115,356		
Income before taxes	$47,507	$49,430	$51,128		
Averages					
Age of reference person	48.1	48.1	48.4		
Number of persons in consumer unit	2.5	2.5	2.5		
Number of earners	1.4	1.4	1.3		
Number of vehicles	1.9	2.0	1.9		
Percent homeowner	66	66	67		
Average annual expenditures	$39,518	$40,677	$40,817	2.9	0.3
Food	5,321	5,375	5,340	1.0	−.7
Food at home	3,086	3,099	3,129	.4	1.0
Cereals and bakery products	452	450	442	−.4	−1.8
Meats, poultry, fish, and eggs	828	798	825	−3.6	3.4
Dairy products	332	328	328	−1.2	.0
Fruits and vegetables	522	552	535	5.7	−3.1
Other food at home	952	970	999	1.9	3.0
Food away from home	2,235	2,276	2,211	1.8	−2.9
Alcoholic beverages	349	376	391	7.7	4.0
Housing	13,011	13,283	13,432	2.1	1.1
Shelter	7,602	7,829	7,887	3.0	.7
Utilities, fuels, and public services	2,767	2,684	2,811	−3.0	4.7
Household operations	676	706	707	4.4	.1
Housekeeping supplies	509	545	529	7.1	−2.9
Housefurnishings and equipment	1,458	1,518	1,497	4.1	−1.4
Apparel and services	1,743	1,749	1,640	.3	−6.2
Transportation	7,633	7,759	7,781	1.7	.3
Vehicle purchases (net outlay)	3,579	3,665	3,732	2.4	1.8
Gasoline and motor oil	1,279	1,235	1,333	−3.4	7.9
Other vehicle expenses	2,375	2,471	2,331	4.0	−5.7
Public transportation	400	389	385	−2.7	−1.0
Healthcare	2,182	2,350	2,416	7.7	2.8
Entertainment	1,953	2,079	2,060	6.5	−.9
Personal care products and services	485	526	527	8.5	.2
Reading	141	139	127	−1.4	−8.6
Education	648	752	783	16.0	4.1
Tobacco products and smoking supplies	308	320	290	3.9	−9.4
Miscellaneous	750	792	606	5.6	−23.5
Cash contributions	1,258	1,277	1,370	1.5	7.3
Personal insurance and pensions	3,737	3,899	4,055	4.3	4.0
Life and other personal insurance	410	406	397	−1.0	2.2
Pensions and Social Security	3,326	3,493	3,658	5.0	4.7

SOURCE: "Table A. Average Annual Expenditures of all Consumer Units and Percent Changes, Consumer Expenditure Survey 2001–2003," in *Consumer Expenditures in 2003*, Report 986, U.S. Department of Labor, U.S. Bureau of Labor Statistics, Washington DC, June 2005, http://www.bls.gov/cex/csxann03.pdf (accessed August 11, 2005)

The data about older drivers are not all bad. According to the Centers for Disease Control and Prevention (CDC), older adults wear safety belts more often than any other age group except infants and preschool children, and they are less likely to drink and drive than other adult drivers. They also take fewer risks than younger drivers, driving when conditions are safest. They limit their driving during bad weather and at night and log fewer miles than younger drivers.

AGE-RELATED CHANGES MAY IMPAIR OLDER DRIVERS' SKILLS

Most older adults retain their driving skills, but some age-related changes in vision, hearing, cognitive functions (attention, memory, and reaction times), reflexes, and flexibility of the head and neck may impair the skills that are critical for safe driving. For example, reaction time declines by about 40% from age thirty-five to seventy-five, and arthritis (inflammation that causes pain and loss of movement of the joints) in the neck or shoulder may limit sufferers' ability to turn their necks well enough to merge into traffic, see when backing up, and navigate intersections where the angle of intersecting roads is less than perpendicular.

Such changes as reduced muscle mass and the resultant reduction in strength, as well as decreases in the efficiency of the circulatory, cardiac, and respiratory systems are strictly related to aging. Others are attributable to the fact that certain diseases, such as arthritis and glaucoma (a disease in which fluid pressure inside the eyes slowly rises, leading to vision loss or blindness), tend to strike at later ages. The functional losses associated with these chronic conditions are usually gradual, and many afflicted older drivers are able to adapt

FIGURE 6.3

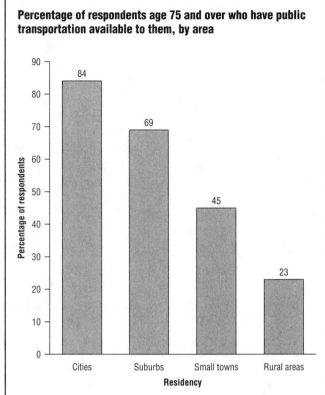

Percentage of respondents age 75 and over who have public transportation available to them, by area

Note: Respondents were asked how they would describe their current residence: as a city, a suburban area around a city, a small town, or in the country.

SOURCE: "Figure 4. Percentage of Respondents Aged 75 and Older Who Have Public Transportation Available to Them, by Area," in *Transportation-Disadvantaged Seniors: Efforts to Enhance Senior Mobility Could Benefit from Additional Guidance and Information*, U.S. Government Accountability Office, Washington, DC, August 2004, http://www.gao.gov/new.items/d04971.pdf (accessed August 11, 2005)

effectively to them. The majority of older adults do not experience declines until very old age, and most learn to adjust to the limitations imposed by age-related changes. Still, a substantial proportion of older adults do stop driving in response to age-related changes. The National Institute on Aging (NIA) reports that each year more than six hundred thousand older adults stop driving because of declines in their fitness level, vision, and ability to think clearly.

The American Medical Association (AMA) identified motor vehicle injuries as the leading cause of injury-related deaths among sixty-five- to seventy-four-year-olds in 2003. Among adults age seventy-five and older, motor vehicle-related injuries followed falls as the second-leading cause of such deaths. The AMA posits that significant growth in the older population and an increase in miles driven by older adults could act to triple the number of traffic fatalities in the coming years. The AMA believes the medical community can help to stem this increase, and it has called upon physicians to help their patients maintain or even improve their driving

skills by periodically assessing them for disease- and medication-related conditions that might impair their capacity to function as safe drivers.

A joint effort of the National Highway Traffic Safety Administration (NHTSA) and the AMA, the 2003 publication *Physician's Guide to Assessing and Counseling Older Drivers* details medical conditions and their potential effect on driving and highlights treatment methods and counseling measures that can minimize those effects. The next sections, which describe health problems with the potential to cause driving hazards, draws heavily from the guide.

Acute and Chronic Medical Problems

Patients discharged from the hospital following treatment for serious illnesses may be temporarily, or even permanently, unable to drive safely. Examples of acute medical problems that can impair driving performance include:

- Acute myocardial infarction (heart attack)
- Stroke (sudden death of a portion of the brain cells due to a lack of blood flow and oxygen) and other traumatic brain injury
- Syncope and vertigo (fainting and dizziness)
- Seizures (sudden attacks or convulsions characterized by generalized muscle spasms and loss of consciousness)
- Surgery
- Delirium (altered mental state characterized by wild, irregular, and incoherent thoughts and actions) from any cause

A variety of chronic medical conditions also can compromise driving function. These could include the following:

- Diseases affecting vision—cataracts, diabetic retinopathy, macular degeneration, glaucoma, retinitis pigmentosa, and low visual acuity (the ability to distinguish fine details) even after correction with lenses. Driving is largely a visual task because about 95% of the information required is obtained visually. Many visual functions such as visual acuity, contrast sensitivity, and glare sensitivity decline with age. Impaired visual acuity can cause difficulty in reading signs. Reduced contrast sensitivity can affect the detection of pedestrians in low-light situations and the ability to see worn lane lines. Glare sensitivity makes driving at night and entering and exiting tunnels difficult, and this condition is aggravated by cataracts.
- Cardiovascular (heart and blood vessels) disease, especially when associated with angina (chest pain

TABLE 6.3

Average annual miles per licensed driver, by driver age and gender, selected years, 1969–2001

							Percent change	
							Annual rate	Total change
Driver age	1969	1977	1983	1990	1995	2001	69–01	69–01
All								
16 to 19	4,633	5,662	4,986	8,485	7,624	7,331	1.44%	58.23%
20 to 34	9,348	11,063	11,531	14,776	15,098	15,650	1.62%	67.42%
35 to 54	9,771	11,539	12,627	14,836	15,291	15,627	1.48%	59.93%
55 to 64	8,611	9,196	9,611	11,436	11,972	13,177	1.34%	53.03%
65+	5,171	5,475	5,386	7,084	7,646	7,684	1.25%	48.60%
All	8,685	10,006	10,536	13,125	13,476	13,785	1.45%	58.72%
Men								
16 to 19	5,461	7,045	5,908	9,543	8,206	8,228	1.29%	50.67%
20 to 34	13,133	15,222	15,844	18,310	17,976	18,634	1.10%	41.89%
35 to 54	12,841	16,097	17,808	18,871	18,858	19,287	1.28%	50.20%
55 to 64	10,696	12,455	13,431	15,224	15,859	16,883	1.44%	57.84%
65+	5,919	6,795	7,198	9,162	10,304	10,163	1.70%	71.70%
All	11,352	13,397	13,962	16,536	16,550	16,920	1.26%	49.05%
Women								
16 to 19	3,586	4,036	3,874	7,387	6,873	6,106	1.68%	70.27%
20 to 34	5,512	6,571	7,121	11,174	12,004	12,266	2.53%	122.53%
35 to 54	6,003	6,534	7,347	10,539	11,464	11,590	2.08%	93.07%
55 to 64	5,375	5,097	5,432	7,211	7,780	8,795	1.55%	63.63%
65+	3,664	3,572	3,308	4,750	4,785	4,803	0.85%	31.09%
All	5,411	5,940	6,382	9,528	10,142	10,233	2.01%	89.11%

Notes:
Table reporting totals could include some unreported characteristics.
In 1995, some drivers indicating that they drove 'no miles' for their average annual miles were changed to 'miles not reported.'

SOURCE: Pat S. Hsu and Timothy R. Reuscher, "Table 23. Average Annual Miles per Licensed Driver by Driver Age and Gender (Driver's Self Estimate) 1969, 1977, 1983, 1990, 1995 NPTS, and 2001 NHTS," in *Summary of Travel Trends 2001 National Household Travel Survey*, U.S. Department of Transportation, Federal Highway Administration, Washington, DC, December 2004, http://nhts.ornl.gov/2001/pub/STT.pdf (accessed August 11, 2005)

TABLE 6.4

Average daily person trips per person, by age and gender, selected years, 1983–2001

	Total					Men					Women				
Age	1983	1990	1990 Adj	1995	2001	1983	1990	1990 Adj	1995	2001	1983	1990	1990 Adj	1995	2001
Total	2.9	3.1	3.8	4.3	4.1	2.9	3.0	3.7	4.3	4.1	2.9	3.1	3.8	4.3	4.1
Under 16	2.3	2.6	3.1	3.7	3.4	2.3	2.6	3.0	3.7	3.5	2.3	2.6	3.1	3.8	3.4
16 to 20	3.3	3.5	4.2	4.6	4.1	3.2	3.5	4.2	4.6	4.0	3.4	3.5	4.2	4.7	4.2
21 to 35	3.5	3.6	4.4	4.6	4.3	3.4	3.5	4.2	4.5	4.2	3.5	3.7	4.6	4.8	4.5
36 to 65	2.9	3.2	3.9	4.6	4.5	2.9	3.1	3.7	4.6	4.4	3.0	3.3	4.1	4.6	4.5
Over 65	1.8	1.9	2.4	3.4	3.4	2.2	2.2	2.8	3.9	3.8	1.5	1.7	2.2	3.0	3.1

Notes:
Table reporting totals could include some unreported characteristics.
2001 data excludes persons aged 0 to 4 since such persons were not included in the 1990 and 1995 surveys.
Only the 1990 data have been adjusted to make them more comparable with the 1995 and 2001 data. Thus, there are limits on the conclusions that can be drawn in comparing travel with earlier survey years. The adjustments to 1990 data affect only person trips, vehicle trips, person miles of travel (PMT) and vehicle miles of travel (VMT).

SOURCE: Pat S. Hsu and Timothy R. Reuscher, "Table 13. Average Daily Person Trips per Person by Age and Gender, 1983, 1990, 1995 NPTS and 2001 NHTS," in *Summary of Travel Trends 2001 National Household Travel Survey*, U.S. Department of Transportation, Federal Highway Administration, Washington, DC, December 2004, http://nhts.ornl.gov/2001/pub/STT.pdf (accessed August 11, 2005)

from a blockage in a coronary artery that prevents oxygen-rich blood from reaching part of the heart), syncope, or cognitive losses

- Neurologic disease including seizures, dementia, multiple sclerosis, Parkinson's disease, peripheral neuropathy (numbness or tingling in the hands and/or feet),

and residual deficits (losses or disability) resulting from stroke

- Psychiatric disease, including mood disorders, anxiety disorders, psychoses (severe mental disorders in which patients suffer hallucinations, irrational thoughts and fears, and are unable to distinguish between the real

TABLE 6.5

Average daily person miles per person, by age and gender, selected years, 1983–2001

Age	Total					Men					Women				
	1983	1990	1990 Adj	1995	2001	1983	1990	1990 Adj	1995	2001	1983	1990	1990 Adj	1995	2001
Total	25.1	28.6	34.9	38.7	40.2	27.7	31.6	38.0	43.9	45.0	22.6	25.8	32.1	33.8	35.7
Under 16	16.2	16.2	20.1	25.0	24.5	16.8	16.3	20.3	23.7	24.6	15.4	16.1	19.9	26.2	24.4
16 to 20	22.2	28.1	34.4	36.4	38.1	23.0	30.1	36.9	37.6	34.1	21.5	26.2	32.2	35.0	42.5
21 to 35	31.1	36.5	44.3	46.0	45.6	32.8	40.4	48.2	51.3	49.8	29.5	32.9	40.7	40.8	41.5
36 to 65	29.2	33.0	40.1	45.1	48.8	33.6	36.5	43.4	53.2	57.7	25.2	29.7	37.0	37.5	40.4
Over 65	12.0	14.2	18.4	24.4	27.5	14.8	17.4	22.5	31.7	32.9	10.2	11.8	15.3	19.2	23.5

Notes:
Table reporting totals could include some unreported characteristics.
2001 data excludes persons aged 0 to 4 since such persons were not included in the 1990 and 1995 surveys.
Only the 1990 data have been adjusted to make them more comparable with the 1995 and 2001 data. Thus, there are limits on the conclusions that can be drawn in comparing travel with earlier survey years. The adjustments to 1990 data affect only person trips, vehicle trips, person miles of travel (PMT) and vehicle miles of travel (VMT).

SOURCE: Pat S. Hsu and Timothy R. Reuscher, "Table 14. Average Daily Person Miles per Person by Age and Gender, 1983, 1990, 1995 NPTS and 2001 NHTS," in *Summary of Travel Trends 2001 National Household Travel Survey,* U.S. Department of Transportation, Federal Highway Administration, Washington, DC, December 2004, http://nhts.ornl.gov/2001/pub/STT.pdf (accessed August 11, 2005)

FIGURE 6.4

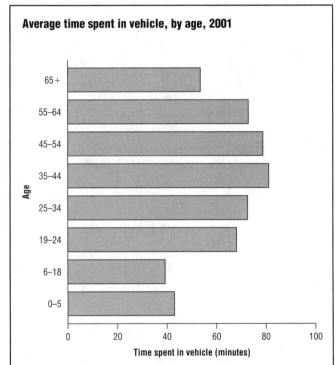

Average time spent in vehicle, by age, 2001

SOURCE: Pat S. Hsu and Timothy R. Reuscher, "Figure 5. Average Time Spent in Vehicle (Minutes) by Age, 2001 NHTS" in *Summary of Travel Trends 2001 National Household Travel Survey*, U.S. Department of Transportation, Federal Highway Administration, Washington, DC, December 2004, http://nhts.ornl.gov/2001/pub/STT.pdf (accessed August 11, 2005)

sugar to produce energy) and hypothyroidism (decreased production of the thyroid hormone by the thyroid gland)

- Musculoskeletal disabilities, including arthritis and foot abnormalities

- Chronic renal (kidney) failure

- Respiratory disease, including chronic obstructive pulmonary disease and obstructive sleep apnea (a breathing disorder characterized by interruptions of breathing during sleep).

Driving requires a range of sophisticated cognitive skills, which is why some cognitive changes can compromise driving ability. It is not unusual for memory, attention, processing speed, and executive skills—the capacity for logical analysis—to decline with advancing age. Weakening memory may make it difficult for some older drivers to process information from traffic signs and to navigate correctly. As multiple demands are made on a driver's attention, they must possess selective attention—the ability to prioritize stimuli and focus on only the most important—in order to attend to vital stimuli such as traffic signs while not being distracted by irrelevant ones such as billboards. Selective attention problems challenge older drivers to distinguish the most critical information when they are faced with many signs and signals. Drivers also must be able to divide their attention in order to focus on the multiple stimuli involved in most driving tasks. Processing speed affects perception-reaction time and is critical in situations where drivers must immediately choose between actions such as accelerating, braking, or steering. Executive skills are required to analyze driving-related stimuli and make appropriate decisions; they enable drivers to decide to stop at a red light or stop at a crosswalk when a pedestrian is crossing the street.

world and the imaginary world), personality disorders, and alcohol or other substance abuse

- Metabolic disease, including Type I and Type II diabetes mellitus (a condition in which there is increased sugar in the blood and urine because the body is unable to use

TABLE 6.6

Death rates for motor vehicle–related injuries, by selected characteristics, selected years, 1950–2002

[Data are based on death certificates]

Sex, race, Hispanic origin, and age	1950[a]	1960[a]	1970	1980	1990	2000	2001	2002
All persons				Deaths per 100,000 resident population				
All ages, age adjusted[b]	24.6	23.1	27.6	22.3	18.5	15.4	15.3	15.7
All ages, crude	23.1	21.3	26.9	23.5	18.8	15.4	15.4	15.7
Under 1 year	8.4	8.1	9.8	7.0	4.9	4.4	3.6	3.0
1–14 years	9.8	8.6	10.5	8.2	6.0	4.3	4.1	3.9
1–4 years	11.5	10.0	11.5	9.2	6.3	4.2	4.1	3.9
5–14 years	8.8	7.9	10.2	7.9	5.9	4.3	4.1	3.9
15–24 years	34.4	38.0	47.2	44.8	34.1	26.9	26.8	28.2
15–19 years	29.6	33.9	43.6	43.0	33.1	26.0	25.7	27.6
20–24 years	38.8	42.9	51.3	46.6	35.0	28.0	28.0	28.8
25–34 years	24.6	24.3	30.9	29.1	23.6	17.3	17.5	17.8
35–44 years	20.3	19.3	24.9	20.9	16.9	15.3	15.7	15.8
45–64 years	25.2	23.0	26.5	18.0	15.7	14.3	14.0	14.5
45–54 years	22.2	21.4	25.5	18.6	15.6	14.2	14.2	14.8
55–64 years	29.0	25.1	27.9	17.4	15.9	14.4	13.7	14.1
65 years and over	43.1	34.7	36.2	22.5	23.1	21.4	21.3	21.5
65–74 years	39.1	31.4	32.8	19.2	18.6	16.5	16.3	17.0
75–84 years	52.7	41.8	43.5	28.1	29.1	25.7	26.3	25.7
85 years and over	45.1	37.9	34.2	27.6	31.2	30.4	27.8	28.0
Male								
All ages, age adjusted[b]	38.5	35.4	41.5	33.6	26.5	21.7	21.8	22.1
All ages, crude	35.4	31.8	39.7	35.3	26.7	21.3	21.5	21.9
Under 1 year	9.1	8.6	9.3	7.3	5.0	4.6	3.2	3.3
1–14 years	12.3	10.7	13.0	10.0	7.0	4.9	4.8	4.6
1–4 years	13.0	11.5	12.9	10.2	6.9	4.7	4.5	4.5
5–14 years	11.9	10.4	13.1	9.9	7.0	5.0	4.9	4.6
15–24 years	56.7	61.2	73.2	68.4	49.5	37.4	38.0	39.3
15–19 years	46.3	51.7	64.1	62.6	45.5	33.9	34.0	36.0
20–24 years	66.7	73.2	84.4	74.3	53.3	41.2	42.1	42.6
25–34 years	40.8	40.1	49.4	46.3	35.7	25.5	26.2	26.5
35–44 years	32.5	29.9	37.7	31.7	24.7	22.0	22.4	22.3
45–64 years	37.7	33.3	38.9	26.5	21.9	20.2	19.9	20.7
45–54 years	33.6	31.6	37.2	27.6	22.0	20.4	20.5	21.3
55–64 years	43.1	35.6	40.9	25.4	21.7	19.8	19.0	19.9
65 years and over	66.6	52.1	54.4	33.9	32.1	29.5	29.5	29.8
65–74 years	59.1	45.8	47.3	27.3	24.2	21.7	21.5	22.7
75–84 years	85.0	66.0	68.2	44.3	41.2	35.6	37.3	35.3
85 years and over	78.1	62.7	63.1	56.1	64.5	57.5	51.1	51.7
Female								
All ages, age adjusted[b]	11.5	11.7	14.9	11.8	11.0	9.5	9.3	9.6
All ages, crude	10.9	11.0	14.7	12.3	11.3	9.7	9.5	9.8
Under 1 year	7.6	7.5	10.4	6.7	4.9	4.2	4.0	2.8
1–14 years	7.2	6.3	7.9	6.3	4.9	3.7	3.4	3.3
1–4 years	10.0	8.4	10.0	8.1	5.6	3.8	3.6	3.3
5–14 years	5.7	5.4	7.2	5.7	4.7	3.6	3.3	3.3
15–24 years	12.6	15.1	21.6	20.8	17.9	15.9	15.1	16.6
15–19 years	12.9	16.0	22.7	22.8	20.0	17.5	16.9	18.9
20–24 years	12.2	14.0	20.4	18.9	16.0	14.2	13.4	14.3
25–34 years	9.3	9.2	13.0	12.2	11.5	8.8	8.7	8.8
35–44 years	8.5	9.1	12.9	10.4	9.2	8.8	9.1	9.3
45–64 years	12.6	13.1	15.3	10.3	10.1	8.7	8.4	8.7
45–54 years	10.9	11.6	14.5	10.2	9.6	8.2	8.1	8.6
55–64 years	14.9	15.2	16.2	10.5	10.8	9.5	8.8	8.9
65 years and over	21.9	20.3	23.1	15.0	17.2	15.8	15.5	15.7
65–74 years	20.6	19.0	21.6	13.0	14.1	12.3	12.0	12.3
75–84 years	25.2	23.0	27.2	18.5	21.9	19.2	19.2	19.3
85 years and over	22.1	22.0	18.0	15.2	18.3	19.3	18.0	17.7

Medications

Many commonly used prescription and over-the-counter (nonprescription) medications can impair driving performance. In general, drugs with strong central nervous system effects, such as antidepressants, antihistamines, muscle relaxants, narcotic analgesics (painkillers), anti-convulsants (used to prevent seizures), and stimulants, have the potential to adversely affect the ability to operate a motor vehicle. The extent to which driving skills are compromised varies from person to person and between different medications used for the same purpose. The effects of prescription and over-the-counter medications may be intensified in combination with other drugs or alcohol.

TABLE 6.6

Death rates for motor vehicle–related injuries, by selected characteristics, selected years, 1950–2002 [CONTINUED]

[Data are based on death certificates]

Sex, race, Hispanic origin, and age	1950[a]	1960[a]	1970	1980	1990	2000	2001	2002
White male[c]				Deaths per 100,000 resident population				
All ages, age adjusted[b]	37.9	34.8	40.4	33.8	26.3	21.8	22.0	22.4
All ages, crude	35.1	31.5	39.1	35.9	26.7	21.6	21.9	22.4
Under 1 year	9.1	8.8	9.1	7.0	4.8	4.2	3.1	2.9
1–14 years	12.4	10.6	12.5	9.8	6.6	4.8	4.6	4.5
15–24 years	58.3	62.7	75.2	73.8	52.5	39.6	40.0	41.9
25–34 years	39.1	38.6	47.0	46.6	35.4	25.1	26.4	26.6
35–44 years	30.9	28.4	35.2	30.7	23.7	21.8	22.4	22.3
45–64 years	36.2	31.7	36.5	25.2	20.6	19.7	19.5	20.6
65 years and over	67.1	52.1	54.2	32.7	31.4	29.4	29.9	29.8
Black or African American male[c]								
All ages, age adjusted[b]	34.8	39.6	51.0	34.2	29.9	24.4	23.5	23.2
All ages, crude	37.2	33.1	44.3	31.1	28.1	22.5	22.0	21.5
Under 1 year	—	*	10.6	7.8	*	6.7	*	*
1–14 years[d]	10.4	11.2	16.3	11.4	8.9	5.5	6.1	5.3
15–24 years	42.5	46.4	58.1	34.9	36.1	30.2	31.4	29.6
25–34 years	54.4	51.0	70.4	44.9	39.5	32.6	29.9	31.7
35–44 years	46.7	43.6	59.5	41.2	33.5	27.2	26.1	25.3
45–64 years	54.6	47.8	61.7	39.5	33.3	27.1	26.7	24.8
65 years and over	52.6	48.2	53.4	42.4	36.3	32.1	28.1	30.4
American Indian or Alaska Native male[c]								
All ages, age adjusted[b]	—	—	—	78.9	48.3	35.8	34.6	39.0
All ages, crude	—	—	—	74.6	47.6	33.6	33.2	37.3
1–14 years	—	—	—	15.1	11.6	7.8	8.4	7.1
15–24 years	—	—	—	126.1	75.2	56.8	55.7	57.2
25–34 years	—	—	—	107.0	78.2	49.8	43.2	49.9
35–44 years	—	—	—	82.8	57.0	36.3	42.3	47.2
45–64 years	—	—	—	77.4	45.9	32.0	30.7	40.7
65 years and over	—	—	—	97.0	43.0	48.5	40.4	45.9
Asian or Pacific Islander male[c]								
All ages, age adjusted[b]	—	—	—	19.0	17.9	10.6	10.4	10.8
All ages, crude	—	—	—	17.1	15.8	9.8	9.7	10.0
1–14 years	—	—	—	8.2	6.3	2.5	2.2	2.5
15–24 years	—	—	—	27.2	25.7	17.0	19.3	20.0
25–34 years	—	—	—	18.8	17.0	10.4	10.0	8.9
35–44 years	—	—	—	13.1	12.2	6.9	7.3	7.8
45–64 years	—	—	—	13.7	15.1	10.1	7.9	8.7
65 years and over	—	—	—	37.3	33.6	21.1	21.8	23.3
Hispanic or Latino male[c,e]								
All ages, age adjusted[b]	—	—	—	—	29.5	21.3	22.2	22.2
All ages, crude	—	—	—	—	29.2	20.1	21.0	21.3
1–14 years	—	—	—	—	7.2	4.4	4.4	5.1
15–24 years	—	—	—	—	48.2	34.7	36.9	38.9
25–34 years	—	—	—	—	41.0	24.9	26.8	26.4
35–44 years	—	—	—	—	28.0	21.6	23.1	22.6
45–64 years	—	—	—	—	28.9	21.7	20.5	19.9
65 years and over	—	—	—	—	35.3	28.9	31.0	30.7
White, not Hispanic or Latino male[e]								
All ages, age adjusted[b]	—	—	—	—	25.7	21.7	21.7	22.2
All ages, crude	—	—	—	—	26.0	21.5	21.7	22.3
1–14 years	—	—	—	—	6.4	4.9	4.6	4.2
15–24 years	—	—	—	—	52.3	40.3	40.1	42.1
25–34 years	—	—	—	—	34.0	24.7	25.9	26.1
35–44 years	—	—	—	—	23.1	21.6	21.9	22.0
45–64 years	—	—	—	—	19.8	19.3	19.2	20.4
65 years and over	—	—	—	—	31.1	29.3	29.7	29.6

Medication side effects that can affect driving performance include drowsiness, dizziness, blurred vision, unsteadiness, fainting, and slowed reaction time. Generally, these side effects are dose-dependent and lessen over time, but older adults are often more sensitive to the effects of medications and may take longer to metabolize them, prolonging their effects. Medications that cause drowsiness, euphoria, or amnesia pose an even greater risk, because they often diminish insight and objectivity, such that the driver may become impaired without any awareness of it.

TABLE 6.6

Death rates for motor vehicle–related injuries, by selected characteristics, selected years, 1950–2002 [CONTINUED]

[Data are based on death certificates]

Sex, race, Hispanic origin, and age	1950[a]	1960[a]	1970	1980	1990	2000	2001	2002
				Deaths per 100,000 resident population				
White female[c]								
All ages, age adjusted[b]	11.4	11.7	14.9	12.2	11.2	9.8	9.5	9.8
All ages, crude	10.9	11.2	14.8	12.8	11.6	10.0	9.8	10.1
Under 1 year	7.8	7.5	10.2	7.1	4.7	3.5	3.8	2.2
1–14 years	7.2	6.2	7.5	6.2	4.8	3.7	3.3	3.2
15–24 years	12.6	15.6	22.7	23.0	19.5	17.1	16.0	17.9
25–34 years	9.0	9.0	12.7	12.2	11.6	8.9	8.8	9.0
35–44 years	8.1	8.9	12.3	10.6	9.2	8.9	9.3	9.4
45–64 years	12.7	13.1	15.1	10.4	9.9	8.7	8.4	8.7
65 years and over	22.2	20.8	23.7	15.3	17.4	16.2	16.0	16.3
Black or African American female[c]								
All ages, age adjusted[b]	9.3	10.4	14.1	8.5	9.6	8.4	8.5	8.2
All ages, crude	10.2	9.7	13.4	8.3	9.4	8.2	8.2	8.0
Under 1 year	—	8.1	11.9	*	7.0	*	*	*
1–14 years[5]	7.2	6.9	10.2	6.3	5.3	3.9	3.7	3.5
15–24 years	11.6	9.9	13.4	8.0	9.9	11.7	11.7	11.6
25–34 years	10.8	9.8	13.3	10.6	11.1	9.4	8.9	8.8
35–44 years	11.1	11.0	16.1	8.3	9.4	8.2	9.2	9.4
45–64 years	11.8	12.7	16.7	9.2	10.7	9.0	8.3	8.4
65 years and over	14.3	13.2	15.7	9.5	13.5	10.4	11.8	9.5
American Indian or Alaska Native female[c]								
All ages, age adjusted[b]	—	—	—	32.0	17.5	19.5	17.6	19.3
All ages, crude	—	—	—	32.0	17.3	18.6	16.9	19.1
1–14 years	—	—	—	15.0	8.1	6.5	7.6	6.8
15–24 years	—	—	—	42.3	31.4	30.3	30.7	29.2
25–34 years	—	—	—	52.5	18.8	22.3	15.5	21.1
35–44 years	—	—	—	38.1	18.2	22.0	13.1	24.4
45–64 years	—	—	—	32.6	17.6	17.8	18.1	20.9
65 years and over	—	—	—	*	*	24.0	25.3	*
Asian or Pacific Islander female[c]								
All ages, age adjusted[b]	—	—	—	9.3	10.4	6.7	6.1	6.2
All ages, crude	—	—	—	8.2	9.0	5.9	5.9	5.7
1–14 years	—	—	—	7.4	3.6	2.3	2.2	1.9
15–24 years	—	—	—	7.4	11.4	6.0	7.6	7.3
25–34 years	—	—	—	7.3	7.3	4.5	4.8	4.4
35–44 years	—	—	—	8.6	7.5	4.9	5.4	3.7
45–64 years	—	—	—	8.5	11.8	6.4	7.0	7.3
65 years and over	—	—	—	18.6	24.3	18.5	11.8	15.6
Hispanic or Latino female[c,e]								
All ages, age adjusted[b]	—	—	—	—	9.6	7.9	7.8	8.1
All ages, crude	—	—	—	—	8.9	7.2	7.2	7.4
1–14 years	—	—	—	—	4.8	3.9	3.3	3.2
15–24 years	—	—	—	—	11.6	10.6	11.2	12.4
25–34 years	—	—	—	—	9.4	6.5	6.5	7.2
35–44 years	—	—	—	—	8.0	7.3	6.9	7.3
45–64 years	—	—	—	—	11.4	8.3	8.4	8.4
65 years and over	—	—	—	—	14.9	13.4	12.9	13.1

Concern about Older Drivers' Safety Prompts Action

As the ranks of older adults swell, many states and organizations—the AMA and NHTSA are chief among these groups—are taking action to ensure driver safety. Concern about older driver safety has intensified in recent years in response to a spate of serious crashes involving older drivers. One particularly horrific example occurred in Southern California when a disoriented eighty-six-year-old man drove at high speed down a street closed for a farmer's market, killing ten people and injuring dozens more. According to the authorities, the driver thought he might have hit the gas instead of the brake as he tried to stop ("Market Crash Raises Age Questions," CBS News online, http://www.cbsnews.com/stories/2003/07/18/national/main564052.shtml, July 18, 2003).

Each state has its own licensing and license renewal criteria for drivers, and some states—California, Delaware, New Jersey, Oregon, and Pennsylvania—require physicians to report unsafe drivers or drivers diagnosed with conditions that may cause lapses of consciousness to the licensing agency. Thirty-four states use medical

TABLE 6.6

Death rates for motor vehicle–related injuries, by selected characteristics, selected years, 1950–2002 [CONTINUED]

[Data are based on death certificates]

Sex, race, Hispanic origin, and age	1950[a]	1960[a]	1970	1980	1990	2000	2001	2002
White, not Hispanic or Latino female[e]				Deaths per 100,000 resident population				
All ages, age adjusted[b]	—	—	—	—	11.3	10.0	9.7	10.1
All ages, crude	—	—	—	—	11.7	10.3	10.1	10.5
1–14 years	—	—	—	—	4.7	3.5	3.2	3.2
15–24 years	—	—	—	—	20.4	18.4	17.0	19.0
25–34 years	—	—	—	—	11.7	9.3	9.3	9.4
35–44 years	—	—	—	—	9.3	9.0	9.6	9.7
45–64 years	—	—	—	—	9.7	8.7	8.3	8.6
65 years and over	—	—	—	—	17.5	16.3	16.1	16.5

— Data not available.

*Rates based on fewer than 20 deaths are considered unreliable and are not shown.

[a]Includes deaths of persons who were not residents of the 50 states and the District of Columbia.

[b]Age-adjusted rates are calculated using the year 2000 standard population.

[c]The race groups, white, black, Asian or Pacific Islander, and American Indian or Alaska Native, include persons of Hispanic and non-Hispanic origin. Persons of Hispanic origin may be of any race. Death rates for the American Indian or Alaska Native and Asian or Pacific Islander populations are known to be underestimated.

[d]In 1950 rate is for the age group under 15 years.

[e]Prior to 1997, excludes data from states lacking an Hispanic-origin item on the death certificate.

Notes: Age groups were selected to minimize the presentation of unstable age-specific death rates based on small numbers of deaths and for consistency among comparison groups.

SOURCE: "Table 44. Death Rates for Motor Vehicle–Related Injuries, According to Sex, Race, Hispanic Origin, and Age: United States, Selected Years 1950–2002," *Health, United States, 2004,* Centers for Disease Control and Prevention, National Center for Health Statistics, Hyattsville, MD, 2004, http://www.cdc.gov/nchs/data/hus/hus04trend.pdf (accessed August 11, 2005)

review boards or medical advisory boards to help determine when a driver should no longer be allowed to drive due to safety or health issues. The boards are comprised of health professionals and physicians and generally do not issue judgments based solely on age. They also recommend licensing standards. For example, some states use accelerated renewal cycles, vision tests, and in-person rather than online or mail renewals for older drivers. Illinois and New Hampshire require road tests for drivers over the age of seventy-five. In 2004 Kansas enacted legislation enabling physicians and optometrists to report drivers they feel are unable to safely operate a motor vehicle.

Ensuring the Safety of Older Drivers

In *Physician's Guide to Assessing and Counseling Older Drivers* the AMA advocates coordinated efforts among the medical and research communities, policy-makers, community planners, automobile industry, and government agencies to achieve the common goal of safe transportation for the older population. The AMA calls for improved diagnostic tools to assist physicians in assessing patients' crash risk, improved access to driver assessment and rehabilitation, safer roads and vehicles, and better alternatives to driving for older adults.

Some auto insurance companies reduce payments for older adults who successfully complete driving classes such as the AARP Driver Safety Program. In 2004 the Driver Safety Program celebrated its twenty-fifth anniversary. More than nine million drivers have taken the eight-hour refresher course, which offers guidance in assessing physical abilities and making adjustments accordingly. Each year approximately thirty-four thousand courses are conducted in communities nationwide. The American Automobile Association (AAA) offers a similar program called Safe Driving for Mature Operators that strives to improve the skills of older drivers. These courses address the aging process and help drivers adjust to age-related changes that can affect driving. Both organizations also provide resources to assist older drivers and their families to determine whether they can safely continue driving.

As of 2005 there were no upper age limits for driving. The National Institute on Aging observes that because people age at different rates, it is not possible to choose a specific age at which to suspend driving. Setting an age limit would leave some drivers on the road too long, while others would be forced to stop driving prematurely. Heredity, general health, lifestyle, and surroundings all influence how people age.

Many states are acting to reduce risks for older drivers by improving roadways to make driving less hazardous. According to the AARP, typical improvements include:

- Wider highway lanes

- Intersections that give drivers a longer view of oncoming traffic and allow more time for left turns

- Road signs with larger, more visible letters and numbers

TABLE 6.7

10 leading causes of nonfatal injury, 2003

Rank	<1	4-Jan	9-May	14-Oct	15–24	25–34	35–44	45–54	55–64	65+	All ages
					Age groups						
1	Unintentional fall 122,276	Unintentional fall 865,209	Unintentional fall 670,107	Unintentional fall 678,897	Unintentional struck by/against 973,073	Unintentional fall 754,691	Unintentional fall 812,270	Unintentional fall 739,365	Unintentional fall 563,973	Unintentional fall 1,822,157	Unintentional fall 7,895,385
2	Unintentional struck by/against 33,132	Unintentional struck by/against 364,168	Unintentional struck by/against 411,733	Unintentional struck by/against 593,148	Unintentional MV-occupant 916,330	Unintentional overexertion 694,464	Unintentional overexertion 657,267	Unintentional overexertion 436,494	Unintentional overexertion 193,361	Unintentional struck by/against 194,435	Unintentional struck by/against 4,422,252
3	Unintentional fire/burn 11,306	Unintentional other bite/sting 134,964	Unintentional cut/pierce 125,350	Unintentional overexertion 278,182	Unintentional fall 866,078	Unintentional struck by/against 675,770	Unintentional struck by/against 594,628	Unintentional struck by/against 390,563	Unintentional struck by/against 191,370	Unintentional MV-occupant 188,278	Unintentional overexertion 3,324,641
4	Unintentional other bite/sting 11,141	Unintentional foreign body 108,037	Unintentional pedal cyclist 113,513	Unintentional cut/pierce 158,011	Unintentional overexertion 746,386	Unintentional MV-occupant 629,739	Unintentional MV-occupant 522,621	Unintentional MV-occupant 351,415	Unintentional MV-occupant 186,101	Unintentional overexertion 168,995	Unintentional MV-occupant 3,026,595
5	Unintentional cut/pierce 7,731	Unintentional cut/pierce 85,140	Unintentional other bite/sting 91,662	Unintentional pedal cyclist 141,252	Unintentional cut/pierce 493,032	Unintentional cut/pierce 441,956	Unintentional cut/pierce 391,061	Unintentional cut/pierce 273,232	Unintentional cut/pierce 143,244	Unintentional cut/pierce 116,915	Unintentional cut/pierce 2,235,869
6	Unintentional MV-occupant 7,713	Unintentional overexertion 67,227	Unintentional other bite/sting 76,045	Unintentional unknown/unspecified 117,463	Other assault* struck by/against 436,395	Other assault* struck by/against 270,689	Other assault* struck by/against 218,136	Unintentional other specified 141,179	Unintentional other bite/sting 65,417	Unintentional other bite/sting 77,191	Other assault* struck by/against 1,247,857
7	Unintentional foreign body 7,465	Unintentional poisoning 62,661	Unintentional MV-occupant 71,653	Other assault* struck by/against 116,873	Unintentional other bite/sting 164,502	Unintentional other bite/sting 141,176	Unintentional other specified 175,356	Unintentional other bite/sting 106,604	Unintentional other specified 51,566	Unintentional poisoning 46,581	Unintentional other bite/sting 998,451
8	Unintentional poisoning 6,095	Unintentional fire/burn 58,931	Unintentional other transport 51,878	Unintentional MV-occupant 108,609	Unintentional unknown/unspecified 164,325	Unintentional other specified 138,591	Unintentional other bite/sting 142,866	Other assault* struck by/against 101,341	Unintentional poisoning 34,436	Unintentional other transport 46,507	Unintentional other specified 763,029
9	Unintentional overexertion 5,975	Unintentional unknown/unspecified 50,343	Unintentional dog bite 49,285	Unintentional other transport 64,821	Unintentional other specified 148,112	Unintentional other transport 102,373	Unintentional poisoning 106,914	Unintentional poisoning 86,187	Unintentional unknown/unspecified 32,529	Unintentional unknown/unspecified 45,837	Unintentional unknown/unspecified 688,779
10	Unintentional unknown/unspecified 5,703	Unintentional MV-occupant 43,495	Unintentional foreign body 48,816	Unintentional other bite/sting 62,926	Unintentional other transport 137,327	Unintentional unknown/unspecified 97,096	Unintentional foreign body 89,692	Unintentional other transport 63,781	Unintentional other transport 32,097	Unintentional other specified 36,156	Unintentional other transport 619,544

*The 'other assault' category includes all assaults that are **not** classified as sexual assault. It represents the majority of assaults.

SOURCE: "10 Leading Causes of Nonfatal Injury, United States 2003, All Races, Both Sexes, Disposition: All Cases," in *WISQARS Leading Causes of Nonfatal Injury Reports*, Centers for Disease Control and Prevention, National Center for Injury Prevention and Control, Office of Statistics and Programming, Atlanta, GA, 2004, http://www.cdc.gov/ncipc/wisqars/nonfatal/quickpicks/quickpicks_2003/allinj.htm (accessed August 11, 2005)

- Bigger orange construction-zone cones
- More rumble strips to reduce speeding

The following are some specific examples of modifications to enhance safety:

- Florida's Elder Roadway User Program includes the installation of reflective pavement markers to illuminate roads when conditions are dark or rainy. Street names are displayed well in advance of intersections. Stop, yield, and warning signs have new, larger lettering.

- The Wisconsin Department of Transportation is making road lanes at least twelve feet wide, using reflective paints, and designing intersections and road curvatures for easier navigation by older drivers.

SPEED-OF-PROCESSING TRAINING MAY REDUCE ACCIDENTS INVOLVING OLDER ADULTS. As outlined in a press release by the American Geriatrics Society (http://www.americangeriatrics.org/news/elderly_training.shtml, May 14, 2005), research suggests that because age-related declines in visual information processing often contribute to older drivers' accidents, special training that enhances visual information processing ability could help prevent accidents involving older drivers. Investigators at the VA Medical Center in Birmingham, Alabama, studied forty-five veterans, ages sixty to eighty, with impaired driving abilities. The veterans were divided into two groups: a control group received training in navigating the Internet, while the rest attended speed-of-processing (SOP) training sessions. Those who received SOP training—improving visual information processing by challenging subjects with increasingly difficult visual attention tasks—showed a marked increase in their ability to process visual information. During timed tests the subjects trained in SOP were much faster at identifying specific items on a computer screen filled with a variety of visual distractions.

PROVIDING FOR ALTERNATIVE MEANS OF TRANSPORTATION

Research conducted by the U.S. Government Accountability Office (GAO) considered issues and services for "transportation-disadvantaged" older adults—those who cannot drive or have limited their driving, or those who have an income restraint, disability, or medical condition that limits their ability to travel. The study aimed to identify federal programs that address this population's mobility issues; the extent to which these programs meet their mobility needs; program practices that enhance their mobility and the cost-effectiveness of service delivery; and obstacles to addressing mobility needs and strategies for overcoming those obstacles. The August 2004 report *Transportation-Disadvantaged Seniors: Efforts to Enhance Senior Mobility Could*

Benefit from Additional Guidance and Information identified fifteen federal programs designed to meet the transportation needs of older adults. Table 6.8 shows the various characteristics of each program, including sponsoring agency, target population served, types of trips covered, and type of service provided. For example the Department of Health and Human Services (HHS) Administration on Aging (AoA) funds Community Services Block Grant Programs, which provide taxicab vouchers and bus tokens that enable low-income older adults to take general trips. However, the AoA's Social Service Block Grants only provide assistance for transport to and from medical or social service appointments.

The GAO also pointed out that in addition to the programs intended to provide assistance specifically to older people, there are other programs designed to aid transportation-disadvantaged segments of the population, including older adults. The Americans with Disabilities Act of 1990 (ADA), for example, required that changes to public transportation be made to provide better accessibility for persons with disabilities; about half of ADA-eligible riders are age sixty-five and older. Also the Transportation Equity Act for the 21st Century (TEA-21), enacted in 1998, authorized funds for several programs, including a formula grant that supported states' efforts to meet the special transportation needs of older adults and people with disabilities.

Types of Transportation for Nondrivers

Transportation for older adults can include door-to-door services such as taxis or van services, public buses that travel along fixed routes, or ridesharing in carpools. According to the AoA, there are three general classes of alternative transportation for older adults:

- Demand response, also known as Dial-a-Ride, generally requires advance reservations and provides door-to-door service from one specific location to another. Such systems offer older adults comfortable and relatively flexible transport, with the potential for adapting to the needs of individual riders. Payment of fares or donations for demand-response transport is usually required on a per-ride basis.

- Fixed route and scheduled services follow a predetermined route, stopping at established locations at specific times to allow passengers to board and disembark. This type of service typically requires payment of fares on a per-ride basis. Older adults are often eligible for discounted rates.

- Ridesharing programs connect people who need rides with drivers who have room in their cars and are willing to take passengers. This system generally offers scheduled transportation to a particular destination, such as a place of employment, senior center, or medical center.

TABLE 6.8

Characteristics of 15 key federal programs that fund transportation for seniors

Agency	Program	Target population	Type of trip allowed	Type of service provided
Department of Education, Office of Special Education and Rehabilitative Services	Independent Living Services for Older Individuals Who Are Blind	Persons aged 55 and older who have significant visual impairment	To access program and related services, or for general trips	Referral, assistance, and training in the use of public transportation
Department of Health and Human Services, Administration for Children and Families	Community Services Block Grant Programs	Low-income persons (including seniors)	General trips	Taxicab vouchers, bus tokens
	Social Service Block Grants	Target population identified by states	To access medical or social services	Any transportation-related use
Department of Health and Human Services, Administration on Aging	Grants for Supportive Services and Senior Centers (Title III-B)	Seniors (aged 60 and older)	To access program services or medical services, or for general trips	Contract for service with existing transportation provider, or directly purchase vehicles (such as vans)
	Program for American Indian, Alaskan Native, and Native Hawaiian Elders (Title VI)	American Indian, Alaskan Native, and Native Hawaiian seniors	To access program services or medical services, or for general trips	Purchase and operation of vehicles (such as vans)
Department of Health and Human Services, Centers for Medicare and Medicaid Services	Medicaid	Generally low-income persons (including seniors), although states determine eligibility	Medicaid medical services (emergency and nonemergency)	Reimbursement for services with existing transportation providers (e.g., transit passes)
Department of Health and Human Services, Health Resources and Services Administration	Rural Health Care Services Outreach Program	Medically underserved populations (including seniors) in rural areas	To access healthcare services	Transit passes, purchase vehicles (such as vans)
Department of Labor, Employment and Training Administration	Senior Community Service Employment Program	Low-income seniors (aged 55 and older)	To access employment opportunities	Reimbursement for mileage
Department of Transportation, Federal Transit Administration	Capital and Training Assistance Program for Over-the-Road Bus Accessibility	Persons with disabilities (including seniors)	General trips	Assistance in purchasing lift equipment and providing driver training
	Capital Assistance Program for Elderly Persons and Persons with Disabilities (Section 5310)	Seniors and persons with disabilities	General trips	Assistance in purchasing vehicles, contract for services with existing transportation providers
	Capital Investment Grants (Section 5309)	General public, although some projects are for the special needs of elderly persons and persons with disabilities	General trips	Assistance for bus and bus-related capital projects
	Job Access and Reverse Commute	Low-income persons (including seniors)	To access employment and related services	Expansion of existing public transportation or initiation of new service
	Nonurbanized Area Formula Program (Section 5311)	General public in rural areas (including seniors)	General trips	Capital and operating assistance for public transportation
	Urbanized Area Formula Program (Section 5307)	General public in urban areas (including seniors)	General trips	Capital assistance, and some operating assistance, for public transportation
Department of Veterans Affairs, Veterans Health Administration	Veterans Medical Care Benefits	Veterans (including seniors) with disabilities or low incomes	To access healthcare services	Mileage reimbursement or contract for service with existing transportation providers

Note: It was not possible to determine the amount spent on transportation services through many of these federal programs.

SOURCE: "Table 1. Characteristics of 15 Key Federal Programs That Fund Transportation for Seniors," in *Transportation-Disadvantaged Seniors: Efforts to Enhance Senior Mobility Could Benefit from Additional Guidance and Information*, U.S. Government Accountability Office, Washington, DC, August 2004, http://www.gao.gov/new.items/d04971.pdf (accessed August 11, 2005)

Meeting the Transportation Needs of Older Adults

In the report *Transportation-Disadvantaged Seniors: Efforts to Enhance Senior Mobility Could Benefit from Additional Guidance and Information*, the GAO cited research by the Beverly Foundation that identified five attributes necessary for alternative transportation services for older adults:

• Availability—older adults can travel to desired locations at the times they want to go.

TABLE 6.9

Obstacles, strategies, and trade-offs associated with meeting transportation-disadvantaged seniors' mobility needs

Obstacles	Strategies	Trade-offs
Seniors are not sufficiently encouraged to plan for driving alternatives	Facilitate a gradual transition from driver to nondriver	Can increase demand for services and, therefore, increase costs
Government policies do not always address seniors' varied needs	Improve alternatives and include seniors in transportation-planning process	Can be expensive and time-consuming
Funding constraints limit local agencies' ability to address needs	Increase funding and funding flexibility and improve coordination	Takes funds away from other uses, flexibility can decrease accountability, and coordination requires sustained effort

SOURCE: "Obstacles, Strategies, and Trade-offs Associated with Meeting Transportation-Disadvantaged Seniors' Mobility Needs, as Identified by Experts and Stakeholders," in *Transportation-Disadvantaged Seniors: Efforts to Enhance Senior Mobility Could Benefit from Additional Guidance and Information*, U.S. Government Accountability Office, Washington, DC, August 2004, http://www.gao.gov/new.items/d04971.pdf (accessed August 11, 2005)

- Accessibility—vehicles can be accessed by those with disabilities; services can be door-to-door or door-through-door as necessary; stops are pedestrian-friendly.

- Acceptability—transport is safe, clean, and easy to use.

- Affordability—financial assistance is available if necessary.

- Adaptability—multiple trips and special equipment can be accommodated.

The GAO study did highlight specific unmet needs, such as transport to multiple destinations or for purposes that involve carrying packages; to life-enhancing activities, such as cultural events; and in rural and suburban areas. However, the investigators discovered that there were limited data available to quantify or assess the extent of the needs that went unmet. The study also identified obstacles to addressing transportation-disadvantaged older adults' mobility needs, potential strategies that federal and other government entities might take to better meet these needs, and trade-offs associated with implementing each strategy. For example, the researchers found that older drivers are not encouraged to investigate or plan for a time when they will be unable to drive. One way to address this obstacle might be to institute educational programs that would ease older adults' transition from driver to nondriver. This strategy does, however, have the potential to increase demand for alternative transportation services and the costs associated with their provision. (See Table 6.9.)

Suggestions garnered by the study for increasing and improving alternative transportation services included enlisting the aid of volunteer drivers; sponsoring demonstration programs, identifying best practices, and increasing cooperation among federal programs; and establishing a central clearinghouse of information that could be accessed by stakeholders in the various programs. The GAO researchers recommended that the AoA improve the value and consistency of information pertaining to older adults' transportation needs that is received from area agencies on aging, including providing guidance for those agencies on assessing mobility needs. The AoA also was called upon to keep older adults and their caregivers better informed of alternative transportation programs, and to ensure that the best methods and practices are shared among transportation and social service providers in order to enhance the older population's mobility.

CHAPTER 7

THE HEALTH AND MEDICAL PROBLEMS
OF OLDER ADULTS

Among the fears many people have about aging is coping with losses—not only declining mental and physical abilities but also the prospect of failing health, chronic illness, and disability. Although aging is associated with physiological changes, the rate and extent of these changes varies widely. One person may be limited by arthritis at age sixty-five, while another is vigorous and active at age ninety.

Despite the increasing proportion of active healthy older adults, it is true that the incidence (the rate of new cases of a disorder over a specified period of time) and prevalence (the total number of cases of a disorder in a given population at a specific time) of selected diseases as well as the utilization of health-care services increase with advancing age. For example, the incidence of diabetes, heart disease, breast cancer, Parkinson's disease, and Alzheimer's disease increases with age. In contrast, the incidence of other diseases, such as HIV infection, multiple sclerosis, and schizophrenia, decreases with age.

This chapter considers the epidemiology of aging—the distribution and determinants of health and illness among older adults. It describes trends in aging and the health of aging Americans; distinctions between healthy aging, disease, and disability; health promotion and prevention as applied to older persons; and selected diseases and conditions common in old age.

GENERAL HEALTH OF OLDER AMERICANS

The proportion of adults rating their health as good to excellent declines with advancing age. In 2004 nearly 82% of persons under age eighteen and 66% of those eighteen to sixty-four consider themselves in very good or excellent health compared with just 37% of adults age sixty-five and older. (See Figure 7.1.)

According to the report *Older Americans 2004: Key Indicators of Well-Being* (Federal Interagency Forum on Aging Related Statistics, http://www.agingstats.gov/chartbook2004/default.htm, November 1, 2004), among non-Hispanic white men, 79% of respondents sixty-five to seventy-four said their health was good or better than good, compared with just 65% of non-Hispanic white men age eighty-five and over. Although the difference is the most dramatic among non-Hispanic white men, men and women of other races and ethnic categories followed the same pattern. Across all older age groups, non-Hispanic white men and women were more likely to report good health than non-Hispanic African-American and Hispanic older adults. (See Figure 7.2.)

According to the same report, most older persons have at least one chronic (long-term) condition and many have several. Among the most frequently occurring conditions of older adults in 2001–02 were hypertension (49.2%), arthritic symptoms (36.1%), all types of heart disease (31.1%), cancer (20.0%), sinusitis (15.1%), and diabetes (15.0%).

Overall, rates of chronic disability among Americans age sixty-five and older decreased from 25% in 1984 to 20% in 1999, however, despite the decline in rates, the number of older Americans with disabilities increased from 6.2 million in 1984 to 6.8 million in 1999. This is because growth of the population of older adults offset the decline in disability rates. In 1999, 15% of noninstitutionalized adults age sixty-five and older were unable to perform one or more activities of daily living (ADLs), such as bathing and dressing, getting in and out of bed, getting around in the home, eating, and toileting. (See Figure 7.3.) Noninstitutionalized individuals are considered chronically disabled if they cannot perform at least one ADL for ninety days or longer.

In addition to ADLs, there are other measures of disability, such as instrumental activities of daily living (IADLs) and measures of physical, cognitive, and social functioning. IADLs include activities such as light housework, meal preparation, laundry, grocery shopping, getting around outside

FIGURE 7.1

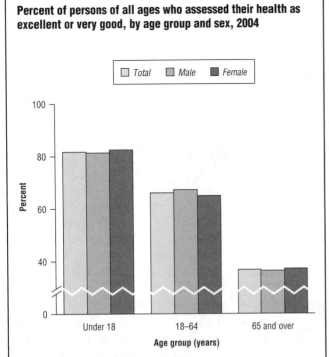

Percent of persons of all ages who assessed their health as excellent or very good, by age group and sex, 2004

Notes: Health status data were obtained by asking respondents to assess their own health and that of family members living in the same household as excellent, very good, good, fair, or poor. The analyses excluded 381 persons (0.41%) with unknown health status.

SOURCE: "Figure 11.3. Percent of Persons of All Ages Who Assessed Their Health as Excellent or Very Good, by Age Group and Sex, 2004," in *Early Release of Selected Estimates Based on Data from the 2004 National Health Interview Survey*, Centers for Disease Control and Prevention, National Center for Health Statistics, Hyattsville, MD, June 29, 2005, http://www.cdc.gov/nchs/data/nhis/earlyrelease/earlyrelease200506.pdf (accessed August 11, 2005)

FIGURE 7.2

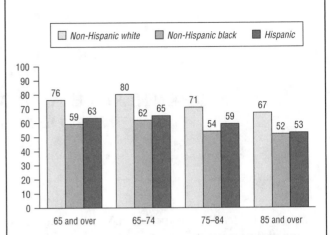

Percentage of people age 65 and over who reported having good to excellent health, by age group, race, and Hispanic origin, 2000–02

Note: Data are based on a 3-year average from 2000–2002. People of Hispanic origin may be of any race.
Reference population: These data refer to the civilian noninstitutionalized population.

SOURCE: "Percentage of People Age 65 and Over Who Reported Having Good to Excellent Health, by Age Group and Race and Hispanic Origin, 2000–2002," in *Older Americans 2004: Key Indicators*, Federal Interagency Forum on Aging Related Statistics, Washington, DC, U.S. Government Printing Office, November 2004, http://www.agingstats.gov/chartbook2004/healthstatus.html#Indicator%2020 (accessed August 11, 2005)

the home, managing money, taking medications as prescribed, and telephoning. Noninstitutionalized individuals are considered chronically disabled if they cannot perform at least one IADL for ninety days or longer. Measures of physical functioning, such as the ability to stoop or kneel, lift heavy objects, walk a few blocks, or reach above the head, are also used to monitor progressive disability.

In 2002 older women reported more difficulties with physical functioning than older men—31% were unable to perform at least one physical function task compared with 18% of men. (See Figure 7.4.) Not surprisingly, problems with physical functioning increased with age. Only 13% of men sixty-five to seventy-four reported difficulty with at least one task compared with 35.1% of men eighty-five and older. One-fifth of women ages sixty-five to seventy-four were unable to perform one task, compared with 57.5% of those age eighty-five and older. (See Table 7.1.)

Hospital Utilization and Physician Visits

Adults age sixty-five and over have the highest rates of inpatient hospitalization and the longest average lengths

of stay (ALOS). In 2002 persons sixty-five to seventy-five had 251 hospital discharges per one thousand population—twice the number of discharges of adults forty-five to sixty-four. The highest number of discharges and longest ALOS were among adults seventy-five and older, 343 and 6.7 days respectively. (See Table 7.2.)

The ALOS for adults age sixty-five and older was 5.8 days in 2002, compared with 4.8 days for people age forty-five to fifty-four. ALOS among all age groups has declined since 1980 from a high of 7.5 days to 4.9 days in 2002. Among patients age seventy-five and older, ALOS decreased by almost one-half, from 11.4 days in 1980 to six days in 2002. (See Table 7.3.)

Shorter stays are in part due to the federal government's introduction of diagnosis-related groups (DRG) in the mid-1980s. (DRGs are categories of illnesses that prescribe, and allow for, set duration of treatment.) DRG-based reimbursement encourages hospitals to discharge patients as quickly as possible by compensating hospitals for a predetermined number of days per diagnosis, regardless of the actual length of stay. Shorter lengths of stay also are attributable to the increasing use of outpatient settings as opposed to hospital admission for an expanding range of procedures such as hernia repairs, gallbladder removal, and cataract surgery.

FIGURE 7.3

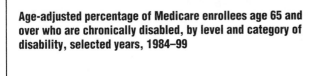

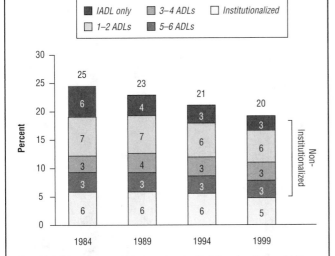

Age-adjusted percentage of Medicare enrollees age 65 and over who are chronically disabled, by level and category of disability, selected years, 1984–99

Note: Disabilities are grouped into two categories: limitations in activities of daily living (ADLs) and limitations in instrumental activities of daily living (IADLs). The six ADLs included are bathing, dressing, getting in or out of bed, getting around inside, toileting, and eating. The eight IADLs included are light housework, laundry, meal preparation, grocery shopping, getting around outside, managing money, taking medications, and telephoning. Individuals are considered to have an ADL disability if they report receiving help or supervision, or using equipment, to perform the activity, or not performing the activity at all. Individuals are considered to have an IADL disability if they report using equipment to perform the activity or not performing the activity at all because of their health or a disability. Individuals are considered to be chronically disabled if they have at least one IADL limitation that is expected to last 90 days or longer, or they are institutionalized. Data for 1989 do not sum to the total because of rounding.
Reference population: These data refer to Medicare enrollees.

SOURCE: "Age-Adjusted Percentage of Medicare Enrollees Age 65 and Over Who Are Chronically Disabled, by Level and Category of Disability, 1984, 1989, 1994, and 1999," in *Older Americans 2004: Key Indicators*, Federal Interagency Forum on Aging Related Statistics, Washington, DC, U.S. Government Printing Office, November 2004, http://www.agingstats.gov/chartbook2004/healthstatus.html#Indicator%2019 (accessed August 11, 2005)

The growing older population also uses more physician services. There were 11,359 physician visits and consultations per one thousand Medicare enrollees in 1992, compared with 13,685 in 2001. Home health care visits peaked at 8,227 per one thousand in 1997 and declined from 1997 to 2001 in response to implementation of the Balanced Budget Act of 1997, which sharply limited Medicare payment for home health care services. (See Figure 7.5.)

CHRONIC DISEASES AND CONDITIONS

Chronic diseases are prolonged illnesses such as arthritis, asthma, heart disease, diabetes, and cancer that do not resolve spontaneously and are rarely cured. According to the Centers for Disease Control and Prevention (CDC), chronic illnesses account for 70% of all deaths in the United States. Five of the six leading causes of death among older adults are chronic diseases—heart disease, cancer, cerebrovascular disease (stroke), chronic lower respiratory diseases, and diabetes mellitus. (The sole acute infectious leading cause of death is influenza and pneumonia.) While other chronic conditions such as arthritis, asthma, and chronic bronchitis are not immediately life threatening, they compromise the quality-of-life of affected individuals and place an enormous financial burden on individuals, families, and the United States health care system.

The prevalence of chronic conditions varies by gender, race, and ethnicity. As illustrated in Figure 7.6, older women suffer from hypertension (high blood pressure), asthma, chronic bronchitis, and arthritis more than older men. Older men have higher levels of heart disease, strokes, cancer, diabetes, and emphysema—a lung disease, most often caused by tobacco smoke, in which the air sacs are enlarged and damaged, impairing breathing. The *Older Americans 2004: Key Indicators of Well-Being* report reveals older non-Hispanic African-Americans have higher levels of hypertension and diabetes than non-Hispanic whites (66% compared with 49% for hypertension and 23% compared with 14% for diabetes). Hispanics also suffer higher rates of diabetes than non-Hispanic whites—24% compared with 14%.

The prevalence of some chronic conditions such as hypertension and diabetes is increasing in the general population and among older adults. In 1998, 47% of older adults suffered from hypertension and 13% had diabetes. By 2002 the percentage of persons sixty-five and older with hypertension and diabetes rose 3%, to 50% and 16% respectively. (See Table 7.4.) The increase in these conditions is largely attributable to increasing rates of obesity, which is implicated in the development of these and many other chronic conditions.

Arthritis

The word "arthritis" literally means joint inflammation, and it is applied to more than one hundred related diseases known as rheumatic diseases. When a joint—the point where two bones meet—becomes inflamed, swelling, redness, pain, and loss of motion occur. In the most serious forms of the disease, the loss of motion can be physically disabling.

Normally, inflammation is the body's response to an injury or a disease. Once the injury heals or the disease is cured, the inflammation stops. In arthritis, however, the inflammation does not subside. Instead, it becomes part of the problem, damaging healthy tissues. This generates more inflammation, and more damage, and the painful cycle continues. The damage can change the shape of bones and other tissues of the joints, making movement difficult and painful.

FIGURE 7.4

Percentage of Medicare enrollees age 65 and over who are unable to perform certain physical functions, by sex, 1991 and 2002

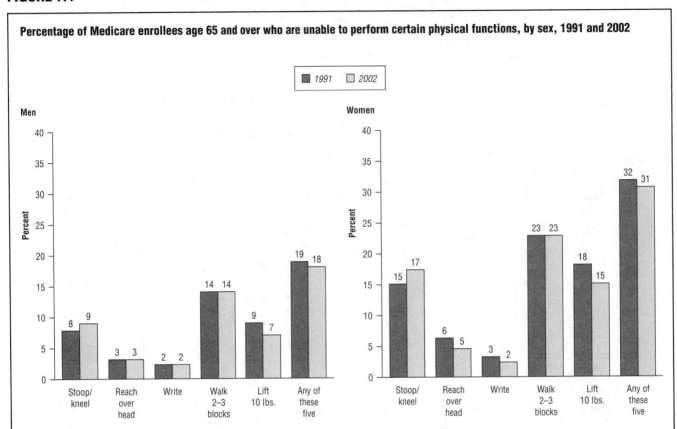

Note: Rates for 1991 are age-adjusted to the 2002 population.
Reference population: These data refer to Medicare enrollees.

SOURCE: "Percentage of Medicare Enrollees Age 65 and Over Who are Unable to Perform Certain Physical Functions, by Sex, 1991 and 2002," in *Older Americans 2004: Key Indicators*, Federal Interagency Forum on Aging Related Statistics, Washington, DC, U.S. Government Printing Office, November 2004, http://www.agingstats.gov/chartbook2004/healthstatus.html#Indicator%2019 (accessed August 11, 2005)

TABLE 7.1

Percentage of Medicare enrollees age 65 and over who are unable to perform any one of five physical functions, by selected characteristics, 2002

Selected characteristic	Percent	
	Men	Women
65–74	13	20
75–84	21.3	32.9
85 and over	35.1	57.5
White, not Hispanic or Latino	17.3	30.4
Black, not Hispanic or Latino	25.5	35.9
Hispanic or Latino	21.7	28.6

Reference population: These data refer to Medicare enrollees.

SOURCE: "Percentage of Medicare Enrollees Age 65 and Over Who are Unable to Perform Any One of Five Physical Functions, by Selected Characteristics, 2002," in *Older Americans 2004: Key Indicators*, Federal Interagency Forum on Aging Related Statistics, Washington, DC, U.S. Government Printing Office, November 2004, http://www.agingstats.gov/chartbook2004/tables-healthstatus.html#Indicator%2019 (accessed August 11, 2005)

More than one hundred types of arthritis have been identified, but four major types affect large numbers of older Americans:

- Osteoarthritis—the most common type, generally affects people as they grow older. Sometimes called degenerative arthritis, it causes the breakdown of bones and cartilage (connective issue attached to bones) and pain and stiffness in the fingers, knees, feet, hips, and back. According to the National Arthritis Data Workgroup, osteoarthritis affects about twenty million Americans, usually after age forty-five.

- Fibromyalgia—affects the muscles and connective tissues and causes widespread pain, as well as fatigue, sleep problems, and stiffness. Fibromyalgia also causes "tender points" that are more sensitive to pain than other areas of the body. According to the National Fibromyalgia Association, ten million Americans, mostly women, suffer from this condition.

- Rheumatoid arthritis—an inflammatory form of arthritis caused by a flaw in the body's immune system. The result is inflammation and swelling in the joint lining, followed by damage to bone and cartilage in the hands, wrists, feet, knees, ankles, shoulders, or elbows. According to the National Women's Health

TABLE 7.2

Discharges, days of care, and average length of stay in short-stay hospitals, selected characteristics, selected years, 1997–2002

[Data are based on household interviews of a sample of the civilian noninstitutionalized population]

Characteristic	Discharges			Days of care			Average length of stay		
	1997	1999	2002	1997	1999	2002	1997	1999	2002
	Number per 1,000 population						Number of days		
Total[b,c]	124.3	119.7	122.9	601.2	555.1	541.0	4.8	4.6	4.4
Age									
Under 18 years	90.8	76.3	80.4	319.0	302.6	267.0	3.5	4.0	3.3
Under 6 years	203.5	183.2	186.7	632.6	664.8	593.5	3.1	3.6	3.2
6–17 years	34.0	24.3	29.0	163.1	126.5*	109.6	4.8	5.2*	3.8
18–44 years	96.8	95.8	95.1	358.8	352.8	313.4	3.7	3.7	3.3
45–64 years	124.9	125.6	124.1	631.1	592.5	573.0	5.1	4.7	4.6
45–54 years	99.2	110.1	106.6	527.5	473.9	493.5	5.3	4.3	4.6
55–64 years	164.8	149.6	150.7	792.4	775.5	693.7	4.8	5.2	4.6
65 years and over	274.4	269.7	293.1	1,852.5	1,620.5	1,738.7	6.8	6.0	5.9
65–74 years	249.1	229.8	250.5	1,595.2	1,386.4	1,270.4	6.4	6.0	5.1
75 years and over	307.3	318.5	342.6	2,188.4	1,907.6	2,283.5	7.1	6.0	6.7
Under 65 years of age									
All persons under 65 years of age[b,d]	102.2	97.6	98.1	416.4	398.9	365.5	4.1	4.1	3.7
Sex[d]									
Male	79.1	77.9	72.8	374.9	374.0	313.2	4.7	4.8	4.3
Female	124.7	116.7	122.7	456.6	422.8	416.2	3.7	3.6	3.4
Race[d,e]									
White only	100.8	94.7	96.4	385.8	368.7	343.0	3.8	3.9	3.6
Black or African American only	126.3	122.8	121.2	688.6	638.3	533.8	5.5	5.2	4.4
American Indian and Alaska Native only	111.9	128.3	122.7*	494.3*	570.0*	707.9*	4.4*	4.4*	5.8*
Asian only	61.7	78.4	44.7*	268.6	249.5	151.0	4.4*	3.2	3.4
Native Hawaiian and Other Pacific Islander only	—	*	*	—	*	*	—	*	*
2 or more races	—	139.1	157.2*	—	688.8*	703.3*	—	5.0*	4.5*
Hispanic origin and race[d,e]									
Hispanic or Latino	109.9	90.1	95.9	416.7	389.8	380.5	3.8	4.3	4.0
Not Hispanic or Latino	101.2	98.7	98.4	415.4	401.5	363.8	4.1	4.1	3.7
White only	99.6	95.4	96.8	382.7	368.4	344.0	3.8	3.9	3.6
Black or African American only	125.7	122.7	121.1	692.6	625.5	515.1	5.5	5.1	4.3
Poverty status[d,f]									
Poor	186.0	168.6	158.3	922.0	875.8	747.9	5.0	5.2	4.7
Near poor	119.3	138.7	124.4	530.5	615.2	492.8	4.4	4.4	4.0
Nonpoor	82.7	78.8	83.0	308.9	285.1	283.3	3.7	3.6	3.4
Hispanic origin and race and poverty status[d,e,f]									
Hispanic or Latino:									
Poor	152.3	119.7	134.1	592.3	558.4	611.6	3.9	4.7	4.6
Near poor	92.7	98.0	105.0	415.0	499.2	381.8	4.5	5.1*	3.6
Nonpoor	92.1	74.7	73.5	294.5	285.2	291.3	3.2	3.8	4.0
Not Hispanic or Latino:									
White only:									
Poor	205.2	182.7	159.2	955.5	907.4	693.8	4.7	5.0	4.4
Near poor	124.3	153.2	128.6	503.4	600.7	486.6	4.0	3.9	3.8
Nonpoor	83.1	78.7	85.0	303.0	284.1	286.1	3.6	3.6	3.4
Black or African American only:									
Poor	199.0	202.4	199.1	1,300.3*	1,216.7	1,165.9*	6.5*	6.0	5.9*
Near poor	139.1	140.9	129.8	819.0	839.1	612.0*	5.9	6.0	4.7*
Nonpoor	85.2	82.4	93.0	402.1	300.9	291.6	4.7	3.7	3.1

Information Center (NWHIC), about 2.1 million persons, mostly women, have this form of arthritis.

- Gout—an inflammation of a joint caused by an accumulation of a natural substance, uric acid, in the joint, usually the big toe, knee, or wrist. The uric acid forms crystals in the affected joint, causing severe pain and swelling. This form affects more men than women, claiming about one million sufferers.

PREVALENCE. Arthritis is a very common problem. In 2005 the CDC reported that more than forty-six million Americans had been diagnosed with arthritis, another twenty-three million suffer chronic joint symptoms but have not yet been diagnosed, and more than seven million are disabled by the disease. The total number is expected to increase to more than sixty million by 2025, with eleven million suffering from a disabling form of the disease. (See Figure 7.7.)

TABLE 7.2

Discharges, days of care, and average length of stay in short-stay hospitals, selected characteristics, selected years, 1997–2002 [CONTINUED]

[Data are based on household interviews of a sample of the civilian noninstitutionalized population]

Characteristic	Discharges			Days of care			Average length of stay		
	1997	1999	2002	1997	1999	2002	1997	1999	2002
	Number per 1,000 population						Number of days		
Health insurance status[d,g]									
Insured	108.1	101.6	104.0	442.5	416.8	389.7	4.1	4.1	3.7
Private	85.6	80.2	84.2	310.2	287.8	274.9	3.6	3.6	3.3
Medicaid	311.6	332.5	278.3	1,575.3	1,695.5	1,305.3	5.1	5.1	4.7
Uninsured	75.3	75.7	69.0	296.3	304.2	249.0	3.9	4.0	3.6

*Estimates are considered unreliable.
— Data not available.
[b]Includes all other races not shown separately and unknown health insurance status.
[c]Estimates for all persons are age adjusted to the year 2000 standard population using six age groups: Under 18 years, 18–44 years, 45–54 years, 55–64 years, 65–74 years, and 75 years of age and over.
[d]Estimates are for persons under 65 years of age and are age adjusted to the year 2000 standard population using four age groups: Under 18 years, 18–14 years, 45–54 years, and 55–64 years of age.
[e]The race groups, white, black, American Indian and Alaska Native (AI/AN), Asian, Native Hawaiian and Other Pacific Islander, and 2 or more races, include persons of Hispanic and non-Hispanic origin. Persons of Hispanic origin may be of any race. The 1999 race-specific estimates are for persons who reported only one racial group; the category "2 or more races" includes persons who reported more than one racial group. Prior to data year 1999, data were tabulated with four racial groups and the category "Asian only" included Native Hawaiian and Other Pacific Islander. Estimates for single race categories prior to 1999 included persons who reported one race or, if they reported more than one race, identified one race as best representing their race.
[f]Poor persons are defined as below the poverty threshold. Near poor persons have incomes of 100 percent to less than 200 percent of the poverty threshold. Nonpoor persons have incomes of 200 percent or greater than the poverty threshold. Starting with Health, United States, 2004 a new methodology for imputing family income was used for data years 1997 and beyond. Missing family income data were imputed for 24–28 percent of persons under 65 years of age in 1997–98 and 30–31 percent in 1999–2002; and 36–11 percent of persons 65 years of age and over in 1997–98 and 44–47 percent in 1999–2002.
[g]Health insurance categories are mutually exclusive. Persons who reported both Medicaid and private coverage are classified as having private coverage. Persons 65 years of age and over who reported Medicare HMO (health maintenance organization) and some other type of health insurance coverage are classified as having Medicare HMO. Starting in 1997 Medicaid includes state-sponsored health plans and State Children's Health Insurance Program (SCHIP). The category "insured" also includes military, other state, and Medicare coverage.

SOURCE: "Table 92. Discharges, Days of Care, and Average Length of Stay in Short-Stay Hospitals, According to Selected Characteristics: United States, Selected Years 1997–2002," in *Health, United States, 2004*, Centers for Disease Control and Prevention, National Center for Health Statistics, Hyattsville, MD, 2004, http://www.cdc.gov/nchs/data/hus/hus04trend.pdf (accessed August 11, 2005)

Arthritis is the leading cause of disability in the United States. Rheumatic and musculoskeletal disorders are the most frequently reported cause of impairment in the adult population, the leading cause of limitation of mobility, and the second-leading cause of activity restriction.

As shown in Table 7.5, about half of all people over age sixty-five will experience some form of arthritis in their lifetimes. In all age groups women have a slightly higher likelihood of developing arthritis, and as they age, women have an increasingly higher prevalence of arthritis than men do. As shown in "Racial/Ethnic Differences in the Prevalence and Impact of Doctor-Diagnosed Arthritis—United States, 2002" (*Morbidity and Mortality Weekly Report*, vol. 54, no. 5, February 2005), between the ages of sixty-five and seventy-four, women have a 20% greater likelihood of developing arthritis than men, and women age seventy-five and older are 40% more likely to develop the disease.

Osteoporosis

Osteoporosis is a skeletal disorder characterized by compromised bone strength, which predisposes affected individuals to increased risk of fracture. The National Osteoporosis Foundation (NOF) defines osteoporosis as about 25% bone loss compared with a healthy young adult, or, on a bone density test, 2.5 standard deviations below normal. Although some bone loss occurs naturally with advancing age, the stooped posture (kyphosis) and loss of height (greater than one to two inches) experienced by many older adults result from vertebral fractures caused by osteoporosis.

In 2004 about ten million Americans over age fifty had been diagnosed with osteoporosis, and another thirty-four million were considered at risk of developing the condition. Like other chronic conditions that disproportionately affect older adults, the prevalence of bone disease and fractures is projected to increase markedly as the population ages. According to a report issued by the U.S. Surgeon General, "Bone Health and Osteoporosis: A Report of the Surgeon General 2004" (U.S. Department of Health and Human Services, http://www.surgeongeneral.gov/library/bonehealth/content.html, April 11, 2005), each year about 1.5 million people suffer an osteoporotic-related fracture, which often leads to a downward spiral in physical and mental health—about 20% of older adults who suffer hip fractures die within one year.

According to the same report, one out of every two women over fifty will have an osteoporosis-related fracture in her lifetime, with the risk of fracture increasing with age. The aging of the population combined with the historic lack of focus on bone health may together cause the number of hip fractures in the United States to double or even triple by the year 2020.

TABLE 7.3

Discharges, days of care, and average length of stay in non-federal short-stay hospitals, selected characteristics, selected years 1980–2002

[Data are based on a sample of hospital records]

Characteristic	1980[a]	1985[a]	1990	1995	1997	1998	2000[b]	2001[b]	2002[b]
	Discharges per 1,000 population								
Total[c]	173.4	151.4	125.2	118.0	116.1	117.9	113.3	115.1	117.3
Age									
Under 18 years	75.6	61.4	46.4	42.4	40.6	40.4	40.3	43.4	43.4
18–44 years	155.3	128.0	102.7	91.4	86.0	88.8	84.9	87.3	90.3
45–54 years	174.8	146.8	112.4	98.5	93.7	92.7	92.1	94.4	95.6
55–64 years	215.4	194.8	163.3	148.3	149.1	155.1	141.5	139.3	146.5
65 years and over	383.7	369.8	334.1	347.7	361.1	365.3	353.4	354.3	357.5
65–74 years	315.8	297.2	261.6	260.0	265.9	267.6	254.6	256.1	254.0
75 years and over	489.3	475.6	434.0	459.1	474.0	477.4	462.0	460.0	466.6
Sex[c]									
Male	153.2	137.3	113.0	104.8	103.0	102.8	99.1	100.0	102.4
Female	195.0	167.3	139.0	131.7	130.0	133.3	127.7	130.6	132.9
Geographic region[c]									
Northeast	162.0	142.6	133.2	133.5	125.5	127.3	127.5	125.2	123.5
Midwest	192.1	158.1	128.8	113.3	115.5	116.4	110.9	113.5	113.6
South	179.7	155.5	132.5	125.2	122.4	126.4	120.9	126.3	126.7
West	150.5	145.7	100.7	96.7	97.9	97.1	89.4	88.8	99.7
	Days of care per 1,000 population								
Total[c]	1,297.0	997.5	818.9	638.6	595.2	598.6	557.7	562.2	570.9
Age									
Under 18 years	341.4	281.2	226.3	184.7	169.8	182.4	179.0	192.5	195.2
18–44 years	818.6	619.2	467.7	351.7	317.4	328.3	309.4	322.7	333.9
45–54 years	1,314.9	967.8	699.7	516.2	460.8	452.9	437.4	455.4	456.7
55–64 years	1,889.4	1,436.9	1,172.3	867.2	821.4	836.1	729.1	732.2	752.2
65 years and over	4,098.3	3,228.0	2,895.6	2,373.7	2,285.6	2,264.2	2,111.9	2,064.2	2,085.1
65–74 years	3,147.0	2,437.3	2,087.8	1,684.7	1,599.3	1,596.1	1,439.0	1,449.5	1,411.9
75 years and over	5,578.8	4,381.3	4,009.1	3,247.8	3,099.6	3,030.8	2,851.9	2,725.5	2,795.0
Sex[c]									
Male	1,239.7	973.3	805.8	623.9	573.8	576.7	535.9	534.5	549.5
Female	1,365.2	1,033.1	840.5	654.9	619.3	622.9	581.0	591.9	596.0
Geographic region[c]									
Northeast	1,400.6	1,113.0	1,026.7	839.0	739.2	731.0	718.6	697.7	690.0
Midwest	1,484.8	1,078.6	830.6	590.9	556.3	552.5	500.5	491.6	502.1
South	1,262.3	957.7	820.4	666.0	629.5	643.9	592.5	623.6	618.6
West	956.9	824.7	575.5	451.1	445.3	450.4	408.2	408.3	454.7

One of the goals of the treatment of osteoporosis is to maintain bone health by preventing bone loss and by building new bone. Another is to minimize the risk and impact of falls, since they can cause fractures. Figure 7.8 shows the pyramid of prevention and treatment of osteoporosis. At its base is nutrition (with adequate intake of calcium, vitamin D, and other minerals), physical exercise, and preventive measures to reduce the risk of falls. The second layer of the pyramid involves identifying and treating diseases that can cause osteoporosis, such as thyroid disease. The peak of the pyramid involves drug therapy for osteoporosis. There are two primary types of drugs used to treat osteoporosis. Antiresorptive agents act to reduce bone loss, and anabolic agents are drugs that build bone. Antiresorptive therapies include use of bisphosphonates, estrogen, selective estrogen receptor modulators (SERMs), and calcitonin. Antiresorptive therapies reduce bone loss, stabilize the architecture of the bone, and decrease bone turnover. In 2005 the Food and Drug Administration (FDA) had approved two bisphosphonates—alendronate and risedronate—for prevention or treatment of osteoporosis and one anabolic agent, a synthetic form of parathyroid hormone known as teriparatide that is administered by injection.

EXERCISE IMPROVES BONE HEALTH IN OLDER ADULTS. The first study to examine the impact of exercise independent of other factors, primarily diet, on bone mineral density and the risk of osteoporosis and fractures confirmed that exercise helps to maintain and, in some cases, improve bone mass in persons ages fifty-five to seventy-five. Kerry Stewart summarized the details of this study in his article "Exercise Effects on Bone Mineral Density: Relationships to Change in Fitness and Fatness" (*American Journal of Preventive Medicine*, vol. 28, no. 5, June 2005). In the study, researchers at Johns Hopkins University School of Medicine in Baltimore, Maryland, followed 104 older men and women and found that six months of aerobic exercise using a bicycle,

TABLE 7.3

Discharges, days of care, and average length of stay in non-federal short-stay hospitals, selected characteristics, selected years 1980–2002 [CONTINUED]

[Data are based on a sample of hospital records]

Characteristic	1980[a]	1985[a]	1990	1995	1997	1998	2000[b]	2001[b]	2002[b]
					Average length of stay in days				
Total[c]	7.5	6.6	6.5	5.4	5.1	5.1	4.9	4.9	4.9
Age									
Under 18 years	4.5	4.6	4.9	4.4	4.2	4.5	4.4	4.4	4.5
18–44 years	5.3	4.8	4.6	3.8	3.7	3.7	3.6	3.7	3.7
45–54 years	7.5	6.6	6.2	5.2	4.9	4.9	4.8	4.8	4.8
55–64 years	8.8	7.4	7.2	5.8	5.5	5.4	5.2	5.3	5.1
65 years and over	10.7	8.7	8.7	6.8	6.3	6.2	6.0	5.8	5.8
65–74 years	10.0	8.2	8.0	6.5	6.0	6.0	5.7	5.7	5.6
75 years and over	11.4	9.2	9.2	7.1	6.5	6.3	6.2	5.9	6.0
Sex[c]									
Male	8.1	7.1	7.1	6.0	5.6	5.6	5.4	5.3	5.4
Female	7.0	6.2	6.0	5.0	4.8	4.7	4.6	4.5	4.5

[a]Comparisons of data from 1980–85 with data from later years should be made with caution as estimates of change may reflect improvements in the design rather than true changes in hospital use.
[b]Rates for 2000 were computed using Census 2000 counts and rates for 2001 and beyond were computed using 2000–based postcensal estimates.
[c]Estimates are age adjusted to the year 2000 standard population using six age groups: under 18 years, 18–44 years, 45–54 years, 55–64 years, 65–74 years, and 75 years and over.
Notes: Rates are based on the civilian population as of July 1.
Rates for 1990–99 are not strictly comparable with rates for 2000 and beyond because population estimates for 1990–99 have not been revised to reflect Census 2000.
Estimates of hospital utilization from the National Health Interview Survey (NHIS) and the National Hospital Discharge Survey (NHDS) may differ because NHIS data are based on household interviews of the civilian noninstitutionalized population, whereas NHDS data are based on hospital discharge records of all persons.

SOURCE: "Table 93. Discharges, Days of Care, and Average Length of Stay in Non-Federal Short-Stay Hospitals, According to Selected Characteristics: United States, Selected Years 1980–2002," in *Health, United States, 2004*, Centers for Disease Control and Prevention, National Center for Health Statistics, Hyattsville, MD, 2004, http://www.cdc.gov/nchs/data/hus/hus04trend.pdf (accessed August 11, 2005)

treadmill, or stepper, combined with weightlifting, resulted in improved overall fitness and fat loss without significant change in bone mineral density. Further, the study participants who exercised the hardest and had the greatest increases in aerobic fitness, muscle strength, and muscle tissue showed bone mass increases of 1% to 2%.

Diabetes

Diabetes is a disease that affects the body's use of food, causing blood glucose (sugar levels in the blood) to become too high. Normally the body converts sugars, starches, and proteins into a form of sugar called glucose. The blood then carries glucose to all cells throughout the body. In the cells, with the help of the hormone insulin, the glucose is either converted into energy for use immediately or stored for the future. Beta cells of the pancreas, a small organ located behind the stomach, manufacture the insulin. The process of turning food into energy via glucose is important because the body depends on glucose for every function.

In diabetes the body can convert food to glucose, but there is a problem with insulin. In one type of diabetes (insulin-dependent diabetes, or Type 1), the pancreas does not manufacture enough insulin, and in another type (non-insulin dependent, or Type 2), the body has insulin but cannot use the insulin effectively (this latter condition is called insulin resistance). When insulin is either absent or ineffective, glucose cannot get into the cells to be used for energy. Instead, the unused glucose builds up in the bloodstream and circulates

through the kidneys. If the blood-glucose level rises high enough, the excess glucose "spills" over into the urine, causing frequent urination. This, in turn, leads to an increased feeling of thirst as the body tries to compensate for the fluid lost through urination.

Type 2—non-insulin-dependent diabetes—is most often seen in adults and is the most common type of diabetes in the United States. In this type the pancreas produces insulin, but it is not used effectively and the body resists responding to it. Heredity may be a predisposing factor in the genesis of type 2 diabetes, but since the pancreas continues to produce insulin, the disease is considered more of a problem of insulin-resistance, in which the body is not using the hormone efficiently.

Because diabetes deprives cells of the glucose needed to function properly, several complications can develop to further threaten the lives of diabetics. The healing process of the body is slowed and there is increased risk of infection. Complications of diabetes include: higher risk and rates of heart disease; circulatory problems, especially in the legs, which are often severe enough to require surgery or even amputation; diabetic retinopathy, a condition that can cause blindness; kidney disease that may require dialysis; and dental problems. Close attention to preventive health care such as regular eye, dental, and foot examinations and tight control of blood sugar levels have been shown to prevent or delay some of the consequences of diabetes.

FIGURE 7.5

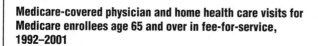

Medicare-covered physician and home health care visits for Medicare enrollees age 65 and over in fee-for-service, 1992–2001

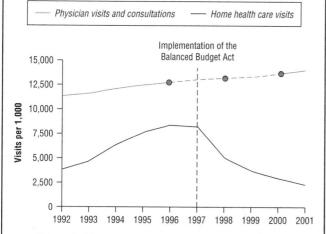

- - - - Data on physician visits and consultations are not available for 1997 and 1999.

Note: Data are for Medicare enrollees in fee-for-service only. Physician visits and consultations include all settings, such as physician offices, hospitals, emergency rooms, and nursing homes. Beginning in 1994, managed care enrollees were excluded from the denominator of all utilization rates because utilization data are not available for them. Prior to 1994, managed care enrollees were included in the denominators; they comprised 7 percent or less of the Medicare population. Reference population: These data refer to Medicare enrollees.

SOURCE: "Medicare-Covered Physician and Home Health Care Visits Per 1,000 Medicare Enrollees Age 65 and Over in Fee-for-Service, 1992–2001," in *Older Americans 2004: Key Indicators*, Federal Interagency Forum on Aging Related Statistics, Washington, DC, U.S. Government Printing Office, November 2004, http://www.agingstats.gov/chartbook2004/healthcare.html#Indicator%2028 (accessed August 11, 2005)

More than 80% of people with type 2 diabetes are overweight, and, in persons prone to type 2 diabetes, becoming overweight can trigger onset of the disease. It is not known precisely how being overweight contributes to causation of this disease. One hypothesis is that being overweight causes cells to change, making them less effective at using sugar from the blood. This then stresses the cells that produce insulin, causing them to gradually fail. Maintaining a healthy weight and keeping physically fit can usually prevent or delay the onset of type 2 diabetes.

The relatively recent rise in type 2 diabetes in the United States is in part attributed to rising obesity among adults. Between 1997 and 2004 the percent of adults diagnosed with diabetes increased from 5.1% to 7.1%. (See Figure 7.9.) Of all adult age groups, the highest rate of diagnosed diabetes was among adults age sixty-five and over. Worse still, these rates may significantly underestimate the true prevalence of diabetes in the United States in view of National Health and Nutrition Surveys findings that showed sizeable numbers of adults have undiagnosed diabetes.

Prostate Problems

Prostate problems typically occur after age fifty. There are three common prostate disorders—prostatitis (inflammation of the prostate gland), benign prostatic hyperplasia (BPH; noncancerous enlargement of the prostate), and prostatic carcinoma (prostate cancer). Prostatitis causes painful or difficult urination and frequently occurs in younger men. BPH also can create problems with urination, however it is most common in older men. According to W. Scott McDougal and Michael J. Berry in their report *Prostate Disease: Finding the Cause and Cure* (Boston, MA: Harvard Medical School, 2004), more than half of men in their sixties and as many as 90% of men in their eighties and nineties suffer from BPH.

Prostate cancer is the second-most common cause of cancer death after lung cancer in American men and the sixth-leading cause of death of men overall. According to the CDC, in the United States approximately 230,110 men were diagnosed with prostate cancer in 2004 and 29,900 died from it. When it is diagnosed and treated early, prostate cancer is generally not life threatening, because it progresses very slowly and remains localized for a long time. As a result, many men who are diagnosed late in life do not die from this disease.

Urinary Incontinence

Urinary incontinence is the uncontrollable loss of urine that is so severe that it has social or hygienic consequences. According to the National Institute on Aging (NIA), at least one out of ten people age sixty-five or older suffers from incontinence ranging from mild leakage to uncontrollable and embarrassing wetting. The problem is more common in women than men. Urinary incontinence can lead to many complications. For example, untreated it increases the risk of developing serious bladder and kidney infections, skin rashes and pressure sores, and falls that result from rushing to use the toilet.

Age-related changes affect the ability to control urination. The maximum capacity of urine that the bladder can hold diminishes as does the ability to postpone urination upon feeling the urge to urinate. As a person ages, the rate of urine flow out of the bladder and through the urethra slows, and the volume of urine remaining in the bladder after urination is finished increases. In women the urethra shortens and its lining becomes thinner as the level of estrogen declines during menopause, decreasing the ability of the urinary sphincter to close tightly. Among older men, the prostate gland enlarges, sometimes blocking the flow of urine through the urethra. While age-related changes increase the risk for incontinence, it typically occurs as a symptom of an illness or other medical disorder.

Although urinary incontinence is common, highly treatable, and frequently curable, it is under-diagnosed and often untreated because sufferers do not seek treatment.

FIGURE 7.6

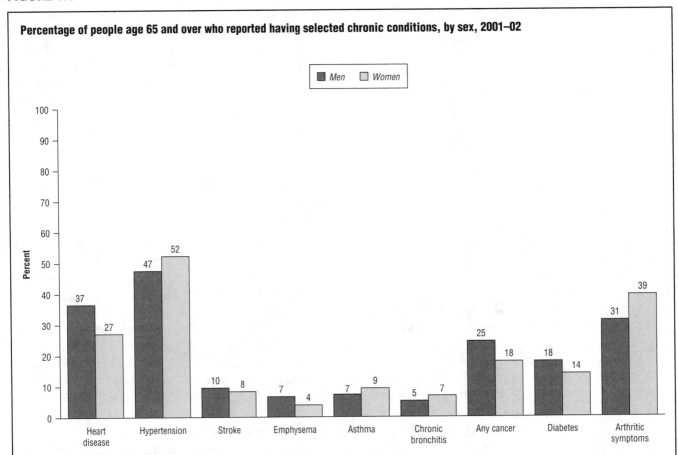

Percentage of people age 65 and over who reported having selected chronic conditions, by sex, 2001–02

Note: Data are based on a 2-year average from 2001–2002. Data for arthritic symptoms are from 2000–2001.
Reference population: These data refer to the civilian noninstitutionalized population.

SOURCE: "Percentage of People Age 65 and Over Who Reported Having Selected Chronic Conditions, by Sex, 2001–2002," in *Older Americans 2004: Key Indicators*, Federal Interagency Forum on Aging Related Statistics, Washington, DC, U.S. Government Printing Office, November 2004, http://www.agingstats.gov/chartbook2004/healthstatus.html#Indicator%2015 (accessed August 11, 2005)

TABLE 7.4

Percentage of people age 65 and over who reported having selected chronic conditions, 1997–2002

Condition	1997–1998	1998–1999	1999–2000	2000–2001	2001–2002
			Percent		
Heart disease	32.3	30.8	29.8	31.1	31.4
Hypertension	46.5	46.1	47.3	49.2	50.2
Stroke	8.2	8.2	8.2	8.8	8.9
Emphysema	5.2	5.1	5.2	5.2	5
Asthma	7.7	7.1	7.4	8.5	8.3
Chronic bronchitis	6.4	6.1	6.2	6.6	6.1
Any cancer	18.7	18.8	19.9	20	20.8
Diabetes	13	13	13.7	14.8	15.5
Arthritic symptoms	37	35.1	35.2	36.1	na

na Comparable data for arthritic symptoms for 2001–2002 are not available.
Note: Data are based on 2-year averages. Data are age-adjusted.
Reference population: These data refer to the civilian noninstitutionalized population.

SOURCE: "Percentage of People Age 65 and Over Who Reported Having Selected Chronic Conditions, 1997–2002," in *Older Americans 2004: Key Indicators*, Federal Interagency Forum on Aging Related Statistics, Washington, DC, U.S. Government Printing Office, November 2004, http://www.agingstats.gov/chartbook2004/tables-healthstatus.html#Indicator%2015 (accessed August 11, 2005)

Many older adults are fearful, embarrassed, or incorrectly assume that incontinence is a normal consequence of growing old. The disorder exacts a serious emotional toll—sufferers are often homebound, isolated or depressed, and are more likely to report their health as fair-to-poor than their peers. In addition, urinary incontinence is often a reason for institutionalization, because three-quarters of those afflicted have some activity limitations and because incontinence is difficult for caregivers to manage. About two-thirds of nursing home residents are incontinent. (See Table 7.6.)

Malnutrition

The older population is especially vulnerable to nutrition-related health problems. As people age, their energy needs decline, and it is vital for them to consume nutrient-dense foods in a lower calorie diet. According to the U.S. Department of Agriculture (USDA), research found that intake of all food groups except fruit and vegetables decline as people age, and fewer than one-half of adults age sixty and older eat the recommended

FIGURE 7.7

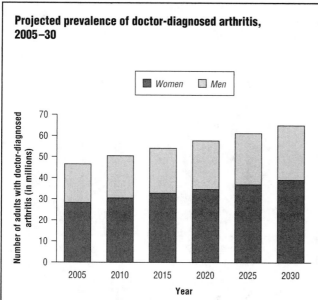

Projected prevalence of doctor-diagnosed arthritis, 2005–30

SOURCE: "Figure X.1. Projected Prevalence of Doctor-Diagnosed Arthritis, US Adults Aged 18+ Years, 2005–2030," in *Future Burden of Arthritis*, Centers for Disease Control and Prevention, National Center for Chronic Disease Prevention and Health Promotion, Hyattsville, MD, May 20, 2005, http://www.cdc.gov/arthritis/data_statistics/national_data_nhis.htm#future (accessed August 11, 2005)

numbers of servings of any food group on a given day. (See Table 7.7.) Just 6% of older men and 3% of older women consumed the recommended number of servings of dairy products, compared with 26% of younger men and 15% of younger women.

Older adults' nutrition may be affected by many factors, including loneliness, depression, a cognitive disorder, poor appetite, and lack of transportation. Poor nutrition may arise in response to a major life change such as the death of a spouse. An older adult may forgo meal preparation when there is no longer someone else to cook for or eat with; and a bereaved or frail older adult may not have the stamina or motivation to shop or cook. Malnutrition also may be the result of poverty. Faced with fixed incomes and competing needs, older adults may be forced to choose between buying food or the prescription medications they need.

Hearing Loss

There are many causes of hearing loss, the most common being age-related changes in the ear's mechanism. Hearing loss is a common problem among older adults and can seriously compromise quality of life. People suffering from hearing loss may withdraw from social contact and are sometimes misdiagnosed as cognitively impaired or mentally ill. In 2002 nearly one-half of older

TABLE 7.5

Number and percentage of adults with doctor-diagnosed arthritis[a], by selected characteristics, 2002

Characteristic	Unweighted no. of respondents	No. (in thousands)	Prevalence of doctor-diagnosed arthritis	
			Crude %	Age-adjusted[b] %
Age group (years)				
18–44	15,693	8,469	7.9	
45–64	9,434	18,523	28.8	
≥65	5,821	15,713	47.8	
Sex				
Women	17,481	25,869	24.3	23.7
Men	13,467	16,835	17.1	17.8
Race/ethnicity[c]				
White, non-Hispanic	20,235	34,325	23.0	21.9
Black, non-Hispanic	4,100	4,464	19.4	22.3
Hispanic	5,255	2,648	11.7	15.8
Other/multiple race[c]	1,358	1,267	12.1	14.4
Total	**30,948**	**42,704**	**20.8**	**20.9**

[a]Respondents with doctor-diagnosed arthritis were defined as those answering "yes" to the question, "Have you ever been told by a doctor or other health professional that you have some form of arthritis, rheumatoid arthritis, gout, lupus, or fibromyalgia?"
[b]Age-adjusted to the standard 2000 U.S. population.
[c]Data for other/multiple radial/ethnic populations are combined because, when analyzed separately, numbers were too small for meaningful analysis. Persons in this category are non-Hispanic.

SOURCE: "Table 1. Number and Percentage of Adults Aged >18 Years with Doctor-Diagnosed Arthritis, by Selected Characteristics—National Health Interview Survey, United States, 2002," in "Racial/Ethnic Differences in the Prevalence and Impact of Doctor-Diagnosed Arthritis—United States, 2002," *Morbidity and Mortality Weekly Report* vol. 54, no. 5, Centers for Disease Control and Prevention. Atlanta GA, February 11, 2005, http://www.cdc.gov/mmwr/preview/mmwrhtml/mm5405a3.htm#tab1 (accessed August 11, 2005)

FIGURE 7.8

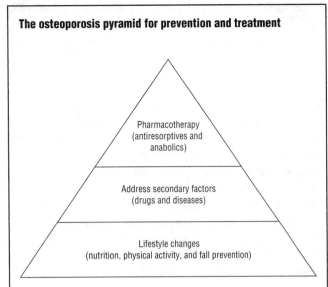

The osteoporosis pyramid for prevention and treatment

Pharmacotherapy
(antiresorptives and
anabolics)

Address secondary factors
(drugs and diseases)

Lifestyle changes
(nutrition, physical activity, and fall prevention)

Note:
The base of the pyramid: The first step in the prevention and treatment of osteoporosis and the prevention of fractures is to build a foundation of nutrition and lifestyle measures that maximize bone health. The diet should not only be adequate in calcium and vitamin D, but should have a healthy balance of other nutrients. A weight-bearing exercise program should be developed. Cigarette smoking and excessive alcohol use must be avoided. In the older individual, at high risk for fractures, the changes in lifestyle would include a plan not only to maximize physical activity, but also to minimize the risk of falls. The use of hip protectors can be considered in some high-risk patients. Diseases that increase the risk of falls by causing visual impairment, postural hypotension (a drop in blood pressure on standing, which leads to dizziness), or poor balance should be treated. Drugs that cause bone loss or increase the risk of falls should be avoided or given at the lowest effective dose.

The second level of the pyramid: The next step is to identify and treat diseases that produce secondary osteoporosis or aggravate primary osteoporosis. These measures are the foundation upon which specific pharmacotherapy is built and should never be forgotten.

The third level of the pyramid: If there is sufficiently high risk of fracture to warrant pharmacotherapy, the patient is usually started on antiresorptives. Anabolic agents are used in individuals in whom antiresorptive therapy is not adequate to prevent bone loss or fractures.

SOURCE: "Figure 9-1. The Osteoporosis Pyramid for Prevention and Treatment," in *Bone Health and Osteoporosis: A Report of the Surgeon General*, U.S. Department of Health and Human Services, Public Health Service, Office of the Surgeon General, Rockville MD, October 14, 2004, http://www.surgeongeneral.gov/library/bonehealth/chapter_9.html#APyramidApproach (accessed August 11, 2005)

FIGURE 7.9

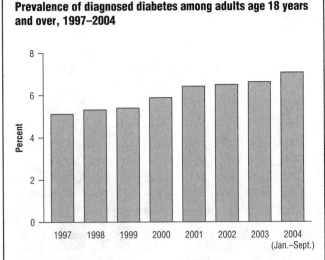

Prevalence of diagnosed diabetes among adults age 18 years and over, 1997–2004

Notes: Prevalence of diagnosed diabetes is based on self-report of ever having been diagnosed with diabetes by a doctor or other health professional. Persons reporting "borderline" diabetes status and women reporting diabetes only during pregnancy were not coded as having diabetes in the analyses. The analyses excluded persons with unknown diabetes status (about 0.1% of respondents each year).

SOURCE: "Figure 14.1. Prevalence of Diagnosed Diabetes among Adults Aged 18 Years and Over: United States, 1997–2004," in *Early Release of Estimates Based on Data from the January–September 2004 National Health Interview Survey*, Centers for Disease Control and Prevention, National Center for Health Statistics, Hyattsville, MD, 2004, http://www.cdc.gov/nchs/data/nhis/earlyrelease/200506.pdf (accessed August 11, 2005)

men and almost one-third of older women reported having trouble hearing. (See Figure 7.10.) This proportion increases to 60% for people age eighty-five and over. Just 10% of older women and 19% of older men reported wearing hearing aids.

Older adults are often reluctant to admit to hearing problems, and sometimes hearing loss is so gradual that even the afflicted person may not be aware of it for some time. For those who seek treatment there is an expanding array of devices and services to mitigate the effects of hearing loss. Hearing-impaired persons may benefit from high-tech hearing aids, amplifiers for doorbells and telephones, infrared amplifiers, and even companion dogs trained to respond to sounds for their owners.

Vision Changes

Almost no one escapes age-related changes in vision. Over time it becomes increasingly difficult to read small print or thread a needle at the usual distance. For many, night vision declines. This is often caused by a condition called presbyopia (tired eyes) and is a very common occurrence. People who were previously nearsighted may actually realize some improvement in eyesight as they become slightly farsighted.

In 2002, 18% of adults age sixty-five and older reported vision problems—16% of older men and 19% of older women. (See Figure 7.10.) Among adults age eighty-four and older, one-third reported trouble seeing.

Book publishers have responded to older adults' declining vision by issuing paperbacks by many popular authors in a bigger size that features larger type and more space between lines. Readers have taken to the enlarged books, despite their higher prices—about $3 more than traditional paperbacks. As reported by Edward Wyatt in "Baby Boomers Labor over the Fine Print" (*New York Times*, August 2005), in August 2005 larger-edition paperbacks of six authors had appeared on the *New York Times* paperback best-seller list.

TABLE 7.6

Nursing home residents age 65 and over, by selected functional status and age, sex, and race, 1985, 1995, and 1999

[Data are based on a sample of nursing home residents]

Age, sex, and race	Functional status[a]											
	Dependent mobility			Incontinent			Dependent eating			Dependent mobility, eating, and incontinent		
	1985	1995	1999	1985	1995	1999	1985	1995	1999	1985	1995	1999
All persons												
65 years and over, age adjusted[b]	75.7	79.0	80.3	55.0	63.8	65.7	40.9	44.9	47.3	32.5	36.5	36.9
65 years and over, crude	74.8	79.0	80.4	54.5	63.8	65.7	40.5	44.9	47.4	32.1	36.5	37.0
65–74 years	61.2	73.0	73.9	42.9	61.9	58.5	33.5	43.8	43.1	25.7	35.8	31.7
75–84 years	70.5	76.5	77.8	55.1	62.5	64.2	39.4	45.2	46.6	30.6	35.3	35.4
85 years and over	83.3	82.4	83.8	58.1	65.3	68.6	43.9	45.0	49.0	35.6	37.5	39.4
Male												
65 years and over, age adjusted[b]	71.2	76.6	76.6	54.2	63.8	66.6	36.0	42.1	45.2	28.0	34.3	35.0
65 years and over, crude	67.8	75.8	75.9	51.9	63.9	66.0	34.9	42.7	45.1	26.9	34.8	35.0
65–74 years	55.8	70.6	70.5	38.8	63.4	59.6	32.8	44.2	45.0	24.1	36.9	34.8
75–84 years	65.7	76.6	76.9	54.4	64.6	68.9	32.6	44.1	44.7	25.5	35.5	35.2
85 years and over	79.2	78.2	78.1	58.1	63.4	66.8	39.2	40.2	45.7	30.9	32.7	34.9
Female												
65 years and over, age adjusted[b]	77.3	79.7	81.5	55.4	63.6	65.0	42.4	45.6	47.8	33.9	36.9	37.2
65 years and over, crude	77.1	80.1	81.9	55.4	63.8	65.6	42.4	45.6	48.1	33.8	37.0	37.7
65–74 years	64.5	74.8	76.4	45.4	60.9	57.7	34.0	43.6	41.6	26.7	35.0	29.3
75–84 years	72.3	76.5	78.2	55.3	61.7	62.2	42.0	45.7	47.4	32.6	35.2	35.6
85 years and over	84.3	83.3	85.2	58.1	65.7	69.0	45.0	46.0	49.7	36.7	38.6	40.4
White[c]												
65 years and over, age adjusted[b]	75.2	78.5	79.9	54.6	63.2	64.9	40.4	44.2	46.1	32.1	35.7	35.7
65 years and over, crude	74.3	78.7	80.2	54.2	63.3	65.1	40.1	44.2	46.2	31.7	35.7	35.8
65–74 years	60.2	71.4	72.6	42.2	60.2	57.1	32.6	41.9	40.7	24.9	33.8	28.8
75–84 years	69.6	76.4	77.5	54.2	61.8	63.8	38.9	44.9	45.8	30.1	34.7	34.8
85 years and over	83.1	81.9	83.6	58.2	65.0	67.8	43.5	44.3	47.7	35.5	36.9	38.1
Black or African American[c]												
65 years and over, age adjusted[b]	83.4	83.2	82.1	61.0	69.3	71.9	49.2	52.2	55.9	38.2	44.0	46.8
65 years and over, crude	81.1	82.1	81.5	59.9	69.1	70.6	47.9	51.7	54.9	37.7	43.7	45.7
65–74 years	70.9	79.6	78.7	48.6	68.3	64.6	43.1	51.2	53.3	33.8	43.1	42.6
75–84 years	82.5	77.8	80.1	70.1	68.9	67.5	47.9	49.5	49.7	40.6	42.3	41.0
85 years and over	87.4	88.0	84.5	57.9	69.8	77.0	51.7	54.3	61.0	37.6	45.5	52.1

[a]Nursing home residents who are dependent in mobility and eating require the assistance of a person or special equipment. Nursing home residents who are incontinent have difficulty in controlling bowels and/or bladder or have an ostomy or indwelling catheter.
[b]Age adjusted by the direct method to the 1995 National Nursing Home Survey population using the following three age groups: 65–74 years, 75–84 years, and 85 years and over.
[c]Beginning in 1999 the instruction for the race item on the current resident questionnaire was changed so that more than one race could be recorded. In previous years only one racial category could be checked. Estimates for racial groups presented in this table are for residents for whom only one race was recorded. Estimates for residents where multiple races were checked are unreliable due to small sample sizes and are not shown.
Notes: Age refers to age at time of interview. Excludes residents in personal care or domiciliary care homes.

SOURCE: "Table 97. Nursing Home Residents 65 Years of Age and Over, According to Selected Functional Status and Age, Sex, and Race: United States, 1985, 1995, and 1999," in *Health United States 2003 Special Excerpt: Trend Tables on 65 and Older Population*, Centers for Disease Control and Prevention, National Center for Health Statistics, Hyattsville, MD, 2004, http://www.cdc.gov/nchs/data/misc/hus2003excerpt.pdf (accessed August 11, 2005)

Major Eye Diseases

Cataract, glaucoma, age-related macular degeneration (AMD), and diabetic retinopathy are the leading causes of vision impairment and blindness in older adults. Cataract is the leading cause of blindness in the world. Glaucoma is a chronic disease that often requires life-long treatment to control. Age-related macular degeneration is the most common cause of blindness and vision impairment in Americans age sixty and older. Diabetic retinopathy is a common complication of diabetes and is considered a leading cause of blindness in the industrialized world.

CATARACT. A cataract is an opacity, or clouding, of the naturally clear lens of the eye. The prevalence of cataracts increases dramatically with age and most develop slowly over time, but they progress causing cloudy vision and eventually almost complete blindness. Once a clouded lens develops, surgery to remove the affected lens and replace it with an artificial lens is the recommended treatment. Each year about 1.5 million cataract surgeries are performed—most are performed as outpatient procedures under local anesthesia—making it the most common operation in the country in people over sixty-five. According to the National Eye Institute

TABLE 7.7

FIGURE 7.10

Percentage of people age 60 and over who eat recommended numbers of servings of any food group on a given day, 2002

	Males		Females	
Food groups	Age 19–59	Age 60 and older	Age 19–59	Age 60 and older
	Percent meeting recommended servings			
Grains	32	26	23	17
Vegetables	46	42	37	38
Fruit	14	29	19	32
Milk, yogurt, and cheese	26	6	15	3
Meat and meat alternates (oz. or equivalent)*	50	36	21	19

Note: These figures also represent the proportion of each population subgroup that meets benchmark food group densities.
*Excludes cooked dry beans and peas, which are included in vegetables.

SOURCE: Joanne F. Guthrie and Biing-Hwan Lin, "Table 3. Fewer Than One-Half of Older Men and Women Eat Recommended Numbers of Servings of Any Food Group on a Given Day," in "Older Americans Need to Make Every Calorie Count," in "The Graying of America," *Food Review*, Food and Rural Economics Division, Economic Research Service, USDA, vol. 25, no. 2, Washington, DC, Summer–Fall 2002, http://www.ers.usda.gov/publications/FoodReview/Sep2002/frvol25i2b.pdf (accessed August 11, 2005)

Percentage of people age 65 and over who reported having any trouble hearing, any trouble seeing, or no natural teeth, by sex, 2002

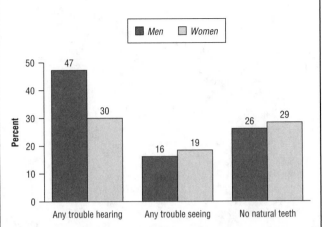

Note: Respondents were asked "Which statement best describes your hearing without a hearing aid: good, a little trouble, a lot of trouble, deaf?" For the purposes of this indicator the category "Any trouble hearing" includes "a little trouble, a lot of trouble, and deaf." Regarding their vision, respondents were asked "Do you have any trouble seeing, even when wearing glasses or contact lenses?" and the category "Any trouble seeing" includes those who in a subsequent question report themselves as blind. Lastly, respondents were asked, in one question, "Have you lost all of your upper and lower natural (permanent) teeth?"
Reference population: These data refer to the civilian noninstitutionalized population.

SOURCE: "Percentage of People Age 65 and Over Who Reported Having Any Trouble Hearing, Any Trouble Seeing, or No Natural Teeth, by Sex, 2002," in *Older Americans 2004: Key Indicators*, Federal Interagency Forum on Aging Related Statistics, Washington, DC, U.S. Government Printing Office, November 2004, http://www.agingstats.gov/chartbook2004/healthstatus.html#Indicator%2016 (accessed August 11, 2005)

(NEI is one of the U.S. National Institutes of Health), by age eighty more than half of all Americans have at least one cataract.

GLAUCOMA. Glaucoma is a disease that causes gradual damage to the optic nerve, which carries visual information from the eye to the brain. The loss of vision is not experienced until a significant amount of nerve damage has occurred. Since the onset is gradual and insidious, as many as half of all people with glaucoma are unaware of having the disease. The NEI reports that in the sixty-five to sixty-nine age group the prevalence of glaucoma is about 1.6% for white women, and three times higher (4.8%) for African-American women. Glaucoma affects more than 10% of African-American men and Hispanic women age eighty and older.

Routine glaucoma testing is especially important for older people. There is no cure for glaucoma and no way to restore lost vision; however, medication can generally manage the condition. At later stages, laser therapy and surgery are effective in preventing further damage.

AGE-RELATED MACULAR DEGENERATION. Age-related macular degeneration (AMD) is a condition in which the macula, a specialized part of the retina responsible for sharp central and reading vision, is damaged. Symptoms include blurred vision, a dark spot in the center of the vision field, and vertical line distortion. AMD rarely affects persons under age sixty, and the National Center for Health Statistics (NCHS) reports that about half of people diagnosed with macular degeneration are over age seventy.

DIABETIC RETINOPATHY. Diabetic retinopathy occurs when the small blood vessels in the retina do not perform properly. Blood vessels can become blocked, break down, leak fluid that distorts vision, and sometimes blood is released into the center of the eye, causing blindness. The NEI reports that 2.5% of Americans age eighteen and older (5.3 million) are affected by diabetic retinopathy, and nearly half of all people with diabetes will develop some degree of diabetic retinopathy during their lifetime; risk increases with age and duration of diabetes. Laser treatment, called photocoagulation, can help to reduce the risk of loss of vision in advanced cases of diabetic retinopathy. The disorder is a leading cause of blindness, but is less common among older adults than other types of visual impairment. The NCHS estimates that about 25% of people with diabetic retinopathy are over age seventy.

Oral Health Problems

According to the American Society on Aging, the proportion of older adults who have lost all of their teeth has declined from the 1950s when more than half of adults age sixty-five and older were toothless to about 28% in

2002. The dramatic improvement is attributable to improvements in oral health such as water fluoridation, improved oral hygiene, advanced dental techniques, and increased utilization of dental services (http://www.asaging.org/media/pressrelease.cfm?id=85). (See Figure 7.10.)

The prevalence of edentulism (having no natural teeth) increases with advancing age—38% of adults age eighty-five and older were toothless in 2002. The condition also is associated with socioeconomic variables. Nearly half (46%) of older adults with family income below the poverty line reported edentulism, compared with 27% of those above the poverty threshold (*Older Americans 2004: Key Indicators of Well-Being*).

Parkinson's Disease

Parkinsonism refers not to a particular disease but to a condition marked by a characteristic set of symptoms that affects more than 1.5 million people in the United States. The American Parkinson Disease Association (APDA) estimates that 1% of the population over age fifty suffers from some manifestation of this disorder.

Parkinson's disease (PD) is caused by the death of about half a million brain cells in the basal ganglia. These cells secrete dopamine, a neurotransmitter (chemical messenger). Dopamine's function is to allow nerve impulses to move smoothly from one nerve cell to another. These nerve cells, in turn, transmit messages to the muscles of the body to begin movement. When the normal supply of dopamine is reduced, the messages are not correctly sent, and the symptoms—mild tremor (shaking), change in walking, or a decreased arm swing—of PD appear.

The four early warning signs of Parkinson's disease are tremors, muscle stiffness, unusual slowness (bradykinesia), and a stooped posture. Medications can control initial symptoms, but over time they become less effective. As the disease worsens, patients develop more severe tremors, causing them to fall or jerk uncontrollably. (The jerky body movements PD patients experience are known as dyskinesias). At other times, rigidity sets in, rendering them unable to move. About one-third of patients also develop dementia, an impairment of cognition.

TREATMENT OF PARKINSON'S DISEASE. Management of PD is individualized and includes not only drug therapy but also a program that stresses daily exercise. Exercise can often lessen the rigidity of muscles, prevent weakness, and improve the ability to walk.

The main goal of drug treatment is to restore the chemical balance between dopamine and another neurotransmitter, acetylcholine. Most patients are given levodopa (L-dopa), a compound that the body converts into dopamine. Treatment with L-dopa does not, however, slow the progressive course of the disease or even delay the changes in the brain PD produces, and it may produce some unpleasant side effects such as dyskinesias.

INFECTIOUS DISEASES

Infectious (contagious) diseases are caused by micro-organisms—viruses, bacteria, parasites, or fungi—transmitted from one person to another through casual contact, such as with the transmittal of influenza, or through bodily fluids, such as with the transmittal of HIV (human immunodeficiency virus), or from contaminated food, air, or water supplies. The CDC reports that in 2002 pneumonia and influenza remained among the top ten causes of death for older adults, responsible for 58,826 deaths (3.2%) of persons age sixty-five and older. (See Table 7.8.) Influenza-related deaths can result from pneumonia as well as from exacerbation of chronic diseases. Older adults account for more than 90% of deaths attributed to pneumonia and influenza.

Influenza

Influenza (flu) is a contagious respiratory disease caused by a virus. The virus is expelled by an infected individual in droplets into the air and may be inhaled by anyone nearby. It can also be transmitted by direct hand contact. The flu primarily affects the lungs, but the whole body experiences symptoms. Influenza is an acute illness characterized by fever, chills, weakness, loss of appetite, and aching muscles in the head, back, arms, and legs. Influenza infection may also produce sore throat, a dry cough, nausea, and burning eyes. The accompanying fever rises quickly—sometimes reaching 104 degrees—but usually subsides after two or three days. Influenza leaves the patient exhausted.

For healthy individuals, the flu is typically a moderately severe illness, with most adults back to work or school within a week. For the very old and older persons who are not in good general health, however, the flu can be very severe and even fatal. Complications such as secondary bacterial infections may develop, taking advantage of the body's weakened condition and lowered resistance. The most common bacterial complication is pneumonia, affecting the lungs, but sinuses, bronchi (larger air passages of the lungs), or inner ears can also become secondarily infected with bacteria. Less common but very serious complications include viral pneumonia, encephalitis (inflammation of the brain), acute renal (kidney) failure, and nervous system disorders. These complications can be fatal.

Influenza can be prevented by inoculation with a current influenza vaccine, which is formulated annually to contain the influenza viruses expected to cause the flu the next year. Immunization produces antibodies to the influenza viruses, which become most effective after one or two months. The CDC advises that older adults get flu

TABLE 7.8

Leading causes of death and numbers of deaths, by age, 1980 and 2002

[Data are based on death certificates]

Age and rank order	1980		2002	
	Cause of death	Deaths	Cause of death	Deaths
25–44 years				
...	All causes	108,658	All causes	132,495
1	Unintentional injuries	26,722	Unintentional injuries	29,279
2	Malignant neoplasms	17,551	Malignant neoplasms	19,957
3	Diseases of heart	14,513	Diseases of heart	16,853
4	Homicide	10,983	Suicide	11,897
5	Suicide	9,855	Homicide	7,728
6	Chronic liver disease and cirrhosis	4,782	Human immunodeficiency virus (HIV) disease	7,546
7	Cerebrovascular diseases	3,154	Chronic liver disease and cirrhosis	3,528
8	Diabetes mellitus	1,472	Cerebrovascular diseases	2,992
9	Pneumonia and influenza	1,467	Diabetes mellitus	2,806
10	Congenital anomalies	817	Influenza and pneumonia	1,316
45–64 years				
...	All causes	425,338	All causes	425,727
1	Diseases of heart	148,322	Malignant neoplasms	143,028
2	Malignant neoplasms	135,675	Diseases of heart	101,804
3	Cerebrovascular diseases	19,909	Unintentional injuries	23,020
4	Unintentional injuries	18,140	Cerebrovascular diseases	15,952
5	Chronic liver disease and cirrhosis	16,089	Diabetes mellitus	15,518
6	Chronic obstructive pulmonary diseases	11,514	Chronic lower respiratory diseases	14,755
7	Diabetes mellitus	7,977	Chronic liver disease and cirrhosis	13,313
8	Suicide	7,079	Suicide	9,926
9	Pneumonia and influenza	5,804	Human immunodeficiency virus (HIV) disease	5,821
10	Homicide	4,019	Septicemia	5,434
65 years and over				
...	All causes	1,341,848	All causes	1,811,720
1	Diseases of heart	595,406	Diseases of heart	576,301
2	Malignant neoplasms	258,389	Malignant neoplasms	391,001
3	Cerebrovascular diseases	146,417	Cerebrovascular diseases	143,293
4	Pneumonia and influenza	45,512	Chronic lower respiratory diseases	108,313
5	Chronic obstructive pulmonary diseases	43,587	Influenza and pneumonia	58,826
6	Atherosclerosis	28,081	Alzheimer's disease	58,289
7	Diabetes mellitus	25,216	Diabetes mellitus	54,715
8	Unintentional injuries	24,844	Nephritis, nephrotic syndrome and nephrosis	34,316
9	Nephritis, nephrotic syndrome, and nephrosis	12,968	Unintentional injuries	33,641
10	Chronic liver disease and cirrhosis	9,519	Septicemia	26,670

... Category not applicable.

SOURCE: Adapted from "Table 32. Leading Causes of Death and Numbers of Deaths, According to Age: United States, 1980 and 2002," in *Health, United States, 2004*, Centers for Disease Control and Prevention, National Center for Health Statistics, Hyattsville, MD, 2004, http://www.cdc.gov/nchs/data/hus/hus04trend.pdf (accessed August 11, 2005)

shots early in the fall, because peak flu activity usually occurs around the beginning of the new calendar year. In 2004, 67.3% of non-Hispanic white, 54.6% of Hispanic, and 45.6% of non-Hispanic African-American older adults reported receiving influenza shots within the past twelve months. (See Figure 7.11.) Immunization reduces hospitalization by about 70% and death by about 85% among noninstitutionalized older adults. Among nursing home residents, the flu shot reduces the risk of hospitalization by about one half, the risk of pneumonia by about 60%, and the risk of death by three-quarters.

Pneumonia

Pneumonia is a serious lung infection. Symptoms of pneumonia are fever, chills, cough, shortness of breath, chest pain, and increased sputum production. Pneumonia

may be caused by viruses, bacteria, or fungi; however, the pneumococcus bacterium is the most important cause of serious pneumonia.

In older adults pneumococcal pneumonia is a common cause of hospitalization and death. About one-quarter of adults age sixty-five and older who contract pneumococcal pneumonia develop bacteremia (bacteria in the blood), and nearly one-quarter of those with bacteremia die from it, even with antibiotic treatment.

Older adults are at high risk—two to three times more likely than other adults—to develop pneumococcal infections. A single vaccination can prevent most cases of pneumococcal pneumonia. The CDC recommends that all persons age sixty-five and older receive the pneumonia vaccine, and, since 1997, an increasing proportion of the older population reports having been

FIGURE 7.11

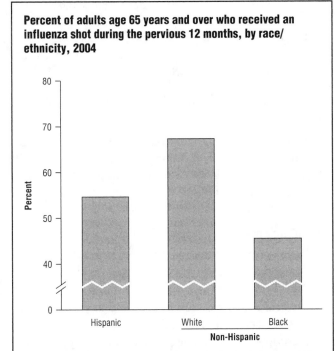

Percent of adults age 65 years and over who received an influenza shot during the pervious 12 months, by race/ethnicity, 2004

Notes: Respondents were asked if they had received a flu shot during the past 12 months. Responses to this question cannot be used to determine when during the preceding 12 months the subject received the flu shot. In addition, estimates are subject to recall error, which will vary depending on when the question is asked because the receipt of a flu shot is seasonal. The analyses excluded 97 adults (1.6%) aged 65 years and over with unknown flu shot status. Beginning in September 2003, respondents were asked about influenza vaccination by nasal spray (sometimes called by the brand name FluMist™) in addition to the question regarding the flu shot. Estimates of nasal spray flu vaccination are not presented.

SOURCE: "Figure 4.3. Percent of Adults Aged 65 Years and Over Who Had Received an Influenza Shot During the Past 12 Months, by Race/Ethnicity: United States, 2004," in *Early Release of Selected Estimates Based on Data from the 2004 National Health Interview Survey*, Centers for Disease Control and Prevention, National Center for Health Statistics, Hyattsville, MD, June 29, 2005, http://www.cdc.gov/nchs/data/nhis/earlyrelease/earlyrelease200506.pdf (accessed August 11, 2005)

FIGURE 7.12

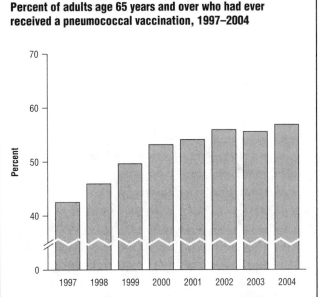

Percent of adults age 65 years and over who had ever received a pneumococcal vaccination, 1997–2004

Notes: The analyses excluded those with unknown pneumococcal vaccination status (about 3% of respondents each year). Beginning with the 2003 data, the National Health Interview Survey transitioned to weights derived from the 2000 census.

SOURCE: "Figure 5.1. Percent of Adults Aged 65 Years and Over Who Had Ever Received a Pneumococcal Vaccination: United States, 1997–2004," in *Early Release of Selected Estimates Based on Data from the 2004 National Health Interview Survey*, Centers for Disease Control and Prevention, National Center for Health Statistics, Hyattsville, MD, June 29, 2005, http://www.cdc.gov/nchs/data/nhis/earlyrelease/earlyrelease200506.pdf (accessed August 11, 2005)

vaccinated. In 2004, 56.8% of adults age sixty-five and older had received a pneumococcal vaccination. (See Figure 7.12.)

MANDATORY IMMUNIZATION FOR NURSING HOME RESIDENTS. As of fall 2005, all of the estimated 1.6 to 2 million residents of the nation's eighteen thousand nursing homes must be immunized against influenza and pneumonia or the nursing homes will risk losing reimbursement from the Medicare and Medicaid programs. This new regulation, issued in August 2005, intends to ensure that the most vulnerable older adults receive their flu shots. Persons sixty-five and older are among the most vulnerable, especially those in the close quarters of nursing homes where infection can spread more easily. As Susan Heavey reported in her article "US to Require Flu Shots for Nursing Home Patients" (Reuters, August 2005), according to a 1999 survey, only two-thirds of nursing home residents had received a flu shot and only 38% had received a pneumonia vaccine.

DISABILITY IN THE OLDER POPULATION

Americans are not only living longer but also are developing fewer chronic diseases and disabilities. The current cohort of older Americans are defying the stereotype that aging is synonymous with increasing disability and dependence.

The proportion of older Americans with a chronic disability declined from one-quarter in 1984 to one-fifth in 1999. (See Figure 7.3.) Despite the 5% decline, the number of chronically disabled adults rose from about 6.2 million in 1984 to 6.8 million in 1999. The increase is attributable to the fact that the decline in disability rates was not great enough to offset growth of the older population. (*Older Americans 2004: Key Indicators of Well-Being.*)

The percentage of older adults with disabilities increases dramatically with age—nearly three-quarters (73.6%) of adults age eighty and older report at least one disability. Over half (57.6%) of those age eighty and older had one or more severe disabilities, and 34.9% of the adults over age eighty reported requiring assistance as a result of disability. (See Figure 7.13.)

The 2003 U.S. Census Bureau's *American Community Survey* provides estimates of disability in the

FIGURE 7.13

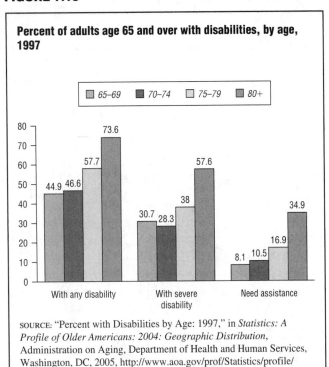

Percent of adults age 65 and over with disabilities, by age, 1997

Legend: 65–69, 70–74, 75–79, 80+

	65–69	70–74	75–79	80+
With any disability	44.9	46.6	57.7	73.6
With severe disability	30.7	28.3	38	57.6
Need assistance	8.1	10.5	16.9	34.9

SOURCE: "Percent with Disabilities by Age: 1997," in *Statistics: A Profile of Older Americans: 2004: Geographic Distribution*, Administration on Aging, Department of Health and Human Services, Washington, DC, 2005, http://www.aoa.gov/prof/Statistics/profile/2004/2004profile.pdf (accessed August 11, 2005)

noninstitutionalized population by age. Of the 14,380,551 men age sixty-five and older, 38% had some form of disability, and 19% had two or more types of disabilities. Of the 19,515,621 women age sixty-five and older, 42% (8,104,133) had some form of disability, and 24% had two or more disabilities. (See Table 7.9.)

Declining rates of disability among older adults may be attributable to:

- Increasing educational attainment of the older population. Educational attainment is associated with improved health and earning power, which enable older adults to obtain adequate nutrition and health care.

- Public health education, which has successfully reduced health risks such as smoking and increased awareness of the importance of a healthy diet and regular exercise.

- Medical advances, such as knee and hip replacements, lens replacements for cataract sufferers, and effective prescription medications, which act to delay or prevent the onset of chronic diseases that disabled previous generations.

TABLE 7.9

Estimates and types of disability for the noninstitutionalized population, 2003

United States	Estimate	Lower bound	Upper bound
Male			
65 years and over	14,380,551	14,359,090	14,402,012
With one type of disability	2,693,238	2,657,836	2,728,640
Sensory disability	895,912	876,338	915,486
Physical disability	1,486,731	1,458,238	1,515,224
Mental disability	187,299	176,521	198,077
Self-care disability	16,141	13,113	19,169
Go-outside-home disability	107,155	100,235	114,075
With two or more types of disability	2,729,446	2,688,514	2,770,378
Includes self-care disability	1,089,580	1,063,664	1,115,496
Does not include self-care disability	1,639,866	1,606,220	1,673,512
No disability	8,957,867	8,898,870	9,017,014
Female			
65 years and over	19,515,621	19,494,235	19,537,007
With one type of disability	3,354,870	3,310,522	3,399,218
Sensory disability	681,808	659,519	704,097
Physical disability	2,148,634	2,111,201	2,186,067
Mental disability	216,484	204,506	228,462
Self-care disability	19,139	15,936	22,342
Go-outside-home disability	288,805	273,763	303,847
With two or more types of disability	4,749,263	4,701,151	4,797,375
Includes self-care disability	2,062,699	2,028,188	2,097,210
Does not include self-care disability	2,686,564	2,649,610	2,723,518
No disability	11,411,488	11,347,546	11,475,430

Notes:
Survey is limited to the household population and excludes the population living in institutions, college dormitories, and other group quarters. Data are based on a sample and are subject to sampling variability.

SOURCE: Adapted from "Population 5 Years and Over–Universe: Civilian Noninstitutionalized Population 5 Years and Over," in *2003 Community Survey Summary Tables*, U.S. Census Bureau, Housing and Household Economic Statistics Division, Washington, DC, December 15, 2004, http://factfinder.census.gov/servlet/DTTable?_bm=y&-geo_id=04000US03&-ds_name=ACS_2003_EST_G00_&-redoLog=false&-mt_name=ACS_2003_EST_G2000_PCT037 (accessed August 11, 2005)

FIGURE 7.14

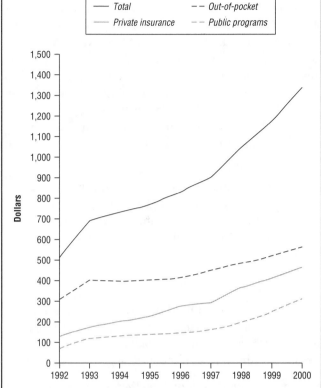

Average annual prescription drug costs and sources of payment among noninstitutionalized Medicare enrollees age 65 and over, 1992–2000

Note: Dollars have been inflation-adjusted to 2000 using the Consumer Price Index. Public programs include Medicare, Medicaid, Department of Veterans Affairs, and other State and Federal programs.
Reference population: These data refer to Medicare enrollees.

SOURCE: "Average Annual Prescription Drug Costs and Sources of Payment Among Noninstitutionalized Medicare Enrollees Age 65 and Over, 1992–2000," in *Older Americans 2004: Key Indicators*, Federal Interagency Forum on Aging Related Statistics, Washington, DC, U.S. Government Printing Office, November 2004, http://www.agingstats .gov/chartbook2004/healthcare.html#Indicator%2030 (accessed August 11, 2005)

- Improved rehabilitation and management of previously disabling conditions such as stroke, heart disease, and vision and hearing deficits.

- The national trend away from institutionalization and toward alternatives in the community such as assisted living facilities, which may help older adults to remain vital and active longer.

DRUG USE AMONG OLDER ADULTS

According to the NIA, adults ages sixty-five and older consume more prescription and over-the-counter medicines than any other age group, and the FDA reports that older adults purchase 30% of all prescription drugs and 40% of all over-the-counter medications. Prescription drug costs have skyrocketed since the early 1990s. Older Americans spend an average total of $3 billion annually on prescription medications. In 2000 the average cost per person was $1,340. (See Figure 7.14.) More than 60% of older adults are taking at least one prescription medication, and most take an average of three to five medications. These estimates do not include over-the-counter medications, dietary supplements, herbal remedies, and other alternative therapies.

Out-of-pocket costs for prescription drugs have increased, creating serious financial hardships for many older adults, especially those Medicare enrollees without supplemental drug coverage. Historically, Medicare has not covered most outpatient prescription drugs; however, Medicare prescription drug discount cards debuted in 2004 and Medicare coverage of prescription drugs began in early 2006. Older Americans paid 60% of prescription drug costs out of pocket in 1992, compared with 42% in 2000. Private insurance paid 35% of prescription drug costs in 2000, and public programs, primarily Medicaid, covered 23%. Average out-of-pocket costs did not increase as rapidly as total costs, because more Medicare enrollees had supplemental prescription drug coverage.

Older Adults Respond Differently to Drugs

Many factors influence the efficacy, safety, and success of drug therapy with older patients. These factors include the effects of aging on pharmacokinetics—the absorption, distribution, metabolism, and excretion of drugs. Of the four, absorption is least affected by aging. In older persons, absorption is generally complete, just slower. Distribution of most medications is related to body weight and composition changes that occur with aging such as decreased lean muscle mass, increased fat mass, and decreased total body water.

Geriatricians (physicians who specialize in the diagnosis and treatment of diseases of older persons) and other health professionals who care for older adults know that drug dosages often must be modified based on changing organ function and estimates of lean body mass. They have coined the adage "start low and go slow" to guide prescribing drugs for older adults. For example, some initial doses of drugs should be lower because older adults have decreased total body water, which might increase the concentration of the drug. Fat-soluble drugs also may have to be administered in lower doses because they may accumulate in fatty tissues, resulting in longer durations of action. The mechanism used to clear a drug via metabolism in the liver or clearance—excretion—through the kidneys changes with aging and is affected by interactions with other medications. Pharmacodynamics, or tissue sensitivity to drugs, also changes with advancing age. Among older adults, complete elimination of a drug from body tissues, including the brain, can take weeks longer than it might in younger persons because of a combination of pharmacokinetic and pharmacodynamic effects.

Adherence, Drug–Drug Interactions, and Polypharmacy

Too often, older people get more drugs without a reassessment of their previous medications. That can be disastrous.

—Madeline Feinberg, pharmacist and former director of the Elder Health program of the University of Maryland School of Pharmacy in *Medications and Older People*, U.S. Food and Drug Administration, September 2003

Adherence—taking prescription medications regularly and correctly— is a challenge for older persons who may suffer from memory loss, impaired vision, or arthritis. The FDA reports that between 40% and 75% of older adults fail to take their medications at the right times, in the right amounts. Strategies to improve adherence include weekly pill boxes, calendars, and easy-to-open bottles with large print labels.

Drug–drug interactions are more frequent among older adults because they are more likely than persons of other ages to be taking multiple medications. The FDA reports that the average older person is taking more than four prescription medications at once plus two over-the-counter medications. Dangerous drug–drug interactions may occur when two or more drugs act together to either intensify or diminish one another's potency and effectiveness or when in combination they produce adverse side effects. For example, a person who takes heparin, a blood-thinning medication, should not take aspirin, which also acts to thin the blood. Similarly, antacids can interfere with absorption of certain drugs used to treat Parkinson's disease, hypertension, and heart disease.

Polypharmacy is the use of many medications at the same time. It also refers to prescribing more medication than is needed or a medication regimen that includes at least one unnecessary medication. The major risk associated with polypharmacy is the potential for adverse drug reactions and interactions. Drug-induced adverse events may masquerade as other illnesses or precipitate confusion, falls, and incontinence, potentially prompting the physician to prescribe yet another drug. This "prescribing cascade" is easily prevented. It requires that physicians ensure that all medications prescribed are appropriate, taken correctly, safe, and effective. It may also be prevented by older adults' maintenance of accurate and complete records of all of their prescription and over-the-counter drug use.

LEADING CAUSES OF DEATH

According to "Health, United States, 2004" (Centers for Disease Control and Prevention, http://www.cdc.gov/nchs/hus.htm, 2004), three-quarters of all deaths in the United States occur among persons sixty-five years of age and over. During the past fifty years, overall death rates have declined by more than one-third for older persons, with chronic diseases responsible for the majority of the deaths throughout this period.

The top three leading causes of death among adults age sixty-five and over—heart disease, malignant neoplasms (cancer), and cerebrovascular diseases—were unchanged from 1980 to 2002. In 2002 Alzheimer's disease, a degenerative disease of the brain that affects many areas of cognitive function, joined the list of leading causes of death in sixth place, and chronic liver disease and cirrhoses (liver disease characterized by irreversible scarring of the liver and impaired liver function), which was responsible for 9,519 deaths in 1980, did not appear on the 2002 list. (See Table 7.8.)

Although diabetes was the seventh-leading cause of death among older adults in 1980 and 2002, in 2002 it claimed more than twice as many lives—54,715 compared with 25,216. In contrast, heart disease retained its first place in 2002 but claimed 19,105 fewer lives.

Heart Disease

While deaths from heart disease have declined, it still kills more Americans than any other single disease. According to the American Heart Association (AHA), about 85% of persons who die of heart disease are age sixty-five or older.

Several factors account for the decreasing numbers of deaths from heart disease, including better control of hypertension and cholesterol levels and changes in exercise and nutrition. The increasing ranks of trained mobile emergency personnel (paramedics) and widespread use of cardiopulmonary resuscitation (CPR) and immediate treatment also increased the likelihood of surviving an initial heart attack.

Growing use of procedures such as cardiac catheterization, coronary bypass surgery, pacemakers, and angioplasty and placement of stents (wire scaffolds that hold arteries open) have improved the quality, and in some instances extended the lives, of persons with heart disease.

Cancer

Cancer is the second-leading cause of death among older adults. (See Table 7.8.) According to the American Cancer Society (ACS), nearly 76% of all cancers are diagnosed after age fifty-five. The likelihood of dying of cancer increases every decade after the age of thirty. In 2002, among persons age sixty-five to seventy-four, there were 792.1 deaths per one hundred thousand persons; for those age seventy-five to eighty-four, this rate was 1,311.9 per one hundred thousand persons; and for those age eighty-five and over, it was 1,723.9 per one hundred thousand persons. (See Table 7.10.)

TABLE 7.10

Death rates for malignant neoplasms, selected characteristics, selected years, 1950–2002

[Data are based on death certificates]

Sex, race, Hispanic origin, and age	1950[a]	1960[a]	1970	1980	1990	2000	2001	2002
All persons				Deaths per 100,000 resident population				
All ages, age adjusted[b]	193.9	193.9	198.6	207.9	216.0	199.6	196.0	193.5
All ages, crude	139.8	149.2	162.8	183.9	203.2	196.5	194.4	193.2
Under 1 year	8.7	7.2	4.7	3.2	2.3	2.4	1.6	1.8
1–4 years	11.7	10.9	7.5	4.5	3.5	2.7	2.7	2.6
5–14 years	6.7	6.8	6.0	4.3	3.1	2.5	2.5	2.6
15–24 years	8.6	8.3	8.3	6.3	4.9	4.4	4.3	4.3
25–34 years	20.0	19.5	16.5	13.7	12.6	9.8	10.1	9.7
35–44 years	62.7	59.7	59.5	48.6	43.3	36.6	36.8	35.8
45–54 years	175.1	177.0	182.5	180.0	158.9	127.5	126.5	123.8
55–64 years	390.7	396.8	423.0	436.1	449.6	366.7	356.5	351.1
65–74 years	698.8	713.9	754.2	817.9	872.3	816.3	802.8	792.1
75–84 years	1,153.3	1,127.4	1,169.2	1,232.3	1,348.5	1,335.6	1,315.8	1,311.9
85 years and over	1,451.0	1,450.0	1,320.7	1,594.6	1,752.9	1,819.4	1,765.6	1,723.9
Male								
All ages, age adjusted[b]	208.1	225.1	247.6	271.2	280.4	248.9	243.7	238.9
All ages, crude	142.9	162.5	182.1	205.3	221.3	207.2	205.3	203.8
Under 1 year	9.7	7.7	4.4	3.7	2.4	2.6	1.5	2.0
1–4 years	12.5	12.4	8.3	5.2	3.7	3.0	2.9	2.7
5–14 years	7.4	7.6	6.7	4.9	3.5	2.7	2.5	2.9
15–24 years	9.7	10.2	10.4	7.8	5.7	5.1	5.0	4.9
25–34 years	17.7	18.8	16.3	13.4	12.6	9.2	9.3	9.2
35–44 years	45.6	48.9	53.0	44.0	38.5	32.7	32.6	31.5
45–54 years	156.2	170.8	183.5	188.7	162.5	130.9	130.3	128.0
55–64 years	413.1	459.9	511.8	520.8	532.9	415.8	405.2	399.8
65–74 years	791.5	890.5	1,006.8	1,093.2	1,122.2	1,001.9	984.6	964.8
75–84 years	1,332.6	1,389.4	1,588.3	1,790.5	1,914.4	1,760.6	1,727.1	1,711.3
85 years and over	1,668.3	1,741.2	1,720.8	2,369.5	2,739.9	2,710.7	2,613.6	2,491.1
Female								
All ages, age adjusted[b]	182.3	168.7	163.2	166.7	175.7	167.6	164.7	163.1
All ages, crude	136.8	136.4	144.4	163.6	186.0	186.2	183.9	183.0
Under 1 year	7.6	6.8	5.0	2.7	2.2	2.3	1.8	1.6
1–4 years	10.8	9.3	6.7	3.7	3.2	2.5	2.5	2.4
5–14 years	6.0	6.0	5.2	3.6	2.8	2.2	2.4	2.4
15–24 years	7.6	6.5	6.2	4.8	4.1	3.6	3.5	3.6
25–34 years	22.2	20.1	16.7	14.0	12.6	10.4	10.9	10.2
35–44 years	79.3	70.0	65.6	53.1	48.1	40.4	41.0	40.0
45–54 years	194.0	183.0	181.5	171.8	155.5	124.2	122.7	119.8
55–64 years	368.2	337.7	343.2	361.7	375.2	321.3	311.5	306.0
65–74 years	612.3	560.2	557.9	607.1	677.4	663.6	652.2	648.5
75–84 years	1,000.7	924.1	891.9	903.1	1,010.3	1,058.5	1,045.4	1,046.7
85 years and over	1,299.7	1,263.9	1,096.7	1,255.7	1,372.1	1,456.4	1,410.7	1,391.1
White male[c]								
All ages, age adjusted[b]	210.0	224.7	244.8	265.1	272.2	243.9	239.2	235.2
All ages, crude	147.2	166.1	185.1	208.7	227.7	218.1	216.4	215.5
25–34 years	17.7	18.8	16.2	13.6	12.3	9.2	9.3	9.1
35–44 years	44.5	46.3	50.1	41.1	35.8	30.9	31.3	30.5
45–54 years	150.8	164.1	172.0	175.4	149.9	123.5	123.6	121.8
55–64 years	409.4	450.9	498.1	497.4	508.2	401.9	392.1	386.0
65–74 years	798.7	887.3	997.0	1,070.7	1,090.7	984.3	969.4	954.8
75–84 years	1,367.6	1,413.7	1,592.7	1,779.7	1,883.2	1,736.0	1,704.6	1,695.3
85 years and over	1,732.7	1,791.4	1,772.2	2,375.6	2,715.1	2,693.7	2,597.6	2,486.8

Success in treating certain cancers, such as Hodgkin's disease and some forms of leukemia, has been offset by the rise in rates of other cancers, such as breast and lung cancers. Table 7.8 shows that the number of cancer deaths among adults age sixty-five and older rose sharply from 258,389 in 1980 to 391,001 in 2002. Progress in treating cancer has largely been related to screenings, early diagnoses, and new drug therapies.

Stroke

Stroke (cerebrovascular disease or "brain attack") is the third-leading cause of death and the principal cause of disability among older adults. (See Table 7.8.) According to "Heart Disease and Stroke Statistics—2005 Update" (American Heart Association, http://www.americanheart.org/presenter.jhtml?identifier=3000090), about three-quarters of stroke sufferers are age sixty-five and older. About 88% of stroke deaths occur in people age sixty-five and older.

TABLE 7.10

Death rates for malignant neoplasms, selected characteristics, selected years, 1950–2002 [CONTINUED]

[Data are based on death certificates]

Sex, race, Hispanic origin, and age	1950[a]	1960[a]	1970	1980	1990	2000	2001	2002
Black or								
African American male[c]					Deaths per 100,000 resident population			
All ages, age adjusted[b]	178.9	227.6	291.9	353.4	397.9	340.3	330.9	319.6
All ages, crude	106.6	136.7	171.6	205.5	221.9	188.5	184.5	181.5
25–34 years	18.0	18.4	18.8	14.1	15.7	10.1	10.5	11.2
35–44 years	55.7	72.9	81.3	73.8	64.3	48.4	44.6	43.0
45–54 years	211.7	244.7	311.2	333.0	302.6	214.2	204.8	197.3
55–64 years	490.8	579.7	689.2	812.5	859.2	626.4	604.2	610.3
65–74 years	636.5	938.5	1,168.9	1,417.2	1,613.9	1,363.8	1,335.3	1,274.7
75–84 years[d]	853.5	1,053.3	1,624.8	2,029.6	2,478.3	2,351.8	2,290.0	2,223.0
85 years and over	—	1,155.2	1,387.0	2,393.9	3,238.3	3,264.8	3,209.9	2,976.1

— Data not available.

*Rates based on fewer than 20 deaths are considered unreliable and are not shown.

[a]Includes deaths of persons who were not residents of the 50 states and the District of Columbia.

[b]Age-adjusted rates are calculated using the year 2000 standard population.

[c]The race groups, white, black, Asian or Pacific Islander, and American Indian or Alaska Native, include persons of Hispanic and non-Hispanic origin. Persons of Hispanic origin may be of any race. Death rates for the American Indian or Alaska Native and Asian or Pacific Islander populations are known to be underestimated.

[d]In 1950 rate is for the age group 75 years and over.

Notes: Rates for 1991–99 were revised using intercensal population estimates based on census 2000. Rates for 2000 were revised based on census 2000 counts. Rates for 2001 and 2002 were computed using 2000-based postcensal estimates. Age groups were selected to minimize the presentation of unstable age-specific death rates based on small numbers of deaths and for consistency among comparison groups.

SOURCE: Adapted from "Table 38. Death Rates for Malignant Neoplasms, According to Sex, Race, Hispanic Origin, and Age: United States, Selected Years 1950–2002," in *Health, United States, 2004*, Centers for Disease Control and Prevention, National Center for Health Statistics, Hyattsville, MD, 2004, http://www.cdc.gov/nchs/data/hus/hus04trend.pdf (accessed August 11, 2005)

For persons over age fifty-five, the incidence of stroke more than doubles in each successive decade.

Table 7.11 shows the death rates for strokes from 1950 to 2000 by age group. Strokes killed 219 people per one hundred thousand in the sixty-five to seventy-four age group in 1980. The death rate was reduced by almost half in 2002, with 120.3 people per one hundred thousand dying of strokes. The rate for persons seventy-five to eighty-four was also cut by almost half between 1980 and 2002. There were 431 deaths per one hundred thousand population for this age group in 2002, down from 786.9 in 1980. The improvement was even greater for persons age eighty-five and older. There were 1,445.9 deaths per one hundred thousand for this age group in 2002, less than half the rate (2,283.7 per one hundred thousand) in 1980.

HEALTHY AGING

The aging of the population is one of the major public health challenges of the 21st century. With more than 70 million baby boomers in the United States poised to join the ranks of those aged 65 or over, the prevention of diseases and injuries is one of the few tools available to reduce the expected growth of health care and long-term care costs.

—Julie Louise Gerberding, MD, MPH, Director, Centers for Disease Control and Prevention

According to the CDC, ample research demonstrates that healthy lifestyles have a greater impact than genetic

factors in helping older people prevent the deterioration traditionally associated with aging. People who are physically active, eat a healthy diet, do not use tobacco, and practice other healthy behaviors reduce their risk for chronic diseases, have half the rate of disability of those who do not, and can delay disability by as many as ten years.

Among the recommended health practices for older adults is participating in screening programs and early detection practices such as screenings for hypertension, cancer, diabetes, and depression. Screening detects diseases early in their course, when they are most treatable; however, many older adults do not obtain the recommended screenings. For example, according to the National Center for Chronic Disease Prevention and Health Promotion (http://www.cdc.gov), 60% of Americans age fifty or older in 2002 did not undergo a sigmoidoscopy or colonoscopy in the previous five years to screen for colorectal cancer, even though Medicare covers the cost. Similarly, immunizations reduce risk for hospitalization and death from influenza and pneumonia, yet in 2004 approximately one-third of older adults had not received flu shots and 43% had not been vaccinated against pneumonia. (See Figure 7.11 and Figure 7.12.)

With falls being the most common cause of injuries to older adults, injury prevention is a vitally important way to prevent disability. According to the CDC, more than one-third of adults age sixty-five or older fall each year, and of those who fall, 10–20% suffer injuries that impair mobility and independence. Removing tripping

TABLE 7.11

Death rates for cerebrovascular diseases, selected characteristics, selected years, 1950–2002

[Data are based on death certificates]

Sex, race, Hispanic origin, and age	1950[a]	1960[a]	1970	1980	1990	2000	2001	2002
All persons				Deaths per 100,000 resident population				
All ages, age adjusted[b]	180.7	177.9	147.7	96.2	65.3	60.9	57.9	56.2
All ages, crude	104.0	108.0	101.9	75.0	57.8	59.6	57.4	56.4
Under 1 year	5.1	4.1	5.0	4.4	3.8	3.3	2.7	2.9
1–4 years	0.9	0.8	1.0	0.5	0.3	0.3	0.4	0.3
5–14 years	0.5	0.7	0.7	0.3	0.2	0.2	0.2	0.2
15–24 years	1.6	1.8	1.6	1.0	0.6	0.5	0.5	0.4
25–34 years	4.2	4.7	4.5	2.6	2.2	1.5	1.5	1.4
35–44 years	18.7	14.7	15.6	8.5	6.4	5.8	5.5	5.4
45–54 years	70.4	49.2	41.6	25.2	18.7	16.0	15.1	15.1
55–64 years	194.2	147.3	115.8	65.1	47.9	41.0	38.0	37.2
65–74 years	554.7	469.2	384.1	219.0	144.2	128.6	123.4	120.3
75–84 years	1,499.6	1,491.3	1,254.2	786.9	498.0	461.3	443.9	431.0
85 years and over	2,990.1	3,680.5	3,014.3	2,283.7	1,628.9	1,589.2	1,500.2	1,445.9
Male								
All ages, age adjusted[b]	186.4	186.1	157.4	102.2	68.5	62.4	59.0	56.5
All ages, crude	102.5	104.5	94.5	63.4	46.7	46.9	45.2	44.2
Under 1 year	6.4	5.0	5.8	5.0	4.4	3.8	3.1	3.2
1–4 years	1.1	0.9	1.2	0.4	0.3	*	0.3	0.4
5–14 years	0.5	0.7	0.8	0.3	0.2	0.2	0.2	0.2
15–24 years	1.8	1.9	1.8	1.1	0.7	0.5	0.5	0.5
25–34 years	4.2	4.5	4.4	2.6	2.1	1.5	1.6	1.4
35–44 years	17.5	14.6	15.7	8.7	6.8	5.8	5.7	5.3
45–54 years	67.9	52.2	44.4	27.2	20.5	17.5	16.7	16.7
55–64 years	205.2	163.8	138.7	74.6	54.3	47.2	43.4	42.7
65–74 years	589.6	530.7	449.5	258.6	166.6	145.0	140.4	135.0
75–84 years	1,543.6	1,555.9	1,361.6	866.3	551.1	490.8	467.3	445.9
85 years and over	3,048.6	3,643.1	2,895.2	2,193.6	1,528.5	1,484.3	1,380.2	1,317.9
Female								
All ages, age adjusted[b]	175.8	170.7	140.0	91.7	62.6	59.1	56.4	55.2
All ages, crude	105.6	111.4	109.0	85.9	68.4	71.8	69.2	68.2
Under 1 year	3.7	3.2	4.0	3.8	3.1	2.7	2.3	2.5
1–4 years	0.7	0.7	0.7	0.5	0.3	0.4	0.4	0.3
5–14 years	0.4	0.6	0.6	0.3	0.2	0.2	0.2	0.2
15–24 years	1.5	1.6	1.4	0.8	0.6	0.5	0.5	0.3
25–34 years	4.3	4.9	4.7	2.6	2.2	1.5	1.5	1.4
35–44 years	19.9	14.8	15.6	8.4	6.1	5.7	5.4	5.5
45–54 years	72.9	46.3	39.0	23.3	17.0	14.5	13.6	13.6
55–64 years	183.1	131.8	95.3	56.8	42.2	35.3	32.9	32.1
65–74 years	522.1	415.7	333.3	188.7	126.7	115.1	109.3	108.1
75–84 years	1,462.2	1,441.1	1,183.1	740.1	466.2	442.1	428.6	421.2
85 years and over	2,949.4	3,704.4	3,081.0	2,323.1	1,667.6	1,632.0	1,550.4	1,501.5
White male[c]								
All ages, age adjusted[b]	182.1	181.6	153.7	98.7	65.5	59.8	56.5	54.2
All ages, crude	100.5	102.7	93.5	63.1	46.9	48.4	46.6	45.7
45–54 years	53.7	40.9	35.6	21.7	15.4	13.6	12.7	12.9
55–64 years	182.2	139.0	119.9	64.0	45.7	39.7	36.1	35.6
65–74 years	569.7	501.0	420.0	239.8	152.9	133.8	128.5	123.8
75–84 years	1,556.3	1,564.8	1,361.6	852.7	539.2	480.0	458.8	437.5
85 years and over	3,127.1	3,734.8	3,018.1	2,230.8	1,545.4	1,490.7	1,386.2	1,327.4

hazards in the home, such as rugs, and installing grab bars in bathrooms are simple measures that can greatly reduce older Americans' risk for falls and fractures.

The current cohort of older adults is better equipped to prevent the illness, disability, and death associated with many chronic diseases than any previous generation. They are less likely to smoke, drink, or experience detrimental stress than younger people, and older adults have better eating habits than their younger counterparts. They are, however, less likely to exercise. Increasing evidence suggests that behavior change, even late in life, is beneficial and can improve disease control and enhanced quality of life.

Maintaining a Healthy Weight

The United States is in the throes of an obesity epidemic. Obesity is defined as body mass index (BMI) greater than or equal to 30kg/m2. In 2004 nearly one-quarter of adults age sixty and over were obese, and the group of adults age forty–fifty-nine that will soon join

TABLE 7.11

Death rates for cerebrovascular diseases, selected characteristics, selected years, 1950–2002 [CONTINUED]

[Data are based on death certificates]

Sex, race, Hispanic origin, and age	1950[a]	1960[a]	1970	1980	1990	2000	2001	2002
				Deaths per 100,000 resident population				
Black or African American male[c]								
All ages, age adjusted[b]	228.8	238.5	206.4	142.0	102.2	89.6	85.4	81.7
All ages, crude	122.0	122.9	108.8	73.0	53.0	46.1	44.6	43.5
45–54 years	211.9	166.1	136.1	82.1	68.4	49.5	48.8	46.5
55–64 years	522.8	439.9	343.4	189.7	141.7	115.4	111.9	110.3
65–74 years	783.6	899.2	780.1	472.3	326.9	268.5	269.2	262.9
75–84 years[d]	1,504.9	1,475.2	1,445.7	1,066.3	721.5	659.2	613.9	587.8
85 years and over	—	2,700.0	1,963.1	1,873.2	1,421.5	1,458.8	1,349.1	1,252.2

— Data not available.

*Rates based on fewer than 20 deaths are considered unreliable and are not shown.

[a]Includes deaths of persons who were not residents of the 50 states and the District of Columbia.

[b]Age-adjusted rates are calculated using the year 2000 standard population.

[c]The race groups, white, black, Asian or Pacific Islander, and American Indian or Alaska Native, include persons of Hispanic and non-Hispanic origin. Persons of Hispanic origin may be of any race. Death rates for the American Indian or Alaska Native and Asian or Pacific Islander populations are known to be underestimated.

[d]In 1950 rate is for the age group 75 years and over.

Notes: Rates for 1991–99 were revised using intercensal population estimates based on census 2000. Rates for 2000 were revised based on census 2000 counts. Rates for 2001 and 2002 were computed using 2000-based postcensal estimates.

SOURCE: Adapted from "Table 37. Death Rates for Cerebrovascular Diseases, According to Sex, Race, Hispanic Origin, and Age: United States, Selected Years 1950–2002," in *Health, United States, 2004*, Centers for Disease Control and Prevention, National Center for Health Statistics, Hyattsville, MD, 2004, http://www.cdc.gov/nchs/data/hus/hus04trend.pdf (accessed August 11, 2005)

the ranks of older Americans reported the highest rate of obesity, 27.7%. (See Figure 7.15.) In addition to older adults who met the criterion for obesity, in 2002, 32% of men and 39% of women age sixty-five–seventy-four, as well as 18% of men and 24% of women ages seventy-five and older, were overweight. Only about a quarter of adults age sixty-five–seventy-four and one-third of adults age seventy-five and older were of healthy weights. (See Table 7.12.)

According to the NCHS, overweight and obese individuals are at increased risk for multiple health problems, including hypertension, high cholesterol, type II diabetes, coronary heart disease, congestive heart failure, stroke, arthritis, obstructive sleep apnea, and other serious conditions.

Smoking

Per capita tobacco consumption declined in the United States in the last decades of the twentieth century. In 2002 fewer people over age sixty-five (10.1% of males and 8.6% of females) smoked than all other age groups (*Older Americans 2004: Key Indicators of Well-Being*).

Smoking hastens the death of more than 440,000 people in the United States each year. Lifelong smokers have a one-in-two chance of dying from a smoking-related disease. Smoking does not simply cut a few months off the end of the smoker's life but reduces the life of the average smoker by twelve years. Smoking is implicated in the development of heart disease, cancer, osteoporosis, and chronic respiratory problems as well as

influenza and pneumonia (*Older Americans 2004: Key Indicators of Well-Being*).

According to the U.S. Surgeon General, even older adult smokers can realize health benefits from quitting. For example, a smoker's risk of heart disease begins to fall almost immediately after quitting, no matter how long the person has smoked.

Physical Activity

Regular physical activity comes closer to being a fountain of youth than any prescription modern medicine can offer. Along with helping older adults to remain mobile and independent, exercise can lower the risk of obesity, heart disease, some cancers, stroke, and diabetes. It can also delay osteoporosis, arthritis, reduce symptoms of depression, and improve sleep quality and memory. Despite these demonstrated benefits, in 2004 just 26.7% of adults age sixty-five–seventy-four and 16% of those age seventy-five and older engaged in regular leisure-time physical activity. Women in these age groups were less likely than men to engage in regular physical activity. (See Figure 7.16.)

The tremendous benefits of physical activity for older adults were reinforced by a study that concluded that people over age seventy who are not active are more likely to develop problems walking or climbing stairs within a few years than those who remain active. According to Marjolein Visser in "Type and Intensity of Activity and Risk or Mobility Limitation: The Mediating Role of Muscle Parameters" (*Journal of the American Geriatrics Society*, vol. 53, no. 5, May 2005), researchers from the

FIGURE 7.15

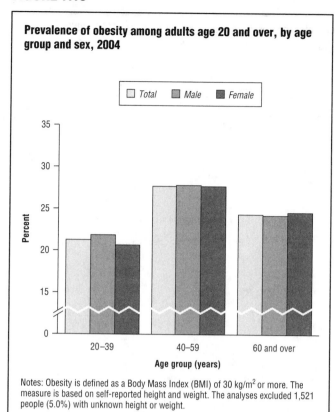

Prevalence of obesity among adults age 20 and over, by age group and sex, 2004

Total · Male · Female

Percent

Age group (years)

Notes: Obesity is defined as a Body Mass Index (BMI) of 30 kg/m² or more. The measure is based on self-reported height and weight. The analyses excluded 1,521 people (5.0%) with unknown height or weight.

SOURCE: "Figure 6.2. Prevalence of Obesity Among Adults Aged 20 and Over, by Age Group and Sex: United States, 2004," in *Early Release of Selected Estimates Based on Data from the 2004 National Health Interview Survey*, Centers for Disease Control and Prevention, National Center for Health Statistics, Hyattsville, MD, June 29, 2005, http://www.cdc.gov/nchs/data/nhis/earlyrelease/earlyrelease200506.pdf (accessed August 11, 2005).

Netherlands interviewed 3,075 men and women between the ages of seventy and seventy-nine, all of whom reported no problems walking one-quarter of a mile or climbing stairs. The investigators followed the subjects for almost five years, noting which subjects developed problems walking and climbing stairs. During the study, 34% of men and 47% of women began to have difficulty walking and climbing stairs. Subjects who were inactive were twice as likely to report these problems as those who said they got regular exercise. Among subjects who were generally inactive, those who walked even a little bit—such as brisk walking for an hour per week—were at reduced risk of mobility problems.

Use of Preventive Health Services

More widespread use of clinical preventive services is a key to preserving and extending the health and quality of life of older Americans. Screening for early detection of selected cancers—breast, cervical, and colorectal—as well as diabetes, cardiovascular disease, and glaucoma has the potential to save lives and slow the progress of chronic disease. Since persons with a regular

source of medical care are more likely to receive basic medical services, such as routine checkups, which present the opportunity to receive preventive services, it is heartening to see that more than 95% of adults sixty-five and older reported having a regular source of medical care. (See Figure 7.17.) Because Medicare covers selected preventive services and screenings, it seems unlikely that cost prevents older adults from obtaining these services. In fact, just 2.6% of the 2004 National Health Interview Survey respondents age sixty-five and older reported that they failed to obtain needed medical care due to cost during the twelve months preceding the interview. (See Figure 7.18.)

Nevertheless, considerable numbers of the older adults did not get preventive screenings in 2002. The CDC Behavioral Risk Factor Surveillance System (BRFSS) and the National Health Interview Survey (NHIS) found that more than 20% of women age sixty-five and older had not had a mammogram during the preceding two years, and only about one-third of older Americans had received other cancer screenings, tests of blood cholesterol levels, and screening for diabetes and heart disease. The Centers for Medicare and Medicaid Services estimates that only 14% of the Medicare population has had any form of colorectal cancer screening, while the American Cancer Society asserts that only 26% of eligible average risk patients have opted to be screened (http://www.acponline.org/journals/news/sep02/colonoscopy.htm). Epidemiologists and health-care planners attribute these low rates of preventive service delivery to older adults' lack of knowledge about prevention and health promotion programs. To address this need for education, the CDC launched a Healthy Aging Web Site (http://www.cdc.gov/aging/), which provides information to health and aging professionals and the public.

SEXUALITY IN AGING

Despite the popular belief that sexuality is exclusively for the young, sexual interest, activity, and capabilities are often lifelong. Although the growing population of older adults will likely spur additional research, to date there are scant data about levels of sexual activity among older adults. The data that are available are often limited to community dwelling older adults, so there is nearly no information about the sexual behavior of institutionalized older adults—those living in nursing homes or other facilities.

After age fifty sexual responses slow; however, very rarely does this natural and gradual diminution cause older adults to end all sexual activity. More important in terms of curtailing older adults' sexual activity is the lack of available partners, which limits opportunities for sexual expression, especially for older women. Another

TABLE 7.12

Overweight, obesity, and healthy weight among persons age 20 and older, selected characteristics, selected years, 1960–2002

[Data are based on measured height and weight of a sample of the civilian noninstitutionalized population]

Sex, age, race, and Hispanic origin[a]	Overweight[b]				
	1960–62	1971–74	1976–80[c]	1988–94	1999–2002
20–74 years, age adjusted[d]			Percent of population		
Both sexes[e,f]	44.8	47.7	47.4	56.0	65.2
Male	49.5	54.7	52.9	61.0	68.8
Female[e]	40.2	41.1	42.0	51.2	61.7
Not Hispanic or Latino					
White only, male	—	—	53.8	61.6	69.5
White only, female[e]	—	—	38.7	47.2	57.0
Black or African American only, male	—	—	51.3	58.2	62.0
Black or African American only, female[e]	—	—	62.6	68.5	77.5
Mexican male	—	—	61.6	69.4	74.1
Mexican female[e]	—	—	61.7	69.6	71.4
20 years and over, age adjusted[d]					
Both sexes[e,f]	—	—	—	56.0	65.1
Male	—	—	—	60.9	68.8
Female[e]	—	—	—	51.4	61.6
Not Hispanic or Latino					
White only, male	—	—	—	61.6	69.4
White only, female[e]	—	—	—	47.5	57.2
Black or African American only, male	—	—	—	57.8	62.6
Black or African American only, female[e]	—	—	—	68.2	77.1
Mexican male	—	—	—	68.9	73.2
Mexican female[e]	—	—	—	68.9	71.2
20 years and over, crude					
Both sexes[e,f]	—	—	—	54.9	65.2
Male	—	—	—	59.4	68.6
Female[e]	—	—	—	50.7	62.0
Not Hispanic or Latino					
White only, male	—	—	—	60.6	69.9
White only, female[e]	—	—	—	47.4	58.2
Black or African American only, male	—	—	—	56.7	61.7
Black or African American only, female[e]	—	—	—	66.0	76.8
Mexican male	—	—	—	63.9	70.1
Mexican female[e]	—	—	—	65.9	69.3
Male					
20–34 years	42.7	42.8	41.2	47.5	57.4
35–4 years	53.5	63.2	57.2	65.5	70.5
45–54 years	53.9	59.7	60.2	66.1	75.7
55–64 years	52.2	58.5	60.2	70.5	75.4
65–74 years	47.8	54.6	54.2	68.5	76.2
75 years and over	—	—	—	56.5	67.4
Female[e]					
20–34 years	21.2	25.8	27.9	37.0	52.8
35–44 years	37.2	40.5	40.7	49.6	60.6
45–54 years	49.3	49.0	48.7	60.3	65.1
55–64 years	59.9	54.5	53.7	66.3	72.2
65–74 years	60.9	55.9	59.5	60.3	70.9
75 years and over	—	—	—	52.3	59.9
20–74 years, age adjusted[d]					
Both sexes[e,f]	13.3	14.6	15.1	23.3	31.1
Male	10.7	12.2	12.8	20.6	28.1
Female[e]	15.7	16.8	17.1	26.0	34.0
Not Hispanic or Latino					
White only, male	—	—	12.4	20.7	28.7
White only, female[e]	—	—	15.4	23.3	31.3
Black or African American only, male	—	—	16.5	21.3	27.9
Black or African American only, female[e]	—	—	31.0	39.1	49.6
Mexican male	—	—	15.7	24.4	29.0
Mexican female[e]	—	—	26.6	36.1	38.9

issue is the greater incidence of illness and progression of chronic diseases that occurs with advancing age. Medical problems with the potential to adversely affect sexual function include diabetes, hypothyroidism, neuropathy, cardiovascular disease, urinary tract infections, prostate cancer, incontinence, arthritis, depression, and dementia. Many pharmacological treatments for chronic illnesses have sexual side effects ranging from diminished libido

TABLE 7.12

Overweight, obesity, and healthy weight among persons age 20 and older, selected characteristics, selected years, 1960–2002 [CONTINUED]

[Data are based on measured height and weight of a sample of the civilian noninstitutionalized population]

Sex, age, race, and Hispanic origin[a]	Obesity[g]				
	1960–62	1971–74	1976–80[c]	1988–94	1999–2002
20 years and over, age adjusted[d]			Percent of population		
Both sexes[e,f]	—	—	—	22.9	30.4
Male	—	—	—	20.2	27.5
Female[e]	—	—	—	25.5	33.2
Not Hispanic or Latino					
White only, male	—	—	—	20.3	28.0
White only, female[e]	—	—	—	22.9	30.7
Black or African American only, male	—	—	—	20.9	27.8
Black or African American only, female[e]	—	—	—	38.3	48.8
Mexican male	—	—	—	23.8	27.8
Mexican female[e]	—	—	—	35.2	38.0
20 years and over, crude					
Both sexes[e,f]	—	—	—	22.3	30.5
Male	—	—	—	19.5	27.5
Female[e]	—	—	—	25.0	33.4
Not Hispanic or Latino					
White only, male	—	—	—	19.9	28.4
White only, female[e]	—	—	—	22.7	31.3
Black or African American only, male	—	—	—	20.7	27.5
Black or African American only, female[e]	—	—	—	36.7	48.8
Mexican male	—	—	—	20.6	26.0
Mexican female[e]	—	—	—	33.3	37.0
Male					
20–34 years	9.2	9.7	8.9	14.1	21.7
35–44 years	12.1	13.5	13.5	21.5	28.5
45–54 years	12.5	13.7	16.7	23.2	30.6
55–64 years	9.2	14.1	14.1	27.2	35.5
65–74 years	10.4	10.9	13.2	24.1	31.9
75 years and over	—	—	—	13.2	18.0
Female[e]					
20–34 years	7.2	9.7	11.0	18.5	28.4
35–44 years	14.7	17.7	17.8	25.5	32.1
45–54 years	20.3	18.9	19.6	32.4	36.9
55–64 years	24.4	24.1	22.9	33.7	42.1
65–74 years	23.2	22.0	21.5	26.9	39.3
75 years and over	—	—	—	19.2	23.6
20–74 years, age adjusted[d]					
Both sexes[e,f]	51.2	48.8	49.6	41.7	32.9
Male	48.3	43.0	45.4	37.9	30.2
Female[e]	54.1	54.3	53.7	45.3	35.6
Not Hispanic or Latino					
White only, male	—	—	45.3	37.4	29.5
White only, female[e]	—	—	56.7	49.2	39.7
Black or African American only, male	—	—	46.6	40.0	35.5
Black or African American only, female[e]	—	—	35.0	28.9	21.3
Mexican male	—	—	37.1	29.8	25.6
Mexican female[e]	—	—	36.4	29.0	27.5
20 years and over, age adjusted[d]					
Both sexes[e,f]	—	—	—	41.6	33.0
Male	—	—	—	37.9	30.2
Female[e]	—	—	—	45.0	35.7
Not Hispanic or Latino					
White only, male	—	—	—	37.3	29.6
White only, female[e]	—	—	—	48.7	39.5
Black or African American only, male	—	—	—	40.1	34.7
Black or African American only, female[e]	—	—	—	29.2	21.7
Mexican male	—	—	—	30.2	26.5
Mexican female[e]	—	—	—	29.7	27.5

(sexual desire and drive) to erectile dysfunction. For example, some medications—antihypertensives, antidepressants, diuretics, steroids, anticonvulsants, and blockers—have high rates of sexual side effects.

In 1998 the National Council on the Aging conducted a landmark study that reported the results of a survey of the sexual behavior of 1,292 people age sixty and older (*Healthy Sexuality and Vital Aging*). Of the survey respondents, 48%

TABLE 7.12

Overweight, obesity, and healthy weight among persons age 20 and older, selected characteristics, selected years, 1960–2002 [CONTINUED]

[Data are based on measured height and weight of a sample of the civilian noninstitutionalized population]

Sex, age, race, and Hispanic origin[a]	Healthy weight[h]				
	1960–62	1971–74	1976–80[c]	1988–94	1999–2002
20 years and over, crude			Percent of population		
Both sexes[e,f]	—	—	—	42.6	32.9
Male	—	—	—	39.4	30.4
Female[e]	—	—	—	45.7	35.4
Not Hispanic or Latino					
White only, male	—	—	—	38.2	29.2
White only, female[e]	—	—	—	48.8	38.7
Black or African American only, male	—	—	—	41.5	35.9
Black or African American only, female[e]	—	—	—	31.2	21.9
Mexican male	—	—	—	35.2	29.4
Mexican female[e]	—	—	—	32.4	29.4
Male					
20–34 years	55.3	54.7	57.1	51.1	40.3
35–44 years	45.2	35.2	41.3	33.4	29.0
45–54 years	44.8	38.5	38.7	33.6	24.0
55–64 years	44.9	38.3	38.7	28.6	23.8
65–74 years	46.2	42.1	42.3	30.1	22.8
75 years and over	—	—	—	40.9	32.0
Female[e]					
20–34 years	67.6	65.8	65.0	57.9	42.6
35–44 years	58.4	56.7	55.6	47.1	37.1
45–54 years	47.6	49.3	48.7	37.2	33.1
55–64 years	38.1	41.1	43.5	31.5	27.6
65–74 years	36.4	40.6	37.8	37.0	26.4
75 years and over	—	—	—	43.0	36.9

— Data not available.
[a]Persons of Mexican origin may be of any race.
The 1999–2002 race-specific estimates are for persons who reported only one racial group. Estimates for single race categories prior to 1999 included persons who reported one race or, if they reported more than one race, identified one race as best representing their race.
[b]Body mass index (BMI) greater than or equal to 25.
[c]Data for Mexicans are for 1982–84.
[d]Age adjusted to the 2000 standard population using five age groups.
[e]Excludes pregnant women.
[f]Includes persons of all races and Hispanic origins, not just those shown separately.
[g]Body mass index (BMI) greater than or equal to 30.
[h]BMI of 18.5 to less than 25 kilograms/meter[2].
Notes: Percents do not sum to 100 because the percent of persons with BMI less than 18.5 is not shown and the percent of persons with obesity is a subset of the percent with overweight. Height was measured without shoes; two pounds were deducted from data for 1960-62 to allow for weight of clothing.

SOURCE: "Table 69. Overweight, Obesity, and Healthy Weight Among Persons 20 Years of Age and Over, According to Sex, Age, Race, and Hispanic Origin: United States, 1960–62, 1971–74, 1976–80, 1988–94, and 1999–2002," in *Health, United States, 2004*, Centers for Disease Control and Prevention, National Center for Health Statistics, Hyattsville, MD, 2004, http://www.cdc.gov/nchs/data/hus/hus04trend.pdf (accessed August 11, 2005)

said they were sexually active, meaning they had engaged in some type of sexual activity at least once a month in the past year. Among those with partners, 80% claimed to be active. Since older men were more likely than older women to have partners, men tended to remain more sexually active throughout their lives. Women with partners, however, were nearly as active as men when in their sixties and seventies, and even more active in their eighties.

Older men were twice as likely as older women to want more sex—56% versus 25%. Of those with partners, 31% reported that the physical aspect of sex was better than it used to be. One in four older Americans said sex was more emotionally satisfying at their current age than when they were in their forties. Men (31%) were much more likely than women (17%) to report that the emotional benefits of sex were greater than they had been in the past.

Ninety percent of survey respondents of both sexes asserted that an honest, moral character and pleasant personality were desirable traits in a romantic partner. More than 80% said they valued humor, good physical health, and intelligence. Men, however, placed substantially more importance on sex than did women, at 78% and 50% respectively. Men wanted partners who enjoyed sexual relationships. Women, on the other hand, valued financial security in a partner far more than men did (82% versus 55%).

In 2004 the AARP updated its 1999 survey, *Sexuality at Midlife and Beyond*, querying nearly seventeen hundred adults age forty-five and older about their relationships and sexual attitudes. One of the biggest changes since the 1999 survey was the older men's use of potency drugs to enhance their performance. Since the drugs had

FIGURE 7.16

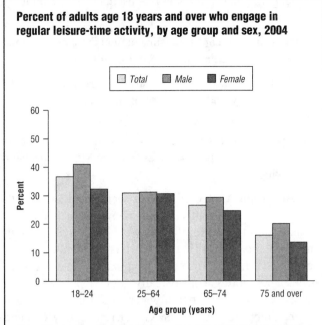

Percent of adults age 18 years and over who engage in regular leisure-time activity, by age group and sex, 2004

Notes: This measure reflects the definition used for the physical activity Leading Health Indicator. Regular leisure-time physical activity is defined as engaging in light-moderate leisure-time physical activity for greater than or equal to 30 minutes at a frequency greater than or equal to five times per week or engaging in vigorous leisure-time physical activity for greater than or equal to 20 minutes at a frequency greater than or equal to three times per week. The analyses excluded persons with unknown physical activity participation (about 3% of respondents each year).

SOURCE: "Figure 7.2. Percent of Adults Aged 18 Years and Over Who Engage in Regular Leisure-Time Activity, by Age Group and Sex: United States, 2004," in *Early Release of Selected Estimates Based on Data from the 2004 National Health Interview Survey*, Centers for Disease Control and Prevention, National Center for Health Statistics, Hyattsville, MD, June 29, 2005, http://www.cdc.gov/nchs/data/nhis/earlyrelease/earlyrelease200506.pdf (accessed August 11, 2005)

FIGURE 7.17

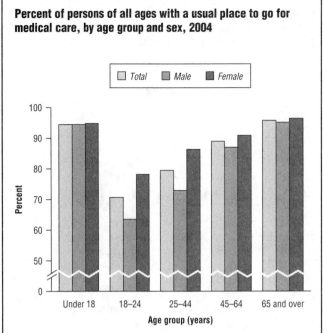

Percent of persons of all ages with a usual place to go for medical care, by age group and sex, 2004

Notes: The usual place to go for medical care does not include a hospital emergency room. The analyses excluded 212 persons (0.5%) with an unknown usual place to go for medical care.

SOURCE: "Figure 2.2. Percent of Persons of All Ages with a Usual Place to Go for Medical Care, by Age Group and Sex: United States, 2004," in *Early Release of Selected Estimates Based on Data from the 2004 National Health Interview Survey*, Centers for Disease Control and Prevention, National Center for Health Statistics, Hyattsville, MD, June 29, 2005, http://www.cdc.gov/nchs/data/nhis/earlyrelease/earlyrelease200506.pdf (accessed August 11, 2005)

debuted just one year before the initial survey, it is no surprise that five years later the proportion of men who had tried the prescription drugs (Viagra, Cialis, and Levitra), hormones, or other treatments more than doubled since 1999, from 10% to 22%.

The 2004 survey found that more older adults had consulted health professionals about this sensitive topic—37% up from 26% in 1999. In 1999 books were the preferred source of information about sexual matters. In 2004 books trailed health professionals with just 30% of respondents consulting them. Nearly one-third of the 2004 respondents said better health would improve their sex lives and nearly one-quarter said better health for their partner would increase their satisfaction. In 2004, 5% more respondents concurred that sexual activity is a critical part of a good relationship.

Two-thirds of men and women with partners said they were either "extremely satisfied" or "somewhat satisfied" with their sex lives. Nearly one-third of respondents with partners described their sex lives as somewhere between "yawn" and "bloody awful." On the whole, mediocre sex

was deemed better than none at all. Nearly 40% of men and 15% of women without regular partners rated their sex lives at the bottom of the satisfaction scale.

The survey revealed that ardor and romance did not diminish with age. Three quarters of those with a regular sexual partner felt that their partners loved them deeply. The older the respondents were, the more likely they were to say that their partner makes them feel important.

THE UNITED STATES LACKS SPECIALISTS IN GERIATRIC MEDICINE

In 1909 Dr. Ignatz L. Nascher coined the term geriatrics from the Greek "geras" (old age) and "iatrikos" (physician). Geriatricians are physicians trained in internal medicine or family practice who obtain additional training and medical board certification in the diagnosis and treatment of older adults.

Geriatric medicine training programs emphasize:

• Management of common conditions that affect older adults such as malnutrition, osteoporosis, incontinence, falls, sensory impairment, depression, and dementia

FIGURE 7.18

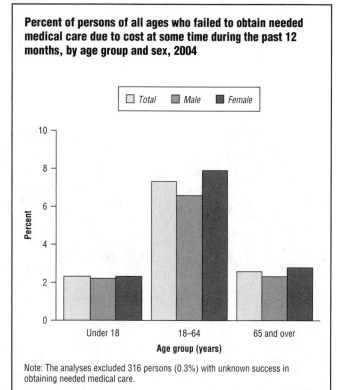

Percent of persons of all ages who failed to obtain needed medical care due to cost at some time during the past 12 months, by age group and sex, 2004

Note: The analyses excluded 316 persons (0.3%) with unknown success in obtaining needed medical care.

SOURCE: "Figure 3.2. Percent of Persons of All Ages Who Failed to Obtain Needed Medical Care Due to Cost at Some Time During the Past 12 Months, by Age Group and Sex: United States, 2004," in *Early Release of Selected Estimates Based on Data from the 2004 National Health Interview Survey*, Centers for Disease Control and Prevention, National Center for Health Statistics, Hyattsville, MD, June 29, 2005, http://www.cdc.gov/nchs/data/nhis/earlyrelease/earlyrelease200506.pdf (accessed August 11, 2005).

- The interaction between aging, disease, and other conditions

- Recognition of the effects of aging on health, physical and mental functioning, and independence

- Appropriate use of medication to prevent the potential dangers and unintended consequences of multiple medications

- Coordinating care to ensure patients' functional independence and enhance overall quality of life

- Organizing health and social services to preserve the productivity and autonomy of older adults

- Assisting families and caregivers as they make decisions about declining capacity, independence, availability and use of support services, and end-of-life decision-making

According to the American Geriatrics Society, the United States currently needs about twenty thousand geriatricians to care for the thirty-six million older adults. In 2004 board-certified geriatricians numbered only seventy-six hundred—fewer than half of the estimated need. The shortage of specially trained physicians will intensify as the baby boom generation joins the ranks of older adults. The American Geriatrics Society contends that financial disincentives pose the greatest barrier to new physicians entering geriatrics. Geriatricians are almost entirely dependent on Medicare reimbursement, and low Medicare reimbursement, which directly influences their earning potential, dissuades many physicians from entering the field. Some prospective geriatricians also may be discouraged by having to spend at least part of their workdays in nursing homes.

In 2005 the American Geriatrics Society called for creating financial and other incentives to attract physicians to obtain specialty training in geriatric medicine. Among their recommendations were medical education loan forgiveness programs, expanded funding for geriatric medicine training programs, and incentives for medical and professional schools to incorporate geriatrics into their curricula.

CHAPTER 8
MENTAL HEALTH AND MENTAL ILLNESS

Changes in mental capabilities are among the most feared aspects of aging. As Mark E. Williams states in "Mild Cognitive Impairment: Who Is Confused?" (*Conference Report Highlights of the American Geriatrics Society 2005 Annual Meeting*, vol. 7, no. 1, May 2005), mental health problems that impair functioning are among the most common age-related changes—their prevalence doubles every five years, increasing from an estimated 1% among those age sixty years old, to 20% at age eighty, and 50% or higher among persons age eighty-five and older.

The aging population has spurred interest in age-related problems in cognition—the process of thinking, learning, and remembering. Cognitive difficulties much milder than those associated with organic brain diseases, such as Alzheimer's disease or dementia, affect a significant proportion of older adults. A study supported by the National Institute on Aging (NIA) and summarized in "Prevalence of Cognitive Impairment: Data from the Indianapolis Study of Health and Aging" (*Neurology*, vol. 57, November 2001) estimated that 23.4% of community-dwelling older adults and 19.2% of nursing home residents suffered some degree of cognitive impairment, in addition to those who suffered from much more serious cognitive impairment. The prevalence of this mild cognitive impairment grew significantly with age, with rates increasing by about 10% for every ten years of age after age sixty-five. The investigators also concluded that "cognitive impairment short of dementia affects nearly one in four community-dwelling elders and is a major risk factor for later development of dementia."

Since the number of persons with mental impairments such as dementia is anticipated to increase as the population ages, and older adults with mental impairment are at risk for institutionalization, the financial costs to individuals and to society are expected to escalate. As such, the mental health and illness of older adults is an increasingly important public health issue.

MENTAL HEALTH

Mental health may be measured in terms of an individual's abilities to think and communicate clearly, learn and grow emotionally, deal productively and realistically with change and stress, and form and maintain fulfilling relationships with others. Mental health is a principle component of wellness—self-esteem, resilience, and the ability to cope with adversity influence how people feel about their themselves.

When mental health is defined and measured in terms of the absence of serious psychological distress, then older adults fare quite well compared with other age groups. The 2004 National Health Interview Survey conducted by the Centers for Disease Control (CDC) posed six questions about the frequency with which respondents experienced certain symptoms of psychological distress within the thirty days preceding the interview. Adults age sixty-five and older were least likely to have experienced serious psychological distress (2.2%) compared with those ages forty-five–sixty-four (3.8%) and adults ages eighteen–forty-four (2.8%).

Experience Shapes Mental Health in Old Age

One theory of aging, termed "continuity theory" and explained in Robert Atchley's book, *The Social Forces in Later Life: An Introduction to Social Gerontology* (Belmont, CA: Wadsworth, 1980), posits that people who age most successfully are those who carry forward the habits, preferences, lifestyles, and relationships from midlife into late life. This theory has gained credence from research studies that have found that traits measured in midlife are strong predictors of outcomes in later life, and that many psychological and social characteristics are stable across the lifespan. For most people, old age does not represent a radical departure from the past; changes often occur gradually and sometimes unnoticeably. Most older adults adapt to the challenges and changes associated with later life using well-practiced coping skills acquired earlier in life.

Not surprisingly, adults who have struggled with mental health problems or mental disorders throughout their lives often continue to suffer these same problems in old age. Few personal problems disappear with old age, and many progress and become more acute. Marital problems, which may have been kept at bay because one or both spouses were away at work, may intensify when a couple spends more time together in retirement. Reduced income, illness, and disability in retirement can aggravate an already troubled marriage and strain even healthy interpersonal, marital, and other family relationships.

Older age can be a period of regrets, which can lead to mutual recriminations. With life expectancy rising, married couples can now expect to spend many years together in retirement. Most older couples manage the transition, but some have problems.

Coping with losses, of friends and family as well as health and independence, may precipitate mental health problems. Hearing loss is common, and close correlations have been found between loss of hearing and depression. Visual impairment limits mobility and the ability to read and watch television. Loss of sight or hearing can cause perceptual disorientation, which in turn may lead to depression, paranoia, fear, and alienation.

A constant awareness of the imminence of death can also become a problem for older adults. Although the majority of older adults resolve their anxieties and concerns about death, some live in denial and fear. How well older adults accept the inevitability of death is a key determinant of satisfaction and emotional well-being in old age.

Memory

Since memory is a key component of cognitive functioning, declining memory that substantially impairs older adults' functioning is a major risk factor for institutionalization. In 2002, 33% of persons age eighty-five and older had moderate to severe memory impairment, compared with 6% of those age sixty-five–sixty-nine. Older men are slightly more likely than older women to suffer memory impairment—15% of men age sixty-five and older compared with 11% of women of the same age. (See Figure 8.1.)

According to "Many Americans Worried about Brain Health, but Only Half Keep Their Brains Fit, According to New Survey" (The Alzheimer's Association, http://www.alz.org/Media/newsreleases/2004/111604_nadm.asp, November 16, 2004), a national survey conducted in October 2004 by the Alzheimer's Association, found that Americans ages fifty-five–sixty-four ranked brain and memory health as their second-greatest health worry, after heart health. Thirty-one percent named heart health

FIGURE 8.1

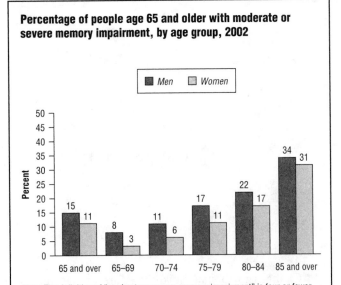

Percentage of people age 65 and older with moderate or severe memory impairment, by age group, 2002

Note: The definition of "moderate or severe memory impairment" is four or fewer words recalled (out of 20) on combined immediate and delayed recall tests among self-respondents. Self-respondents who refused either the immediate or delayed word recall test were excluded from the analysis. Proxy respondents with an overall memory rating of "poor" were included as having moderate or severe memory impairment.
Reference population: These data refer to the civilian noninstitutionalized population.

SOURCE: "Percentage of People Age 65 and Older with Moderate or Severe Memory Impairment, by Age Group, 2002," in *Older Americans 2004: Key Indicators*, Federal Interagency Forum on Aging Related Statistics, Washington, DC, U.S. Government Printing Office, November 2004, http://www.agingstats.gov/chartbook2004/healthstatus.html#Indicator%2017 (accessed August 11, 2005)

as their greatest worry, followed by brain and memory health (23%) and cancer (19%).

Despite the reported high levels of concern, the survey found that only about one-half (52%) of the survey respondents said they engaged in activities aimed at exercising their brains and building capacity for memory. Women were more likely than men to say they engage in such activities—56% versus 47%. Queried about the specific activities they engaged in to exercise their brains and build memory, more than half (53%) named reading, and almost one-third (31%) said puzzles or games. Although the respondents did not necessarily associate their activities with boosting brain health, many reported engaging in activities that exercise and build brain memory. For example, more than three-quarters (77%) said they "make a special effort to choose foods that are healthier" and "read books" (76%), and more than one-half (57%) claimed they "walk a mile or more."

ORGANIC BRAIN DISEASES—DEMENTIAS

Dementia refers to a range of mental and behavioral changes caused by cerebrovascular or neurological diseases that permanently damage the brain, impairing the activity of brain cells. These changes can affect memory, speech, and the ability to perform the activities of daily living.

It is important to remember that occasional forgetfulness and memory lapses are not signs of dementia. Dementia is caused by disease and is not the inevitable result of growing older. Many disorders may cause or simulate dementia, which is not a single disorder—dementia refers to a condition caused by a variety of diseases and disorders, a small proportion of which are potentially reversible.

Multi-Infarct Dementia

According to the NIA, multi-infarct dementia is the most common form of vascular dementia and accounts for 10–20% of all cases of progressive dementia. It usually affects people between the ages of sixty and seventy-five and is more likely to occur in men than women. Multi-infarct dementia is caused by a series of small strokes that disrupt blood flow and damage or destroy brain tissue. Sometimes these small strokes are "silent"—they produce no obvious symptoms and are detected only on imaging studies, such as computerized tomography (CT) or magnetic resonance imaging (MRI) scans of the brain. An older adult may suffer several small strokes before noticing serious changes in memory, reasoning or other signs of multi-infarct dementia.

Because strokes occur suddenly, loss of cognitive skills and memory present quickly, although some affected individuals may appear to improve for short periods of time, then decline again after having more strokes. Establishing the diagnosis of multi-infarct dementia is challenging because its symptoms are difficult to distinguish from those of Alzheimer's disease. Treatment cannot reverse the damage already done to the brain. Instead it focuses on preventing further damage by reducing the risk of additional strokes. This entails treating the underlying causes of stroke—hypertension, diabetes, high cholesterol, and heart disease. Surgical procedures to improve blood flow to the brain, such as carotid endarterectomy, angioplasty, or stenting, as well as medications to reduce the risk of stroke, are also used to treat this condition.

Alzheimer's Disease

The most prevalent form of dementia is Alzheimer's disease (AD), named after German neurologist Alois Alzheimer, who in 1906 discovered the neurofibrillary tangles, which along with amyloid plaques in the brain, are characteristic markers of this progressive, degenerative disease that affects the brain and results in severely impaired memory, thinking, and behavior.

The United States Department of Health and Human Services (HHS) estimates that 4.5 million Americans suffered from AD in 2004. The NIA reports that approximately 10% of the population over age sixty-five and nearly half of those over age eighty-five—the fastest-growing segment of United States society—have the disease, and its prevalence doubles every five years beyond age sixty-five. According to the U.S. Census Bureau, the numbers of cases of AD are expected to increase by more than 12% every five years through 2015. Prevalence is partially determined by the length of time people with AD survive. While average survival is eight years after diagnosis, some AD patients have lived longer than twenty years with the disease. Therefore, improvements in AD care, as well as increased length of life of the older adult population in general, will increase the numbers of AD patients.

The Alzheimer's Association asserts that if a cure or prevention is not found by 2050, the number of Americans with AD is estimated to range from 11.3 million to sixteen million, with a middle estimate of 13.2 million. On the other hand, discovery of a treatment that could delay the onset of AD by five years could reduce the number of individuals with the disease by nearly 50% after fifty years.

SYMPTOMS. AD begins slowly between the ages of fifty-five and eighty with mild episodes of forgetfulness and disorientation. As the disease progresses, memory loss increases and mood swings are frequent, accompanied by confusion, irritability, restlessness, and speech impairment. The symptoms include difficulty with memory and a loss of cognitive function. The AD patient may also experience trouble finding words; impaired judgment; disorientation in place and time; and changes in behavior and personality. How quickly these changes occur varies from person to person, but eventually the disease leaves its victims unable to care for themselves. In their terminal stages, AD victims require care twenty-four hours a day. They no longer recognize family members or themselves, and they need help with such daily activities as eating, dressing, bathing, and using the toilet. Eventually, they may become incontinent, blind, and unable to communicate. Finally, their bodies may "forget" how to breathe or make the heart beat. Many AD patients die from pneumonia.

DEATH RATES. AD is the eighth-leading cause of death in adults of all ages. In 2003 it claimed 63,343 lives, up 6% from 2002, and it was the fifth-leading cause of death among adults age sixty-five and older. (See Table 8.1.) AD also contributes to many more deaths that are attributed to other causes, such as pneumonia and heart and respiratory failure.

From the time of diagnosis, people with Alzheimer's disease survive about half as long as those of similar age without dementia. Average survival time is affected by age at diagnosis and severity of other medical conditions.

TABLE 8.1

Deaths and death rates for the 10 leading causes of death in specified age groups, preliminary 2003

[Data are based on a continuous file of records received from the states. Rates are per 100,000 population in specified group. Figures are based on weighted data rounded to the nearest individual, so categories may not add to totals or subtotals.]

Rank[a]	Cause of death and age	Number	Rate
	All ages[b]		
...	All causes	2,443,930	840.4
1	Diseases of heart	684,462	235.4
2	Malignant neoplasms	554,643	190.7
3	Cerebrovascular diseases	157,803	54.3
4	Chronic lower respiratory diseases	126,128	43.4
5	Accidents (unintentional injuries)	105,695	36.3
...	Motor vehicle accidents	44,059	15.2
...	All other accidents	61,636	21.2
6	Diabetes mellitus	73,965	25.4
7	Influenza and pneumonia	64,847	22.3
8	Alzheimer's disease	63,343	21.8
9	Nephritis, nephrotic syndrome and nephrosis	42,536	14.6
10	Septicemia	34,243	11.8
...	All other causes	536,265	184.4
	1–4 years		
...	All causes	4,911	31.1
1	Accidents (unintentional injuries)	1,679	10.6
...	Motor vehicle accidents	591	3.7
...	All other accidents	1,088	6.9
2	Congenital malformations, deformations and chromosomal abnormalities	514	3.3
3	Malignant neoplasms	383	2.4
4	Assault (homicide)	342	2.2
5	Diseases of heart	186	1.2
6	Influenza and pneumonia	151	1.0
7	Septicemia	82	0.5
8	Certain conditions originating in the perinatal period	76	0.5
9	In situ neoplasms, benign neoplasms and neoplasms of uncertain or unknown behavior	53	0.3
10	Chronic lower respiratory diseases	47	0.3
...	All other causes	1,398	8.9
	5–14 years		
...	All causes	6,930	16.9
1	Accidents (unintentional injuries)	2,561	6.3
...	Motor vehicle accidents	1,592	3.9
...	All other accidents	970	2.4
2	Malignant neoplasms	1,060	2.6
3	Congenital malformations, deformations and chromosomal abnormalities	370	0.9
4	Assault (homicide)	310	0.8
5	Intentional self-harm (suicide)	255	0.6
6	Diseases of heart	252	0.6
7	Influenza and pneumonia	134	0.3
8	Chronic lower respiratory diseases	107	0.3
9	Septicemia	77	0.2
10	In situ neoplasms, benign neoplasms and neoplasms of uncertain or unknown behavior	76	0.2
...	All other causes	1,728	4.2

SUSPECTED CAUSES. AD is not a normal consequence of growing older, and researchers continue to seek its cause. It is a disease of the brain that is influenced by genetic and nongenetic factors.

Researchers have found some promising genetic clues to the disease and have observed the different patterns of inheritance, ages of onset (when symptoms begin), genes, chromosomes, and proteins linked to the development of AD. Mutations in four genes, situated

[Data are based on a continuous file of records received from the states. Rates are per 100,000 population in specified group. Figures are based on weighted data rounded to the nearest individual, so categories may not add to totals or subtotals.]

Rank[a]	Cause of death and age	Number	Rate
	15–24 years		
...	All causes	33,022	80.1
1	Accidents (unintentional injuries)	14,966	36.3
...	Motor vehicle accidents	10,857	26.3
...	All other accidents	4,109	10.0
2	Assault (homicide)	5,148	12.5
3	Intentional self-harm (suicide)	3,921	9.5
4	Malignant neoplasms	1,628	4.0
5	Diseases of heart	1,083	2.6
6	Congenital malformations, deformations and chromosomal abnormalities	425	1.0
7	Influenza and pneumonia	216	0.5
8	Cerebrovascular diseases	204	0.5
9	Chronic lower respiratory diseases	172	0.4
10	Human immunodeficiency virus (HIV) disease	171	0.4
...	All other causes	5,088	12.3
	25–44 years		
...	All causes	128,924	153.0
1	Accidents (unintentional injuries)	27,844	33.1
...	Motor vehicle accidents	13,582	16.1
...	All other accidents	14,261	16.9
2	Malignant neoplasms	19,041	22.6
3	Diseases of heart	16,283	19.3
4	Intentional self-harm (suicide)	11,251	13.4
5	Assault (homicide)	7,367	8.7
6	Human immunodeficiency virus (HIV) disease	6,879	8.2
7	Chronic liver disease and cirrhosis	3,288	3.9
8	Cerebrovascular diseases	3,004	3.6
9	Diabetes mellitus	2,662	3.2
10	Influenza and pneumonia	1,337	1.6
...	All other causes	29,968	35.6
	45–64 years		
...	All causes	437,058	636.1
1	Malignant neoplasms	144,936	211.0
2	Diseases of heart	101,713	148.0
3	Accidents (unintentional injuries)	23,669	34.5
...	Motor vehicle accidents	9,891	14.4
...	All other accidents	13,778	20.1
4	Diabetes mellitus	16,326	23.8
5	Cerebrovascular diseases	15,971	23.2
6	Chronic lower respiratory diseases	15,409	22.4
7	Chronic liver disease and cirrhosis	13,649	19.9
8	Intentional self-harm (suicide)	10,057	14.6
9	Human immunodeficiency virus (HIV) disease	5,917	8.6
10	Septicemia	5,827	8.5
...	All other causes	83,584	121.7

on chromosomes 1, 14, 19, and 21, are thought to be involved in the disease.

The first genetic breakthrough was reported in the February 1991 issue of the British journal *Nature*. Investigators reported that they had discovered that a mutation in a single gene could cause this progressive neurological illness. Scientists found the defect in the gene that directs cells to produce a substance called amyloid protein. Researchers at the Massachusetts Institute of Technology found that low levels of the brain chemical acetylcholine contribute to the formation of hard deposits of amyloid protein that accumulate in the brain tissue of AD patients.

TABLE 8.1

Deaths and death rates for the 10 leading causes of death in specified age groups, preliminary 2003 [CONTINUED]

[Data are based on a continuous file of records received from the states. Rates are per 100,000 population in specified group. Figures are based on weighted data rounded to the nearest individual, so categories may not add to totals or subtotals.]

Rank[a]	Cause of death and age	Number	Rate
	65 years and over		
...	All causes	1,804,131	5,022.8
1	Diseases of heart	564,204	1,570.8
2	Malignant neoplasms	387,475	1,078.7
3	Cerebrovascular diseases	138,397	385.3
4	Chronic lower respiratory diseases	109,199	304.0
5	Alzheimer's disease	62,707	174.6
6	Influenza and pneumonia	57,507	160.1
7	Diabetes mellitus	54,770	152.5
8	Nephritis, nephrotic syndrome and nephrosis	35,392	98.5
9	Accidents (unintentional injuries)	33,976	94.6
...	Motor vehicle accidents	7,379	20.5
...	All other accidents	26,597	74.0
10	Septicemia	26,609	74.1
...	All other causes	333,895	929.6

... Category not applicable.
[a]Rank based on number of deaths.
[b]Includes deaths under 1 year of age.
Note: Data are subject to sampling or random variation.

SOURCE: Donna L. Hoyert, Hsiang-Ching Kung, and Betty L. Smith, "Table 7. Deaths and Death Rates for the 10 Leading Causes of Death in Specified Age Groups: United States, Preliminary 2003," in "Death: Preliminary Data for 2003," *National Vital Statistics Reports*, vol. 53, no. 15, Centers for Disease Control and Prevention, National Center for Health Statistics, Hyattsville, MD, February 28, 2005, http://www.cdc.gov/nchs/data/nvsr/nvsr53/nvsr53_15.pdf (accessed August 11, 2005)

In normal people the protein fragments are broken down and excreted by the body. Amyloid protein is found in cells throughout the body, and researchers do not know how it becomes a deadly substance in the brain cells of some people and not others.

In 1995 three more genes linked to AD were identified. One gene appears to be related to the most devastating form of early-onset AD, which can strike people in their thirties. When defective, the gene may prevent brain cells from correctly processing a substance called beta amyloid precursor protein. The second gene is linked to another early-onset form of AD that strikes people before age sixty-five. This gene also appears to be involved in producing beta amyloid. Researchers believe that the discovery of these two genes will allow them to narrow their search for the proteins responsible for early-onset AD and give them clues to the causes of AD in older people.

The third gene, known as apolipoprotein E (apoE), was reported as associated with AD in 1993, but its role in the body was not known at that time. Researchers have since found that the gene plays several roles. Within the body, it regulates lipid metabolism within the organs and helps to redistribute cholesterol. In the brain, apoE participates in repairing nerve tissue that has been injured. There are three forms (alleles) of the gene: apoE-2,

apoE-3, and apoE-4. Until recently, people with two copies of apoE-4, one from each parent, were thought to have a greatly increased risk of developing AD before age seventy. From one-half to one-third of all AD patients have at least one apoE-4 gene, while only 15% of the general population has an apoE-4 gene. In 1998 researchers discovered that the apoE-4 gene seems to affect when a person may develop AD, not whether the person will develop the disease.

Another recently discovered gene, A2M-2, appears to affect whether a person will develop AD. Researchers estimate that nearly one-third (30%) of Americans may carry A2M-2, a genetic variant that more than triples their risk of developing late-onset AD compared with siblings with the normal version of the A2M gene. The discovery of A2M-2 opens up the possibility of developing a drug that mimics the A2M gene's normal function. This has the potential to protect susceptible persons against brain damage or perhaps even reverse it.

TESTING FOR AD. A complete physical, psychiatric, and neurological evaluation can usually produce a diagnosis of AD that is about 90% accurate. For many years, the only sure way to diagnose the disease was to examine brain tissue under a microscope, which was not possible while the AD victim was still alive. An autopsy of someone who has died of AD reveals a characteristic pattern that is the hallmark of the disease—tangles of fibers (neurofibrillary tangles) and clusters of degenerated nerve endings (neuritic plaques) in areas of the brain that are crucial for memory and intellect. Also, the cortex of the brain is shrunken.

In 1996 a San Francisco biotechnology firm developed a diagnostic test for AD. The test, which involves analysis of blood and spinal fluid, produced conclusive results in 60% of older patients with dementia attributed to AD.

In 2000 researchers at Brigham and Women's Hospital in Boston found that by using magnetic resonance imaging (MRI) they could measure the volume of brain tissue in areas of the brain used for memory, organizational ability, and planning, and using these measurements could accurately identify persons with AD and predict which people would develop AD in the future. The same year other scientists, at New York University Medical Center, the Mayo Clinic, and the National Hospital for Neurology and Neurosurgery in London, reported using MRI to identify parts of the brain affected by AD before symptoms appear and to measure brain atrophy to monitor the progression of AD.

In early 2005 researchers Chad Mirkin and William Klein at Northwestern University announced development of yet another diagnostic test that detects small amounts of protein in spinal fluid ("Nanoparticle-based Detection in Cerebral Spinal Fluid of a Soluble Pathogenic Biomarker for Alzheimer's Disease," Proceedings of the National Academy of Science, http://www.pnas.org, February 15, 2005). The test is called a bio-barcode assay and is as many as a million times more sensitive than other tests. First used to identify a marker for prostate cancer, the test is used to detect a protein in the brain called amyloid-beta-derived diffusible ligand (ADDL). ADDLs are small soluble proteins. To detect them, the researchers used nanoscale particles that had antibodies specific to ADDL.

Investigators continue to look at other biological markers, such as blood tests, for AD and at neuropsychological tests, which measure memory, orientation, judgment, and problem solving, to see if they can accurately predict whether healthy, unaffected older adults will develop AD or whether those with mild cognitive impairment will go on to develop AD.

Physicians and neuroscientists have long been eager for a simple and accurate test that can distinguish persons with AD from those with cognitive problems or dementias arising from other causes. An accurate test would allow the detection of AD early enough for the use of experimental medications to slow the progression of the disease, as well as identify persons at risk of developing AD. But the availability of tests raises ethical and practical questions: Do people really want to know their risks of developing AD? Will health insurers use genetic or other diagnostic test results to deny insurance coverage to persons at risk for the disease?

TREATMENT. There is still no cure or prevention for AD, and treatment focuses on managing symptoms. Medication may slow the appearance of some symptoms and can lessen others, such as agitation, anxiety, unpredictable behavior, and depression. Physical exercise and good nutrition are important, as is a calm and highly structured environment. The object is to help the AD patient maintain as much comfort, normalcy, and dignity for as long as possible.

Until 1997 tacrine (marketed as Cognex) was the nation's only Alzheimer's medication. But in early 1997 the Food and Drug Administration (FDA) approved a new drug, donepezil, to be marketed under the trade name Aricept. Both drugs are cholinesterase inhibitors, which produce some delay in the deterioration of memory and other cognitive skills. They offer only mild benefits at best.

By 2005 there were five FDA-approved prescription drugs for the treatment of AD, and the National Institutes of Health (NIH) affiliates and pharmaceutical companies were involved in clinical trials of more than twenty new drugs to treat AD. All of the drugs being tested are intended to improve the symptoms of AD and slow its progression, but none is expected to "cure" AD. The investigational drugs aim to address three aspects of AD: to improve cognitive function in persons with early AD,

slow or postpone the progression of the disease, and control behavioral problems such as wandering, aggression, and agitation of patients with AD.

Other research is examining the roles of the hormones estrogen and progesterone on memory and cognitive function. Since AD involves inflammatory processes in the brain, scientists are also studying the use of anti-inflammatory agents such as ibuprofen or prednisone to reduce the risk of developing AD. Researchers are also investigating the relationship between the various gene sites, particularly the mutation on chromosome 21, and environmental influences that may increase susceptibility to AD. Another NIA-funded study is trying to find out whether antioxidants, such as vitamin E, can prevent persons with mild memory impairment from progressing to AD.

In 2005 the NIA and Alzheimer's Association launched the AD Genetics Study, recruiting subjects from families in which two siblings developed AD after age sixty. They hope to compare the genes of the afflicted siblings with those from another family member who does not have AD in an effort to find the genes that contribute to AD.

CARING FOR THE AD PATIENT. AD affects members of the patient's family. While medication may suppress some symptoms and occasionally slow the progression of the disease, eventually most AD patients require constant care and supervision. Until recently, nursing homes and residential care facilities were not equipped to provide this kind of care and, if they accepted AD patients at all, admitted only those in the very earliest stages of the disease. Since 2000, a growing number of nursing homes have welcomed AD patients despite the fact that they are more difficult and costly to care for than older adults without AD. Although this change was primarily financially motivated, as nursing home occupancy rates dropped in response to the growth of alternative housing for older adults, it does offer families with ample financial resources—the average annual stay ranges from $46,000 to $75,000 depending on geography and intensity of services—an alternative to caring for the AD patient at home.

Many children and other relatives of AD patients cannot afford institutional care or feel a moral obligation to care for the affected family member at home as long as possible. No matter how willing and devoted the caregiver, the time, patience, and resources required to provide care over a long period of time are immense, and the task is often overwhelming. As the patient's condition progresses, caregivers often find themselves socially isolated. Research reveals that the average caregiver misses more than three weeks of work a year and that as many as 20% of caregivers quit their jobs altogether. Caregiving has been linked to increased rates of depression, compromised immune function, and a greater use of medication and psychotropic drugs—medications used to improve mood and relieve symptoms of mental distress. Few caregivers are prepared for this impact on their health and lives.

Caregivers who participate in support groups, and make use of home health aids, adult day care, and respite care (facilities where patients stay for a limited number of days), not only feel healthier but also are better able to care for AD patients and maintain them at home longer than those who do not.

MENTAL ILLNESS

Older people with mental illnesses were once considered "senile"—mentally debilitated as a result of old age. Serious forgetfulness, emotional disturbances, and other behavioral changes do not, however, occur as a normal part of aging. They may be caused by chronic illnesses such as heart disease, thyroid disorders, or anemia; infections, poor diet, or lack of sleep; or prescription drugs, such as narcotic painkillers, sedatives, and antihistamines. Social isolation, loneliness, boredom, or depression also may cause memory lapses. When accurately diagnosed and treated, these types of problems frequently can be reversed.

Mental illness refers to all identifiable mental health disorders and mental health problems. *Mental Health: A Report of the Surgeon General, 1999* (http://www.surgeongeneral.gov/library/mentalhealth/home.html) defines mental disorders as "health conditions that are characterized by alterations in thinking, mood, or behavior (or some combination thereof) associated with distress and/or impaired functioning." The report distinguishes mental health disorders from mental health problems, describing the signs and symptoms of mental health problems as less intense and of shorter duration than those of mental health disorders, but it acknowledges that both mental health disorders and problems may be distressing and disabling.

The Surgeon General's report observed that nearly 20% of people age fifty-five years and older experience mental disorders that are not part of normal aging. The most common disorders, in order of estimated prevalence rates, are anxiety (11.4%), severe cognitive impairment (6.6%), and mood disorders (4.4%) such as depression. The report also points out that mental disorders in older adults are frequently unrecognized, underreported, and undertreated.

Diagnosing mental disorders in older adults is challenging, because their symptoms and presentation may be different from that of other adults. For example, many older individuals volunteer physical as opposed to emotional or psychological complaints, and they present symptoms of depression and anxiety that are not typical of depressive or anxiety disorders. Accurate identification, detection, and diagnosis of mental disorders in older adults also are complicated by the following:

- Mental disorders often coexist with other medical problems.
- The symptoms of some chronic diseases may imitate or conceal psychological disorders.
- Older adults are more likely to report physical symptoms than psychological ones, because there is less stigma associated with physical health or medical problems than with mental health problems.

Depression

Symptoms of depression are an important indicator of physical and mental health in older adults, because persons who experience many symptoms of depression also are more likely to report higher rates of physical illness, disability, and higher rates of health service utilization.

The prevalence of clinically relevant depressive symptoms (as distinguished from brief periods of sadness or depressed mood) increases with advancing age. In 2002, 19% of adults age eighty-five and older experienced these symptoms, compared with 13% of those age sixty-five–sixty-nine. Older women in all age groups reported depressive symptoms more than older men did. Sixteen percent of women age sixty-five–sixty-nine reported depressive symptoms, compared with 10% of men the same age. Among those age eighty-five and older, 22% of women reported symptoms, compared with 15% of men. (See Figure 8.2.)

Often, illness itself can trigger depression in older adults by altering the chemicals in the brain. Examples of illnesses that can touch off depression are diabetes, hypothyroidism, kidney or liver dysfunction, heart disease, and infection. In patients with these ailments, treating the underlying disease usually eliminates the depression. About one-quarter of older adults with chronic diseases also suffer from depression. Understandably, persons with disabling chronic illnesses such as arthritis, stroke, and pulmonary diseases are likely to become depressed. Some prescription medications, as well as over-the-counter drugs, also may cause depression.

Research conducted in 2005 at the University of Rochester Sleep and Neurophysiology Research Laboratory and summarized by Alan Mozes in "Insomnia Linked to Depression in Elderly" (*HealthDay*, Jun 27, 2005) found that chronic insomnia may trigger and foster depression among older adults. One study found that older patients with a history of depression were more likely to continue being depressed if they also suffered from persistent insomnia. The second study indicated that even without a history of depression, older patients—particularly

FIGURE 8.2

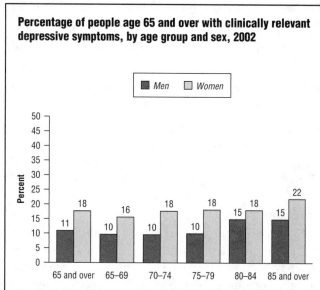

Percentage of people age 65 and over with clinically relevant depressive symptoms, by age group and sex, 2002

Note: The definition of "clinically relevant depressive symptoms" is four or more symptoms out of a list of eight depressive symptoms from an abbreviated version of the Center for Epidemiological Studies Depression Scale (CES-D) adapted by the Health and Retirement Study. The CES-D scale is a measure of depressive symptoms and is not to be used as a diagnosis of clinical depression.
Reference population: These data refer to the civilian noninstitutionalized population.

SOURCE: "Percentage of People Age 65 and Over with Clinically Relevant Depressive Symptoms by Age Group and Sex, 2002," in *Older Americans 2004: Key Indicators*, Federal Interagency Forum on Aging Related Statistics, Washington, DC, U.S. Government Printing Office, November 2004, http://www.agingstats.gov/chartbook2004/healthstatus.html#Indicator%2018 (accessed August 11, 2005)

women—who suffer from chronic sleeplessness are at a higher risk for becoming severely depressed than those who have no trouble sleeping. The findings support the hypothesis that insomnia may be more than a symptom of depression; it may also be a cause. The investigators concluded that older patients with persistent insomnia are six times more likely to experience serious new-onset depression than individuals who sleep easily.

Depression causes some older adults to deliberately neglect or disregard their medical needs—failing to take prescribed medication or taking it incorrectly, and eating poorly. These may be "covert" acts of suicide. Actual suicide, which is frequently a consequence of serious depression, is highest among older adults relative to all other age groups. In 2002 the death rate for suicide among persons age seventy-five to eighty-four was 17.7 per one hundred thousand, and among adults age eighty-five and older it was 18. Older men had the highest rates—38.1 per one hundred thousand in men age seventy-five to eighty-four and 50.7 in men age eighty-five and older. (See Table 8.2.)

TREATMENT OF DEPRESSION. According to the Surgeon General's report, despite the availability of effective treatments for depression, a substantial fraction of affected older adults do not receive treatment, largely because they either do not seek it or because their depression is not identified, accurately diagnosed, or effectively treated. For example, although older patients respond well to antidepressant medications, some physicians do not prescribe them to older patients already taking many drugs for chronic medical conditions because they do not want to risk drug–drug interactions or add another drug to an already complicated regimen. As a result, only a minority of older adults diagnosed with depression receives the appropriate drug dose and duration of treatment for depression.

Studies of the brain show that depression has a biological and chemical basis. Research suggests that the problem may be caused by the complex neurotransmission (chemical messaging) system of the brain and that persons suffering depression have either too much or too little of certain neurochemicals in the brain. Investigators believe that depressed patients with normal levels of neurotransmitters may suffer from an inability to regulate them. Most antidepressant drugs currently used to treat the disorder attempt to correct these chemical imbalances.

In 2005 a study of two hundred older patients admitted to a psychiatric hospital found that antidepressants reduced the risk of suicide attempts by about 50%. Treatment with benzodiazepines, often used to treat anxiety, in addition to antidepressants reduced the risk of attempted suicides by another 10%. These findings are detailed in "Antidepressants May Help Reduce Suicides in Elderly" (*Medscape*, http://www.medscape.com/viewarticle/505332).

Other common treatments for depression include psychotherapy, with or without the use of antidepressant medications, and electroconvulsive therapy (ECT). Psychotherapy is most often used to treat mild to moderate depression and is prescribed for a limited, defined period, generally ranging from ten to twenty weeks. ECT is used for life-threatening depression that does not respond to treatment with antidepressant drugs.

Anxiety Disorders

Anxiety disorders—extreme nervousness and apprehension or sudden attacks of anxiety without apparent external causes—can be debilitating and destructive. Symptoms may include fear, a "knot" in the stomach, sweating, or elevated blood pressure. If the anxiety is severe and long lasting, more serious problems may develop. Persons suffering from anxiety over an extended period may have headaches, ulcers, irritable bowel syndrome, insomnia, and depression. Because anxiety tends to create various other emotional and physical symptoms, a "cascade" effect can occur in which these new or additional problems produce even more anxiety.

TABLE 8.2

Death rates for suicide, by selected characteristics, selected years 1950–2002

[Data are based on death certificates]

Sex, race, Hispanic origin, and age	1950[a]	1960[a]	1970	1980	1990	2000	2001	2002
All persons				Deaths per 100,000 resident population				
All ages, age adjusted[b]	13.2	12.5	13.1	12.2	12.5	10.4	10.7	10.9
All ages, crude	11.4	10.6	11.6	11.9	12.4	10.4	10.8	11.0
Under 1 year	...	...	...	...	...	...	...	...
1–4 years	...	...	...	...	...	...	...	...
5–14 years	0.2	0.3	0.3	0.4	0.8	0.7	0.7	0.6
15–24 years	4.5	5.2	8.8	12.3	13.2	10.2	9.9	9.9
15–19 years	2.7	3.6	5.9	8.5	11.1	8.0	7.9	7.4
20–24 years	6.2	7.1	12.2	16.1	15.1	12.5	12.0	12.4
25–44 years	11.6	12.2	15.4	15.6	15.2	13.4	13.8	14.0
25–34 years	9.1	10.0	14.1	16.0	15.2	12.0	12.8	12.6
35–44 years	14.3	14.2	16.9	15.4	15.3	14.5	14.7	15.3
45–64 years	23.5	22.0	20.6	15.9	15.3	13.5	14.4	14.9
45–54 years	20.9	20.7	20.0	15.9	14.8	14.4	15.2	15.7
55–64 years	26.8	23.7	21.4	15.9	16.0	12.1	13.1	13.6
65 years and over	30.0	24.5	20.8	17.6	20.5	15.2	15.3	15.6
65–74 years	29.6	23.0	20.8	16.9	17.9	12.5	13.3	13.5
75–84 years	31.1	27.9	21.2	19.1	24.9	17.6	17.4	17.7
85 years and over	28.8	26.0	19.0	19.2	22.2	19.6	17.5	18.0
Male								
All ages, age adjusted[b]	21.2	20.0	19.8	19.9	21.5	17.7	18.2	18.4
All ages, crude	17.8	16.5	16.8	18.6	20.4	17.1	17.6	17.9
Under 1 year	...	...	...	...	...	...	...	...
1–4 years	...	...	...	...	...	...	...	...
5–14 years	0.3	0.4	0.5	0.6	1.1	1.2	1.0	0.9
15–24 years	6.5	8.2	13.5	20.2	22.0	17.1	16.6	16.5
15–19 years	3.5	5.6	8.8	13.8	18.1	13.0	12.9	12.2
20–24 years	9.3	11.5	19.3	26.8	25.7	21.4	20.5	20.8
25–44 years	17.2	17.9	20.9	24.0	24.4	21.3	22.1	22.2
25–34 years	13.4	14.7	19.8	25.0	24.8	19.6	21.0	20.5
35–44 years	21.3	21.0	22.1	22.5	23.9	22.8	23.1	23.7
45–64 years	37.1	34.4	30.0	23.7	24.3	21.3	22.5	23.5
45–54 years	32.0	31.6	27.9	22.9	23.2	22.4	23.4	24.4
55–64 years	43.6	38.1	32.7	24.5	25.7	19.4	21.1	22.2
65 years and over	52.8	44.0	38.4	35.0	41.6	31.1	31.5	31.8
65–74 years	50.5	39.6	36.0	30.4	32.2	22.7	24.6	24.7
75–84 years	58.3	52.5	42.8	42.3	56.1	38.6	37.8	38.1
85 years and over	58.3	57.4	42.4	50.6	65.9	57.5	51.1	50.7
Female								
All ages, age adjusted[b]	5.6	5.6	7.4	5.7	4.8	4.0	4.0	4.2
All ages, crude	5.1	4.9	6.6	5.5	4.8	4.0	4.1	4.3
Under 1 year	...	...	...	...	...	...	...	...
1–4 years	...	...	...	...	...	...	...	...
5–14 years	0.1	0.1	0.2	0.2	0.4	0.3	0.3	0.3
15–24 years	2.6	2.2	4.2	4.3	3.9	3.0	2.9	2.9
15–19 years	1.8	1.6	2.9	3.0	3.7	2.7	2.7	2.4
20–24 years	3.3	2.9	5.7	5.5	4.1	3.2	3.1	3.5

Unrelenting anxiety that appears unrelated to specific environments or situations is called *generalized anxiety disorder*. Persons suffering from this disorder worry excessively about the events of daily life and the future. They are also more likely to experience physical symptoms such as shortness of breath, dizziness, rapid heart rate, nausea, stomach pains, and muscle tension than persons afflicted with other panic disorders, social phobias, or agoraphobia (fear of being in an open space or a place where escape is difficult).

The Surgeon General's report estimated the prevalence of anxiety disorder as about 11.4% in adults age fifty-five years and older. Phobic anxiety disorders such as social phobia, which causes extreme discomfort in social settings, are among the most common mental disturbances in late life. In contrast, the prevalence of panic disorder (0.5%) and obsessive-compulsive disorder (1.5%) is very low in older adults. Generalized anxiety disorder, rather than specific anxiety syndromes, may be more prevalent in older people.

Effective treatment for anxiety involves medication, primarily benzodiazepines such as Valium, Librium, and Xanax, as well as psychotherapy. Like other medications, the duration of action of benzodiazepines may be longer in older adults, and their side effects may include drowsiness, fatigue, physical impairment, memory or other cognitive

TABLE 8.2

Death rates for suicide, by selected characteristics, selected years 1950–2002 [CONTINUED]

[Data are based on death certificates]

Sex, race, Hispanic origin, and age	1950[a]	1960[a]	1970	1980	1990	2000	2001	2002
25–44 years	6.2	6.6	10.2	7.7	6.2	5.4	5.5	5.8
25–34 years	4.9	5.5	8.6	7.1	5.6	4.3	4.4	4.6
35–44 years	7.5	7.7	11.9	8.5	6.8	6.4	6.4	6.9
45–64 years	9.9	10.2	12.0	8.9	7.1	6.2	6.6	6.7
45–54 years	9.9	10.2	12.6	9.4	6.9	6.7	7.2	7.4
55–64 years	9.9	10.2	11.4	8.4	7.3	5.4	5.7	5.7
65 years and over	9.4	8.4	8.1	6.1	6.4	4.0	3.9	4.1
65–74 years	10.1	8.4	9.0	6.5	6.7	4.0	3.9	4.1
75–84 years	8.1	8.9	7.0	5.5	6.3	4.0	4.0	4.2
85 years and over	8.2	6.0	5.9	5.5	5.4	4.2	3.4	3.8

… Category not applicable.
[a]Includes deaths of persons who were not residents of the 50 states and the District of Columbia.
[b]Age-adjusted rates are calculated using the year 2000 standard population.
Notes: Rates for 1991–99 were revised using intercensal population estimates based on census 2000. Rates for 2000 were revised based on census 2000 counts. Rates for 2001 and 2002 were computed using 2000-based postcensal estimates.
Figures for 2001 include September 11 related deaths for which death certificates were filed as of October 24, 2002.
Age groups were selected to minimize the presentation of unstable age-specific death rates based on small numbers of deaths and for consistency among comparison groups.

SOURCE: Adapted from "Table 46. Death Rates for Suicide, According to Sex, Race, Hispanic Origin, and Age: United States, Selected Years 1950–2002," in *Health, United States, 2004*, Centers for Disease Control and Prevention, National Center for Health Statistics, Hyattsville, MD, 2004, http://www.cdc.gov/nchs/data/hus/hus04trend.pdf (accessed August 11, 2005)

impairment, confusion, depression, respiratory problems, abuse or dependence problems, and withdrawal reactions.

Schizophrenia

Schizophrenia is an extremely disabling form of mental illness. Its symptoms include hallucinations, paranoia, delusions, and social isolation. Persons suffering from schizophrenia "hear voices," and over time the voices take over in the schizophrenic's mind, obliterating reality and directing all kinds of erratic behaviors. Suicide attempts and violent attacks are common in the lives of schizophrenics. Many schizophrenics turn to drugs in an attempt to escape the torment inflicted by their brains. The National Institute of Mental Health (NIMH) estimates that as many as half of all schizophrenics are also drug abusers.

The prevalence of schizophrenia among adults age sixty-five years or older is estimated as 0.6%, less than half of the 1.3% that is estimated for the population age eighteen to fifty-four. However, the economic burden of late-life schizophrenia is high. While the use of nursing homes and state hospitals for patients with all mental disorders has declined over the past two decades, this decline is very slight for older patients with schizophrenia.

Drug treatment of schizophrenia in older adults is complicated. The medications used to treat schizophrenia, such as haloperidol, effectively reduce such symptoms as delusions and hallucinations of many older patients, but they also have a high risk of disabling side effects, such as tardive dyskinesia—involuntary, rhythmic movements of the face, jaw, mouth, tongue, and trunk.

MISUSE OF ALCOHOL AND PRESCRIPTION DRUGS

The Surgeon General's report observes that older adults are more likely to misuse, as opposed to abuse, alcohol and prescription drugs. The report estimated the prevalence of heavy drinking (twelve to twenty-one drinks per week) in the current cohort of older adults is 3% to 9%. The prevalence rates are expected to rise as the baby boomer cohort, with its history of alcohol and illegal drug use, joins the ranks of older adults. The current group of older adults is more likely to suffer substance misuse problems, such as drug dependence, arising from underuse, overuse, or erratic use of prescription and over-the-counter medications.

According to the 2004 National Health Interview Survey (NHIS), adults age sixty-five and older had the lowest rate of excessive alcohol consumption—just 3.8%—of all age groups. Older men were much more likely than older women to have met the NHIS criteria for excessive alcohol consumption—five or more drinks in one day at least once in the past year—7.1% versus 1.4%. (See Figure 8.3.)

The National Institute on Alcohol Abuse and Alcoholism (NIAAA), an institute of the NIH, reports in "Module 10C: Older Adults and Alcohol Problems, NIAA: Social Work Education for the Prevention and Treatment of Alcohol Use Disorders" (The National Institute on Alcohol Abuse and Alcoholism, http://www.niaaa.nih.gov/publications/social/Module10COlderAdults/Module10C-text.html) that surveys conducted in health-care settings find higher prevalence of alcoholism in the older population than reported in community surveys.

FIGURE 8.3

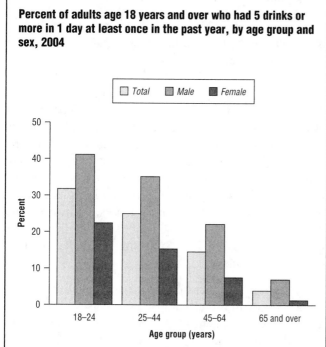

Percent of adults age 18 years and over who had 5 drinks or more in 1 day at least once in the past year, by age group and sex, 2004

Note: The analyses excluded 783 adults (2.5%) with unknown alcohol consumption.

SOURCE: "Figure 9.2. Percent of Adults Aged 18 Years and Over Who Had 5 or More Drinks in 1 Day at Least Once in the Past Year, by Age Group and Sex: United States, 2004," in *Early Release of Selected Estimates Based on Data from the 2004 National Health Interview Survey*, Centers for Disease Control and Prevention, National Center for Health Statistics, Hyattsville, MD, June 29, 2005, http://www.cdc.gov/nchs/data/nhis/earlyrelease/earlyrelease200506.pdf (accessed August 11, 2005)

FIGURE 8.4

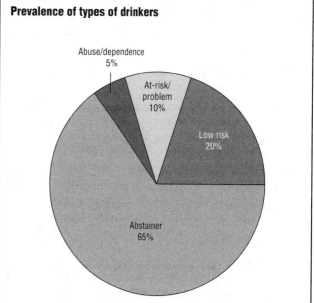

Prevalence of types of drinkers

Notes: At-risk drinking is characterized by alcohol use that increases the chances that a person will develop alcohol-related problems and complications. Problem drinking among older adults is when alcohol is consumed at a level that has already resulted in adverse medical (e.g., injury, medication interactions), psychological, family, financial/economic, self-care, legal, or social consequences. Alcohol or drug dependence refers to a medical disorder characterized by loss of control over consumption, preoccupation with alcohol or drugs, continued use despite adverse consequences, and physiological symptoms such as tolerance and withdrawal.

SOURCE: "Figure 3. Prevalence of Types of Drinkers," in *Module 10C: Older Adults and Alcohol Problems, NIAA: Social Work Education for the Prevention and Treatment of Alcohol Use Disorders*, National Institute on Alcohol Abuse and Alcoholism, Bethesda, MD, October 2004, http://www.niaaa.nih.gov/publications/social/Module10COlder Adults/Module10C-text.html (accessed August 11, 2005)

Research has revealed that between 6% and 11% of patients age sixty-five and older admitted to hospitals exhibited symptoms of alcoholism, as did 20% of older patients hospitalized in psychiatric units and 14% of older patients seen in emergency departments. The prevalence of problem drinking in nursing homes has been reported as high as 49% in some studies, but this high percentage may reflect utilization of nursing homes for short-term alcoholism rehabilitation treatment.

Prevalence of Types of Older Problem Drinkers

The NIAAA describes the prevalence of three types of problem drinkers. They are at-risk drinkers, problem drinkers, and alcohol-dependent drinkers.

- At-risk drinking is alcohol use that increases the risk of developing alcohol-related problems and complications. Persons over age sixty-five who drink more than seven drinks per week (one per day) are considered at-risk of developing health, social, or emotional problems caused by alcohol.

- Problem drinkers have already suffered medical, psychological, family, financial/economic, self-care, legal, or social consequences of alcohol abuse.

- Alcohol dependent drinkers suffer from a medical disorder characterized by loss of control over consumption, preoccupation with alcohol, and continued use despite adverse health, social, legal, and financial consequences.

Figure 8.4 shows the estimated prevalence rates of these different types of drinkers as well as the majority (65%) of older adults that abstains from alcohol consumption.

Types of Older Problem Drinkers

Another way to characterize older problem drinkers is by the duration and the patterns of their drinking histories. The first group is composed of those over age sixty who have been drinking most of their lives. This group is termed "survivors" or "early onset problem drinkers." They have beaten the statistical odds by living to old age despite heavy drinking. These are the persons most likely to suffer medical problems such as cirrhosis of the liver and mental health disorders such as depression.

The second group, termed "intermittents," has historically engaged in "binges" or "bout" drinking interspersed with periods of relative sobriety. These drinkers are at risk for alcohol abuse, because they are more likely than others to self-medicate with alcohol to relieve physical pain and emotional distress or to assuage loneliness and social isolation.

The third group is characterized as "reactors" or "late-onset problem drinkers." The stresses of later life, particularly the loss of work or a spouse, may precipitate heavy drinking. These people show few of the physical consequences of prolonged drinking and fewer disruptions of their lives. About two-thirds of those age sixty-five and older who suffer from alcoholism have had long-standing alcohol addictions; in the remaining one-third, alcohol abuse develops late in life.

Alcohol-Related Issues Unique to Older Adults

Older adults generally have a decreased tolerance to alcohol. Consumption of a given amount of alcohol by older adults usually produces higher blood-alcohol levels than it would in a younger population. Chronic medical problems such as cirrhosis may be present, but older adults are less likely to require detoxification and treatment of alcohol-withdrawal problems. One possible explanation is that few lifelong alcohol abusers survive to old age.

Because older adults usually take more medication than people in other age groups, they are more susceptible to drug–alcohol interactions. Alcohol reduces the safety and efficacy of many medications and, in combination with some drugs, may produce coma or death. Adverse consequences of alcohol consumption in older adults are not limited to problem drinkers. Older adults with medical problems, including diabetes, heart disease, liver disease, and central nervous system degeneration, also may suffer adverse reactions from alcohol consumption.

SCREENING, DIAGNOSIS, AND TREATMENT. The NIAAA advocates screening to identify at-risk drinkers, problem drinkers, and dependent drinkers to determine the need for further diagnostic evaluation and treatment. The Center for Substance Abuse Treatment, part of the Substance Abuse and Mental Health Services Administration (SAMHSA), has a screening protocol stipulating that:

- All adults age sixty and over should be screened for alcohol and prescription drug use/abuse as part of any medical examination or application for health or social services.

- Annual rescreening should be performed if certain physical symptoms emerge or if the individual is undergoing major life changes, stresses, or transitions.

- These screening criteria apply to any health, social, work, or recreation setting that serves older adults and

is not limited to medical-care and substance-treatment settings.

Diagnosis of problem drinking in the older population is complicated by the fact that many psychological, behavioral, and physical symptoms of problem drinking also occur in people who do not have drinking problems. For example, brain damage, heart disease, and gastrointestinal disorders often develop in older adults independent of alcohol use, but may also occur with drinking. In addition, mood disorders, depression, and changes in employment, economic, or marital status often accompany aging but can also be symptoms of alcoholism. Alcohol-induced organic brain syndrome (OBS) is characterized by cognitive impairment—memory lapses, confusion, and disorientation. As a result, some older alcoholics may be incorrectly diagnosed as suffering from dementia or other mental illness.

Older problem drinkers make up a relatively small proportion of the total number of clients seen by most agencies for treatment of alcohol abuse. There is very little data about the effectiveness of intervention and treatment, which usually consists of some combination of counseling and education, in the older population. Nonetheless, the chances for recovery among older drinkers are considered good, because older clients tend to complete the full course of therapy more often than younger clients.

MORE GEROPSYCHIATRISTS AND RESEARCHERS ARE NEEDED

Geropsychiatry, the subspecialty of psychiatry that focuses on the diagnosis and treatment of mental illness in older people, is a relatively new field, and research is just beginning in this area. A significant obstacle, however, is the shortage of trained researchers. In the editorial "Research Training in Mental Health and Aging: The Harvest Is Plentiful; the Laborers, Few" (*American Journal of Geriatric Psychiatry*, vol. 11, June 2003), Charles Reynolds and Margaret Gatz assert that "there are more scientific opportunities than there are researchers to do the work." The authors contend that mental disorders in the older population are treatable but that research on causation and treatment is necessary in order to provide the optimal treatment. They observe that despite the urgent public health need to grow the next generation of researchers in aging and mental health, there are a disproportionately low number of young scientists in the career-development pipeline. To remedy this shortage, they recommended:

- Recruiting physicians early in their careers to interest them in geropsychiatric career training

- Removing financial obstacles to research careers in geriatric mental health

- Identifying areas where further research training in geriatric psychology, psychiatry, and related disciplines is critical to public health
- Enhancing cooperation and partnerships among stakeholders in government (NIMH and the NIA), academia, industry, and foundations

The authors also observed that because research on aging and mental health is multidisciplinary, research training and mentoring in mental health and aging also should be provided to professionals in epidemiology, health economics, pharmacy, nursing, and social work.

CHAPTER 9
CARING FOR OLDER ADULTS—CAREGIVERS

In the United States most long-term care of older adults continues to be provided by families as opposed to nursing homes, assisted living facilities, social service agencies, or government programs. This continuing commitment to family care of older adults in the community is remarkable in view of relatively recent changes in the fabric of American society. American family life has undergone significant changes in the past three decades. Most households require two incomes, and greater numbers of women have entered the workforce. Delayed marriage and childbearing has produced a "sandwich generation" of family caregivers that is simultaneously caring for two generations—their children and their parents. For the first time in history adults may spend more years caring for a parent than for a child. Increased geographic separation of families further compounds the difficulties of family caregiving.

Another challenge is that the supply of caregivers is not keeping pace with the growth in the older population. The number of older adults for every one hundred adults of working age (from eighteen to sixty-four) is called the "dependency ratio." According to the U.S. Census Bureau, in 1990 there were twenty-one older adults for every one hundred working-age adults. When the baby boomer generation (those born between 1946 and 1964) begin approaching retirement age in 2025, there will be thirty-two older adults for every one hundred people of working age.

In *Families and Work* (New York: Oxford University Press, 2000) Andrew Scharlach, a professor in the School of Social Welfare at the University of California, Berkeley, predicts that by 2020 one in three people will have to provide care for an aging parent, with much of that care in the form of financial assistance.

PROFILE OF AMERICA'S CAREGIVERS

We envision an America in which patients and their families are at the center of all health-care planning.

We envision an America in which care for those with chronic conditions is holistic and integrated across medical and social settings, regardless of age or economic status. We envision an America in which family caregivers lead full and productive lives, as free as possible from depression, pain, isolation, and loneliness. We envision an America in which the contributions of family caregivers to the welfare of their loved ones and to society is recognized and supported by all societal sectors: government, employers, faith, health care, philanthropy, family and friends. In short, we envision an America in which the work of family caregiving is recognized and rewarded in a manner commensurate with its importance.

—"Our Vision," The National Family Caregivers Association (http://www.thefamilycaregiver.org/about/)

According to the Family Caregiver Alliance, a 1999 survey found that about one in four households—approximately twenty-three million households—was involved in some form of caregiving for persons age fifty and over. By 2007 this number is expected to grow to thirty-nine million households.

Figure 9.1 shows that, historically, the percentage of older adults with chronic disabilities that obtained care from "informal" sources—family and friends—has far outstripped the percentages receiving formal or paid long-term care services as well as the percentages of older adults receiving a combination of formal and informal care. In 1999 two-thirds of adults age sixty-five and over with chronic disabilities received only informal care; an additional 26% received a combination of informal and paid services; and 9% relied exclusively on paid care.

More Caregivers Are Women

A survey of caregivers conducted in 2000 by the National Family Caregivers Association (NFCA) asserts that while family caregiving has historically fallen to women—wives, daughters, and daughters-in-law—it is

FIGURE 9.1

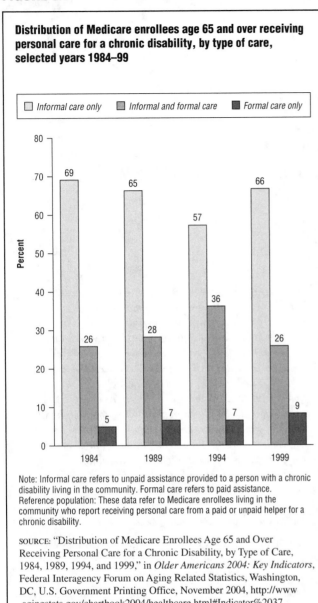

Distribution of Medicare enrollees age 65 and over receiving personal care for a chronic disability, by type of care, selected years 1984–99

Note: Informal care refers to unpaid assistance provided to a person with a chronic disability living in the community. Formal care refers to paid assistance. Reference population: These data refer to Medicare enrollees living in the community who report receiving personal care from a paid or unpaid helper for a chronic disability.

SOURCE: "Distribution of Medicare Enrollees Age 65 and Over Receiving Personal Care for a Chronic Disability, by Type of Care, 1984, 1989, 1994, and 1999," in *Older Americans 2004: Key Indicators*, Federal Interagency Forum on Aging Related Statistics, Washington, DC, U.S. Government Printing Office, November 2004, http://www.agingstats.gov/chartbook2004/healthcare.html#Indicator%2037 (accessed August 11, 2005)

responsibilities for older adults, and nearly two-thirds of Americans under age sixty anticipate assuming elder care responsibilities in the next ten years.

A survey, "MetLife Juggling Act Study, Balancing Caregiving with Work and the Costs of Caregiving" (MetLife, http://www.metlife.com/WPSAssets/12949500 261100547900V1FJuggling%20Study%20-111004.pdf, November 1999), found that caregivers for family members age fifty and older generally underestimated the length of time they would spend as caregivers—less than half (46%) the survey participants anticipated providing care for more than two years. The survey found that average duration of caregiving was about eight years, with approximately one-third of respondents providing care for more than ten years.

Caregiving in the U.S.

In April 2004 the National Alliance for Caregiving and AARP conducted a national survey of 1,247 caregivers. Entitled *Caregiving in the U.S.* and funded by the MetLife Foundation, the survey set out to determine the number and characteristics of caregivers in the United States and how caregiving affects their lives. When completed, the study estimated that 44.4 million caregivers age eighteen and older in 22.9 million households—21% of U.S. households—currently provide unpaid care to adult relatives. Caregivers provided an average of twenty-one hours of care per week—essentially making caregiving a part-time job, and 17% said they provide more than forty hours per week of care. Although most caregivers reported little emotional stress, physical difficulty, or financial hardship, the 10% to 31% of caregivers that provide the most intense care, in terms of hours worked and the difficulty of caregiving tasks, felt that caregiving took a toll on their health and their lives.

The survey found that more caregivers were between the ages of eighteen and forty-nine (58%) than age fifty and older (42%), and more women (61%) than men (39%) performed caregiving. Nearly two-thirds of working caregivers (62%) said they had to make some adjustments to their work lives to accommodate their caregiving responsibilities. Female caregivers provided more hours of care and more intense care than did males. Because they provide more care, it is not surprising that female caregivers reported higher levels of emotional stress—40% compared with 26% of men in the highest levels of stress rating.

This survey described the "typical" caregiver as a forty-six-year-old woman with some college education who works and spends more than twenty hours per week caring for her mother. The average duration of caregiving is 4.3 years, but three in ten caregivers provided care for more than five years, and caregivers age fifty and older, who tend to care for mothers and grandmothers, are

no longer predominantly a women's issue. Men now comprise as much as 44% of the caregiving population. Despite the rise in men serving as caregivers, women still devote about 50% more time to caregiving than do men.

Family Caregivers Online (http://www.familycare giversonline.com), an education and information resource funded by the area agencies on aging, describes the demographics of the "sandwich generation," the Americans between the ages of forty-five and fifty-five who have aging parents or in-laws and children under age twenty-one. In 2000 between 59% and 75% of these caregivers were women. The average caregiver was forty-six years old, married, worked outside the home, and earned an annual income of $35,000. About half of all baby boomers have children living at home and among those most likely to have provided care for twenty years or more.

More than one-third (35%) of caregivers said they did not have enough time for themselves. Twenty-nine percent felt unable to manage emotional and physical stress, and the same percentage said they needed help balancing work and family responsibilities. Other caregiver needs and concerns include:

- Concern about keeping the persons they care for safe (30%)
- Identifying activities they can share with the persons they care for (27%)
- The need for help communicating with physicians and other health-care professionals (22%)
- The need for help making end-of-life decisions (20%)

More than one-quarter (29%) of caregivers sought information to help them on the Internet, and 28% turned to physicians for information. Nearly three-quarters (73%) of caregivers said praying helped them to cope with stress, 61% said they talked with friends or relatives, and 44% obtained information about caregiving from books or other print materials.

Caregivers varied in their use of support services. Those caring for persons suffering from Alzheimer's disease or dementia were more likely to use outside support services than other caregivers. Similarly, caregivers living in cities (58%) and those living with the recipients of care were more likely to use support services than caregivers in suburbs (42%) or rural area (44%) and caregivers living within an hour of the persons they cared for. The use of support services increased with advancing age of the caregiver—40% of younger caregivers, 55% of those ages fifty–sixty-four, and 56% of caregivers age sixty-five and older sought and obtained supportive services.

Caregiving Can Compromise Health and Well-Being

For many people, caring for an ill or disabled older adult can, over time, become an enormous burden. Caregivers may neglect their own health and other needs, because no one else is available to care for their aging spouse or parent.

Deputy Secretary of Health and Human Services Claude Allen and panelists Michael O'Grady, John Hoff, Josefina Carbonell, Donald Showers, Katryna Gould, and Bill Kays at a town hall meeting ("Ensuring the Health and Wellness of Our Nation's Family Caregivers," U.S. Administration on Aging, http://www.aoa.gov/prof/aoaprog/caregiver/careprof/TownHall/townhall_12_16_03.asp, December 16, 2003) reported that about one third of caregivers describe their own health as "fair to poor." The stress associated with family caregiving has been found to compromise immune function, increasing the risks of infectious diseases such as colds and flu. It also is linked to increased risk for depressive symptoms and chronic diseases, such as heart disease, diabetes, and cancer.

The key research findings about the relationship between caregiving and compromised health include:

- Richard Schulz and Scott Beach in "Caregiving as a Risk Factor for Mortality" (*Journal of the American Medical Association*, vol. 282, no. 23, December 15, 1999) stated that spouses who suffer from chronic conditions, serve as caregivers, and report stress related to their caregiving efforts have a mortality rate that is nearly two-thirds (63%) higher than their noncaregiving peers. Caregivers experienced more depression and anxiety and a reduced level of health. They also were less likely to get adequate rest, to have time to rest when they were sick, or to have time to exercise.

- Janice Kiecolt Glaser and Ronald Glaser in "Chronic Stress and Age-Related Increases in the Proinflammatory Cytokine IL-6" (*Proceedings of the National Academy of Sciences*, June 30, 2003) found that the stress of caring for older adults with dementia has been shown to compromise caregivers' immune systems for as long as three years after their caregiving ends.

- Richard Schulz et al, in "Long-term Care Placement of Dementia Patients and Caregivers Health and Well-being" (*Journal of the American Medical Association*, vol. 292, no. 8, August 25, 2004) found caregivers remain at risk for depression and anxiety after the older adults with dementia they have cared for are placed in long-term health-care facilities. Depressive symptoms and anxiety in caregivers were as severe after caregivers institutionalized their relatives compared with when they served as in-home caregivers.

- According to Carolyn Cannuscio et al in "Reverberation of Family Illness: A Longitudinal Assessment of Informal Caregiver and Mental Health Status in the Nurses' Health Study" (*American Journal of Public Health*, vol. 92, no. 8, August 2002), caregivers who provide care thirty-six or more hours weekly are more likely than noncaregivers to experience symptoms of depression or anxiety. For spouses serving as caregivers the rate is six times higher; for those caring for a parent the rate is twice as high.

Research also has demonstrated that at-risk caregivers are less likely than their peers who do not provide care for older relatives to engage in health-promoting behaviors that are important for chronic disease prevention and health promotion. The aforementioned town hall panelists observed that in view of caregivers' risks of developing health problems, there is an urgent need to exhort family caregivers to engage in activities such as regular exercise and preventive medical care that will benefit their own health, well-being, and longevity.

The Economics of Caregiving

The majority of the costs and responsibility for long-term care for older adults rests with family caregivers in the community. The shift toward increasing reliance on this informal system of care was spurred by changes in the health-care delivery financing system that resulted in shorter hospital stays along with the high cost of nursing home care, older adults' preference for home care over institutional care, and the shortage of workers in all long-term care settings. Taken together, these factors continue to increase the likelihood that frail, disabled, and ill older adults will be cared for by relatives in the community.

During the next few decades, as the number of older persons needing assistance to remain independent increases dramatically, the burden and cost of providing care to an ill or disabled relative will affect almost every United States household. In 2000 the Administration on Aging (AoA) estimated that the economic value alone of the unpaid family caregiving provided by more than 22.4 million persons was a staggering $257 billion per year—two times the amount spent on nursing homes and home health-care services (Peter S. Arno, "Economic Value of Informal Caregiving," presented at the American Association of Geriatric Psychiatry, Orlando, FL, February 24, 2002). In 2003 the AoA calculated that if the services of family caregivers for older adults were replaced by paid home health-care staff, the cost would range from $45 billion to $94 billion per year.

Research conducted by the NFCA reveals that families that are caring for an older adult relative tend to have lower incomes than noncaregiving families. Thirty-five percent of average American households have incomes of under $30,000. In contrast, 43% of caregiving families have incomes below $30,000 ("Random Sample Survey of Family Caregivers," National Family Caregivers Association, 2000).

PROMOTING THE HEALTH OF CAREGIVERS

This section offers a brief overview of selected state or local initiatives designed to help caregivers eat better, increase physical activity and exercise, maintain a healthy weight, stop smoking, reduce alcohol use, improve sleep, reduce stress, identify available health resources, and increase their use of recommended preventive health services. These programs were described in *A Compendium of Intervention and Descriptive Studies Designed to Promote the Health of Caregivers for Older Adults*, a report prepared by RTI International for the Assistant Secretary for Planning and Evaluation of the Department of Health and Human Services in 2003. Since the majority of these programs commenced in

2002 or later, their results, in terms of outcomes and effectiveness, were not yet published in 2005.

Hospital-Based Programs

The United Hospital Fund sponsored seven hospital-based programs to assist caregivers between 1998 and 2002. Each program targeted a specific community of caregivers, and two of the seven projects focused on helping caregivers take better care of themselves. In New York City the Brooklyn Hospital Center/Wartburg Lutheran Home for the Aging offered information and training for caregivers of neurologically impaired African-American patients and encouraged caregivers to acknowledge, and endeavor to meet, their own needs. The program evaluated caregivers' stress levels and needs for home care assistance and provided in-home visits to help patients and caregivers make smooth transitions from hospital to home.

Another New York City hospital program, Maimonides Medical Center/First to Care Home Care program, offered caregivers community referrals to health-care providers for their own health-care needs, as well as a hotline to use during and after their relatives' hospitalizations. Caregivers considered high risk by virtue of advanced age, poor health, or having many other responsibilities such as child care or care for another ill person participated in the program, as well as those considered at average risk. The high-risk group received information on benefits and entitlements to Medicare, Meals on Wheels, food stamps, and other community resources while their relatives were still in the hospital. They also met with a social worker both while their relatives were in the hospital and within twenty-four hours of their relative's discharge to learn about how to take care of their own health during the transition home. The average risk caregivers received the same information materials as the high-risk group but did not visit with a social worker.

The projects' self-evaluations revealed that caregivers who participated in the Brooklyn/Wartburg project reported having less caregiver strain and a greater understanding of the health promotion benefits available to them under the Medicare and Medicaid programs than caregivers who had not participated in the program. The Maimonides program was so successful that it expanded from two inpatient units in 2000 to fifteen units in 2002.

Programs Sponsored by Government Agencies

"Health First Study: Caregivers Take Time to Stay Active" is a research project sponsored by the National Institute on Aging (NIA) designed to promote physical activity among female caregivers whose spouses have been diagnosed with Alzheimer's disease or a related disorder. The program provides caregivers with telephone counseling from a behavior-change specialist.

Together, the caregiver and counselor agree on an exercise goal the caregiver can achieve by the end of the project period. In regular telephone calls the caregivers set short-term goals and learn problem-solving skills to help improve their chances of success. The counselor offers the option of home-based exercise, but caregivers also may achieve their goals by joining group exercise programs.

"REACH II: Resources for Enhancing Alzheimer's Caregiver Health" is a program for caregivers of frail older adults sponsored by the NIA and the National Institute for Nursing Research that aims to increase caregiver knowledge, skills, and well-being. The program begins with a health risk appraisal for each caregiver and development of an approach to address risk in multiple health areas including caregiver health and self-care, caregiver depression, social support, and safety of both the patient and caregiver. The program offers ten home visits and five contacts with trained staff using an innovative computer/telephone technology system over a six-month period. Interventions offered include home-based exercise programs, computer-based monitoring systems, and individual consultations with medical providers.

"Teaching Healthy Lifestyles for Caregivers Study" is a research project sponsored by the NIA designed to determine the health and quality-of-life effects of moderate exercise among older female caregivers. The project involved one hundred female subjects ages forty-nine to eighty-two that were sedentary, free of cardiovascular disease, providing at least ten hours per week of unpaid care for a relative with dementia, and not participating in regular physical activity. Study participants were offered twelve months of home-based, telephone-supervised, moderate-intensity exercise training that began with an in-person introductory counseling session. The training consisted of thirty to forty minutes of endurance exercise four times a week. Participants were also encouraged to increase other forms of routine activity throughout the day, such as walking, stationary cycling, or gardening. Participants were taught how to take their heart rates, monitor their perceived exertion, and record their exercise frequency, intensity, and duration. Telephone contacts were used to monitor progress, answer questions, and provide individual support.

The research and evaluation focused on measuring participants' self-rated cardiovascular fitness, sleep quality, adherence to protocols, caloric intake, and psychological stress. Study participants kept their own records and were examined by medical professionals before the project and twelve months later, after they had completed the exercise program. Compared with a control group that did not participate in the exercise program, the participants showed significant improvements in total energy expenditure, stress-induced blood pressure, self-rated sleep quality, and level of psychological distress. These results underscored the importance of exercise in helping caregivers relieve stress and improve their health.

The "Maine Primary Partners in Caregiving Program" is sponsored by the AoA. It identifies stressed caregivers in rural Maine communities and encourages them to obtain support and assistance. Specialists contact the at-risk caregivers and offer them education, training resources, and access to a statewide telephone hotline. During the first year of operations—April 2002 to March 2003—approximately five hundred caregivers under stress were identified, and the majority chose to receive assistance from specialists. Most caregivers wanted to learn about potential service options for the future but did not yet want to obtain respite services.

The "Making the Link Program" is sponsored by the AoA and is intended to increase physicians' awareness of the toll caregiving can take on the health of caregivers. The program also aims to remind physicians that caregivers are an important part of the health-care team and that services to support caregivers are available through local Area Agencies on Aging (AAAs) and Title VI–Native American aging programs. The program's goals are to actively involve physicians in identifying caregivers and referring them to National Family Caregiver Support Program (NFCSP) services, and to promote the idea that caregiving is a public health issue and increase awareness of the important health-care role of family caregivers. The program has engaged professional societies and government agencies including the American Medical Association, American College of Physicians–American Society of Internal Medicine, American Geriatrics Society, American Association of Medical Society Executives, National Medical Association, American Project Access Network, Indian Health Service, National Alliance for Caregiving, the Families and Health Care Project at the United Hospital Fund, Health Resources and Services Administration, the American Academy of Family Physicians, and the National Health Care Council to participate in disseminating educational materials.

Public–Private Collaborative Projects

PREP (PReparedness, Enrichment, and Predictability) is a program for caregivers of frail older adults sponsored by the NIA, National Institute for Nursing Research, and Northwest Region of Kaiser Permanente. PREP provides frail older persons and their families with a range of services chosen by the families. Each family is assessed to measure both family and caregiver health and well-being. The family considers its needs and decides which services and social supports it would like to receive. If the family decides to select caregiver health supports as part of its service package, then an in-depth health assessment is conducted to determine the types of caregiving services needed. PREP nurses deliver the services with guidance from an interdisciplinary team of experts from Kaiser Permanente's health-care system. Families receive in-person and telephone support services for a twelve-month period. Researchers will then compare caregivers who participated in PREP to a control group of caregivers to determine whether PREP participation has an effect on variables such as caregiver skill and stress, as well as the health status of the caregiver and the older adults receiving care.

The "Powerful Tools for Caregiving Program" offers self-care training to caregivers to help them to take better physical and emotional care of themselves. Initiated in 1995 in Oregon, the program has since been expanded to California, North Carolina, Washington, and Wisconsin. The Legacy Health System, Mather LifeWays Foundation, Robert Wood Johnson Foundation, Northwest Health Foundation, Good Samaritan Foundation, the AoA, Oregon Community Foundation, and other community agencies sponsor it. The program is quite extensive. Caregivers attend six 2.5 hour classes over a six-week period to help them cultivate self-care tools to reduce personal stress, learn to take better physical and emotional care of themselves, communicate their needs to family members, and make difficult caregiving decisions such as the determination that a family member can no longer live alone, drive safely, and/or manage finances. Caregivers receive a three-hundred-page book, entitled *The Caregiver Helpbook*, developed specifically for the program. The book describes wellness practices for caregivers, including proper diet, adequate sleep, and regular exercise. The project also recruits and trains current and former caregivers to facilitate the classes.

Evaluation of more than seven hundred family caregivers in Oregon found that the program produced enduring improvements in caregivers' health and well-being. It reduced caregiver guilt and anger; increased self-care behavior including increased physical exercise; increased positive feelings about caregiving; reduced depression; and improved knowledge and use of services available in the community.

The "Rosalynn Carter Institute and Johnson & Johnson Caregivers Program and the CARE-NET Project" is sponsored by the Rosalynn Carter Institute for Caregiving, Georgia Southwestern State University in Americus, Johnson & Johnson, the AoA, and private donors. It seeks to promote the mental health and well-being of individuals, families, and professional caregivers; encourage effective caregiving practices; build public awareness of caregiving needs; and advance public and social policies that enhance caring communities through three initiatives. The "Practice in Action" program awards grants of $25,000 to five programs per year that advance science and contribute to knowledge in

caregiving. The "Science to Practice Initiative" convenes expert panels to consider caregiving issues. In 2002 four expert panels met and prepared monographs based on their areas of expertise and in response to the questions "what is known?" and "what is needed?" in the field of caregiving. The "Caring for You, Caring for Me," program helps caregivers to take better care of themselves.

THE CONTINUUM OF FORMAL SERVICES

As the older population increases, the segment of the population available to provide unpaid care, generally composed of family members, has decreased. Since the availability of caregivers has diminished, increasing numbers of older adults in need of assistance will have to rely on a combination of family caregiving and paid professional services or on professional services alone.

Home Health Care

Home health-care agencies provide a wide variety of services. Services range from helping with activities of daily living, such as bathing, light housekeeping, and meals, to skilled nursing care. About 20% of the personnel employed by home health agencies are registered nurses, another 7% are licensed practical nurses, and 13% are nursing or home health aides. Other personnel involved in home health care include physical therapists, social workers, and speech–language pathologists.

Home health care grew faster in the early 1990s than any other segment of health services. Its growth may be attributable to the observation that in many cases, caring for patients at home is preferable to and more cost-effective than care provided in a hospital, nursing home, or some other residential facility. Oftentimes, older adults are more comfortable and much happier living in their own homes or with family members.

Prior to the year 2000 Medicare coverage for home health care was limited to patients immediately following discharge from the hospital. By the year 2000 Medicare covered beneficiaries' home health-care services with no requirement for prior hospitalization. There were also no limits to the number of professional visits or to the length of coverage. As long as the patient's condition warranted it, the following services were provided:

- Part-time or intermittent skilled nursing and home health aide services

- Speech–language pathology services

- Physical and occupational therapy

- Medical social services

- Medical supplies

- Durable medical equipment (with a 20% co-payment)

Over time, the population receiving home care services has changed. Today much of home health care is associated with rehabilitation from critical illnesses, and fewer users are long-term patients with chronic conditions. This changing pattern of use reflects a shift from longer-term care for chronic conditions to short-term, post-acute care. Compared with post-acute care users, the long-term patients are older, more functionally disabled, more likely to be incontinent, and more expensive to serve.

In 2000, the most recent year for which data were available, nearly 1.4 million persons received home health services. More women received home health services—62% were women and 35% were men. More than two-thirds of all home health-care recipients were age sixty-five or older. Among ten thousand adults age eighty-five and over, 694 used home health-care services in 2000. (See Table 9.1.)

Respite Care and Adult Day Care

Respite care enables caregivers to take much-needed breaks from the demands of caregiving. It offers relief for families who may be overwhelmed and exhausted by the demands of caregiving and may be neglecting their own needs for rest and relaxation.

Respite care takes many forms. In some cases the respite worker comes to the home to take care of the older adult so that the caregiver can take a few hours off for personal needs, relaxation, or rest. Inpatient respite care, offered by some nursing homes and board-and-care facilities, provides an alternative to in-home care. Respite care also is available for longer periods so that caregivers can recuperate from their own illnesses or even take vacations.

Adult day-care programs, freestanding or based in hospitals, provide structured daytime programs where older adults may receive the social, health, and recreational services they need to restore or maintain optimal functioning. Although they are not specifically intended to provide respite for caregivers, adult day-care programs temporarily relieve families of the physical and emotional stress of caregiving.

Community Services

In addition to home health-care services, many communities offer a variety of services to help older adults and their caregivers. They include:

- Home-care aides to assist with chores such as housecleaning, grocery shopping, or laundry, as well as assistance with the activities of daily living

- Repair services to help with basic home maintenance, as well as minor changes to make homes secure and safe, such as the installation of grab bars in bathrooms, special seats in the shower, or ramps for wheelchairs

- Home-delivered meal programs offering nutritious meals to those who can no longer shop for groceries or cook

- Companion and telephone reassurance services to keep in touch with older adults living alone (volunteers make regular visits or phone calls to check on, and maintain contact with, isolated older adults)

- Trained postal or utility workers to spot signs of trouble at the homes of the older persons

- Personal Emergency Response Systems devices that allow older adults to summon help in emergencies (when the user pushes the button on the wearable device, it sends a message to a response center or police station)

- Senior centers offering recreation programs, social activities, educational programs, health screenings, and meals

- Communities providing transportation to help older adults run errands, attend medical appointments, and make related trips (such services are often subsidized or free-of-charge)

- Adult day-care centers providing care for older adults who need supervised assistance (services may include health care, recreation, meals, rehabilitative therapy, and respite care)

Home and Community-Based Services

Home and community-based services refer to the entire array of supportive services that help older persons live independently in their homes and communities. In 1981 former president Ronald Reagan signed the federal law that implemented the Medicaid Home and Community-Based Services (HCBS) waiver program. Prior to the passage of this legislation, Medicaid long-term care benefits were primarily limited to nursing homes. The HCBS legislation provided a vehicle for states, for the first time, to offer services not otherwise available through their Medicaid programs to serve people in their own homes and communities, preserving their independence and ties to family and friends at a cost no higher than that of institutional care. States have the flexibility to design HCBS waiver programs to meet the specific needs of defined groups.

Seven specific services may be provided under HCBS waivers: case management services, homemaker services, home health aide services, personal care services, adult day health-care services, respite care services, and rehabilitation services. Other services may be provided at the request of the state if approved by the federal government. Services must be cost-effective and necessary for the prevention of institutionalization. Services may be provided to older adults and persons

TABLE 9.1

Home health care patients, according to age, sex, and diagnosis, selected years 1992–2000

[Data are based on a survey of current home health care patients]

Age, sex, and diagnosis	1992	1994	1996	1998	2000
			Number of current patients		
Total home health care patients	**1,232,200**	**1,889,327**	**2,427,483**	**1,881,768**	**1,355,290**
			Current patients per 10,000 population		
Total	**47.8**	**71.8**	**90.6**	**69.6**	**48.7**
Age at time of survey					
Under 65 years, crude	12.6	21.0	27.8	25.0	16.4
65 years and over, crude	295.4	424.9	526.3	375.7	277.0
65 years and over, age adjusted[a]	315.8	449.6	546.6	381.0	276.5
65–74 years	151.7	209.1	240.1	202.0	130.2
75–84 years	398.3	542.2	753.6	470.3	347.6
85 years and over	775.9	1,206.1	1,253.4	885.4	694.1
Sex					
Male, total	**32.6**	**47.8**	**60.9**	**47.9**	**35.1**
Under 65 years, crude	10.9	17.8	22.1	22.9	15.6
65 years and over, crude	219.2	303.1	386.4	255.2	199.6
65 years and over, age adjusted[a]	255.8	350.0	438.3	277.6	216.4
65–74 years	121.8	169.9	187.0	159.7	100.7
75–84 years	322.0	427.5	598.7	321.4	270.0
85 years and over	635.2	893.1	1,044.3	653.0	553.9
Female, total	**62.4**	**94.7**	**118.9**	**90.4**	**61.8**
Under 65 years, crude	14.3	24.2	33.6	27.0	17.2
65 years and over, crude	347.4	508.9	623.9	460.4	332.6
65 years and over, age adjusted[a]	351.5	506.6	615.0	445.8	315.5
65–74 years	175.3	240.6	283.2	236.3	154.6
75–84 years	445.3	614.5	854.0	568.8	400.4
85 years and over	830.7	1,327.6	1,337.0	981.7	754.9
Age at time of survey[b]			**Percent distribution**		
Under 65 years	23.1	25.7	27.0	31.3	29.5
65 years and over	76.9	74.3	73.0	68.7	70.5
65–74 years	22.6	20.6	18.4	19.7	17.3
75–84 years	33.9	31.2	35.3	29.9	31.3
85 years and over	20.4	22.4	19.4	19.1	21.9
Sex					
Male	33.2	32.5	32.9	33.6	35.2
Female	66.8	67.5	67.1	66.4	64.8
Primary admission diagnosis[c]					
Malignant neoplasms	5.7	5.7	4.8	3.8	4.9
Diabetes	7.7	8.1	8.5	6.1	7.8
Diseases of the nervous system and sense organs	6.3	8.0	5.8	7.6	6.1
Diseases of the circulatory system	25.9	27.2	25.6	23.6	23.6
Diseases of heart	12.6	14.3	10.9	12.3	10.9
Cerebrovascular diseases	5.8	6.1	7.8	5.1	7.3
Diseases of the respiratory system	6.6	6.1	7.7	7.9	6.8
Decubitus ulcers	1.9	1.1	1.0	1.2	1.9
Diseases of the musculoskeletal system and connective tissue	9.4	8.3	8.8	8.3	9.8
Osteoarthritis	2.5	2.8	3.2	2.7	3.5
Fractures, all sites	3.8	3.7	3.3	4.0	4.1
Fracture of neck of femur (hip)	1.4	1.7	1.3	1.1	1.5
Other	32.7	31.8	34.6	37.5	34.9

[a]Age adjusted by the direct method to the year 2000 standard population using the following three age groups: 65–74 years, 75–84 years, and 85 years and over.
[b]Denominator excludes persons with unknown age.
[c]Denominator excludes persons with unknown diagnosis.
Notes: Current home health care patients are those who were on the rolls of the agency as of midnight on the day immediately before the date of the survey. Rates are based on the civilian population as of July 1.

SOURCE: "Table 90. Home Health Care Patients, According to Age, Sex, and Diagnosis: United States, Selected Years 1992–2000," in *Health, United States, 2004*, Centers for Disease Control and Prevention, National Center for Health Statistics, Hyattsville, MD, 2004, http://www.cdc.gov/nchs/data/hus/hus04trend.pdf (accessed August 11, 2005)

with disabilities, persons with developmental disabilities or mental retardation, and persons with physical or mental illness. States have flexibility in designing their waiver programs; this allows them to tailor their programs to the specific needs of the populations they want to serve.

The HCBS waiver program has experienced tremendous growth since its enactment in 1981. In 2005 there were more than 285 approved waiver programs operating in forty-four states.

National Network on Aging

The National Network on Aging, funded by the Older Americans Act (OAA), serves about seven million older persons and their caregivers through twenty-nine thousand service providers, 655 area agencies on aging, 233 tribal and native organizations, fifty-six state units on aging, two organizations that serve native Hawaiians, and thousands of volunteers. These organizations provide assistance and services to older individuals and their families in urban, suburban, and rural areas throughout the United States. The AoA, an agency in the U.S. Department of Health and Human Services, is the federal headquarters for the network.

While all older Americans may receive services through the OAA, it targets vulnerable older populations—those older adults disadvantaged by social or health disparities.

SERVICES FUNDED BY THE OAA. The core services funded by the OAA are:

- Supportive services enable communities to provide a range of programs including information and referral services, transportation to medical appointments and grocery and drug stores, and handyman, chore, and personal-care services.

- Nutrition services are more than simply the provision of food. The OAA Nutrition Program funds meals served in senior centers, nutrition education, health screenings, and counseling at senior centers. For many homebound older adults the daily delivery of a hot meal enables them to remain in their homes. Many elderly people happily welcome the volunteer who delivers their meals and who may be their only visitor. In 2002 the OAA Nutrition Program celebrated thirty years of service.

- Preventive and health promotion programs and services educate and enable older persons to make healthy lifestyle choices. Every year illness and disability that result from chronic disease affect the quality of life for millions of older adults and their caregivers. Many chronic diseases can be prevented through healthy lifestyles, physical activity, appropriate diet and nutrition, smoking cessation, active and meaningful social engagement, and regular health screenings. The ultimate goal of the OAA health promotion and disease prevention services is to increase the quality and years of healthy life.

- The National Family Caregiver Support Program (NFCSP), funded for the first time in 2000, is a sig-

nificant addition to the OAA. It was created to help the millions of people who provide primary care for spouses, parents, older relatives, and friends. The program provides information to caregivers about available services; assistance to caregivers in gaining access to services; individual counseling; and organization of support groups and training to assist caregivers to make decisions and solve problems related to caregiving.

- Services that protect the rights of vulnerable older persons are designed to empower older persons and their family members to detect and prevent elder abuse and consumer fraud, as well as to enhance the physical, mental, emotional, and financial well-being of the older population. An example of these services is pension counseling to help older Americans access their pensions and make informed insurance and health-care choices, and long-term care ombudsman programs that serve to investigate and resolve complaints made by or for residents of nursing homes and board-and-care facilities. The AoA supports the training of thousands of paid and volunteer long-term care ombudsmen, insurance counselors, and other professionals who assist with reporting waste, fraud, and abuse in nursing homes and other settings. The AoA also funds Medicare patrol projects, which operate in forty-seven states and the District of Columbia and Puerto Rico. The AoA awards grants to state units on aging, area agencies on aging, and community organizations to train senior volunteers so they can educate other older Americans about how to take a more active role in monitoring and understanding their health and health care.

- Services to Native Americans include nutrition and supportive services designed to meet the unique cultural and social traditions of tribal and native organizations and organizations serving native Hawaiians. Native American elders are among the most disadvantaged groups in the country.

Eldercare Locator

The AoA sponsors the Eldercare Locator service, a nationwide toll-free service that helps older adults and their caregivers find local services. The service also is available online (http://www.eldercare.gov) so that consumers can easily link to information and referral services.

The Eldercare Locator program connects callers to an information specialist with access to a database of more than forty-eight hundred entries. The toll-free Eldercare Locator service operates Monday through Friday, 9:00 A.M. to 8:00 P.M., Eastern Standard Time, and can be reached at (800) 677-1116.

BenefitsCheckup

The National Council on Aging offers the online BenefitsCheckup program (http://www.benefitscheckup.org), which examines a database of more than thirteen hundred programs to determine older adults' eligibility for federal, state, and some local private and public benefits and programs. Users respond to a few confidential questions, and the database tells them which federal, state, and local programs they might be eligible for and how to apply. It is the first Internet-based service designed to help older Americans, their families, caregivers, and community organizations determine quickly and easily which benefits they qualify for and how to claim them.

There are about fifty to seventy programs available to individuals per state. Among the programs included are those that help older adults find income support, prescription drug savings, government health programs, energy assistance, property tax relief, nutrition programs, in-home services, veterans' programs, and volunteer, educational, and training programs.

The On Lok/PACE Program

One comprehensive-care model program for frail older adults is based on a San Francisco model. On Lok Senior Health in San Francisco, California (http://www.onlok.org), combines medical care, home care, social services, and case management into a complete program of care. Founded in 1979, the On Lok Senior Health Services derives its name from the Chinese words for "peaceful" and "happy."

Clients sign over their Medicare and Medicaid benefits to join the program. In return, they receive housing and comprehensive medical care, as long as they use the program's doctors and nurses. Central to the On Lok model is the day health center, an expanded version of the social adult day programs that proliferated in the 1970s. In addition to recreational activities, the centers have health services with on-site geriatricians, rehabilitation therapists, nurse practitioners, and other health professionals. Clients may also receive, if necessary, intravenous antibiotic or hydration therapy at the center.

Participants like the program because they are guaranteed lifelong health care, including hospitalization or nursing home care. Even with the provision of comprehensive support services, which are more extensive than would be covered by Medicare and Medicaid, the program is less expensive than nursing home care. Because the participants' health is constantly monitored, their use of hospitals is sharply reduced, which enables On Lok facilities to use the funds saved on hospitalization to pay for the extra services that the model provides.

The On Lok model is the basis for a comprehensive service delivery system called PACE, the Program of All-Inclusive Care for the Elderly. When the Balanced Budget Act of 1997 (PL 105-33) was passed, PACE became a key provider under Medicare and a voluntary state option under Medicaid. At the time the Balanced Budget Act was enacted, there were fifteen PACE demonstration programs up and running successfully. Forty were opened in the first year after passage, and about twenty have opened every year thereafter. Figure 9.2 shows the distribution of PACE activity across the United States as of June 2005.

The PACE model centers on the belief that it is better for the well-being of older adults with chronic care needs (as well as the well-being of their families) to be served in their communities than in nursing homes. To be eligible for PACE, a person must be age fifty-five or older, certified by the state as eligible for nursing home care, and live in an area served by a PACE program.

PACE serves individuals who are able to live safely in the community at the time of enrollment. Although all PACE participants must be certified to need nursing home care to enroll in PACE, only about 7% of PACE participants reside in a nursing home nationally. Should a PACE enrollee require nursing home care, the PACE program pays for it and continues to coordinate the enrollee's care.

PACE provides and pays for all needed services including:

- Adult day care that offers nursing; physical, occupational, and recreational therapies; meals; nutritional counseling; social work; and personal care

- Medical care provided by a PACE physician familiar with the history, needs, and preferences of each enrollee

- Home health care and personal care

- Prescription drugs

- Social services

- Allied health services such as audiologists, dentists, optometrists, podiatrists, and speech therapists

- Hospital and nursing home care

Geriatric Care Managers Help Older Adults Age in Place

The increasing complexity of arranging care for older adults, especially when families live at a distance from the older adults in need of care, has given rise to a relatively new service profession—geriatric care management. Geriatric care managers have varied educational backgrounds and professional credentials. They may be gerontologists, nurses, social workers, or psychologists who specialize in issues related to aging and services for older adults. Care managers generally work with a formal or informal network of social workers, nurses, psychologists, elder law attorneys, advocates, and agencies that serve older adults.

Geriatric care managers work with families and increasingly with corporations wishing to assist employees,

FIGURE 9.2

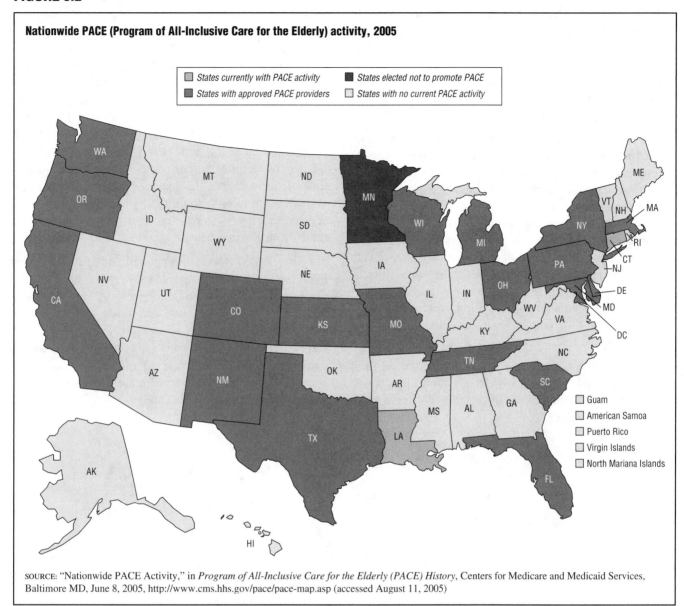

Nationwide PACE (Program of All-Inclusive Care for the Elderly) activity, 2005

☐ States currently with PACE activity   ■ States elected not to promote PACE
■ States with approved PACE providers   ☐ States with no current PACE activity

☐ Guam
☐ American Samoa
☐ Puerto Rico
☐ Virgin Islands
☐ North Mariana Islands

SOURCE: "Nationwide PACE Activity," in *Program of All-Inclusive Care for the Elderly (PACE) History*, Centers for Medicare and Medicaid Services, Baltimore MD, June 8, 2005, http://www.cms.hhs.gov/pace/pace-map.asp (accessed August 11, 2005)

to create flexible plans of care to meet the needs of the older adults. They oversee home-health staffing needs, monitor the quality of in-home services and equipment, and serve as liaisons for families at a distance from their older relatives. Fees range from $180 to $250 for an initial evaluation to approximately $60 to $75 per hour for follow-up, monitoring, and communicating with the family.

Hired homemakers/caregivers, transportation services, home modifications, and other services add to the bill. The total monthly cost of "aging in place" varies. An older adult who needs light housekeeping or companionship for three hours twice a week might spend around $300 a month, while one who needs twenty-four-hour-a-day supervision might pay $5,000 per month or more—much more if care from a certified home health aide or licensed vocational nurse (LVN) is required.

CORPORATE INVOLVEMENT

The "sandwich generation" of baby boomers torn between work, caring for their children, and assisting aging parents is having an impact on the workplace. The Office of Personnel Management (OPM), the federal government's Human Resource Agency, reports that as increasing numbers of employees confront the responsibilities of caring for aging relatives, many employers are seeking ways to ease the stress caused by these mounting pressures and help their employees balance the demands of caregiving and work.

The 2004 National Alliance for Caregiving and an AARP national survey of caregivers determined in *Caregiving in the United States* that caregiving has a substantial impact on the workplace. Nearly six in ten (59%) caregivers have left work or worked while providing care, and almost two-thirds (62%) said they had to make some work-related adjustments—going into work late (57%) or leaving early or taking time off during the day to provide care. Seventeen percent said they had taken leaves of absence, 10% went from working full-time to part-time, and 6% reported quitting work entirely. Five percent sacrificed their job benefits, 4% turned down promotions, and 3% took early retirement to fulfill their caregiving responsibilities.

The OPM observes that employees overwhelmed by their caregiving responsibilities may be less productive on the job, use up their allotted sick leave time, drop back to part-time status, or quit the workforce altogether. The costs to employers in terms of lost productivity, absenteeism, workday interruptions, employee turnover, and attrition were estimated as more than $11 billion per year in 2003 by a MetLife survey. The OPM recommends that private employers institute the kinds of workplace accommodations already in place in many federal agencies, such as flextime, telecommuting, job-sharing, extended family leave, and part-time employment, as well as provision of information and referral services to assist caregivers.

Although employers may realize that increased flexibility and understanding results in more productive employees, just 21% percent of companies offered elder care referral services, according to the "2005 Benefits Survey" (SHRMOnline, http://www.shrm.org/hrresources/surveys_published/AllSurveysTOC.asp, June 2005) conducted by the Society for Human Resource Management (SHRM). About one-quarter of employers said they offered more elder care leave than is required under the 1993 federal Family and Medical Leave Act (FMLA). Just 1% of employers surveyed subsidized the cost of elder care or offered a company-supported elder care center, and none offered paid elder care. About one-quarter of employers permitted workers to use paid time-off for vacation, sick leave, child care, or elder care; allowed them to use unpaid family and medical leave; or enabled employees to pay for elder care programs using funds from flexible benefit accounts.

The SHRM survey found that the industries most likely to offer elder care referral services were finance (27%) and nonprofit service agencies (25%), and those least likely were wholesale and retail trade industries (5%) and manufacturers of durable goods (15%). Not surprisingly, the health-care industry and government employers were most likely to offer elder care leave above and beyond federal and state FMLA provisions, as well as emergency elder care.

CHAPTER 10
HEALTH-CARE USE, EXPENDITURES, AND FINANCING

Health-care use and expenditures tend to be concentrated among older adults. Because older adults often suffer multiple chronic conditions, they are hospitalized more frequently, use the most prescription and over-the-counter drugs, make the highest number of physician visits, and require care from more physician–specialists and other health-care providers—such as podiatrists and physical therapists—than any other age group.

Nearly all older Americans have health insurance through Medicare, which covers inpatient hospitalization, outpatient care, physician services, home health care, short-term skilled nursing facility care, and hospice (end-of-life care) services. Historically, older adults' use of health-care services has changed in response to physician practice patterns, advances in medical technology, and Medicare reimbursement for services. For example, advances in medical technology and physician practice patterns have shifted many medical procedures once performed in hospitals to outpatient settings such as ambulatory surgery centers.

Another example of changes in utilization occurred during the 1980s when hospital lengths of stay for Medicare patients declined in response to the introduction of prospective payment and diagnostic related groups (DRGs)—methods used to reimburse various providers for services performed. *Older Americans 2004: Key Indicators of Well-Being* (http://www.agingstats.gov/chartbook2004/default.htm) states that between 1992 and 2001 the hospitalization rate increased from 306 to 365 hospital stays per one thousand Medicare enrollees. (See Figure 10.1.) However, during the same period the average length of stay (ALOS) decreased from eight days to six days.

Older adults account for 12% of the United States population but are responsible for disproportionate health-care expenditures. The Center for Medicare & Medicaid Services (CMS was formerly known as the Health Care Financing Administration, or simply HCFA), an agency of the U.S. Department of Health and Human Services (HHS), has projected that the national health expenditure will grow to $3.4 trillion by 2013, almost twice as much as the 2004 expenditure of $1.8 trillion. (See Table 10.1.) (Because the numbers in Table 10.1 are projections, they necessarily differ from the actual numbers presented in other tables and figures.) Medicare is projected to reach $532.1 billion by 2013, accounting for almost 16% of all health-care expenditures.

FINANCING HEALTH CARE FOR OLDER ADULTS

The United States is the only industrialized nation that does not have a national health-care program. In nearly all other developed countries, government national medical-care programs cover almost all health-related costs, from birth to long-term care.

In the United States the major government health-care entitlement programs are Medicare and Medicaid. They provide financial assistance for persons age sixty-five and older, the poor, and persons with disabilities. Before the existence of these programs, a large number of older Americans could not afford adequate medical care. For older adults who are beneficiaries, the Medicare program provides reimbursement for hospital and physician care, while Medicaid pays for the cost of nursing home care.

MEDICARE

The spirit in which this law is written draws deeply upon the ancient dreams of all mankind. In Leviticus, it is written, "Thou shall rise up before the hoary head, and honor the face of an old man."

—Russell B. Long, Democratic senator from Louisiana, at the original vote for Medicare in 1965

FIGURE 10.1

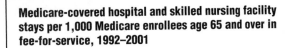

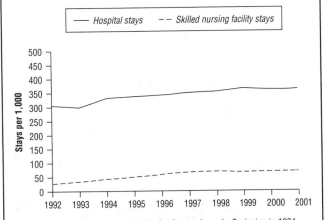

Medicare-covered hospital and skilled nursing facility stays per 1,000 Medicare enrollees age 65 and over in fee-for-service, 1992–2001

Note: Data are for Medicare enrollees in fee-for-service only. Beginning in 1994, managed care enrollees were excluded from the denominator of all utilization rates because utilization data are not available for them. Prior to 1994, managed care enrollees were included in the denominators; they comprised 7 percent or less of the Medicare population.
Reference population: These data refer to Medicare enrollees.

SOURCE: "Medicare-Covered Hospital and Skilled Nursing Facility Stays per 1,000 Medicare Enrollees Age 65 and Over in Fee-for-Service, 1992–2001," in *Older Americans 2004: Key Indicators*, Federal Interagency Forum on Aging Related Statistics, Washington, DC, U.S. Government Printing Office, November 2004, http://www.agingstats.gov/chartbook2004/healthcare.html#Indicator%2028 (accessed August 11, 2005)

The Medicare program, enacted under Title XVIII ("Health Insurance for the Aged") of the Social Security Act (PL 89-97), was signed into law by President Lyndon B. Johnson and went into effect on July 1, 1966. That year nineteen million older adults entered the program. The CMS forecasts that by 2030 the number of Americans insured by Medicare will exceed seventy million.

The establishment of the Medicare program in 1966 served to improve equity in health care. Before the creation of Medicare about half of the older population was uninsured, and the insured population was often limited to benefits of just $10 per day. Further, because poverty rates among older adults hovered at about 30%, the older population could not be expected to pay for private health insurance. The Medicare program extended health-care coverage to a population with growing health needs and little income.

Forty years after its inception the Medicare program covers about half of the health-care costs of older Americans. In 2001 Medicare financed 54% of the health-care costs of older Americans. Medicaid covered 10%, and other payers, primarily private health insurers, covered 15%. Older adults paid 21% of their health-care costs out of pocket. (See Figure 10.2.) Historically, Medicare pay-

ment has focused almost exclusively on acute care services such as hospitals, physicians, and short-term rehabilitation and home health care, but in 2005 Medicare offered its first prescription drug benefits. Other public and private payers finance long-term care.

The Medicare program is composed of several parts:

- Part A provides hospital insurance. Coverage includes physicians' fees, nursing services, meals, semiprivate rooms, special care units, operating room costs, laboratory tests, and some drugs and supplies. Part A also covers rehabilitation services, limited post–hospital skilled nursing facility care, home health care, and hospice care for the terminally ill.

- Part B (Supplemental Medical Insurance, or SMI) is elective medical insurance; enrollees must pay premiums to get coverage. It covers private physicians' services, diagnostic tests, outpatient hospital services, outpatient physical therapy, speech pathology services, home health services, and medical equipment and supplies.

- A newer, third part of Medicare, sometimes known as Part C, is the Medicare Advantage (formerly Medicare + Choice) program, which was established by the Balanced Budget Act (BBA) of 1997 to expand beneficiaries' options and allow them to participate in private-sector health plans.

- Part D, the Medicare prescription drug benefit, was enacted after Congress passed the Prescription Drug, Improvement, and Modernization Act of 2003 (see below).

In 2003 more than $283 million was spent to provide coverage for the forty million persons enrolled in Medicare. (See Table 10.2.) Most Medicare recipients were age sixty-five and older; more than half of these older adults were between the ages of sixty-five and seventy-four; a third were between the ages of seventy-five and eighty-four; and 12.1% was eighty-five and older. The CMS estimates that by 2050 sixty-nine million people age sixty-five and older will be eligible for Medicare; of those, fifteen million will be eighty-five or older.

Reimbursement under Medicare

In general, Medicare reimburses physicians on a fee-for-service basis, as opposed to per capita (per head) or per member per month. In response to the increasing administrative burden of paperwork, reduced compensation, and delays in reimbursements, some physicians opt out of Medicare participation—they do not provide services under the Medicare program and choose not to accept Medicare patients into their practices. Others continue to provide services to Medicare beneficiaries, but they do not "accept assignment," meaning that their

TABLE 10.1

National health expenditures aggregate and per capita amounts, percent distribution and average annual percent change by source of funds, selected years, 1990–2013

Year	Total	Out-of-pocket payments	Third-party payments							
			Total	Private health insurance	Other private funds	Public				
						Total	Federal[a]	State and local[a]	Medicare[b]	Medicaid[c]
Historical estimates					Amount in billions					
1990	$696.00	$137.30	$558.70	$233.50	$42.80	$282.50	$192.70	$89.80	$110.20	$73.60
1998	1,150.30	175.3	975	382.9	70.8	521.3	368.4	152.9	210.2	171.5
1999	1,222.60	184.5	1,038.10	412.7	72.6	552.9	386.4	166.4	213.5	186.8
2000	1,309.40	192.6	1,116.90	449.3	72.9	594.6	416	178.6	225.1	203.4
2001	1,420.70	200.5	1,220.20	495.6	72.3	652.3	460.3	192	246.5	224.3
2002	1,553.00	212.5	1,340.50	549.6	77.5	713.4	504.7	208.7	267.1	250.4
Projected										
2003	1,673.60	227	1,446.60	606.7	80.9	759	535.2	223.8	280.9	269.2
2004	1,793.60	243	1,550.60	656.5	84.5	809.6	569.1	240.5	295.2	292.7
2005	1,920.80	260.9	1,660.00	707	88.7	864.2	605	259.3	309.3	319.2
2006	2,064.00	279.7	1,784.30	762.2	93.8	928.2	648.1	280.1	328.3	348.4
2007	2,219.20	299.3	1,919.90	821.9	99.5	998.5	695.5	303	349.3	380.4
2008	2,387.70	319.9	2,067.80	887.7	105.3	1,074.80	747.1	327.7	372.9	414.9
2009	2,565.00	341.7	2,223.30	954.6	111.3	1,157.40	803.5	354	399.3	452.2
2010	2,751.00	364.3	2,386.70	1,022.20	117.6	1,246.90	864.9	382	428.9	492.1
2011	2,945.60	387.4	2,558.20	1,092.00	123.7	1,342.50	930.6	411.9	460.8	534.8
2012	3,145.80	411.3	2,734.50	1,160.60	129.9	1,444.00	1,000.30	443.6	495.1	580.2
2013	3,358.10	436.2	2,921.80	1,233.40	136.3	1,552.10	1,074.80	477.3	532.1	628.5
Historical estimates					Per capita amount					
1990	$2,738	$540	$2,198	$919	$168	$1,111	$758	$353	*	*
1998	4,179	637	3,542	1,391	257	1,894	1,339	556	*	*
1999	4,402	664	3,738	1,486	261	1,991	1,391	599	*	*
2000	4,670	687	3,983	1,603	260	2,121	1,483	637	*	*
2001	5,021	709	4,313	1,752	256	2,306	1,627	679	*	*
2002	5,440	744	4,696	1,925	271	2,499	1,768	731	*	*
Projected										
2003	5,808	788	5,020	2,105	281	2,634	1,857	777	*	*
2004	6,167	836	5,332	2,257	291	2,784	1,957	827	*	*
2005	6,546	889	5,657	2,409	302	2,945	2,062	883	*	*
2006	6,972	945	6,027	2,575	317	3,135	2,189	946	*	*
2007	7,431	1,002	6,429	2,752	333	3,344	2,329	1,015	*	*
2008	7,928	1,062	6,866	2,947	350	3,569	2,481	1,088	*	*
2009	8,446	1,125	7,321	3,143	367	3,811	2,646	1,166	*	*
2010	8,984	1,190	7,795	3,338	384	4,072	2,825	1,248	*	*
2011	9,543	1,255	8,288	3,538	401	4,349	3,015	1,334	*	*
2012	10,110	1,322	8,789	3,730	417	4,641	3,215	1,426	*	*
2013	10,709	1,391	9,318	3,933	435	4,950	3,428	1,522	*	*

TABLE 10.1

National health expenditures aggregate and per capita amounts, percent distribution and average annual percent change by source of funds, selected years, 1990–2013 [CONTINUED]

Year	Total	Out-of-pocket payments	Third-party payments			Public				
			Total	Private health insurance	Other private funds	Total	Federal[a]	State and local[a]	Medicare[b]	Medicaid[c]
Historical estimates					*Percent distribution*					
1990	100	19.7	80.3	33.5	6.1	40.6	27.7	12.9	15.8	10.6
1998	100	15.2	84.8	33.3	6.2	45.3	32	13.3	18.3	14.9
1999	100	15.1	84.9	33.8	5.9	45.2	31.6	13.6	17.5	15.3
2000	100	14.7	85.3	34.3	5.6	45.4	31.8	13.6	17.2	15.5
2001	100	14.1	85.9	34.9	5.1	45.9	32.4	13.5	17.4	15.8
2002	100	13.7	86.3	35.4	5	45.9	32.5	13.4	17.2	16.1
Projected										
2003	100	13.6	86.4	36.3	4.8	45.4	32	13.4	16.8	16.1
2004	100	13.5	86.5	36.6	4.7	45.1	31.7	13.4	16.5	16.3
2005	100	13.6	86.4	36.8	4.6	45	31.5	13.5	16.1	16.6
2006	100	13.6	86.4	36.9	4.5	45	31.4	13.6	15.9	16.9
2007	100	13.5	86.5	37	4.5	45	31.3	13.7	15.7	17.1
2008	100	13.4	86.6	37.2	4.4	45	31.3	13.7	15.6	17.4
2009	100	13.3	86.7	37.2	4.3	45.1	31.3	13.8	15.6	17.6
2010	100	13.2	86.8	37.2	4.3	45.3	31.4	13.9	15.6	17.9
2011	100	13.2	86.8	37.1	4.2	45.6	31.6	14	15.6	18.2
2012	100	13.1	86.9	36.9	4.1	45.9	31.8	14.1	15.7	18.4
2013	100	13	87	36.7	4.1	46.2	32	14.2	15.8	18.7
				Average annual percent change from previous year shown						
Historical estimates										
1990	—	3.1	7.2	6.4	6.5	8	8.4	6.9	8.4	11.1
1998	6.5	5.2	6.5	7.8	2.5	6	4.9	8.8	1.6	8.9
1999	6.3	4.4	7.6	8.9	0.5	7.5	7.6	7.3	5.4	8.9
2000	7.1	4.1	9.2	10.3	−0.9	9.7	10.7	7.5	9.5	10.2
2001	8.5	6	9.9	10.9	7.2	9.4	9.7	8.7	8.4	11.7
2002	9.3									
Projected										
2003	7.8	6.8	7.9	10.4	4.4	6.4	6	7.2	5.2	7.5
2004	7.2	7.1	7.2	8.2	4.5	6.7	6.3	7.5	5.1	8.7
2005	7.1	7.3	7.1	7.7	4.9	6.8	6.3	7.8	4.8	9
2006	7.5	7.2	7.5	7.8	5.8	7.4	7.1	8	6.1	9.2
2007	7.5	7	7.6	7.8	6	7.6	7.3	8.2	6.4	9.2
2008	7.6	6.9	7.7	8	5.9	7.6	7.4	8.1	6.8	9.1
2009	7.4	6.8	7.5	7.5	5.7	7.7	7.5	8	7.1	9
2010	7.3	6.6	7.3	7.1	5.6	7.7	7.6	7.9	7.4	8.8
2011	7.1	6.3	7.2	6.8	5.3	7.7	7.6	7.8	7.5	8.7
2012	6.8	6.2	6.9	6.3	5	7.6	7.5	7.7	7.4	8.5
2013	6.7	6.1	6.9	6.3	5	7.5	7.4	7.6	7.5	8.3

*Calculation of per capita estimates is inappropriate.

[a]Includes Medicaid SCHIP (State Children's Health Insurance Program) Expansion and SCHIP.

[b]Subset of federal funds.

[c]Subset of federal and state and local funds. Includes Medicaid SCHIP Expansion.

Notes: Per capita amounts based on July 1 census resident based population estimates. Numbers and percents may not add to totals because of rounding.

SOURCE: "Table 3. National Health Expenditures Aggregate and Per Capita Amounts, Percent Distribution and Average Annual Percent Change by Source of Funds: Selected Calendar Years 1990–2013," in *National Health Care Expenditures Projections—Tables*, Centers for Medicare and Medicaid Services, Office of the Actuary, Baltimore, MD, January 2004, http://www.cms.hhs.gov/statistics/nhe/projections-2003/t3.asp (accessed August 11, 2005)

FIGURE 10.2

Sources of payment for health care services for Medicare enrollees age 65 and over, by type of service, 2001

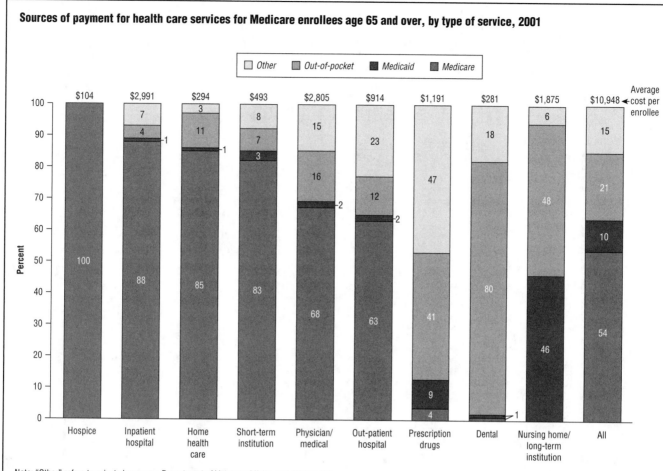

Note: "Other" refers to private insurance, Department of Veterans Affairs, and other public programs.
Reference population: These data refer to Medicare enrollees.

SOURCE: "Sources of Payment for Health Care Services for Medicare Enrollees Age 65 and Over, by Type of Service, 2001," in *Older Americans 2004: Key Indicators*, Federal Interagency Forum on Aging Related Statistics, Washington, DC, U.S. Government Printing Office, November 2004, http://www .agingstats.gov/chartbook2004/healthcare.html#Indicator%2033 (accessed August 11, 2005)

patients must pay out-of-pocket for services and then seek reimbursement from Medicare.

The Tax Equity and Fiscal Responsibility Act of 1982 (PL 97-248) authorized a "risk managed care" option for Medicare, based on agreed-upon prepayments. Beginning in 1985, the HCFA (now known as CMS) could contract to pay health-care providers, such as HMOs or other prepaid plans, to serve Medicare and Medicaid patients. These groups were paid a predetermined amount per enrollee for their services. These became known as Medicare-risk HMOs.

During the 1980s and 1990s the federal government, employers that provided health coverage for retiring employees, and many states sought to control costs by encouraging Medicare and Medicaid beneficiaries to enroll in Medicare-risk HMOs. Medicare-risk HMOs kept costs down because, essentially, the federal government paid the health plans that operated them with fixed

fees—a predetermined dollar amount per member per month (PMPM). For this fixed fee, Medicare recipients were to receive a fairly comprehensive, preset array of benefits. PMPM payment financially incentivized Medicare-risk HMO physicians to control costs, unlike physicians who were reimbursed on a fee-for-service basis (paid for each visit, procedure, or treatment delivered).

Although Medicare recipients were generally satisfied with these HMOs (even when enrolling meant they had to change physicians and thereby end longstanding relationships with their family doctors), many of the health plans did not fare as well. The health plans suffered for a variety of reasons: some plans had underestimated the service utilization rates of older adults, and some were unable to provide the stipulated range of services as cost effectively as they had believed possible. Other plans found that the PMPM payment was simply not sufficient to enable them to cover all the clinical services and their administrative overhead.

TABLE 10.2

Expenditures for health services and supplies under public programs, by type of expenditure and program, 2003

Program area	All expenditures	Total	Personal health care										Administration	Public health activities
			Hospital care	Physician and clinical services	Dental services	Other professional services	Home health care	Prescription drugs	Other non durable medical products	Durable medical equipment	Nursing home care	Other personal health care		
			Amount in billions											
Public and private spending	$1,614.2	$1,440.8	$515.9	$369.7	$74.3	$48.5	$40.0	$179.2	$32.5	$20.4	$110.8	$49.5	$119.7	$53.8
All public programs	721.7	631.5	300.8	123.0	4.9	13.6	24.9	43.2	1.7	7.6	67.3	44.6	36.4	53.8
Federal funds	507.5	479.8	242.1	101.3	2.9	8.8	18.6	25.2	1.7	7.4	45.5	26.3	20.2	7.4
State and local funds	214.2	151.7	58.7	21.7	1.9	4.8	6.3	18.0	—	0.2	21.8	18.3	16.2	46.3
Medicare[a]	283.1	274.9	156.4	73.8	0.1	6.9	12.9	2.8	1.7	6.6	13.7	—	8.2	—
Medicaid[a]	267.0	248.5	87.0	26.1	4.0	2.5	9.9	33.7	—	—	51.0	34.2	18.4	—
Federal	157.5	147.1	52.6	15.8	2.3	1.5	5.5	19.9	—	—	29.5	20.0	10.4	—
State and local	109.5	101.4	34.4	10.4	1.7	1.0	4.4	13.7	—	—	21.6	14.2	8.1	—
Other state and local														
Public assistance programs	5.5	5.5	1.9	0.6	0.0	0.1	0.0	2.6	—	0.0	0.2	0.1	0.1	—
Department of Veterans Affairs	24.5	24.4	18.1	1.5	0.0	—	0.2	0.1	—	0.7	2.3	1.5	0.1	—
Department of Defense[b]	17.2	16.5	10.6	3.3	0.0	—	—	1.3	—	—	—	1.2	0.8	—
Workers' compensation	34.0	26.3	11.2	10.3	—	3.5	—	1.2	0.1	0.1	—	—	7.7	—
Federal	0.8	0.4	0.4	0.2	—	0.2	—	0.0	0.0	0.0	—	—	0.0	—
State and local	33.2	25.5	10.8	10.1	—	3.4	—	1.1	0.1	0.1	—	—	7.7	—
State and local hospitals[c]	15.5	15.5	10.9	—	—	—	1.9	—	—	—	—	2.7	—	—
Other public programs for personal health care[d]	21.1	19.9	4.7	7.4	0.7	0.6	0.0	1.5	—	0.2	0.0	4.9	1.2	—
Federal	16.9	16.1	3.9	6.7	0.5	0.3	0.0	1.0	—	0.1	0.0	3.6	0.8	—
State and local	4.3	3.8	0.8	0.7	0.2	0.4	0.0	0.5	—	0.1	0.0	1.2	0.5	—
Government public health activities	53.8	—	—	—	—	—	—	—	—	—	—	—	—	53.8
Federal	7.4	—	—	—	—	—	—	—	—	—	—	—	—	7.4
State and local	46.3	—	—	—	—	—	—	—	—	—	—	—	—	46.3
CMS programs Medicare, Medicaid and SCHIP	556.7	529.1	245.3	101.4	4.7	9.5	22.8	37.8	1.7	6.7	64.8	34.6	27.5	—

[a]Excludes funds paid into the Medicare trust funds by states under buy-in agreements to cover premiums for Medicaid recipients.

[b]Includes care for retirees and military dependents.

[c]Expenditures not offset by revenues.

[d]Includes program spending for Medicaid SCHIP (State Children's Health Insurance Program) Expansion & SCHIP; maternal and child health; vocational rehabilitation medical payments; Public Health Service and other federal hospitals; Indian health services; alcoholism, drug abuse, and mental health; and school health.

Notes: The figure 0.0 denotes amounts less than $50 million. Numbers may not add to total because of rounding.

SOURCE: "Table 10. Expenditures for Health Services and Supplies Under Public Programs, by Type of Expenditure and Program: Calendar Year 2003," Centers for Medicare and Medicaid Services, Baltimore, MD, January 2005. http://www.cms.hhs.gov/statistics/nhe/historical/t10.asp (accessed August 11, 2005)

Still, the health plans providing these "senior HMOs" competed fiercely to market to and enroll older adults. Some health plans feared that closing their Medicare-risk programs would be viewed negatively by employer groups, which, when faced with the choice of plans that offered coverage for both younger workers and retirees or one that only covered the younger workers, would choose the plans that covered both. Despite losing money, most health plans maintained their Medicare-risk programs to avoid alienating the employers they depended on to enroll workers who were younger, healthier, and less expensive to serve than the older adults.

About ten years in to operations, some of the Medicare-risk plans faced a challenge that proved unbeatable. Their enrollees had aged and required even more health-care services than they had previously. For example, a senior HMO member who had joined as a healthy sixty-five-year-old could now be a frail seventy-five-year-old with multiple chronic health conditions requiring many costly health-care services. While the PMPM had increased over the years, for some plans it was simply insufficient to cover their costs. Many Medicare-risk plans, especially those operated by smaller health plans, were forced to end their programs abruptly, leaving thousands of older adults scrambling to join other health plans. Others have endured to the year 2006, offering older adults comprehensive care and generating substantial cost savings for employers and the federal government.

"Medicare Advantage"

The Balanced Budget Act of 1997 produced another plan for Medicare recipients—taking the place of the Medicare-risk plans—called Medicare + Choice, which later became known as Medicare Advantage. These plans offer Medicare beneficiaries a wider range of managed care plan options than just HMOs—older adults could join preferred provider organizations (PPOs) and provider-sponsored organizations (PSOs) that generally offer greater freedom of choice of providers (physicians and hospitals) than available through HMO membership.

When older adults join Medicare Advantage plans that have entered into contracts with the CMS, the plans are paid a fixed amount per member per month, which represents Medicare's share of the cost of the services. The attraction of these plans is that members no longer have to pay the regular Medicare deductibles and co-payments for Medicare-covered services. Some plans charge modest monthly premiums, and/or nominal co-payments as services are used, but there are no other charges by the plan for physician visits, hospitalization, or use of other covered services. Members of Medicare Advantage plans must continue to pay the Medicare Part B monthly premium.

According to Mathematica Policy Research Inc., an independent research firm that conducts policy research

and surveys for federal and state governments, and the Kaiser Family Foundation, the plans have experienced declining enrollment despite growing diversity in choice. In 1999, 17% of Medicare beneficiaries were enrolled in private plans; by late 2003 enrollment dropped to 12%. Reduced choice in coordinated care plans, as well as declining benefits and higher premiums for enrollment, accounted for declining enrollments.

By 2005, 179 plans, most of which were HMOs, enrolled 12% of the Medicare population. Enrollment varies widely based on geography. Less than 1% of Medicare beneficiaries are enrolled in HMO plans in sixteen states and Washington, D.C., while in Arizona, California, Colorado, Oregon, Pennsylvania and Rhode Island, 20% or more are enrolled in HMOs.

Insurance to Supplement Medicare Benefits

In 2002 approximately 61% of older adults—twenty million persons—had private health insurance coverage, and 35% (11.5 million older adults) had private insurance obtained through the workplace to supplement their Medicare coverage. (See Table 10.3.) The most popular private insurance is supplemental insurance known as Medigap insurance. Federal regulations mandate that all Medigap policies sold offer a standard, minimum set of benefits, but there are ten standard variations that offer additional coverage and benefits.

In addition to Medigap policies, older adults also may purchase Medicare supplemental health insurance called "Medicare SELECT," which offers essentially the same coverage as Medigap policies but requires use of preferred providers—specific hospitals and in some cases plan physicians—to receive full benefits. Although Medicare SELECT policies restrict older adults' choices, they are generally less expensive than Medigap policies.

A less popular option is hospital indemnity coverage—insurance that pays a fixed cash amount for each day of hospitalization up to a designated number of days. Some coverage may have added benefits such as surgical benefits or skilled nursing home benefits. Most policies have a maximum annual number of days or a lifetime maximum payment amount.

The Prescription Drug, Improvement, and Modernization Act of 2003

Congress passed the Prescription Drug, Improvement, and Modernization Act of 2003, which represents the largest expansion of Medicare since its creation in 1965. The legislation established a Medicare prescription drug benefit. Among other things, it provides help for low-income beneficiaries and those with the highest drug costs. It also contains some measures to help keep prescription drugs affordable and includes $88 billion in subsidies to maintain current employer-provided coverage.

TABLE 10.3

Health insurance coverage for persons age 65 and over, according to type of coverage and selected chracteristics, selected years, 1989–2002

[Data are based on household interviews of a sample of the civilian noninstitutionalized population]

Characteristic	Private insurance[a]						Private insurance obtained through workplace[a,b]					
	1989	1995	1999	2000	2001	2002	1989	1995	1999	2000	2001	2002
						Number in millions						
Total[c]	22.4	23.5	20.8	20.6	20.6	20.0	11.2	12.4	11.3	11.7	11.9	11.5
						Percent of population						
Total, age adjusted[c,d]	76.1	74.5	64.0	63.1	62.7	60.6	37.3	38.9	34.6	35.6	36.0	34.7
Total, crude[3]	76.5	74.6	64.1	63.1	62.7	60.6	38.4	39.5	34.9	35.8	36.1	34.8
Age												
65–74 years	78.2	75.1	64.5	62.7	63.0	60.5	43.7	43.3	38.6	39.4	39.7	37.8
75 years and over	73.9	73.9	63.5	63.6	62.4	60.6	30.2	34.1	30.3	31.4	31.9	31.4
75–84 years	75.9	75.7	64.6	64.6	63.9	61.4	32.0	36.0	32.3	33.1	33.3	33.1
85 years and over	65.5	67.3	59.6	59.5	57.0	57.5	22.8	27.3	23.2	24.7	26.7	25.4
Sex[d]												
Male	77.4	76.6	64.5	64.3	63.8	62.0	42.1	43.3	38.6	39.7	40.1	38.9
Female	75.4	73.2	63.8	62.2	61.9	59.6	34.0	35.8	31.8	32.5	33.0	31.8
Race[d,e]												
White only	79.8	78.3	67.6	66.9	66.4	64.0	38.7	40.4	35.8	37.2	37.4	35.9
Black or African American only	42.3	40.3	39.9	35.6	37.6	36.4	23.7	24.6	27.5	25.0	27.9	26.9
American Indian and Alaska Native only	*	*	*35.2	*	*31.8	*	*	*	*33.3	*	*	*
Asian only	#	#	33.1	43.3	40.9	40.0	#	#	21.4	23.2	23.5	27.8
Native Hawaiian and Other Pacific Islander only	...	...	*	*	*	*	...	...	*	*	*	
2 or more races	...	...	56.0	63.1	50.0	55.0	...	...	26.9	48.4	32.3	35.4
Hispanic origin and race[d,e]												
Hispanic or Latino	42.3	39.8	26.9	23.4	24.0	23.1	22.2	18.4	17.4	15.1	16.2	16.3
Mexican	33.5	31.8	27.4	20.3	24.8	21.4	20.2	15.9	16.9	12.8	16.8	15.6
Not Hispanic or Latino	77.2	76.2	66.2	65.5	65.2	63.0	37.7	39.9	35.7	36.8	37.2	35.9
White only	81.0	80.3	69.7	69.1	68.8	66.4	39.3	41.7	36.8	38.3	38.6	37.1
Black or African American only	42.4	40.1	40.1	35.6	37.6	36.5	23.7	24.4	27.6	25.0	28.0	27.0
Percent of poverty level[d,f]												
Below 100 percent	46.1	40.0	31.8	33.3	32.2	30.0	11.6	13.8	11.7	12.5	15.0	12.6
100–149 percent	67.7	67.6	46.5	46.0	47.5	45.4	22.2	26.7	17.6	18.7	22.6	19.3
150–199 percent	81.1	76.0	60.0	61.2	61.3	58.0	39.0	38.7	28.0	29.1	28.6	28.6
200 percent or more	85.5	85.3	73.4	72.6	71.3	69.5	49.4	49.3	43.0	44.9	43.7	43.1
Geographic region[d]												
Northeast	76.1	76.2	66.0	66.7	66.1	65.6	42.2	44.6	39.7	38.7	38.8	39.8
Midwest	81.9	82.3	77.0	75.9	72.4	71.6	40.0	44.7	38.5	41.2	40.5	37.2
South	73.0	70.7	60.2	58.4	60.2	57.2	32.0	33.7	31.0	31.9	34.1	33.1
West	74.7	68.8	51.5	51.5	51.7	47.8	37.1	33.6	30.63	31.7	30.6	29.1
Location of residence[d]												
Within MSA[g]	76.6	74.7	62.8	61.4	61.2	59.7	39.9	40.9	36.0	36.9	36.5	35.7
Outside MSA[g]	74.8	73.9	68.2	68.5	68.1	63.4	30.2	32.2	30.0	31.5	34.1	31.5

The prescription drug benefit includes:

- A $35 monthly premium

- A $250 annual deductible

- 75% coverage until $2,250 total costs

- No coverage between $2,250 and $5,100

- An annual out-of-pocket limit of $3,600 per year (plus 5% over $5,100)

- 95% coverage above $5,100 total

Beginning in 2004, a drug discount card was made available to Medicare beneficiaries. The discount card offered an average of about 13% off the cost of prescription drugs. Medicare beneficiaries could buy the cards for up to $30 and obtain discounts on drugs they purchase at neighborhood pharmacies or by mail order. Beneficiaries with household incomes below about $12,000 for an individual ($16,000 for a couple) received the cards for free and were given $600 a year to fill their prescriptions. The card program was a temporary measure that was replaced by prescription drug coverage under Medicare in 2006.

As detailed in Robert Pear's article "Lower Costs Seen for Premium in Medicare Drug Benefit Plan" (*New York Times*, August 10, 2005), beginning January 2006, Medicare beneficiaries can apply for prescription drug

TABLE 10.3

Health insurance coverage for persons age 65 and over, according to type of coverage and selected chracteristics, selected years, 1989–2002 [CONTINUED]

[Data are based on household interviews of a sample of the civilian noninstitutionalized population]

Characteristic	Medicare health maintenance organization[a,h]						Medicaid[a,i]					
	1989	1995	1999	2000	2001	2002	1989	1995	1999	2000	2001	2002
						Number in millions						
Total[c]	...	...	5.2	5.0	4.2	3.9	2.0	3.0	2.4	2.5	2.7	2.6
						Percent of population						
Total, age adjusted[c,d]	...	...	16.0	15.2	12.9	11.9	7.2	9.6	7.4	7.6	8.1	8.0
Total, crude[3]	...	...	16.0	15.2	12.9	11.9	7.0	9.4	7.3	7.6	8.1	8.0
Age												
65–74 years	...	...	16.1	15.8	12.8	11.8	6.3	8.4	6.6	7.7	7.8	8.1
75 years and over	...	...	15.9	14.6	13.1	12.0	8.2	10.9	8.1	7.5	8.5	7.9
75–84 years	...	...	16.5	15.5	13.4	12.7	7.9	9.9	7.2	7.2	8.1	8.0
85 years and over	...	...	13.7	11.1	11.9	9.2	9.7	14.3	11.4	8.6	10.3	7.5
Sex[d]												
Male	...	...	16.5	15.6	12.5	12.4	5.2	5.8	5.3	5.5	6.1	5.7
Female	...	...	15.6	15.0	13.3	11.5	8.6	12.2	8.8	9.2	9.7	9.7
Race[d,e]												
White only	...	...	15.8	15.2	13.0	11.7	5.6	7.4	5.6	5.6	6.2	6.3
Black or African American only	...	...	16.5	14.7	11.2	10.8	21.2	28.4	18.2	19.6	20.0	19.4
American Indian and Alaska Native only	...	...	*	*	*	*	*	*	*	*35.8	*	*
Asian only	...	...	18.9	16.0	13.4	19.1	#	#	28.2	21.3	23.7	20.0
Native Hawaiian and Other Pacific Islander only	...	...	*	*	*	*	...	...	*	*	*	*
2 or more races	...	...	*21.8	*29.8	*16.3	*15.0	...	...	*	*	*19.9	*
Hispanic origin and race[d,e]												
Hispanic or Latino	...	...	25.7	25.0	20.1	22.1	26.4	32.7	24.0	29.6	30.1	28.6
Mexican	...	...	26.0	24.5	18.9	20.1	#	#	17.5	28.1	25.6	24.6
Not Hispanic or Latino	...	...	15.4	14.6	12.5	11.2	6.6	8.5	6.4	6.3	6.8	6.6
White only	...	...	15.2	14.5	12.5	11.1	4.9	6.1	4.7	4.6	4.9	5.0
Black or African American only	...	...	16.5	14.7	11.2	10.6	21.1	28.5	18.1	19.5	20.0	19.4
Percent of poverty level[d,f]												
Below 100 percent	...	...	13.9	15.1	9.1	9.2	28.2	36.4	30.1	28.6	31.4	30.0
100–149 percent	...	...	17.4	16.6	12.9	11.8	9.0	12.8	13.9	14.2	15.4	13.5
150–199 percent	...	...	18.8	15.9	14.0	12.9	4.7	5.9	5.2	5.5	7.0	6.9
200 percent or more	...	...	15.4	14.8	13.3	12.1	2.4	2.4	2.8	2.9	3.1	3.2
Geographic region[d]												
Northeast	...	...	17.5	12.5	13.5	10.3	5.4	8.9	7.3	7.4	7.9	7.7
Midwest	...	...	9.0	8.4	7.5	6.0	3.7	5.8	5.7	4.5	5.1	5.1
South	...	...	12.2	13.2	10.2	9.0	9.7	11.8	8.2	9.4	9.3	9.4
West	...	...	31.0	30.6	23.8	26.4	9.4	11.5	8.2	8.6	10.0	9.3

coverage. There is a premium for the prescription drug coverage of about $32 per month, and the government pays the full premium for low-income people eligible for both Medicare and Medicaid, up to preset limits. The maximum payment for low-income beneficiaries varies from a low of $23 a month in California to a high of $36 a month in Maine, Mississippi, New Hampshire, and North Carolina.

The poorest beneficiaries are eligible for additional assistance valued at about $2,300 per recipient. Beneficiaries with incomes up to 135% of the poverty level—about $1,100 per month for an individual—can essentially obtain their medicines for free except for copayments of $2 to $5 per prescription.

Many advocates for older adults fear that the beneficiaries most in need of this assistance will not apply for it. In 2005 about 7.8 million people were eligible for the $600 credit toward prescription drug purchases, but only about a quarter of those eligible actually enrolled for the credit and many were automatically enrolled. About half of the Medicare beneficiaries eligible for the prescription drug subsidy will be automatically enrolled because of their participation in other government programs. But about 7.5 million beneficiaries will have to apply for the benefit.

According to Kevin Freking's article "Seniors May Be Wary of Drug Subsidy" (*Associated Press*, May 5, 2005), social service workers worry that the poorest, most vulnerable older adults—the population that is eligible for free prescription drugs—may be deterred by the complicated six-page application that requires details of their finances, asks them to compute the face value of insurance policies, requires them to calculate how much help

TABLE 10.3

Health insurance coverage for persons age 65 and over, according to type of coverage and selected chracteristics, selected years, 1989–2002 [CONTINUED]

[Data are based on household interviews of a sample of the civilian noninstitutionalized population]

Characteristic	Medicare health maintenance organization[a,h]						Medicaid[a,i]					
	1989	1995	1999	2000	2001	2002	1989	1995	1999	2000	2001	2002
							Number in millions					
Location of residence[d]												
Within MSA[g]	...	...	19.7	18.7	15.8	14.5	6.5	8.9	6.9	7.2	8.1	7.6
Outside MSA[g]	...	...	3.4	4.4	3.1	3.0	8.8	11.7	8.8	9.0	8.3	9.3

*Estimates are considered unreliable.
Estimates calculated upon request.
— Data not available.
[a]Almost all persons 65 years of age and over are covered by Medicare also.
[b]Private insurance originally obtained through a present or former employer or union. Starting in 1997 also includes private insurance obtained through workplace, self-employed, or professional association.
[c]Includes all other races not shown separately and, in 1984 and 1989, unknown poverty level.
[d]Estimates are for persons 65 years of age and over and are age adjusted to the year 2000 standard using two age groups: 65–74 years and 75 years and over.
[e]The race groups, white, black, American Indian and Alaska Native (AI/AN), Asian, Native Hawaiian and Other Pacific Islander, and 2 or more races, include persons of Hispanic and non-Hispanic origin. Persons of Hispanic origin may be of any race. The 1999 and later race-specific estimates are for persons who reported only one racial group; the category "2 or more races" includes persons who reported more than one racial group. Estimates for single race categories prior to 1999 included persons who reported one race or, if they reported more than one race, identified one race as best representing their race.
[f]Poverty status was unknown for 15–18 percent of persons 65 years of age and over in 1984 and 1989. Missing family income data were imputed for 22–25 percent of persons 65 years of age and over in 1994–96. Missing family income data were imputed for 36 percent of persons 65 years of age and over in 1997, 41 percent in 1998, and 44–47 percent in 1999–2002.
[g]MSA is metropolitan statistical area.
[h]Persons reporting Medicare coverage are considered to have health maintenance organization (HMO) coverage if they responded yes when asked if they were under a Medicare managed care arrangement such as an HMO.
[i]Includes public assistance through 1996. Starting in 1997 includes state-sponsored health plans. In 2002 the age-adjusted percent of the population 65 years of age and over covered by Medicaid was 7.3 percent, and 0.7 percent were covered by State-sponsored health plans.
Notes: Percents do not add to 100 because (1) elderly persons with more than one type of insurance in addition to Medicare appear in more than one column, (2) elderly persons with Medicare fee-for-service only are not shown, and (3) the percent of elderly persons without health insurance (1.3 percent in 2002) is not shown.

SOURCE: "Table 132. Health Insurance Coverage for Persons 65 Years of Age and Over, According to Type of Coverage and Selected Characteristics: United States, Selected Years 1989–2002," in *Health, United States, 2004*, Centers for Disease Control and Prevention, National Center for Health Statistics, Hyattsville, MD, 2004, http://www.cdc.gov/nchs/data/hus/hus04trend.pdf (accessed August 11, 2005).

---

they receive from relatives to pay for food, utilities, and other bills, and warns that anyone who gives false information could go to prison.

PRESCRIPTION DRUG PRICES ROSE IN 2004–05. A survey conducted by David Gross, Susan Raetzman, and Professor Stephen Schondelmeyer for the AARP found that pharmaceutical companies increased the prices they charge drug wholesalers for the top two hundred brand-name drugs an average of 3.4% in the first three months of 2004, while inflation in general was 1.2%. The study *Trends in Manufacturer Prices of Prescription Drugs Used by Older Americans*, released in June 2004 by the AARP Public Policy Institute, found that 29% of the drugs studied had increases in the first quarter (from December 31, 2003, to March 31, 2004) of more than 5%, or more than four times the rate of inflation for the same period. First quarter increases of more than 7.5% were found in almost 11% of the drugs. Of the twenty-five brand-name drugs with the greatest sales in 2003, nearly two-thirds had price increases in the first quarter of 2004.

This increase occurred just after enactment of Medicare legislation intended to increase government spending for prescription drugs that promised prescription drug savings for older Americans. The price increase also preceded the June 2004 implementation of the pharmacy discount card program aimed at providing Medicare recipients savings on brand-name drugs ranging from 11% to 18%.

An AARP Public Policy Institute report, "Trends in Manufacturer Prices of Brand Name Prescription Drugs Used by Older Americans—Second Quarter 2005 Update" (AARP, http://assets.aarp.org/rgcenter/health/dd128_drugprices.pdf), found that manufacturer prices for brand-name drugs rose 6.1% during the twelve months ending in June 2005, which was more than twice the general rate of inflation (3%). The average annual manufacturer price increase through mid-2005 revealed continued slowing from the 7.1% average increase for calendar year 2004. Of the twenty-five brand-name drugs with the greatest sales in 2003, twenty-two had price increases in the first quarter of 2005.

Medicare Faces Challenges

Like Social Security, the Medicare program's continuing financial viability is in jeopardy. In 1995, for the first time since 1972, the Medicare trust fund lost money, a sign that the financial condition of Medicare was worse than previously assumed. The CMS had not expected a deficit until 1997. However, income to the trust fund, primarily from payroll taxes, was less than expected,

FIGURE 10.3

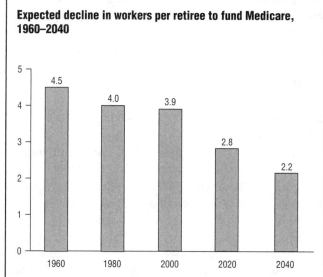

Expected decline in workers per retiree to fund Medicare, 1960–2040

SOURCE: National Bipartisan Commission on the Future of Medicare, "Fewer Workers Per Retiree to Fund Medicare," in *The Facts About Medicare*, Health Care Financing Administration, Baltimore, MD, 1999, http://thomas.loc.gov/medicare/factpage4.html (accessed August 11, 2005)

FIGURE 10.4

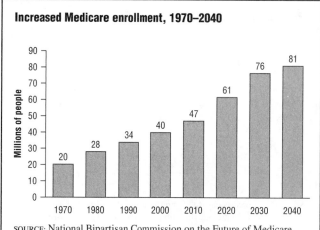

Increased Medicare enrollment, 1970–2040

SOURCE: National Bipartisan Commission on the Future of Medicare, "Medicare Enrollment Soars," in *The Facts About Medicare*, Health Care Financing Administration, Baltimore, MD, 1999, http://thomas.loc.gov/medicare/factpage4.html (accessed August 11, 2005)

and spending was higher. The deficit is significant because losses are anticipated to grow from year to year. No tax increases are scheduled under current law, and there is no reason to expect a reduction in the rate of spending.

A NATIONAL BIPARTISAN COMMISSION CONSIDERS THE FUTURE OF MEDICARE. The National Bipartisan Commission on the Future of Medicare was created by Congress in the Balanced Budget Act of 1997. The Commission was chaired by Senator John Breaux, a Democrat from Louisiana, and Representative William Thomas, a Republican from California, and was charged with examining the Medicare program and drafting recommendations to avert a future financial crisis and reinforce the program in anticipation of the retirement of the baby boomers.

The commission observed that like Social Security, Medicare would suffer because there would be fewer workers per retiree to fund it. (See Figure 10.3.) It predicted that beneficiaries' out-of-pocket costs would rise and forecasted soaring Medicare enrollment. (See Figure 10.4.) Perhaps the direst prediction was the commission's determination that that, without reform, the Medicare Part A fund would be bankrupt in the year 2008. (See Figure 10.5.)

When the commission disbanded in March 1999, it was unable to forward an official recommendation to Congress, because a plan endorsed by Senator Breaux fell one vote short of the required majority needed to authorize an official recommendation. The plan backed by Senator Breaux would have changed Medicare into a premium system, where instead of Medicare directly covering beneficiaries, the beneficiaries would be given a fixed amount of money to purchase private health insurance. The plan also would have raised the age of eligibility from sixty-five to sixty-seven, as has already been done with Social Security, and provided prescription drug coverage for low-income beneficiaries, much like the Medicare Prescription Drug, Improvement, and Modernization Act of 2003.

THE MEDICARE PRESCRIPTION DRUG, IMPROVEMENT, AND MODERNIZATION ACT AIMS TO REFORM MEDICARE. Supported by Senator Breaux, the Medicare Prescription Drug, Improvement, and Modernization Act of 2003 is a measure intended to introduce private-sector enterprise into a Medicare model in urgent need of a reform. The Part D drug benefit is one of the biggest components of the Medicare reform in terms of political capital and dollars and is projected to cost $724 billion between 2006 and 2015.

Under the Act, premiums and deductibles may rise quickly, because they are indexed to the growth in per-capita Medicare expenditures. For example, the deductible for Medicare Part D, the drug benefit, is expected to rise from $250 to $445 by 2013, and the threshold for drug coverage that covers 95% of expenses is expected to rise to $9,066 from $5,100.

Older adults with substantial incomes will face increasing premium costs. In 2005 older adults paid 25% of the Medicare Part B premium cost, and the government paid the remaining 75%. Beginning in 2007, older adults with annual incomes of $80,000 to $100,000 (or couples earning $160,000 to $200,000) will pay 35%; those earning between $100,000 and $150,000

FIGURE 10.5

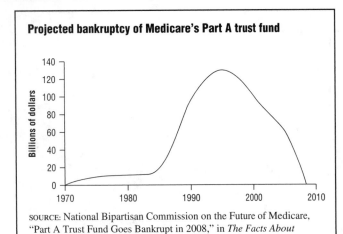

Projected bankruptcy of Medicare's Part A trust fund

SOURCE: National Bipartisan Commission on the Future of Medicare, "Part A Trust Fund Goes Bankrupt in 2008," in *The Facts About Medicare*, Health Care Financing Administration, Baltimore, MD, 1999, http://thomas.loc.gov/medicare/factpage4.html (accessed August 11, 2005)

($200,000 to $300,000 for couples) will pay 50%; those earning $150,000 to $200,000 ($300,000 to $400,000 for couples) will pay 65%; and anyone earning more than $200,000 ($400,000 for couples) will pay 80% of the premium cost.

The Act also expanded coverage of preventive medical services. According to the CMS, new beneficiaries will receive a free physical examination along with laboratory tests to screen for heart disease and diabetes. The Act also provides employers with $89 billion in subsidies and tax breaks to help offset the costs associated with maintaining retiree health benefits.

Medicare reform continues to be hotly contested. One of the issues that attracted attention from policy makers, legislators, and the public in 2005 was the safe, legal reimportation of prescription drugs from other countries. In the face of skyrocketing drug prices, many older adults traveled to Canada to purchase prescription drugs, because the costs were 40% less than those in the United States. A study conducted by investigators, "Do Drug Makers Lose Money on Canadian Imports" (Boston University School of Public Health, http://www.bu.edu/dbin/sph/departments/health_services/documents/health_reform/Canadian_importing_break_even_14_Apr04_FINAL.pdf, April 15, 2004), estimated savings of $59.7 billion in 2004 had Americans been permitted to pay the Canadian price for brand-name prescription drugs.

Other issues debated included drug prices, gaps in prescription drug coverage under the new legislation, allowances to change coverage plans from traditional fee-for-service Medicare to competing private health plans, and the role of health savings accounts and other cost sharing proposals. Health-care industry observers predict that increased federal spending as a result of the new drug benefit will intensify demands for cost contain-

ment, which will amplify as the baby boomer generation becomes eligible for Medicare coverage. The immediate and long-term impact of private plan participation is not yet known, although the increase in Medicare Advantage payments may generate new insurance options and benefits as health plans compete and expand coverage to attract enrollees.

Medicare Health Support Helps Older Adults Choose and Access Health Services

In 2005 the CMS launched Medicare Health Support, a pilot program to offer approximately 180,000 chronically ill fee-for-service Medicare recipients (Medicare recipients who are not enrolled in managed care plans) access to health coaches. Free to participants, the program coaches will counsel participants about medical choices and preventive care. The number of coaches in each area will vary. Most will serve in the regions where they reside, but others will travel to visit participants who require personal assistance. The coaches will offer customized care plans and twenty-four-hour hot lines to help and advise patients on issues ranging from treatment to living wills.

Medicare Health Support began in Oklahoma, Maryland, and Washington, D.C., in August 2005 and in Florida, western Pennsylvania, Mississippi, greater Chicago, northern Georgia, Queens and Brooklyn in New York, and thirty-five counties in Tennessee in late 2005, with full implementation anticipated in 2006. Federal officials hope the new program will simultaneously save money and improve the health of chronically ill Medicare recipients.

MEDICAID

Medicaid was enacted by Congress in 1965 under "Grants to States for Medical Assistance Programs," Title XIX of the Social Security Act. It is a joint federal/state program that provides medical assistance to selected categories of low-income Americans: the aged, persons who are blind, persons who are disabled, or families with dependent children. Medicaid covers hospitalization, physicians' fees, laboratory and radiology fees, and long-term care in nursing homes. It is the largest source of funds for medical and health-related services for the United States' poorest people and the second-largest public payer of health-care costs, after Medicare.

In 2002 Medicaid provided coverage for 8%—2.6 million—of adults age sixty-five and over. Older Medicaid recipients were more likely to be female (9.7%) than male (5.7%), and nearly 29% were of Hispanic origin. There were a greater number of older Medicaid recipients in the South and West, 9.4% and 9.3% respectively, than in the Northeast (7.7%) or Midwest (5.1%). (See Table 10.3.)

According to John Holahan and Arunabh Ghosh in "Understanding the Recent Growth in Medicaid Spending, 2000–2003" (Health Affairs, http://content.healthaffairs.org/cgi/reprint/hlthaff.w5.52v1, January 26, 2005), Medicaid spending increased to $276 billion by fiscal year 2003, up one-third from 2000, according to an analysis conducted by the director of the Urban Institute's Health Policy Center in Washington, D.C. From 2000 to 2003 Medicaid spending grew at an average of 10.2% annually. State Medicaid cost containment efforts such as curbing provider payment rates, reducing benefits, and a slowing of enrollment growth served to moderate Medicaid spending growth in 2003. The 7.1% growth in 2003 is comparable to the increases the program experienced in the late 1990s, and Medicaid costs actually grew at a slower rate than private insurance costs. Although families accounted for most of Medicaid enrollment growth from 2000 to 2003, they only accounted for 44% of Medicaid spending growth. Older adults and persons with disabilities accounted for 56% of spending growth. Although older adults and persons with disabilities are a minority of the Medicaid population, they are responsible for the majority of program costs due to their intensive use of services.

Medicaid is the largest third-party payer of long-term care in the United States, financing about one half of all nursing home care. Under current law, an older person must have less than $2,500 in savings or assets (with some exceptions) to qualify for nursing home care paid for by Medicaid. Although home health services currently account for a small share of Medicaid expenditures for older adults, they are the fastest-growing expense. In 2003 they accounted for nearly one-third of all Medicaid long-term care costs.

According to CMS, Medicaid long-term care expenditures in 2003 totaled $83.8 billion, approximately 32% of total Medicaid expenditures of $259.6 billion. Long term care expenditures increased by 0.3% from 2002. Medicaid spending for nursing home expenditures decreased 3.8% in 2003, from $46.5 billion to $44.8 billion. However, this decrease, the first in at least fifteen years, is likely attributable to the use of upper payment limit (UPL) programs in selected states, rather than a real decline in fee-for-service payments to nursing facilities. UPL programs allow states to pay selected providers—usually county- and state-owned nursing facilities—more than the actual cost of services, as long as total Medicaid payments do not exceed the amount Medicare would pay for the same services. Some states use UPL programs to draw down additional federal matching dollars without having to contribute additional state funds. They make extra payments to providers and then require them to return some or all of the excess funds as an intergovernmental transfer. Expenditures for services provided in intermediate care facilities (ICFs) rose 0.7%, from $11.2 to $11.3 billion.

Expenditures for community-based long-term care services continued to increase in 2003. Total home and community-based services increased by 7.6%, to $27.8 billion. Expenditures for Medicaid home health-care benefits increased 4.7%, to $2.9 billion, and expenditures under the Medicaid personal care services benefit increased 4%, to $6.3 billion. This trend is expected to persist as Medicaid programs continue to invest more resources in alternatives to institutional services.

VETERANS' BENEFITS

Persons who have served in the U.S. military are entitled to medical treatment at any veterans' facility in the nation. According to the Department of Veterans Affairs (VA), between 2000 and 2010, the total veteran population is projected to decline by 17.7%, from 24.3 to 20.0 million. However, this projection may change as a result of the current armed conflicts. During the same time period, the percent of veterans over the age of sixty-five will decline by only 9%, from 9.3 million to 8.5 million, while the population of veterans age seventy-five and older will increase 12%, from four to 4.5 million. After 2010 there is a projected increase in older veterans as the large Vietnam-era cohort ages. Throughout this period the number of veterans age eighty-five and older is expected to increase steadily and significantly to reach 1.4 million by 2012.

The number of veterans age sixty-five and older that received health care from the Veterans Health Administration (VHA) increased steadily from 1990 through 2003. This increase may in part be attributable to the fact that VHA benefits cover services not covered by Medicare, such as prescription drugs, mental health care, long-term care (nursing home and community-based care) and specialized services for persons with disabilities. The VHA estimates that 91% of its patients age sixty-five and older are covered by Medicare Part A, 83% by Medicare Part B, 48% by Medigap insurance, 8% by Medicaid, 14% by private insurance, and 7% by TRI-CARE for Life—expanded medical coverage for military retirees and veterans. Just 4% have no additional public or private coverage. In 2003 approximately 2.3 million veterans age sixty-five and older received health care from the VHA. An additional one million older veterans were enrolled to receive health care but did not use services in 2003. (See Figure 10.6.)

Despite a short-term decline in the total number of veterans, there has been increased demand for health-care service in response to VHA initiatives such as opening the system to all veterans in 1995; initiating enrollment for VHA health care in 1999; increasing access to outpatient treatment; and shifting care from inpatient to

FIGURE 10.6

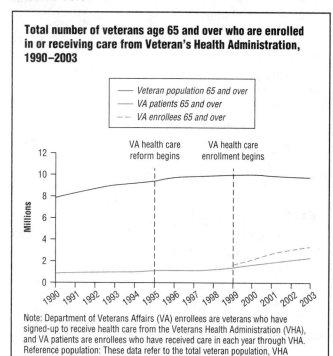

Total number of veterans age 65 and over who are enrolled in or receiving care from Veteran's Health Administration, 1990–2003

— Veteran population 65 and over
— VA patients 65 and over
- - - VA enrollees 65 and over

VA health care reform begins

VA health care enrollment begins

Note: Department of Veterans Affairs (VA) enrollees are veterans who have signed-up to receive health care from the Veterans Health Administration (VHA), and VA patients are enrollees who have received care in each year through VHA. Reference population: These data refer to the total veteran population, VHA enrollment population, and VHA patient population.

SOURCE: "Total Number of Veterans Age 65 and Over Who Are Enrolled In or Receiving Care from Veteran's Health Administration, 1990–2003," in *Older Americans 2004: Key Indicators*, Federal Interagency Forum on Aging Related Statistics, Washington, DC, U.S. Government Printing Office, November 2004, http://www.agingstats .gov/chartbook2004/healthcare.html#Indicator%2034 (accessed August 11, 2005)

outpatient settings. Figure 10.6 shows the effects of these initiatives on enrollment and receipt of health-care services.

LONG-TERM HEALTH CARE

The options for quality, affordable long-term care in the United States are limited but improving. Nursing home costs range from $50,000 to $75,000 per year depending on services and location. The Congressional Budget Office (CBO) reports that in 2003 nursing home care cost an average of $181 per day for a private room, or about $66,000 per year. Many nursing home residents rely on Medicaid to pay these fees. In 2001 Medicaid covered 46% of nursing home costs for older Americans. (See Figure 10.2.) The second most common source of payment at admission is private insurance, the prospective resident's own income, or family support, followed by Medicare (which only pays for short-term stays after hospitalization). The primary source of payment changes as a stay lengthens. After their funds are "spent down," nursing home residents on Medicare shift to Medicaid.

Although nursing home care may seem cost prohibitive, even an unskilled caregiver who makes home visits can cost more than $25,000 a year; skilled care costs much more. The CBO reports that in 2003 a visit by a home health aide averaged $18 per hour. Most older adults cannot afford this expense. Lifetime savings may be exhausted long before the need for care ends. The CBO estimated that total expenditures for long-term care (LTC) services for the older adults in 2004—excluding the value of donated care from relatives and friends— totaled about $135 billion, or approximately $15,000 per older adult.

The Future of Spending for Long-Term Care

The CBO reports that the population over age eighty-five, those most likely to require LTC, will more than triple by 2040. Even though disability rates among older adults have declined in recent years, reducing somewhat the need for LTC, the CBO projects that spending for LTC will grow by more than 2.5 times by 2040, reaching $346 billion (in inflation-adjusted dollars) for the older population alone.

Who Pays for Long-Term Care?

Payment for LTC is derived from three major sources: Medicaid, private insurance (LTC insurance), and out-of-pocket spending. As Figure 10.7 shows, the proportions of the contributions vary depending on whether the older adult receives formal or informal care. For example, without informal care, out-of-pocket payments account for 33% of spending, compared with 21% for older adults receiving informal care from relatives or friends.

According to the CBO, in 2004 out-of-pocket expenditures accounted for about one-third of total LTC expenditures, or about $5,000 per older adult. The federal government reduces the cost of some LTC through the tax code's treatment of certain LTC expenses. The Health Insurance Portability and Accountability Act of 1996 (HIPAA) allows a taxpayer (or his or her dependent) who incurs such expenses, and has a specified degree of physical or cognitive impairment, to deduct them from taxable income along with other medical costs. Qualifying expenses include payments for nursing home care; home care services; medical equipment and supplies, such as oxygen, wheelchairs, and walkers; and home modifications, such as the installation of grab bars in the shower.

Medicare, Medicaid, and Long-Term Care

Medicare does not cover custodial or long-term nursing home care but, under specific conditions, will pay for short-term rehabilitative stays in nursing homes and for some home health care. Medicaid is the only public program with LTC coverage.

Medicaid, however, does not work like private insurance, which offers protection from catastrophic expense.

FIGURE 10.7

Estimated percentage shares of spending on long-term care for the elderly, 2004

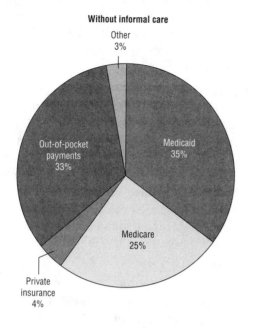

Without informal care

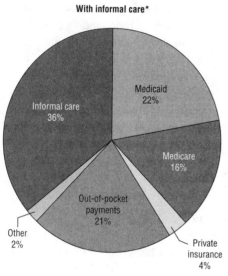

With informal care*

*Values are calculated on the basis of how much such care would cost if it were provided through formal means.

SOURCE: "Summary Figure 1. Estimated Percentage Shares of Spending on Long-Term Care for the Elderly, 2004," in *Financing Long-Term Care for the Elderly*, Congressional Budget Office, Washington, DC, April 2004, http://www.cbo.gov/showdoc.cfm?index=5400&sequence=1&from=0#summaryfigure1 (accessed August 11, 2005)

Medicaid is a means-tested program, so middle-income persons needing nursing home care become eligible for Medicaid only after they "spend down" their own personal income and assets ($2,000 for a single person and $3,000 for couples).

Even then, Medicaid will not necessarily pay the entire nursing home bill. Nursing home residents must

TABLE 10.4

Long-term care expenditures for the elderly, by source of payment, 2004

[Billions of dollars]

Payment source	Institutional care	Home care	Total
Medicaid	36.5	10.8	47.3
Medicare	15.9	17.7	33.6
Private insurance	2.4	3.3	5.6
Out of pocket	35.7	8.3	44
Other	2	2.5	4.4
Total	**92.4**	**42.5**	**134.9**

SOURCE: "Table 1-2. Long-Term Care Expenditures for the Elderly, by Source of Payment, 2004," in *Financing Long-Term Care for the Elderly*, Congressional Budget Office, Washington, DC, April 2004, http://www.cbo.gov/showdoc.cfm?index=5400&sequence=2&from=0#table1-2 (accessed August 11, 2005)

meet income eligibility standards as well. In some states older adults with incomes too high for regular Medicaid eligibility, but with substantial medical bills, are allowed to spend down to become income-eligible for Medicaid. They must incur medical bills until their income for a given period, minus the medical expenses, falls below the Medicaid threshold.

While every state's Medicaid program covers LTC, each has made different choices about the parameters of its program. Eligibility rules and protection for the finances of spouses of nursing home residents vary widely, but federal law requires states to allow the community spouse to retain enough of the institutionalized spouse's income to maintain a monthly allowance for minimum living costs. The allowance is set by the state according to federal guidelines—in 2004 no less than $1,515 per month and no more than $2,319. The community spouse also is allowed to retain joint assets—either an amount equal to one-half of the couple's resources at the time the spouse enters the institution, up to a federally specified maximum ($92,760 in 2004), or the state standard, whichever is greater. Federal law requires that the state standard be no less than a predetermined amount—$18,552 in 2004.

Table 10.4 shows the breakdown of LTC expenditures for older adults by the source of payment. In 2004 Medicaid paid the largest proportion of institutional expenses ($36.5 billion), but almost the same amount ($35.7 billion) was paid out of pocket. Medicare expenditures for institutional care ($15.9 billion) were less than half of Medicaid expenditures, and private insurance paid $2.4 billion toward institutional care. Medicare made the largest contribution ($17.7 billion) toward home care services, while Medicaid paid $10.8 billion and $8.3 billion was paid out of pocket. In 2004 private insurance paid nearly $6 billion, or about 4% of total LTC expenditures for older adults.

MEDICARE TO PAY FOR SOME ADULT DAY CARE. As Susan Heavey reported in her article "U.S. Medicare to Take Close Look at Adult Day Care" (Reuters, August 14, 2005), in 2006, Medicare will begin a three-year test program that will cover adult day-care services for older adults recovering from ailments who would otherwise have entered nursing homes or required home nursing care. There are about thirty-four hundred adult day-care facilities across the United States, and more than 60% offer some health as well as social services. The test program aims to keep some older patients out of hospitals and nursing homes, which are costlier settings. Advocates of this program assert that the additional support services at most adult day-care centers, such as opportunities for socialization and on-site nurses, are likely to speed recovery and prevent costly complications that Medicare would have to pay for later. At the very least, the trial's sponsors believe it will introduce adult day care to persons who may have never considered it. It could also act to reduce stress and improve the health of caregivers, many of whom are also Medicare beneficiaries.

Private Long-Term Care Insurance

Another source of financing is LTC insurance. Private LTC insurance policies typically cover some portion of the cost of nursing home care and home health-care services. According to America's Health Insurance Plans (formerly the Health Insurance Association of America), about 8.3 million policies were sold from 1987 through 2001, and almost three-quarters of these policies were still in force in 2005.

Typically, LTC insurance policies pay for nursing home care and home care but stipulate a maximum daily benefit such as $100 or $150, as well as a pre-established maximum lifetime amount. Policies with inflation protection increase the dollar value of their benefits by a contractually specified percentage each year, usually 5%. Policyholders become eligible for benefits when they reach a specific minimum level of impairment, usually defined as being unable to perform two or three activities of daily living (ADLs) or when they are cognitively impaired to the extent that they require continuous supervision.

LTC insurance premiums take into account the cost of services and the risk that policyholders will need long-term care as they age. In 2002 the average annual premium for a LTC policy was $2,014 if the policy was purchased at age sixty-five; the premium more than doubled if the policy was purchased at age seventy-five. (See Table 10.5.) The lower premiums offered to younger people assume that their risk of requiring LTC services is low and that they will pay premiums over a longer period than will persons who obtain LTC insurance when they are older.

LTC insurance policies feature fixed premiums—the premiums do not increase as policyholders age or as their health declines, even though the risk of using services increases. To establish these fixed premiums, actuaries calculate amounts to ensure that the premiums paid over the life of a policy, along with the interest accrued from investing the premiums, more than adequately cover the claims of policyholders while ensuring profit for the insurance company.

Premiums for private LTC insurance are tax deductible. Policies purchased before the Health Insurance Portability and Accountability Act of 1996 (HIPAA) was enacted are automatically deductible, but policies purchased afterward must conform to the HIPPA requirements in order for their premiums to be tax deductible. The tax benefit is limited to taxpayers who itemize deductions and whose total medical and dental expenditures exceed 7.5% of their adjusted gross income.

HOME HEALTH CARE

The National Center for Health Statistics (NCHS) describes home health care as "provided to individuals and families in their places of residence for the purpose of promoting, maintaining, or restoring health or for maximizing the level of independence while minimizing the effects of disability and illness, including terminal illness." Figure 10.8 and Figure 10.9 show that Medicare and Medicaid spending for home health care have increased steadily since 2000. The CBO estimated that Medicare spent $17 billion for home health care in 2004 and projects steady growth in spending through 2014.

The NCHS 2000 National Home and Hospice Care Survey (NHHCS) described the characteristics of agencies providing home health and hospice care and the patients they served. Approximately 1,355,300 patients received home health-care services from 7,200 agencies at the time of the 2000 NHHCS. The number of agencies peaked in 1996, but between 1996 and 2000 the number declined by nearly one-third. Similarly, the number of patients served almost doubled between 1992 and 1996, but by 2000 the number of patients decreased to levels comparable to 1992. Between 1990 and 1996 home health care was the fastest-growing segment of the health-care industry—expenditures for home health-care services more than doubled, from $13 billion to $30 billion. During the 1990s alarm about inappropriate, excessive, and fraudulent home health-care claims and the rapidly growing older population prompted the CMS, the major public payer for home health care, to institute major cost-containment strategies to contain escalating costs.

The 2000 NHHCS found that nearly three-quarters (70%) of home health-care patients were ages sixty-five and older. More than half (52%) of all payment for home

TABLE 10.5

Average annual premiums for private long-term care insurance, 2002

[Dollars]

If policy is purchased at age	Policies with terms averaging three to six years		Policy with lifetime term	
	No inflation protection	Inflation protection of 5 percent compounded	No inflation protection	Inflation protection of 5 percent compounded
30	284	622	437	1,016
35	299	667	467	1,089
40	336	743	515	1,171
45	375	822	592	1,319
50	427	925	687	1,499
55	537	1,140	874	1,839
60	740	1,474	1,170	2,345
65	1,086	2,014	1,675	3,160
70	1,771	2,987	2,700	4,647
75	3,015	4,607	4,461	7,029
80	4,822	6,791	7,077	10,378
85	6,528	7,718	10,700	13,869

Note: The table reflects policies offering comprehensive benefits (nursing home care, in-home care (including respite care), and community-based care (for example, hospice or adult day care) with a $100 daily benefit for a three- to six-year period, a 30- to 100-day elimination period, and a pool-of-money contract.

SOURCE: "Table 1-3. Average Annual Premiums for Private Long-Term Care Insurance, 2002," in *Financing Long-Term Care for the Elderly*, Congressional Budget Office, Washington, DC, April 2004, http://www.cbo.gov/showdoc.cfm?index=5400&sequence=2&from=0#table1-3 (accessed August 11, 2005)

health care was derived from Medicare, while Medicaid contributed 20% of payments and private sources accounted for 17%.

Three-quarters of home health-care patients received skilled nursing services, 44% received personal care services, and 37% received therapeutic services. More than half (52%) of home care patients received help with at least one ADL, and among patients receiving help with ADLs, 83% received help with bathing or showering.

Community Housing with Home Care Services

Some older adults have access to a variety of home care services through their place of residence. Assisted living facilities, retirement communities, and continuing care retirement facilities are community housing alternatives that often provide services such as meal preparation, laundry and cleaning services, transportation, and assistance adhering to prescribed medication regimens.

In 2002 just 2% of Medicare recipients age sixty-five and older lived in community housing that offered at least one home care service, and an additional 5% lived in long-term care facilities. The percentage of persons residing in community housing that offered home care services was higher in the older age groups. Among persons age eighty-five and older, 7% lived in community hous-

ing with services, and 19% lived in long-term care facilities. (See Figure 10.10.)

Among older adult residents of community housing with services, 86% had access to meal preparation services, 80% had housekeeping/cleaning services, 68% had laundry services, and 47% said they could receive help with medications. More than half (53%) of the residents of community housing with services reported that there were additional charges for at least some services (*Older Americans 2004: Key Indicators of Well-Being*).

Older adults living in community housing with support services had more functional limitations than those living in the community but fewer than residents of long-term care facilities. Almost half (45%) of older adults living in community housing with services had at least one ADL limitation compared with 28% of older adults living in the community, but more than one-third (37%) of older adults living in community housing with services reported no ADL limitations. (See Figure 10.11.) More than half (53%) of older residents in community housing with services said they could remain in their residences even if they required substantial personal care and assistance with the activities of daily living.

FIGURE 10.8

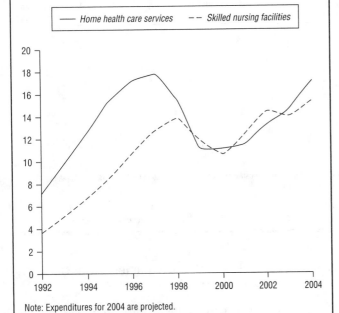

Medicare's expenditures on long-term care for elderly beneficiaries, fiscal years 1992–2004

[Billions of dollars]

Note: Expenditures for 2004 are projected.

SOURCE: "Figure 1-5. Medicare's Expenditures on Long-Term Care for Elderly Beneficiaries, Fiscal Years 1992 to 2004," in *Financing Long-Term Care for the Elderly*, Congressional Budget Office, Washington, DC, April 2004, http://www.cbo.gov/showdoc.cfm?index =5400&sequence=2&from=0#figure1–5 (accessed August 11, 2005)

FIGURE 10.9

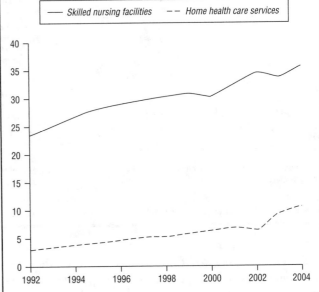

Medicaid's expenditures on long-term care for elderly beneficiaries, fiscal years 1992–2004

[Billions of dollars]

Note: Expenditures for 2004 are projected.

SOURCE: "Figure 1–4. Medicaid's Expenditures on Long-Term Care for Elderly Beneficiaries, Fiscal Years 1992 to 2004," in *Financing Long-Term Care for the Elderly*, Congressional Budget Office, Washington, DC, April 2004, http://www.cbo.gov/showdoc.cfm?index =5400&sequence=2&from=0#figure1-4 (accessed August 11, 2005)

FIGURE 10.10

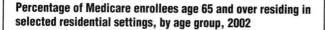

Percentage of Medicare enrollees age 65 and over residing in selected residential settings, by age group, 2002

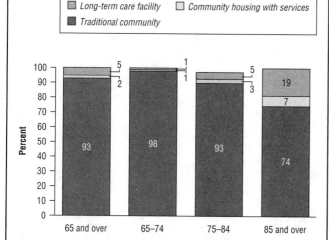

Note: Community housing with services applies to respondents who reported they lived in retirement communities or apartments, senior citizen housing, continuing care retirement facilities, assisted living facilities, staged living communities, board and care facilities/homes, and other similar situations, AND who reported they had access to one or more of the following services through their place of residence: meal preparation, cleaning or housekeeping services, laundry services, help with medications. Respondents were asked about access to these services but not whether they actually used the services. A residence is considered a long-term care facility if it is certified by Medicare or Medicaid; or has 3 or more beds and is licensed as a nursing home or other long-term care facility and provides at least one personal care service; or provide 24-hour, 7-day-a-week supervision by a caregiver.
Reference population: These data refer to Medicare enrollees.

SOURCE: "Percentage of Medicare Enrollees Age 65 and Over Residing in Selected Residential Settings, by Age Group, 2002," in *Older Americans 2004: Key Indicators*, Federal Interagency Forum on Aging Related Statistics, Washington, DC, U.S. Government Printing Office, November 2004, http://www.agingstats.gov/chartbook2004/healthcare .html#Indicator%2036 (accessed August 11, 2005)

FIGURE 10.11

Percentage of Medicare enrollees age 65 and over with functional limitations, by residential setting, 2002

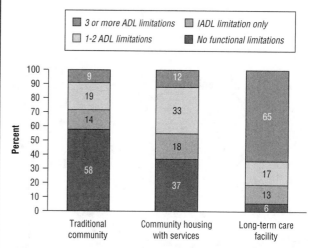

Note: Community housing with services applies to respondents who reported they lived in retirement communities or apartments, senior citizen housing, continuing care retirement facilities, assisted living facilities, staged living communities, board and care facilities/homes, and other similar situations, AND who reported they had access to one or more of the following services through their place of residence: meal preparation, cleaning or housekeeping services, laundry services, help with medications. Respondents were asked about access to these services but not whether they actually used the services. A residence is considered a long-term care facility if it is certified by Medicare or Medicaid; or has 3 or more beds and is licensed as a nursing home or other long-term care facility and provides at least one personal care service; or provides 24-hour, 7-day-a-week supervision by a caregiver. IADL limitations refer to difficulty performing (or inability to perform, for a health reason) one or more of the following tasks: using the telephone, light housework, heavy housework, meal preparation, shopping, managing money. ADL limitations refer to difficulty performing (or inability to perform, for a health reason) the following tasks: bathing, dressing, eating, getting in/out of chairs, walking using the toilet. Long-term care facility residents with no limitations may include individuals with limitatations in certain IADLS: doing light or heavy housework or meal preparation. These questions were not asked of facility residents.
Reference population: These data refer to Medicare enrollees.

SOURCE: "Percentage of Medicare Enrollees Age 65 and Over with Functional Limitations, by Residential Setting, 2002," in *Older Americans 2004: Key Indicators*, Federal Interagency Forum on Aging Related Statistics, Washington, DC, U.S. Government Printing Office, November 2004, http://www.agingstats.gov/chartbook2004/healthcare .html#Indicator%2036 (accessed August 11, 2005)

CHAPTER 11
CRIME AND ABUSE OF OLDER ADULTS

Population-based surveys of elder mistreatment occurrence are feasible and should be given a high priority.

—National Research Council to Review Risk and Prevalence of Elder Abuse and Neglect, 2003

According to Professionals against Confidence Crimes (PACC), a nonprofit, nonpartisan organization of law enforcement professionals, national surveys reveal that the crimes older adults believe that they are most susceptible to are murder, aggravated assault and rape, armed robbery, theft from their person, burglary, and fraud. Their fears are not, however, entirely consistent with reality. Older adults are the least likely to become victims of violent crimes. The crimes more often committed against older adults are thefts of their purses or wallets, fraud and confidence crimes, mail theft, vandalism, and burglary.

The PACC attributes older adults' misplaced fears in part to sensational media reports that do not correctly convey the real crime risks for older adults. As a result, older adults do not have an accurate understanding about the crimes that affect them. The PACC contends that unless older adults understand the real risks, they will not take the proper steps to protect themselves.

CRIME AGAINST OLDER ADULTS

The Bureau of Justice Statistics reports that adults age sixty-five or older experienced much less violence and victimization as well as fewer property crimes than younger persons did between 1993 and 2002. Table 11.1 reveals that adults age sixty-five and older had the lowest rates of violent victimization of any age group—with older white women experiencing the lowest rates, just three per one thousand population, during this period. Furthermore, there was a 22.6% decrease in violent crimes against persons age sixty-five and older from 2001 to 2003. Victimization rates for violent crime were

2.7 per one thousand persons age sixty-five or older, down from 3.5 per one thousand persons in 2001.

Rather than violent crimes, property crimes, which include household burglary, motor vehicle theft, and other theft, accounted for the highest percentage of crime against adults age sixty-five or older. (See Figure 11.1.) Compared with other age groups, older adults were disproportionately affected by property crimes, although households headed by adults age sixty-five and older suffered property crimes at a relatively low rate—about a fourth of that for households headed by persons under age twenty-five: ninety-three per one thousand households versus 406 per one thousand. Property crimes accounted for 93% of victimizations of older adults or households headed by adults sixty-five and over. About one in five of personal crimes against older adults were thefts, compared with about one in thirty-three for persons ages twelve to forty-nine. (See Figure 11.2.)

Property crime against households headed by persons of all ages declined from 1993 to 2002. For older adults property crime rates were less than half the rates reported in 1993—sixty-three per one thousand households versus 133 per one thousand. (See Figure 11.3.)

Older adults also were disproportionately victimized by purse snatching and pocket picking—theft of their purses or wallets. More than 20% of personal crimes against older adults were thefts of purses and wallets, compared with about 6% among adults age fifty to sixty-four. (See Figure 11.2.)

Violent Crimes

Like property crimes, nonfatal violence also declined between 1993 and 2002. Older adults had the lowest rates of any age group for nonfatal violence during these years. (See Figure 11.4.) Older adults also have lower rates of murder than other age groups, with the murder rate staying stable from 1998 to 2002. (See Figure 11.5.)

TABLE 11.1

Violent crime victimization rates, by age groups, race, and gender, 1993–2002

Average annual rate violent victimization per 1,000 persons, 1993–2002

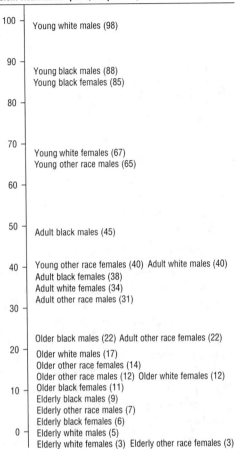

Note: The four age categories used throughout the report are referred to in this chart as "young," ages 12–24, "adult," ages 25–49, "older," ages 50–64, and "elderly," age 65 or older. Hispanics do not appear in a separate category but are included in the racial categories shown.

SOURCE: Patsy Klaus, "The Elderly, Age 65 or Older, Had Lower Violent Victimization Rates Than Other Age Groups, When Comparing Race and Gender," in *Crimes Against Persons Age 65 or Older, 1993–2002*, Bureau of Justice Statistics Special Report, U.S. Department of Justice, Washington, DC, January 2005, http://www.ojp.usdoj.gov/bjs/abstract/cpa6502.htm (accessed August 11, 2005)

While older adults are less likely than younger persons to be victims of violent crimes, when they are victimized they are just as likely to face attackers armed with weapons and to receive serious injuries as persons ages twelve to sixty-four. (See Table 11.2.) Not surprisingly, older adults were less likely (45%) to offer resistance when attacked than victims ages twelve to sixty-four (29%). Nonetheless, more than half of the older adult population (55%) did resist violent victimizations.

According to "Crimes against Persons Age 65 or Older, 1993–2002" (Bureau of Justice Statistics Special Report, Washington, DC: U.S. Department of Justice,

FIGURE 11.1

Percent of violent and property crimes, by age of victim, 1993–2002

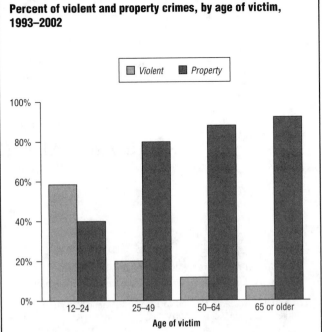

SOURCE: Patsy Klaus, "Figure 1. Percent of Violent and Property Crimes, by Age of Victim, 1993–2002," in *Crimes Against Persons Age 65 or Older, 1993–2002*, Bureau of Justice Statistics Special Report, U.S. Department of Justice, Washington, DC, January 2005, http://www.ojp.usdoj.gov/bjs/abstract/cpa6502.htm (accessed August 11, 2005)

FIGURE 11.2

Purse snatching and pocket picking as a percentage of all crimes against persons, by age of victim, 1993–2002

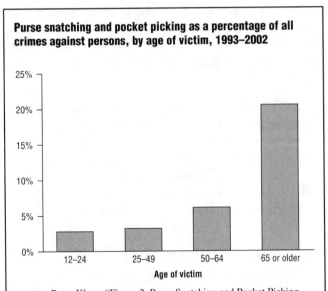

SOURCE: Patsy Klaus, "Figure 2. Purse Snatching and Pocket Picking as a Percentage of All Crimes Against Persons, by Age of Victim, 1993–2002," in *Crimes Against Persons Age 65 or Older, 1993–2002*, Bureau of Justice Statistics Special Report, U.S. Department of Justice, Washington, DC, January 2005, http://www.ojp.usdoj.gov/bjs/abstract/cpa6502.htm (accessed August 11, 2005)

2005), older adults were more likely to be victimized by strangers than younger persons—53% compared with 46%—and were more likely to be victimized by persons

FIGURE 11.3

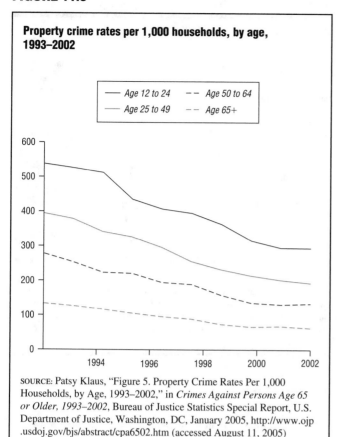

Property crime rates per 1,000 households, by age, 1993–2002

SOURCE: Patsy Klaus, "Figure 5. Property Crime Rates Per 1,000 Households, by Age, 1993–2002," in *Crimes Against Persons Age 65 or Older, 1993–2002*, Bureau of Justice Statistics Special Report, U.S. Department of Justice, Washington, DC, January 2005, http://www.ojp.usdoj.gov/bjs/abstract/cpa6502.htm (accessed August 11, 2005)

FIGURE 11.4

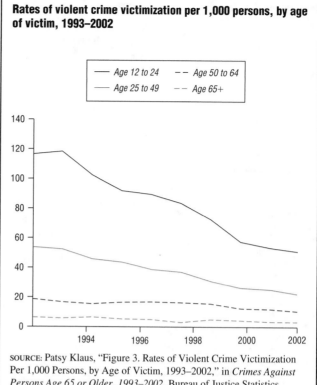

Rates of violent crime victimization per 1,000 persons, by age of victim, 1993–2002

SOURCE: Patsy Klaus, "Figure 3. Rates of Violent Crime Victimization Per 1,000 Persons, by Age of Victim, 1993–2002," in *Crimes Against Persons Age 65 or Older, 1993–2002*, Bureau of Justice Statistics Special Report, U.S. Department of Justice, Washington, DC, January 2005, http://www.ojp.usdoj.gov/bjs/abstract/cpa6502.htm (accessed August 11, 2005)

over age thirty—48% versus 30%. Fewer crimes against older adults occurred at night, compared with crimes committed against persons twelve to sixty-four—about half as many crimes involving violent victimization against older adults occurred at night. This is probably because older adults are more likely than younger people to be at home at night. (See Table 11.3.)

Older adults were more likely than persons ages twelve to sixty-four to be victimized in or near their homes. Nearly half (46%) of violent crimes and 67% of property crimes against older adults occurred at or near their homes. Among persons of all ages, purse snatching and pocket picking rarely occurred near home.

Older adults also were more likely than persons ages twelve to sixty-four to report violence (53% compared with 44%) and purse snatching or pocket picking (42% compared with 32%) to the police. Only about one-third of households of all ages reported property crimes to the police.

The Physical and Emotional Impact of Crime

According to the United States Bureau of Justice Statistics Special Report, most older Americans who are the victims of violent crime are not physically injured. On average, each year from 1993 to 2002 about 22% of violent crime victims age sixty-five and older were

FIGURE 11.5

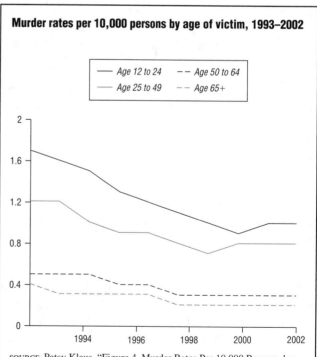

Murder rates per 10,000 persons by age of victim, 1993–2002

SOURCE: Patsy Klaus, "Figure 4. Murder Rates Per 10,000 Persons, by Age of Victim, 1993–2002," in *Crimes Against Persons Age 65 or Older, 1993–2002*, Bureau of Justice Statistics Special Report, U.S. Department of Justice, Washington, DC, January 2005, http://www.ojp.usdoj.gov/bjs/abstract/cpa6502.htm (accessed August 11, 2005)

TABLE 11.2

Nonfatal violent victimizations, 1993–2002

	Age of victim	
Total	12–64	65 or older
Percent facing weapons	25.7%	30.2%
Firearm	9.4	12.7
Knife	6.3	6.4
Other type	8.7	9.3
Don't know type	1.2	1.8
Percent resisting	71.0%	55.5%
Threatened/attacked with weapon	2.2	2.5
Threatened/attacked without weapon	27.9	15.3
Nonconfrontational resistance	29.5	24.9
Other or unknown type	11.3	12.9
Percent not resisting	29.0%	44.5%
Percent injured	25.9%	21.8%
Types of injury		
Serious	3.3	2.8
Minor	21.2	18.7
Rape without other injury	1.2	0.3*
Don't know type	0.1	0.0*

*Based on 10 or fewer cases.

SOURCE: Patsy Klaus, "Table 2. Nonfatal Violent Victimizations, 1993–2002," in *Crimes Against Persons Age 65 or Older, 1993–2002*, Bureau of Justice Statistics Special Report, U.S. Department of Justice, Washington, DC, January 2005, http://www.ojp.usdoj.gov/bjs/abstract/cpa6502.htm (accessed August 11, 2005)

TABLE 11.3

Characteristics of crimes, 1993–2002

	Age of victim	
	12–64	65 or older
Percent occurring at night		
Violence	45.8%	27.2%
Personal theft	34.4	14.8
Property crimes	29.2	20.9
Percent occurring at/near home		
Violence	27.0%	45.5%
Personal theft	5.4	5.8*
Property crimes	54.3	67.0
Percent reported to police		
Violence	43.9%	53.0%
Personal theft	32.1	42.3
Property crimes	34.7	35.5

Note: Some persons did not know when crimes occurred, especially property crimes.
*Based on 10 or fewer cases.

SOURCE: Patsy Klaus, "Table 3. Characteristics of Crimes, 1993–2002," in *Crimes Against Persons Age 65 or Older, 1993–2002*, Bureau of Justice Statistics Special Report, U.S. Department of Justice, Washington, DC, January 2005, http://www.ojp.usdoj.gov/bjs/abstract/cpa6502.htm (accessed August 11, 2005)

FIGURE 11.6

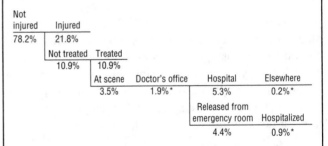

Injury and treatment status of persons age 65 or older who reported being a victim of violence, 1993–2002

*Based on 10 or fewer cases.

SOURCE: Patsy Klaus, "Figure 6. On Average Each Year 1993–2002, of Persons Age 65 or Older Who Reported Being a Victim of Violence, 22% Were Injured and 1% Were Hospitalized Overnight," in *Crimes Against Persons Age 65 or Older, 1993–2002*, Bureau of Justice Statistics Special Report, U.S. Department of Justice, Washington, DC, January 2005, http://www.ojp.usdoj.gov/bjs/abstract/cpa6502.htm (accessed August 11, 2005)

physically injured, 11% of these injured adults required treatment for their injuries, and just 1% were hospitalized overnight for treatment. (See Figure 11.6.) The physical injuries do not, however, tell the whole story. Victimization and fear of victimization can have far more serious effects on the quality of older adults' lives than they might for younger persons.

Older adults are often less resilient than younger people. Even so-called nonviolent crimes, such as purse snatching, vandalism, and burglary, can be devastating. Stolen or damaged articles and property are often irreplaceable, either because of their sentimental or monetary value. Even nonviolent crimes leave victims with a sense of violation and heightened vulnerability.

Once victimized, older adults may become reluctant to leave their homes because they fear contact with strangers. Their fears are not entirely without merit. An article by the Centers for Disease Control and Prevention (CDC), "Non-fatal Physical Assault-Related Injuries among Persons Aged 60 Years Treated in Hospital Emergency Departments—United States, 2001" (*Morbidity and Mortality Weekly Report*, vol. 52, no. 34, August 2003), observed that of the more than thirty-three thousand persons age sixty and older treated for nonfatal assault-related injuries in hospital emergency room departments in 2001, the assaults occurred almost equally at home (25.9%) and in public places (27.5%).

Older People Are Considered Easy Prey

Because of their physical limitations, older adults are often considered easy prey. They are less likely than younger victims to resist criminal attacks. Their reluctance to resist may be based on awareness that they lack the strength to repel a younger aggressor and the understanding they are physically frail and at risk of injuries that could permanently disable them. The U.S. Bureau of Justice reports that crime victims over age sixty-five who try to protect themselves most often use nonphysical actions, such as arguing, reasoning, or screaming. Younger victims are more likely to use physical action, such as attacking, resisting, or running from or chasing offenders.

FRAUD

Older adults are also considered easy prey for fraud, deception, and exploitation. They are more readily accessible to con artists than other age groups because they are likely to be at home to receive visits from door-to-door salespersons, e-mails, or calls from telemarketers. Older adults who are homebound or otherwise isolated may not have regular contact with others who might help them to identify possible schemes or frauds. Law enforcement officials and consumer advocates assert that older people are targeted because:

- They are more likely than younger people to have substantial financial savings, home equity, or credit, all of which are tempting to fraud perpetrators.

- They are often reluctant to be rude to others, so they may be more likely to hear out a con's story. They also may be overly trusting.

- Older adults are less likely to report frauds, either because they are embarrassed, do not know how or to whom to report the crimes, or because they fear appearing incapable of handling their personal finances.

- Older adults who do report fraud may not make very good witnesses. Their memories may fade over the often protracted span of time between the crime and the trial, and on the witness stand they may be unable to provide detailed enough information to lead to a conviction.

According to the National Fraud Information Center's "2004 Telemarketing Fraud Report" (National Consumer League, http://www.fraud.org/telemarketing/2004-telemarketing%20scams.pdf), older consumers—age sixty and over—reported a higher percentage of complaints for telemarketing frauds in 2004. Older victims made one-third of all complaints that year. Older consumers are especially vulnerable to certain kinds of telemarketing fraud. In 2004 two-thirds of the reports of sweepstakes fraud, 59% of the reports of lottery club scams, and more than half of the reports of magazine sales scams were made by adults age sixty or older. The National Fraud Information Center's report "Telemarketing Scams—January–June 2005" (National Consumer League, http://www.fraud.org/telemarketing/tele_scam_halfyear_2005.pdf) states that from January through June 2005 nearly half (49%) of scams with the most victims over age sixty involved medical care products or services followed by investments (46%), prizes/sweepstakes (41%), and magazine sales (40%).

The Federal Trade Commission (FTC) is the federal government's lead consumer protection agency. FTC authority extends over practically the entire economy, including business and consumer transactions via telephone and the Internet. The FTC's consumer mission includes prohibiting unfair or deceptive acts or practices.

The Food and Drug Administration (FDA) and the FTC actively work to prevent health fraud and scams. The agencies identify products with substandard or entirely useless ingredients as well as those with fraudulent or misleading advertising to prevent the dissemination of unsubstantiated or deceptive claims about the health benefits of particular products or services.

The FTC monitors practices and industries such as dietary supplements, arthritis remedies, and memory aids that especially appeal to older consumers. In 2002 the FTC issued a report, *Activities Affecting Older Americans*, that described FTC law enforcement initiatives within its consumer protection purview that are important to older consumers, including health-care initiatives, financial practices initiatives, sales and promotional practices initiatives, and enforcement initiatives against fraud.

Health Fraud

Older adults may be particularly susceptible to false or misleading claims about the safety and efficacy of over-the-counter (OTC) drugs, devices, foods, dietary supplements, and health-care services, because the marketing of such products and services often relates to conditions associated with aging. Also, many of these unproven treatments promise false hope and offer immediate cures for chronic diseases or complete relief from pain. It is easy to understand how older adults who are frightened or in pain might be seduced by false promises of quick cures.

In June 1999 the FTC launched Operation Cure.all—a law enforcement and consumer education campaign aimed at protecting consumers from Internet health fraud—and announced settlements of four cases in which respondents made deceptive and unsubstantiated health claims of "miracle cures" for serious illnesses. In April 2000 the FTC announced settlements with three additional Internet companies arising from the firms' marketing of products as effective treatments or cures for diseases such as arthritis, cancer, and diabetes. In July 2001 Operation Cure.all also investigated cases targeting companies marketing a variety of devices, herbal products, and other dietary supplements as professed treatments or cures for cancer, arthritis, Alzheimer's disease, diabetes, and other diseases.

The FTC Commission also pursued legal action against firms making unsubstantiated or otherwise deceptive claims for products and health-care services. For example, in Novartis Corp., et al., Docket No. 9279, the Commission alleged that deceptive representations were made about Doan's Pills—nationally advertised OTC pain relievers. The FTC contested the claim that Doan's Pills were more effective in relieving back pain than other OTC pain relievers. Ultimately, the FTC required the respondents to disseminate corrective advertising.

In September 2001 Howard Beales, the director of the United States Bureau of Consumer Protection of the FTC, testified before the U.S. Senate Special Committee on Aging at its hearing "Health Fraud and the Elderly: A Continuing Health Epidemic." Beales observed that at the consumer level the costs of these products and services range from a few dollars to tens of thousands of dollars for questionable cancer treatments. In most cases these products and services are not covered by insurance. In addition to economic losses, some products and services can pose serious health threats by deterring patients from seeking the best available treatments. In some instances marketers advise consumers that it is not necessary for them to seek conventional medical treatment. Delaying or deferring treatment is not the only risk, however; some products and services are themselves dangerous.

COUNTERFEIT PRESCRIPTION DRUGS. Skyrocketing Internet sales of prescription drugs has created a relatively new form of health fraud—counterfeit drugs. Because older adults often take multiple prescription medications, they are an ideal target market for this type of health fraud. According to a May 2004 survey released by the National Consumers League (NCL), "Consumer Group Says Americans Vulnerable to, Unaware of Counterfeit Drugs" (NCL News, http://www.nclnet.org/news/2004/counterfeit_drugs.htm, June 21, 2004), more than one-quarter (26%) of adults age fifty-five or older have purchased medications online, and most consumers purchasing prescription drugs online do not know how to tell whether the drugs they receive are legitimate. The survey revealed that more than half of those who purchased drugs online felt there was no way to tell if the drugs they obtained were real or counterfeit, and nearly one-third of purchasers said they were not required to have a prescription to make their purchases.

Financial Fraud and Exploitation

Financial crimes against older adults are on the rise. Along with telemarketing, mail fraud, Internet scams, and health-care and insurance fraud, there have been pension and trust fund fraud, mail theft, reverse mortgage fraud, and many others. The National Fraud Information Center estimates that there are fourteen thousand illegal telemarketing operations in the United States, swindling the older population out of more than $40 billion each year.

The Internet Fraud Complaint Center, a partnership between the Federal Bureau of Investigation (FBI) and National White Collar Crime Center reports in "2004 Internet Fraud Crime Report" (Internet Fraud Complaint Center, http://www.ifccfbi.gov/strategy/2004_IC3Report.pdf) that

in 2004 more than one-quarter of complainants were age sixty and older, and this group reported higher losses—an average of $252.50 per complaint—than other age groups.

In a new twist on identity theft—stealing an individual's personal information for illegal purposes—identity thieves trick unsuspecting consumers into providing their Social Security numbers, financial account numbers, mothers' maiden names, and even credit card data by pretending to be people they are not—bankers, retailers, or representatives of government agencies. This practice is known as "phishing." The most common form of phishing is conducted via email, but it may also be performed by telephone. Phishers request personal information for some fabricated reason—the victim's account is about to be closed, an order has been placed in the victim's name, or information has been lost because of a computer problem. Some phishers claim they are from the fraud departments of well-known companies and ask to verify personal information to avert identity theft. According to the National Consumer League's Internet Fraud Watch, in one instance a phisher claimed to be from a state lottery commission and requested people's banking information to deposit their "winnings" into their accounts.

Other common financial schemes frequently used by fraudulent direct mail marketers are "sweepstakes" or "free giveaways." Consumers receive postcards announcing that they are entitled to claim one or more prizes. The postcards bear a toll-free telephone number to phone to claim the prizes. Once the toll-free number is accessed, a recording instructs the consumer to touch numbers on the telephone key pad that correspond with a "claim number" that appears on the postcard.

Ultimately, the consumer receives no prize. Instead the unsuspecting victim receives a telephone bill that reflects a substantial charge for the call, just as if a 900 number had been called. The entry of the sequence of numbers that matched the claim number engages an automated information service for which the consumer is charged.

Medicare Fraud

Medicare loses millions of dollars every year due to fraud and abuse. The most common forms of Medicare fraud are:

- Billing for services not furnished
- Misrepresenting a diagnosis to justify a higher payment
- Soliciting, offering, or receiving a kickback
- Charging Medicare higher fees than normal for certain procedures
- Falsifying certificates of medical necessity, plans of treatment, and medical records to justify payment
- Billing for a service not furnished as billed

In 1996 Congress enacted the Health Insurance Portability and Accountability Act (HIPPA), which allocated funding to protect Medicare's program integrity and prevent fraud. In one of the largest efforts in the history of Medicare, the program has undertaken a major campaign to help eliminate Medicare fraud, waste, and abuse. According to the Office of Inspector General, as a result of the campaign, the federal government recovered $1.2 billion in fines, settlements, and judgments for the Medicare program during fiscal year 2000.

In order to combat Medicare fraud at the level of the beneficiary, the United States Administration on Aging (AoA) provides grants to local organizations to help older Americans become more vigilant health-care consumers so that they can help to identify and prevent fraudulent health-care practices. Senior Medicare Patrol projects train volunteer retired professionals, such as doctors, nurses, accountants, investigators, law enforcement personnel, attorneys, and teachers to help Medicare and Medicaid beneficiaries become better health-care consumers. Since 1997 these projects and other AoA grants have trained more than twenty-five thousand volunteers, conducted more than sixty thousand community education events, and counseled more than one million beneficiaries.

The "Who Pays? You Pay" campaign is an example of a successful outreach effort to combat Medicare fraud. It is a partnership between AARP, the U.S. Department of Health and Human Services, and the U.S. Department of Justice. It establishes a line of defense against a problem that costs the Medicare program billions of dollars each year.

The campaign asks beneficiaries to regularly review their Medicare statements and ask such questions as: "Did I receive the services or products for which Medicare is being billed? Did my doctor order the service or product for me? And, to the best of my judgment, is the service or product necessary given my health condition?" If the answer to any of these questions is no, the partners emphasize working first with the health-care provider or Medicare insurance company. If there is still doubt, beneficiaries are advised to call a hotline (1-800-HHS-TIPS). Medicare beneficiaries receive rewards of up to $1,000 for successfully identifying fraud and abuse.

MEDICARE PRESCRIPTION CARD FRAUD. In 2004 several state health departments began receiving reports of the sale of fake Medicare prescription cards to older adults under the recently enacted Medicare Prescription Drug, Improvement, and Modernization Act of 2003. Apparently, con artists capitalizing on the confusion surrounding the new and complex Medicare prescription drug benefit began selling the phony Medicare discount cards to seniors in Idaho and Georgia. In response to these reports, some states initiated campaigns to educate older adults about the discount cards. In April 2004 the federal Centers for Medicare and Medicaid Services (CMS) mailed informational letters to Medicare recipients that contained an illustration of the official federal government seal that appears on the authentic cards to help older adults distinguish the authentic cards from counterfeits.

ABUSE AND MISTREATMENT OF OLDER ADULTS

Domestic violence against older adults is a phenomenon that first gained public attention during the late 1970s when Congressman Claude Pepper held widely publicized hearings about the mistreatment of older adults. In the three decades since those hearings, policy makers, health professionals, social service personnel, and advocates for older Americans have sought ways to protect the older population from physical, psychological, and financial abuse.

The Magnitude of the Problem

It is difficult to determine exactly how many older adults are the victims of abuse or mistreatment. As with child abuse and domestic violence among younger adults, the number of actual cases is larger than the number of reported cases. There is consensus among professionals and agencies that deal with issues of elder abuse that it is far less likely to be reported than child or spousal abuse. The challenge of estimating the incidence and prevalence of this problem is further compounded by the varying definitions of abuse and varying reporting practices used by the states, government, and voluntary agencies, as well as the fact that comprehensive national data are not collected. Further, research suggests that abuse often occurs over long periods of time and that only when it reaches a critical juncture, such as instances of severe injury, will the neglect or abuse become evident to health, social service, or legal professionals.

Although the magnitude of the problem of abuse and mistreatment of older adults is unknown, its social and moral importance is obvious. Abuse and neglect of older individuals in society violates a sacred trust and moral commitment to protect vulnerable individuals and groups from harm and to ensure their well-being and security.

The report *Elder Mistreatment: Abuse, Neglect, and Exploitation in an Aging America—Panel to Review Risk and Prevalence of Elder Abuse and Neglect* (Washington, DC: The National Academies Press, 2002), issued by the National Research Council Panel to Review Risk and Prevalence of Elder Abuse, estimated that between one and two million Americans age sixty-five or older have been injured, exploited, or otherwise mistreated by someone on whom they depended for care or protection. It is likely that the frequency of occurrence of mistreatment of older adults will increase during the next several decades, as the population ages.

Nationwide, reports of elder abuse have increased every year. The National Center on Elder Abuse (NCEA) observes that in 2002 there were more than six hundred thousand reported instances of abuse of Americans age sixty and over. The NCEA opines that this number probably represents the tip of the iceberg and that more than one million older adults were victims of abuse that year and another million suffered from neglect. The U.S. Senate Special Committee on Aging estimates that there may be as many as five million victims every year.

Types of Mistreatment

Federal definitions of elder abuse, neglect, and exploitation appeared for the first time in the Older Americans Act Amendments of 1987. Broadly defined, there are three basic categories of abuse: domestic elder abuse, institutional elder abuse, and self-neglect or self-abuse.

Sadly, most documented instances of elder abuse refer to a form of maltreatment of an older person by someone who has a special relationship with the older adult, such as a spouse, sibling, child, friend, or caregiver. Until recently, most data indicated that adult children were the most common abusers of older family members, but an NCEA study conducted in 2000 and summarized by Pamela Teaster in *A Response to the Abuse of Vulnerable Adults: The 2000 Survey of State Adult Protective Services* (Washington, DC: The National Center on Elder Abuse, 2000) found that spouses are the most common perpetrators of abuse and mistreatment. The major types of elder abuse and mistreatment include:

- Physical abuse—inflicting physical pain or bodily injury

- Sexual abuse—nonconsensual sexual contact of any kind with an older person

- Emotional or psychological abuse—inflicting mental anguish by, for example, name calling, humiliation, threats, or isolation

- Neglect—willful or unintentional failure to provide basic necessities, such as food and medical care, as a result of caregiver indifference, inability, or ignorance

- Material or financial abuse—exploiting or misusing an older person's funds or assets

- Abandonment—the desertion of an older adult by an individual who has physical custody of the elder or who has assumed responsibility for providing care for the older person

- Self-neglect—behaviors of an older person that threaten his or her own health or safety

Theft by Family and Friends

The criminal justice system has documented the fact that money and property are stolen from older adults at alarming rates. John Wasik writes in "The Fleecing of America's Elderly" (*Consumers Digest*, March/April 2000) that just one in twenty-five cases of financial abuse of older adults is reported, which suggests that there may be five million financial abuse victims each year. Because financial abuse is difficult to define, it also is difficult to identify, investigate, and prosecute. One challenge that even stymies law enforcement agents is to distinguish an unwise but legitimate financial transaction from an exploitative one resulting from undue influence, duress, or fraud. The crimes are even more complicated to resolve because a large portion are committed not by professional criminals but by relatives, friends, home health aides, household workers, and neighbors. In-home care for older adults frequently offers hired caregivers ready access to the financial and property assets of the older adults in their care.

Financial abuse also differs from physical and emotional mistreatment in that it is more likely to occur with the unspoken permission of the older adult and, as a result, may be more difficult to detect and confirm. In some instances the older adult and the perpetrator may feel that the perpetrator is entitled to the older person's assets. Older adults may want to compensate their relatives and caregivers. These complex family and caregiver dynamics may make it difficult to distinguish between a transfer of assets made with consent from one performed in response to coercion. Like other forms of mistreatment, financial abuse in a family is generally not a single identifiable event. Instead it reflects actions that may have started out as legitimate efforts to be helpful but over time became abusive. As a result, determining when financial abuse began can be very difficult.

Who Are the Abuse Victims?

According to the NCEA, the majority of the reported cases of mistreatment are older women; this may simply be the result of the disproportionate number of female older adults, or it may mean that older women are at greater risk for mistreatment than are older men.

The findings of thirty research studies published between 1988 and 2000 were reviewed by Bonnie Brandl and Loree Cook-Daniels in "Domestic Abuse in Later Life, Victims" (National Center on Elder Abuse, http://www.elderabusecenter.org/pdf/research/victims.pdf). The researchers found that there was not a single profile that characterized the typical abused older adult. Most studies confirmed a higher percentage of female victims than male—older women accounted for two-thirds to 100% of victims in these studies. Some victims perceived abuse as normal behavior, while others minimized it or believed it was their fault. Physical and cognitive impairments were common among victims, as were symptoms of depression, unhappiness, shame, guilt, and suicidal ideation—thoughts about ending their own lives. It is unclear, however, whether these impairments rendered the older adults more susceptible to abuse or whether over time, the effects of abuse caused the victims to become depressed or cognitively impaired.

Reporting Abuse

Like child abuse and sexual assault crimes, many crimes against older adults are not reported because the victims are physically or mentally unable to summon help or because they are reluctant or afraid to publicly accuse relatives or caregivers. Loneliness or dependency prevents many victims from reporting the crimes, even when they are aware of them, simply because they are afraid to lose the companionship and care of the perpetrator. When financial abuse is reported, the source of the information is likely to be someone other than the victim: a police officer, ambulance attendant, bank teller, neighbor, or other family member.

Since 1983 most states have required physicians and other social service professionals to report evidence of abuse, neglect, and exploitation. Teaster's survey *A Response to the Abuse of Vulnerable Adults: The 2000 Survey of State Adult Protective Services* found that reporting requirements varied widely. Thirty-four states stipulated time frames for reports ranging from immediately (twenty-three states) to more than four days in one state. The most common penalty for failing to report abuse was a misdemeanor with possible fines ranging from $100 to $10,000 and/or jail sentences. Nine states had prosecuted individuals for failing to report abuse.

Causes of Elder Abuse

According to the NCEA, no single theory can explain why older people are abused. The causes of abuse are diverse and complicated. Some relate to the personality of the abuser, some reflect the relationship between the abuser and the abused, and some are reactions to stressful situations. While some children truly dislike their parents and the role of caregiver, many others want to care for their parents or feel it is the right thing to do but may be emotionally or financially unable to meet the challenges of caregiving.

STRESS. Meeting the daily needs of a frail and dependent older adult is demanding and may be overwhelming for some family members who serve as caregivers. When the older person lives in the same household as the caregiver, crowding, differences of opinion, and constant demands often add to the strain of providing physical care. When the older person lives in a different house, the pressure of commuting and managing two households may be unduly stressful.

Stress may be a reality in the life of caregivers, but research does not support its role as a contributing factor in abuse of older adults. The findings of thirteen research studies published between 1988 and 2000 were reviewed by Bonnie Brandl and Loree Cook-Daniels in "Domestic Abuse in Later Life, Causation Theories" (National Center on Elder Abuse, http://www.elderabusecenter.org/pdf/research/risks.pdf). Brandl and Daniels's report strove to explain why perpetrators abuse older adults and served to dispel the popular belief that the stress of caregiving prompted abuse. Just two studies suggested a possible link between the stress of caregiving and abuse.

FINANCIAL BURDEN. Caring for an older adult often places a financial strain on a family. Older parents may need financial assistance at the same time that their children are raising their own families. Instead of an occasional night out, a long-awaited vacation, or a badly needed newer car, families may find themselves paying for ever-increasing medical care, prescription drugs, special dietary supplements, extra food and clothing, or therapy. Saving for their children's college education, for a daughter's wedding, or for retirement may be difficult or impossible. While it seems intuitively correct that resentment might provoke emotional or physical abuse of older adults by their caregivers, there are no data to support the hypothesis that financial strain is a major contributor to mistreatment of older adults.

THE CYCLE OF ABUSE. One theory of the causation of abuse of older adults posits that persons who abuse an older parent or relative were themselves abused as children. Suzanne K. Steinmetz, the director for Resources for Older Americans at the University of Delaware and a recognized expert on domestic violence, found support for this hypothesis in her study of abusers entitled *Duty Bound: Elder Abuse and Family Care* (Newbury Park, CA: Sage Publications, 1988). She found only one out of four hundred children treated nonviolently when they were raised attacked their older parents; on the other hand, one out of two children who were violently mistreated as children abused their older parents.

Psychiatrist Mitchell Messer of the Violence Institute of Chicago, who treats adults who care for elderly parents, concurred: "We find parent beatings when the parents set the example of solving problems through brutality when the children were growing up.... The response is simply following the example...set." As adults, formerly abused children often have financial, marital, or drug problems that they blame on their parents, which may make them even more abusive.

INVASION OF PRIVACY. Research suggests that a shared living arrangement is a major risk factor for mistreatment of older adults, with older persons living alone at lowest risk for abuse. A shared residence increases the opportunities for contact, conflict, and mistreatment.

When the home must be shared, there is an inevitable loss of a certain amount of control and privacy. Movement may be restricted, habits may need to change, rivalries between generations may ensue. Frustration and anxiety may result as both older parent and supporting child try to suppress anger, with varying degrees of success (Richard J. Bonnie and Robert B. Wallace, *Elder Mistreatment: Abuse, Neglect, and Exploitation in an Aging America*, Washington, DC: National Academies Press, 2002).

SOCIAL ISOLATION. Social isolation has been linked to abuse and mistreatment of older adults. Several studies have found that low levels of social support were associated with verbal and physical abuse by caregivers. To a certain extent, families that are socially isolated are better able to hide unacceptable behaviors from friends, kin, and neighbors who might sanction abusers or report them. Although there are not yet data to support the corollary to this finding, it is hypothesized that mistreatment is less likely in families rooted in strong social networks (*Elder Mistreatment: Abuse, Neglect, and Exploitation in an Aging America*).

ALZHEIMER'S DISEASE OR OTHER DEMENTIA. The diagnosis of Alzheimer's disease or other dementia is a risk factor for the physical abuse of older adults. Several studies have estimated prevalence rates of mistreatment in samples of dementia patient caregivers and compared them with rates in general population surveys. Since the prevalence findings of rates of physical abuse fall in the 1% to 3% range in the general population, and between 5% and 12% among dementia patients, it would appear that persons suffering from dementia are at greater risk for mistreatment. Research has not pinpointed the relationship between dementia and the risk for abuse; however, it may be that dementia itself is not the risk factor but rather the disruptive behaviors that result from dementia. This hypothesis is consistent with research that has shown that the disruptive behavior of Alzheimer's disease patients is an especially strong predictor and cause of caregiver stress (*Elder Mistreatment: Abuse, Neglect, and Exploitation in an Aging America*).

REVERSE DEPENDENCY. Some sources believe that abusers may be quite dependent, emotionally and financially, on their victims. Research has revealed that abused older adults were no more likely to have had a recent decline in health or be seriously ill or hospitalized previously than nonabused older adults. In fact, as a group, the abused older persons were more self-sufficient in preparing meals, doing ordinary housework, and climbing stairs than were the nonabused older adults.

On the other hand, abusing caregivers often seem more dependent on their victims for housing, financial assistance, and transportation than are nonabusing caregivers. They appear to have fewer resources and are frequently unable to meet their own basic needs. Rather than having power in the relationship, they are relatively powerless. From these observations, some researchers speculate that abusing caregivers may not always be driven to violence by the physical and emotional burden of caring for a seriously disabled older person but may have mental health problems of their own that can lead to violent behavior. Several studies have specifically pointed to depression as characteristic of perpetrators of elder mistreatment (*Elder Mistreatment: Abuse, Neglect, and Exploitation in an Aging America*).

The Abusive Spouse

The high rate of spousal abuse among the older population is possibly because many older adults live with their spouses, so the opportunity for spousal violence is great. Violence against an older spouse may be the continuation of an abusive relationship that began years earlier—abuse does not end simply because a couple ages. Sometimes, however, the abuse may not begin until later years, in which case it is often associated with mental illness, alcohol abuse, unemployment, postretirement depression, and/or loss of self-esteem.

Intervention and Prevention

All fifty states and the District of Columbia have laws addressing abuse of older adults, but like laws aiming to prevent and reduce child abuse and domestic violence among younger people, they are often ineffective. The effectiveness of laws and the enforcing agencies vary from state to state and even from county to county within a given state. No standard definition of abuse exists among enforcement agencies. In many cases authorities cannot legally intervene and terminate an abusive condition unless a report is filed, the abuse is verified, and the victim files a formal complaint. An older adult could understandably be reluctant, physically unable, or too fearful to accuse or prosecute an abuser.

As of mid-2005 forty-three states and the District of Columbia operated "mandatory reporting systems," that require selected professionals to report suspected abuse. In eight states reporting is voluntary. In eight of the mandatory reporting states—Delaware, Indiana, Kentucky, New Mexico, North Carolina, Rhode Island, Texas, and Wyoming—any person who suspects mistreatment is required to report it. Although it is thought to reduce instances of abuse, mandatory reporting has never been evaluated to determine whether it is an effective measure for preventing or reducing mistreatment of older persons.

Clearly, the best way to stop elder abuse is to prevent its occurrence. Older people who know that they will eventually need outside help should carefully analyze the potential challenges of living with their families and, if necessary and possible, make alternate arrangements. All older adults should take action to protect their money and assets to ensure that their valuables cannot be easily taken from them.

Families or individuals who must serve as caregivers for older adults, voluntarily or otherwise, must be helped to realize that their frustration and despair do not have to result in abuse. Health and social service agencies offer myriad interventions including group support programs and counseling to help caregivers and their families. Many communities have allocated resources to assist families to offset the financial burden of elder care, for example, through tax deductions or subsidies for respite care.

INSTITUTIONAL ABUSE—A FORGOTTEN POPULATION?

The elderly in skilled nursing facilities are among the most vulnerable members of our society. They are dependent on the . . . nursing facility operator for their food, medicine, medical care, dental care, and a bed; a roof over their heads; for assistance with virtually every daily activity.

—Eric Z. Shapira, "Elder Abuse: Society's Forgotten Issue," *General Dentistry*, 2000

Abuse of the older population can and does occur in the institutions—nursing homes, board and care facilities, and retirement homes—charged with, and compensated for, caring for the nation's older population. "Institutional abuse" generally refers to the same forms of abuse as domestic abuse crimes but perpetrated by persons who have legal or contractual obligations to provide older adults with care and protection. Despite the fact that, according to the Omnibus Budget Reconciliation Act of 1987, nursing homes must take steps to attain or maintain the "highest practicable physical, mental, and psychosocial well-being of each resident," too many residents are the victims of neglect or abuse by these facilities or their employees.

Older adult residents of long-term care facilities or supportive housing are thought to be at higher risk for abuse and neglect than community dwelling older adults. They are particularly vulnerable because most suffer from one or more chronic diseases that impair their physical and cognitive functioning, rendering them dependent on others. Further, many are either unable to report abuse or neglect, or they are fearful that reporting may generate reprisals from the facility staff or otherwise adversely affect their lives. Others are unaware of the availability of help.

Although there are federal laws and regulations that govern nursing homes, there are no federal standards that oversee or regulate residential care facilities, such as personal care homes, adult congregate living facilities, residential care homes, homes for the aged, domiciliary care homes, board and care homes, and assisted living facilities. As a result, it is much more difficult than with nursing homes to estimate the prevalence or nature of abuse or neglect in these facilities. Despite reports in recent years

that have raised the specter of widespread and serious abuse of institutionalized older persons, as of 2005 there had never been a systematic study of the prevalence of abuse in nursing homes or other residential facilities.

Types of Abuse and Neglect

Nursing home neglect and/or abuse can take many forms, including:

- Failure to provide proper diet and hydration
- Failure to assist with personal hygiene
- Overmedication or undermedication
- Failure to answer call lights promptly
- Failure to turn residents in their beds to promote circulation and prevent decubitus ulcers (bedsores)
- Slapping or other physical abuse
- Leaving residents in soiled garments or beds or failure to take them to the toilet
- Use of unwarranted restraints
- Emotional or verbal abuse
- Retaliation for making a complaint
- Failure to provide appropriate medical care
- Sexual assault, unwanted touching, indecent exposure, or rape
- Theft of the resident's property or money

Surveys conducted with certified nursing assistants (CNAs) who work in long-term care facilities are summarized in "Preventing Abuse and Neglect in Nursing Homes: The Role of Staffing and Training" (Texas A&M University System Health Science Center, http://srphmain. tamu.edu/centers/srhrc/PPT/nh2_gsa03.ppt, November 23, 2003). The findings revealed that more than one-third of CNAs have witnessed abuses including incidents that included elements of physical and verbal or psychological abuse, such as:

- Aggressiveness with a resident and rough handling
- Pulling too hard on a resident
- Yelling in anger
- Threatening behavior
- Punching, slapping, kicking, hitting
- Speaking in a harsh tone, cursing at a resident, or saying harsh or mean things to a resident

The CNAs also offered examples of neglect, which is often more difficult to detect and measure, including:

- Neglecting oral/dental care
- Failing to perform prescribed range of motion exercises

- Failing to change residents after an episode of incontinence

- Ignoring residents who are bedfast, particularly not offering activities to them

- Not performing prescribed wound care

- Failing to bathe residents regularly

- Performing a one-person transfer (move from bed to chair or wheelchair) when the resident required a two-person transfer

- Not providing cuing or task segmentation to residents who need that kind of assistance to maximize their independence

- Failing to perform scheduled toileting or helping residents when they ask

- Not keeping residents hydrated

- Turning off a call light and taking no action on the resident's request

Resident Risk Factors

Although there has been scant research describing the factors that contribute to risk for abuse of institutionalized older adults, some studies indicate that the risk for abuse increases in direct relationship to the older resident's dependence on the facility's staff for safety, protection, and care. A patient with a diagnosis of Alzheimer's disease, another dementia, or some type of memory loss or confusion also was higher among nursing home residents who had been abused than in the average nursing home population. Another study suggested that residents with behavioral symptoms, such as physical aggressiveness, appeared to be at higher risk for abuse by staff; this finding was supported by interviews with CNAs. These studies are summarized by Catherine Hawes et al. in "Preventing Abuse and Neglect in Nursing Homes: The Role of the Nurse Aide Registries" (*Report to the Centers for Medicare and Medicaid Services*, College Station, TX: School of Rural Public Health, Texas A&M University System Health Science Center, 2001).

Social isolation also may increase the risk for abuse. Residents who have no visitors are especially vulnerable, because they lack family or friends who could oversee their care, bear witness to and report any abuses, and advocate on their behalf.

Efforts to Identify and Reduce Abuse

In an effort to improve the quality of care and eliminate abuse in nursing homes, government regulations and laws have been enacted that require greater supervision and scrutiny of nursing homes. In 1987 President Ronald Reagan signed the Omnibus Budget Reconciliation Act (OBRA, or PL 100-203), which included protections for patient rights and treatment. The law went into effect October 1990, but compliance with the law varies from state to state and from one nursing facility to another.

Many states have adopted additional legislation to help stem instances of institutional abuse and neglect. For example, in 1998 New York State enacted "Kathy's Law," which created the new felony-level crime of "abuse of a vulnerable elderly person." At the state level there are many agencies involved in identifying and investigating cases of abuse or neglect. These agencies differ across states but may include ombudsmen, adult protective services, the state survey agency responsible for licensing nursing homes, the state agency responsible for the operation of the nurse aide registry, Medicaid fraud units in the attorney general's office, and professional licensing boards.

CMS has also taken this issue seriously. As stated in the report "Progress in Nursing Home Quality" (Centers for Medicare and Medicaid Services, http://www.cms. hhs.gov/quality/nhqi/NHprogressrpt.pdf, December 2004), CMS has instilled several key communication tools and quality measures. CMS has concentrated its efforts in four ways:

- Raising nursing home consumer awareness and assistance. For example, consumers can locate standardized data on Medicare- and Medicaid-certified nursing home facilities via the Nursing Home Compare Web site (http://www.medicare.gov/NHCompare/Include/Data Section/Questions/SearchCriteria.asp?version=default &browser=IE%7C6%7CWinXP&language=English &defaultstatus=0&pagelist=Home&CookiesEnabled Status=True).

- Enhancing the survey, standards, and enforcement processes. More than six thousand federal and state surveyors review 98% of all nursing homes at least once every fifteen months. CMS also enhanced this survey to facilitate the detection of dehydration, malnutrition, pressure ulcers, ineffective drug use, and abuse.

- Improving quality of care. CMS increased training for care providers and state agencies on abuse and quality of life issues. CMS also clarified the quality of care requirements among the surveyors and established new goals in the Government Performance and Results Act (GPRA).

- Effectively partnering with representatives from the nursing home industry, professional associations representing home health-care providers, and advocacy groups. Members of these groups meet frequently as a committee and advise CMS on the Nursing Home Quality Initiative (NHQI).

ADEQUATE STAFFING AND TRAINING CAN AMELIO-RATE ABUSE. Testifying before the U.S. Senate Committee on Finance on July 17, 2003, Catherine Hawes, a professor of Health Policy and Management and director of the Southwest Rural Health Research Center, School of Rural Public Health at Texas A&M University System Health Science Center (http://finance.senate.gov/hearings/testimony/2003test/071703chtest.pdf), asserted that quality improved immediately after the implementation of the nursing home reform provisions of the OBRA, but that there is evidence that quality has deteriorated in recent years. Hawes attributed this decline in part to inadequate regulatory processes but said the major cause of poor nursing home quality was inadequate staffing, compounded by insufficient staff training.

To illustrate her concerns about training, Hawes compared the Texas requirements of manicurists, who must complete six hundred hours of approved training and pass an examination, with the relatively lax requirement—just seventy-five hours of training—for CNAs who provide daily hands-on care in settings where residents suffer from multiple and/or chronic diseases, may be incontinent, have some form of significant cognitive impairment, and need help with more than four basic activities of daily living, including bathing, dressing, locomotion, and using the toilet. Based on research she and her colleagues conducted, Hawes contended that 85% of abuse and neglect resulted from inadequate staffing—too few staff, bad staff-to-resident ratios, difficulty hiring qualified staff, poor training, poor supervision and management, staff turnover, and low wages.

Hawes acknowledged that the total cost of increasing staffing levels, providing adequate training, and paying CNAs a living wage would be high, but she observed that without these actions and the funding to support them, conditions would not improve. She concluded her testimony with a plea for expanded funding, explaining that the nation's "1.6 million nursing home residents don't have that much time to wait."

LONG-TERM CARE OMBUDSMAN PROGRAMS. Long-term care ombudsmen are advocates for residents of nursing homes, board and care homes, assisted living facilities and other adult care facilities. The Ombudsman Program was established under the Older Americans Act, which is administered by the AoA. Since the program began in 1972, thousands of paid and volunteer ombudsmen have advocated on behalf of individuals and groups of residents, provided information to residents and their families about the long-term care system, investigated

more than 260,000 complaints each year, and worked to effect systems changes at the local, state, and national level. They serve as an ongoing presence in long-term care facilities, monitoring care and conditions.

According to the AoA, in 2004 state long-term care ombudsman programs investigated 227,721 complaints. Table 11.4 shows the increasing number of nursing facility complaints from the late 1990s through 2003 and lists the top complaint categories. Table 11.5 lists the complaint categories and number of board and care facility complaints investigated by ombudsman programs for the same time period.

ADULT PROTECTIVE SERVICES LEGISLATION. An analysis of adult protective services legislation performed for the NCEA by the American Bar Association Commission on Law and Aging found that seven states—Iowa, Kansas, Maine, Massachusetts, South Carolina, Tennessee and Virginia—amended their Adult Protective Services (APS) laws in 2004. The recently enacted legislation acted to:

- Amend definitions of elder abuse
- Enhance the ability of APS to access victims
- Revise provisions related to mandatory and voluntary reporters
- Add provisions related to notifying licensing and regulatory agencies when mandated reporters fail to make reports
- Add or change provisions related to disclosure of records
- Add or change provisions related to elder abuse fatality teams
- Revise APS investigation procedures
- Add provisions related to case referrals to the medical examiner and/or law enforcement
- Add provisions requiring APS to work collaboratively with other agencies
- Add provisions regarding training of newly mandated reporters
- Create penalties for filing false reports and failing to file mandated reports
- Change provisions regarding involuntary APS
- Address the problem of employers/supervisors who fail to report when an employee/supervisee who is a mandatory reporter expresses to the employer/supervisor a suspicion of abuse

TABLE 11.4

Top 20 complaints by category for nursing facilities, 1997–2003

Complaint categories	1997 Total	1997 %	1997 Rank	1998 Total	1998 %	1998 Rank	1999 Total	1999 %	1999 Rank	2000 Total	2000 %	2000 Rank	2001 Total	2001 %	2001 Rank	2002 Total	2002 %	2002 Rank	2003 Total	2003 %	2003 Rank
	157,380			163,540			172,662			186,234			209,633			208,762			226,376		
Call lights, requests for assistance	6,189	3.93%	1	7,026	4.30%	1	7,644	4.43%	1	8,676	4.66%	1	10,126	4.83%	1	9,885	4.74%	1	11,240	4.97%	1
Accidents, improper handling	5,701	3.62%	2	6,032	3.69%	3	6,804	3.94%	3	7,675	4.12%	2	7,810	3.73%	4	8,082	3.87%	4	9,514	4.20%	2
Care plan/resident assessment	5,445	3.46%	3	5,242	3.21%	7	6,412	3.71%	5	7,550	4.05%	3	8,572	4.09%	3	8,842	4.24%	2	8,758	3.87%	3
Dignity, respect-staff attitudes	5,318	3.38%	4	5,710	3.49%	4	6,453	3.74%	4	7,351	3.95%	4	8,838	4.22%	2	8,583	4.11%	3	8,326	3.68%	4
Personal hygiene	5,299	3.37%	5	6,411	3.92%	2	7,110	4.12%	2	7,279	3.91%	5	7,712	3.68%	5	7,519	3.60%	6	7,531	3.33%	5
Discharge/eviction-planning, notice, procedure	4,794	3.05%	6	5,407	3.31%	6	5,455	3.16%	7	5,762	3.09%	7	6,699	3.20%	6	7,670	3.67%	5	7,465	3.30%	6
Menu-quantity, quality, variation, choice	4,082	2.59%	8	4,554	2.78%	9	5,063	2.93%	8	5,540	2.97%	8	6,161	2.94%	8	6,185	2.96%	7	7,074	3.12%	7
Medications-administration, organization	3,366	2.14%	12	3,885	2.38%	11	4,397	2.55%	10	4,914	2.64%	9	5,734	2.74%	9	5,841	2.80%	8	6,931	3.06%	8
Symptoms unattended, no notice to others of change in condition	3,529	2.24%	11	3,818	2.33%	12	4,077	2.36%	12	4,617	2.48%	10	5,075	2.42%	10	4,886	2.34%	11	5,600	2.47%	9
Physical abuse	4,080	2.59%	9	5,426	3.32%	5	4,591	2.66%	9	4,350	2.34%	11	4,842	2.31%	11	4,777	2.29%	12	5,163	2.28%	10
Resident to resident	2,565	1.63%	17	2,577	1.58%	19	2,851	1.65%	17	3,034	1.63%	18	3,569	1.70%	17	3,746	1.79%	17	5,010	2.21%	11
Personal property lost, stolen, used by others, destroyed	3,621	2.30%	10	3,993	2.44%	10	4,229	2.45%	11	4,227	2.27%	12	4,680	2.23%	12	4,531	2.17%	13	4,919	2.17%	12
Staff unresponsive, unavailable	3,050	1.94%	13	3,248	1.99%	13	3,286	1.90%	15	3,700	1.99%	15	4,605	2.20%	13	4,964	2.38%	10	4,627	2.04%	13
Equipment/building-disrepair, hazard, poor lighting, fire safety	2,400	1.52%	21	1,952	1.19%	26	2,541	1.47%	20	2,899	1.56%	19	3,472	1.66%	18	3,657	1.75%	18	4,323	1.91%	14
Shortage of staff	4,351	2.76%	7	4,887	2.99%	8	5,740	3.32%	6	6,625	3.56%	6	6,664	3.18%	7	5,503	2.64%	9	4,308	1.90%	15
Exercise choice and/or civil rights	2,375	1.51%	22	2,851	1.74%	15	3,479	2.01%	13	3,803	2.04%	14	4,109	1.96%	15	3,939	1.89%	15	4,237	1.87%	16
Supervision	2,202	1.40%	25	1,925	1.18%	27	2,325	1.35%	24	3,326	1.79%	16	3,607	1.72%	16	3,872	1.85%	16	4,218	1.86%	17
Cleanliness, pests	2,919	1.85%	14	3,123	1.91%	14	3,458	2.00%	14	3,832	2.06%	13	4,199	2.00%	14	4,002	1.92%	14	3,912	1.73%	18
Toileting	2,193	1.39%	26	2,720	1.66%	16	3,022	1.75%	16	3,093	1.66%	17	3,377	1.61%	19	3,107	1.49%	21	3,713	1.64%	19
Verbal/mental abuse	2,676	1.70%	15	2,598	1.59%	18	2,601	1.51%	18	2,787	1.50%	20	3,171	1.51%	21	3,256	1.56%	20	3,618	1.60%	20

SOURCE: "Top 20 Complaints by Category for Nursing Facilities (FFY 1996–2003)," in 2003 National Ombudsman Reporting System Data Tables, Administration on Aging, Department of Health and Human Services, Washington, DC, 2004, http://www.aoa.gov/prof/aoaprog/elder_rights/LTCombudsman/National_and_State_Data/2003nors/2003nors.asp (accessed August 11, 2005)

TABLE 11.5

Top 20 complaints by category for board and care facilities, 1997–2003

Complaint categories	1997 Total	%	Rank	1998 Total	%	Rank	1999 Total	%	Rank	2000 Total	%	Rank	2001 Total	%	Rank	2002 Total	%	Rank	2003 Total	%	Rank
	30,783			34,696			37,953			41,397			50,152			49,463			56,470		
Medications-administration, organization	1,113	3.62%	2	1,433	4.13%	2	1,682	4.43%	2	1,844	4.45%	2	2,234	4.45%	2	2,335	4.72%	1	2,528	4.48%	1
Menu-quantity, quality, variation, choice	1,499	4.87%	1	1,792	5.16%	1	1,816	4.78%	1	2,060	4.98%	1	2,736	5.46%	1	2,035	4.11%	2	2,350	4.16%	2
Discharge/eviction-planning, notice, procedure	1,000	3.25%	5	1,216	3.50%	3	1,365	3.60%	3	1,421	3.43%	4	1,691	3.37%	4	1,867	3.77%	3	2,231	3.95%	3
Dignity, respect-staff attitudes	918	2.98%	7	1,129	3.25%	4	1,336	3.52%	4	1,491	3.60%	3	1,915	3.82%	3	1,787	3.61%	4	1,763	3.12%	4
Equipment/building-disrepair, hazard, poor lighting, fire safety	1,058	3.44%	4	1,023	2.95%	6	1,300	3.43%	5	1,261	3.05%	5	1,486	2.96%	5	1,358	2.75%	5	1,577	2.79%	5
Care plan/resident assessment	505	1.64%	18	664	1.91%	15	754	1.99%	15	1,025	2.48%	8	1,146	2.29%	9	1,278	2.58%	6	1,482	2.62%	6
Accidents, improper handling	546	1.77%	16	698	2.01%	13	843	2.22%	10	886	2.14%	11	1,009	2.01%	13	1,059	2.14%	10	1,434	2.54%	7
Cleanliness, pests	909	2.95%	8	927	2.67%	8	1,133	2.99%	6	1,091	2.64%	6	1,419	2.83%	6	1,109	2.24%	8	1,233	2.18%	8
Physical abuse	938	3.05%	6	1,044	3.01%	5	901	2.37%	9	847	2.05%	13	979	1.95%	15	1,076	2.18%	9	1,189	2.11%	9
Personal hygiene	1,093	3.55%	3	940	2.71%	7	914	2.41%	8	1,061	2.56%	7	1,163	2.32%	7	965	1.95%	15	1,169	2.07%	10
Exercise choice and/or civil rights	539	1.75%	17	644	1.86%	16	719	1.89%	16	701	1.69%	17	1,009	2.01%	13	895	1.81%	16	1,154	2.04%	11
Personal property lost, stolen, used by others, destroyed	576	1.87%	14	691	1.99%	14	789	2.08%	14	867	2.09%	12	1,080	2.15%	10	973	1.97%	14	1,151	2.04%	12
Billing/charges notice, approval, questionable, accounting wrong or denied	676	2.20%	11	724	2.09%	11	825	2.17%	13	928	2.24%	10	1,061	2.12%	11	1,133	2.29%	7	1,117	1.98%	13
Supervision	389	1.26%	25	460	1.33%	26	431	1.14%	29	581	1.40%	21	755	1.51%	24	854	1.73%	17	1,088	1.93%	14
Symptoms unattended, no notice to others of change in condition	464	1.51%	20	577	1.66%	17	644	1.70%	17	703	1.70%	16	895	1.78%	16	819	1.66%	20	1,029	1.82%	15
Verbal/mental abuse	652	2.12%	12	797	2.30%	10	843	2.22%	10	802	1.94%	15	895	1.78%	16	1,025	2.07%	12	1,023	1.81%	16
Resident to resident	348	1.13%	30	424	1.22%	30	329	0.87%	36	505	1.22%	32	529	1.05%	35	695	1.41%	27	997	1.77%	17
Shortage of staff	614	1.99%	13	720	2.08%	12	836	2.20%	12	1,001	2.42%	9	1,149	2.29%	8	1,029	2.08%	11	979	1.73%	18
Personal funds-mismanaged, access denied, deposits & other money not returned	728	2.36%	9	887	2.56%	9	929	2.45%	7	806	1.95%	14	1,012	2.02%	12	975	1.97%	13	955	1.69%	19
Legal-guardianship, conservatorship, power of attorney, wills	440	1.43%	23	506	1.46%	23	458	1.21%	28	610	1.47%	19	591	1.18%	28	823	1.66%	19	903	1.60%	20

SOURCE: "Top 20 Complaints by Category for Board and Care Facilities (FFY 1996–2003)," in *2003 National Ombudsman Reporting System Data Tables*, Administration on Aging, Department of Health and Human Services, Washington, DC, 2004, http://www.aoa.gov/prof/aoaprog/elder_rights/LTCombudsman/National_and_State_Data/2003nors/2003nors.asp (accessed August 11, 2005)

IMPORTANT NAMES AND ADDRESSES

AARP (formerly American Association of Retired Persons)
601 E St., NW
Washington, DC 20049
1-888-687-2277
URL: http://www.aarp.org

Administration on Aging
Washington, DC 20201
(202) 619-0724
E-mail: aoainfo@aoa.gov
URL: http://www.aoa.dhhs.gov

Alliance for Aging Research
2021 K St., NW, Suite 305
Washington, DC 20006
(202) 293-2856
FAX: (202) 785-8574
E-mail: info@agingresearch.org
URL: http://www.agingresearch.org

Alzheimer's Association
225 N. Michigan Ave., Floor 17
Chicago, IL 60601-7633
(312) 335-8700
1-800-272-3900
FAX: (312) 335-1110
E-mail: info@alz.org
URL: http://www.alz.org

American Association for Geriatric Psychiatry
7910 Woodmont Ave., Suite 1050
Bethesda, MD 20814-3004
(301) 654-7850
FAX: (301) 654-4137
E-mail: main@aagponline.org
URL: http://www.aagponline.org

American Association of Homes and Services for the Aging
2519 Connecticut Ave., NW
Washington, DC 20008-1520
(202) 783-2242
FAX: (202) 783-2255
E-mail: info@aahsa.org
URL: http://www.aahsa.org

American Geriatrics Society
350 Fifth Ave., Suite 801
New York, NY 10118
(212) 308-1414
FAX: (212) 832-8646
E-mail: info@americangeriatrics.org
URL: http://www.americangeriatrics.org

American Heart Association
7272 Greenville Ave.
Dallas, TX 75231
(214) 373-6300
1-800-AHA-USA1
FAX: (214) 706-1341
URL: http://www.americanheart.org

American Society on Aging
833 Market St., Suite 511
San Francisco, CA 94103-1824
(415) 974-9600
1-800-537-9728
FAX: (415) 974-0300
E-mail: info@asaging.org
URL: http://www.asaging.org

Arthritis Foundation
P.O. Box 7669
Atlanta, GA 30357
(404) 872-7100
1-800-568-4045
FAX: (404) 872-0457
E-mail: help@arthritis.org
URL: http://www.arthritis.org

Asociacion Nacional por Personas Mayores/National Association for Hispanic Elderly
234 E. Colorado Blvd., Suite 300
Pasadena, CA 91101
(626) 564-1988
FAX: (626) 564-2659
E-mail: support@anppm.org

Assisted Living Federation of America
11200 Waples Mill Rd., Suite 150
Fairfax, VA 22030
(703) 691-8100

FAX: (703) 691-8106
E-mail: info@alfa.org
URL: http://www.alfa.org

The Boomer Project
2325 West Broad Street
Richmond, VA 23220
(804) 690-4837
URL: http://www.boomerproject.com

Centers for Disease Control and Prevention
1600 Clifton Rd.
Atlanta, GA 30333
(404) 639-3311
1-800-311-3435
URL: http://www.cdc.gov

Centers for Medicare and Medicaid Services
7500 Security Blvd.
Baltimore, MD 21244-1850
(410) 786-3000
1-877-267-2323
URL: http://www.cms.gov

Children of Aging Parents
P.O. Box 167
Richboro, PA 18954
1-800-227-7294
E-mail: info@caps4caregivers.org
URL: http://www.caps4caregivers.org

Civic Ventures
139 Townsend Street, Suite 505
San Francisco, CA 94107
(415) 430-0141
E-mail: info@civicventures.org
URL: http://www.civicventures.org

Eldercare Locator Directory
1-800-677-1116
FAX: (202) 296-8134
E-mail: eldercarelocatoror@spherix.com
URL: http://www.eldercare.gov

Family Caregiver Alliance
180 Montgomery St., Suite 1100
San Francisco, CA 94104
(415) 434-3388
1-800-445-8106
FAX: (415) 434-3508
E-mail: info@caregiver.org
URL: http://www.caregiver.org

The Gerontological Society of America
1030 15th St., NW, Suite 250
Washington, DC 20005
(202) 842-1275
FAX: (202) 842-1150
E-mail: geron@geron.org
URL: http://www.geron.org

Gray Panthers
733 15th St., NW, Suite 437
Washington, DC 20005
(202) 737-6637
1-800-280-5362
FAX: (202) 737-1160
E-mail: info@graypanthers.org
URL: http://www.graypanthers.org

Insurance Institute for Highway Safety
1005 N. Glebe Road, Suite 800
Arlington, VA 22201
(703) 247-1500
FAX: (703) 247-1588
URL: http://www.highwaysafety.org

Jewish Council for the Aging
11820 Parklawn Dr., Suite 200
Rockville, MD 20852
(301) 255-4200
FAX: (301) 231-9360
E-mail: jcagw@jcagw.org
URL: http://www.jcagw.org

Mature Workers Employment Alliance
826 Euclid Ave.
Syracuse, NY 13210
(315) 446-3587
E-mail: mwea4cny@connections4.com
URL: http://www.connections4.com/mwea/
index.php

Medicare Rights Center
1460 Broadway, 17th Floor
New York, NY 10036
(212) 869-3850
FAX: (212) 869-3532
E-mail: info@medicarerights.org
URL: http://www.medicarerights.org

National Academy of Elder Law Attorneys, Inc.
1604 N. Country Club Rd.
Tucson, AZ 85716
(520) 881-4005
FAX: (520) 325-7925
URL: http://www.naela.org

National Alliance for Caregiving
4720 Montgomery Ln., 5th Floor
Bethesda, MD 20814

E-mail: info@caregiving.org
URL: http://www.caregiving.org

National Alliance of Senior Citizens
2525 Wilson Blvd.
Arlington, VA 22201
FAX: (703) 528-4380

National Association for Home Care and Hospice
228 Seventh St., SE
Washington, DC 20003
(202) 547-7424
FAX: (202) 547-3540
URL: http://www.nahc.org

National Caregiving Foundation
801 N. Pitt St., Suite 116
Alexandria, VA 22314-1765
1-800-930-1357
E-mail: info@caregivingfoundation.org
URL: http://www.caregivingfoundation.org

The National Caucus and Center on Black Aged, Inc.
1220 L St., NW, Suite 800
Washington, DC 20005
(202) 637-8400
E-mail: info@ncba-aged.org
URL: http://www.ncba-aged.org

National Center on Elder Abuse
1201 15th St., NW, Suite 350
Washington, DC 20005-2842
(202) 898-2586
FAX: (202) 898-2583
E-mail: ncea@nasua.org
URL: http://www.elderabusecenter.org

National Center for Health Statistics Division of Data Services
3311 Toledo Rd.
Hyattsville, MD 20782
(301) 458-4000
URL: http://www.cdc.gov/nchs

National Citizens' Coalition for Nursing Home Reform
1828 L St., NW, Suite 801
Washington, DC 20036
(202) 332-2276
FAX: (202) 332-2949
URL: http://www.nccnhr.org

National Council on the Aging
300 D St., SW, Suite 801
Washington, DC 20024
(202) 479-1200
FAX: (202) 479-0735
E-mail: info@ncoa.org
URL: http://www.ncoa.org

National Family Caregivers Association
10400 Connecticut Ave., Suite 500
Kensington, MD 20895-3944
(301) 942-6430
1-800-896-3650

FAX: (301) 942-2302
E-mail: info@thefamilycaregiver.org
URL: http://www.thefamilycaregiver.org

National Hispanic Council on Aging
1341 Connecticut Ave., 4th Floor, Suite 4.2
Washington, DC 20036
(202) 429-0787
FAX: (202) 429-0789
E-mail: nhcoa@nhcoa.org
URL: http://www.nhcoa.org

National Hospice and Palliative Care Organization
1700 Diagonal Rd., Suite 625
Alexandria, VA 22314
(703) 837-1500
FAX: (703) 837-1233
E-mail: nhpco_info@nhpco.org
URL: http://www.nhpco.org

National Indian Council on Aging
10501 Montgomery Blvd. NE, Suite 210
Albuquerque, NM 87111-3846
(505) 292-2001
URL: http://www.nicoa.org/

National Institute on Aging
Building 31, Room 5C27
31 Center Dr., MSC 2292
Bethesda, MD 20892
(301) 496-1752
E-mail: karpf@nia.nih.gov
URL: http://www.nih.gov/nia

National Osteoporosis Foundation
1232 22nd Street NW
Washington, DC 20037-1292
(202) 223-2226
URL: http://www.nof.org

National PACE Association
801 N. Fairfax St., Suite 309
Alexandria, VA 22314
(703) 535-1565
FAX: (703) 535-1566
E-mail: info@npaonline.org
URL: http://www.npaonline.org

National Respite Locator Service
ARCH National Respite Network and Resource Center
Chapel Hill Training-Outreach Project
800 Eastowne Dr., Suite 105
Chapel Hill, NC 27514
(919) 490-5577
FAX: (919) 490-4905
URL: http://www.respitelocator.org

National Senior Citizens Law Center
1101 14th St., NW, Suite 400
Washington, DC 20005
(202) 289-6976
FAX: (202) 289-7224
E-mail: nsclc@nsclc.org
URL: http://www.nsclc.org

National Society for American Indian Elderly
1326 N. Central Avenue, Unit 208
Phoenix, AZ 85004
(602) 253-9211, ext. 161
FAX: (602) 253-9135
E-mail: info@nsaie.org
URL: http://www.nsaie.dreamhosters.com/

National Urban League
120 Wall St., 8th Floor
New York, NY 10005
(212) 558-5300
FAX: (212) 344-5332
E-mail: info@nul.org
URL: http://www.nul.org

Older Women's League
1750 New York Ave. NW, Suite 350
Washington, DC 20006

(202) 783-6686
1-800-825-3695
FAX: (202) 628-0458
E-mail: owlinfo@owl-national.org
URL: http://www.owl-national.org

Pension Benefit Guaranty Corporation
1200 K St., NW, Suite 240
Washington, DC 20005-4026
(202) 326-4343
FAX: (202) 326-4344
URL: http://www.pbgc.gov

Pension Rights Center
1350 Connecticut Ave., NW, Suite 206
Washington, DC 20036-6608
URL: http://www.pensionrights.org

SCORE
409 3rd St., SW, 6th Floor
Washington, DC 20024

1-800-634-0245
URL: http://www.score.org

SeniorNet
1171 Homestead Road, Suite 280
Santa Clara, CA 95050
(408) 615-0699
FAX: (408) 615-0928
URL: http://www.seniornet.org

U.S. Census Bureau
4700 Silver Hill Rd.
Washington, DC 20233-0001
E-mail: webmaster@census.gov
URL: http://www.census.gov

U.S. Department of Veterans Affairs
Washington, DC 20011
1-800-827-1000
URL: http://www.va.gov

RESOURCES

Many of the demographics data cited in this text were drawn from U.S. Census Bureau reports, including *Americans 55 and Older: A Changing Market* (Sharon Yntema ed., American Generations Series, New Strategist Publications, 3rd edition, 2001); *Current Population Survey: Annual Social and Economic Supplement*; *Income, Poverty, and Health Insurance Coverage in the United States: 2003*; *Household Net Worth and Asset Ownership 1998 and 2000*; *2003 Current Population Survey* (CPS); and the *2003 American Community Survey* (ACS). The Administration on Aging (AoA) report *A Profile of Older Americans: 2004* was helpful, and *Older Americans 2004: Key Indicators of Well-Being*, prepared by the Federal Interagency Forum on Aging Related Statistics (Forum), also provided useful data about older adults. The Forum is a consortium of twelve federal agencies—AoA, Agency for Healthcare Research and Quality, Bureau of Labor Statistics, U.S. Census Bureau, Centers for Medicare and Medicaid Services (CMS), Department of Veterans Affairs, Environmental Protection Agency, National Center for Health Statistics (NCHS), National Institute on Aging, Office of the Assistant Secretary for Planning and Evaluation, Office of Management and Budget, and the Social Security Administration— dedicated to encouraging cooperation and collaboration among federal agencies to improve the quality and utility of data on the aging population. Additional population data were drawn from *The World Factbook*, published by the Central Intelligence Agency and the NCHS of the Centers for Disease Control and Prevention (CDC). The U.S. Interagency Council on Homelessness provided estimates of homelessness among older Americans.

A study conducted by the National Council on the Aging (NCOA), titled *Myths and Realities of Aging 2000*, offered insight into older adults' feelings and impressions about growing older, and publications including the *2004 Retirement Confidence Survey* from the Employee Benefits Research Institute provided information about pension plans and other employee benefits. The NCOA and International Longevity Center publication *American Perceptions of Aging in the 21st Century* depicts trends in work and retirement among older adults. The Women's Bureau of the U.S. Department of Labor and the National Economic Council Interagency Working Group on Social Security described trends in labor force participation. The *New Face of Work*, a MetLife Foundation/Civic Ventures 2005 study, characterized new trends in working and retirement. The Equal Employment Opportunity Commission offers information about age discrimination issues and claims. *Forces Shaping the Future Workforce and Workplace in the United States* (Santa Monica, CA: RAND Labor and Population, 2004) discusses how the participation of older workers will itself shape the face of the workforce and workplace. The Independent Sector, a national coalition of philanthropic organizations, conducts surveys about volunteerism in America. The Social Security Administration provides information about the history and future of this vital social program as well as benefits and eligibility in publications such as the *2005 OASDI Trustees Report*.

The National Center for Education Statistics report *The Condition of Education 2004* provides information about trends in adult education. The Media Audit measures older adults' Internet use, and the *Pew Internet & American Life Project* tracks Internet use by age. *The 2004 Political Landscape: Evenly Divided and Increasingly Polarized* (Washington, DC: Pew Research Center for the People and the Press, 2005) characterized older adults' political allegiances. The Brookings Institution Series on Transportation Reform offered information about the transportation needs of older persons in *The Mobility Needs of Older Americans: Implications for Transportation Reauthorization* (Washington DC: Center on Urban and Metropolitan Policy, July 2003). The U.S.

Department of Transportation and the Federal Highway Administration report the number of older drivers; the *National Household Travel Survey* (NHTS) is the nation's inventory of daily and long-distance travel; and the Insurance Institute for Highway Safety reports accident data. The National Highway Traffic Safety Administration and American Medical Association developed a reference, the *Physician's Guide to Assessing and Counseling Older Drivers*, which details medical conditions and their potential effect on driving skills.

The CDC's *National Nursing Home Survey* (NNHS) is a continuing series of national sample surveys of nursing homes, their residents, and their staff. A Commonwealth Fund report published in 2002 described an innovation in nursing home care in eastern Wisconsin, *Evaluation of the Wellspring Model for Improving Nursing Home Quality*. The National Low-Income Housing Coalition report *Out of Reach 2004* documents income and rental housing cost data for the fifty states, the District of Columbia, and Puerto Rico. The Housing Research Foundation 2002 report *Public Housing for Seniors: Past, Present and Future* described the characteristics of older public housing residents and the properties and neighborhoods in which they live.

The Social Security Administration publications *Fast Facts and Figures about Social Security, 2004* and *The Future of Social Security* detail the contributions of Social Security to Americans' overall incomes. The U.S. Department of Labor's Bureau of Labor Statistics publishes the *Consumer Expenditure Survey*, which provided insight into how older adults spend their money.

CMS (formerly the Health Care Financing Administration) is the agency of the U.S. Department of Health and Human Services (HHS) that coordinates Medicare and Medicaid. CMS provides information about the history, the beneficiaries, and the future of these entitlement programs. Another agency within the HHS is the CDC's NCH, which provides vital health statistics. NCHSS publications of interest in the study of older Americans are *Deaths: Preliminary Data for 2003*; *Health, United States, 2004*; *Morbidity and Mortality Weekly Report*; *National Vital Statistics Reports*; *2004 National Health Interview Survey*; and *National Home and Hospice Care Survey*. The Congressional Budget Office report *Financing Long-Term Care for the Elderly* details spending on long-term care.

AARP (formerly the American Association of Retired Persons) underwrites research about older Americans. Examples of their research cited in this text are *Political Behavior and Values across the Generations*; *Global Report on Aging: Spring 2005*; *Trends in Manufacturer Prices of Prescription Drugs Used by Older Americans*; and *Sexuality at Midlife and Beyond*. The AARP/Roper ASW survey about grandparenting, *The Grandparent Study 2002 Report*, describes homes in which grandparents were raising grandchildren.

The National Family Caregivers Association (NFCA) produced *NFCA's 2001 Survey of Self-Identified Family Caregivers*, which describes the economic, health, and social costs of family caregiving as well as the demographics of caregivers, and *National Family Caregivers Association Random Sample Survey of Family Caregivers, Summer 2000*. An additional caregiver resource includes the Family Caregiver Alliance. The National Alliance for Caregiving and AARP produced *Caregiving in the United States, 2004*, and the MetLife Company produced *MetLife Juggling Act Study, Balancing Caregiving with Work and the Costs of Caregiving*. Selected state or local initiatives designed to help caregivers are described in *A Compendium of Intervention and Descriptive Studies Designed to Promote the Health of Caregivers for Older Adults*, a report prepared by RTI International for the Assistant Secretary for Planning and Evaluation of the HHS in 2003. The *2005 Benefits Survey* by the Society for Human Resource Management reported employers' elder care policies and practices.

Many organizations and publications provide information on specific health and medical problems of older adults. The 2003 U.S. Census Bureau's American Community Survey provided estimates of disability in the noninstitutionalized population by age. Among the many publications cited in this text are *Bone Health and Osteoporosis: A Report of the Surgeon General*; *Heart Disease and Stroke Statistics—2005 Update* (American Heart Association); *Many Americans Worried about Brain Health, but Only Half Keep Their Brains Fit, According to New Survey* (The Alzheimer's Association); *Mental Health: A Report of the Surgeon General, 1999*; *Older Adults and Alcohol Problems, NIAA: Social Work Education for the Prevention and Treatment of Alcohol Use Disorders* (National Institute on Alcohol Abuse and Alcoholism); *Prostate Disease: Finding the Cause and Cure* (Harvard Medical School); *Cancer Facts and Figures: 2004* (American Cancer Society); *Fast Facts on Osteoporosis* (National Osteoporosis Foundation); *Parkinson's Disease: What You and Your Family Should Know* by Paul Nausieda and Gloria Bock (National Parkinson Foundation); *The Graying of America, Food Review* by Joanne Guthrie and Biing-Hwan Lin (Food and Rural Economics Division, Economic Research Service, USDA, vol. 25, no. 2, summer–fall 2002); *Medications and Older People* (U.S. Food and Drug Administration, September 2003); *Healthy Aging: Preventing Disease and Improving Quality of Life among Older Americans—At a Glance, 2002* (CDC); and *Healthy Sexuality and Vital Aging* (NCOA).

Professional medical journals offer research findings and information about health and disease among older adults as well as health service utilization and financing.

Articles from the following journals were cited in this text: *Aging & Mental Health, General Dentistry, Health Affairs, Journal of Personality and Social Psychology, American Journal of Geriatric Psychiatry, American Journal of Preventive Medicine, Neurology, American Journal of Public Health, Morbidity and Mortality Weekly Report, New England Journal of Medicine, Journal of the American Medical Association, Journal of the American Geriatrics Society*, and *Proceedings of the National Academy of Science.*

Similarly, many agencies, organizations, and professional organizations, notably the American Society on Aging, National Council on the Aging, RAND Corporation, National Center for Education Statistics, Mature Workers Employment Alliance, American Geriatrics Society, and American Psychiatric Association, offer data and analysis of myriad issues of importance to older Americans.

Since the aging population affects nearly every aspect of society, from employment and housing to health care and politics, consumer publications frequently feature articles about and of interest to older adults. Articles cited in this volume were drawn from *Suddenly Senior, HR Magazine, Wall Street Journal, New York Times, New Standard, CNN Money Online, Washington Post, Health-Day*, and *Consumers Digest.*

Information about abuse and mistreatment of older adults can be found in the National Fraud Information Center's *2004 Telemarketing Fraud Report* (Washington, DC: National Consumer League, 2005); *Crimes against Persons Age 65 or Older, 1993–2002 (Bureau of Justice Statistics Special Report, Washington, DC: U.S. Department of Justice, January 2005); 2004 Internet Fraud—Crime Report* (Internet Fraud Complaint Center, National White Collar Crime Center, and Federal Bureau of Investigation, 2005); *Elder Mistreatment: Abuse, Neglect, and Exploitation in an Aging America* (Richard J. Bonnie and Robert B. Wallace, editors, National Research Council, Washington, DC: National Academies Press, 2003); "A Response to the Abuse of Vulnerable Adults: The 2000 Survey of State Adult Protective Services" (Washington, DC: National Center on Elder Abuse, 2000); "Domestic Abuse in Later Life, Victims" (Bonnie Brandl and Loree Cook-Daniels, Washington, DC: National Center on Elder Abuse, 2003); and *Preventing Abuse and Neglect in Nursing Homes: The Role of the Nurse Aide Registries—Report to the Centers for Medicare and Medicaid Services* (Catherine Hawes et al., School of Rural Public Health, Texas A&M University System Health Science Center, 2001).

We are very grateful to the Gallup Organization for permitting us to present the results of their renowned opinion polls and graphics, and to the Boomer Project for granting permission to cite data and reproduce graphics from *50 Things Every Marketer Needs to Know about Boomers over 50.*

INDEX